Beginning JSP,™ JSF,™ and Tomcat Web Development

From Novice to Professional

Giulio Zambon
with Michael Sekler

Apress®

Beginning JSP™, JSF™, and Tomcat Web Development: From Novice to Professional

Copyright © 2007 by Giulio Zambon with Michael Sekler

ISBN-13 (pbk): 978-1-59059-904-4

ISBN-10 (pbk): 1-59059-904-7

Printed and bound in the United States of America 9 8 7 6 5 4 3 2 1

Lead Editor: Steve Anglin
Technical Reviewer: Kunal Mittal
Editorial Board: Steve Anglin, Ewan Buckingham, Tony Campbell, Gary Cornell, Jonathan Gennick, Jason Gilmore, Kevin Goff, Jonathan Hassell, Matthew Moodie, Joseph Ottinger, Jeffrey Pepper, Ben Renow-Clarke, Dominic Shakeshaft, Matt Wade, Tom Welsh
Project Manager: Richard Dal Porto
Copy Editor: Nicole Abramowitz
Associate Production Director: Kari Brooks-Copony
Production Editor: Janet Vail
Compositor: Linda Weidemann, Wolf Creek Press
Proofreader: Linda Seifert
Indexer: Toma Mulligan, Book Indexers
Artist: April Milne
Cover Designer: Kurt Krames
Manufacturing Director: Tom Debolski

Distributed to the book trade worldwide by Springer-Verlag New York, Inc., 233 Spring Street, 6th Floor, New York, NY 10013. Phone 1-800-SPRINGER, fax 201-348-4505, e-mail orders-ny@springer-sbm.com, or visit http://www.springeronline.com.

For information on translations, please contact Apress directly at 2855 Telegraph Avenue, Suite 600, Berkeley, CA 94705. Phone 510-549-5930, fax 510-549-5939, e-mail info@apress.com, or visit http://www.apress.com.

The source code for this book is available to readers at http://www.apress.com.

Contents at a Glance

Contents

About the Authors

GIULIO ZAMBON's first love was physics, but he left it more than 30 years ago to dedicate himself to software development—back when computers were still made of transistors and core memories, programs were punched on cards, and Fortran only had arithmetic IFs. Over the years, he learned a dozen computer languages and worked with all sorts of operating systems. He concentrated his interests in telecom and real-time systems, and he managed several projects to their successful completion.

In 2001, Giulio founded his own company offering computer telephony integration (CTI) services, and he used JSP and Tomcat exclusively to develop the web side of the service platform.

He has lived and worked in nine cities of five countries, can speak four languages fluently, and is a dedicated Trekker.

MICHAEL SEKLER graduated from the University of Western Australia in 1987 and has worked as a software engineer, developer, software architect, and consultant for several large and small companies. Michael's expertise lies mainly in design, development, and support with databases, the Web, and content management systems. In the last few years, he has worked with open source systems, gaining experience with Linux and Java technologies. In his spare time, Michael enjoys good music and walks in the countryside.

About the Technical Reviewer

■**KUNAL MITTAL** serves as the director of technology for the domestic TV group at Sony Pictures Entertainment and is responsible for the technology strategy and application development for the group. Kunal is active in several enterprise initiatives, such as the service-oriented architecture (SOA) strategy and road map and the implementation of several Information Technology Infrastructure Library (ITIL) processes within Sony Pictures.

Kunal has authored and edited several books and written more than 20 articles on Java Platform, Enterprise Edition (Java EE), BEA WebLogic, and SOA. Some of his works include *Pro Apache Beehive* (Apress, 2005), *BEA WebLogic Server 8.1 Unleashed* (Sams, 2003), and a three-part series of articles entitled "Build your SOA: Maturity and Methodology" (www.soainstitute.org, 2006). For a full list of Kunal's publications, visit his web site at www.kunalmittal.com/html/publications.shtml.

Kunal holds a master's degree in software engineering and is a licensed private pilot.

Introduction

Welcome to *Beginning JSP, JSF, and Tomcat Web Development: From Novice to Professional.*
This book has the ambitious goal of teaching you how to develop dynamic web pages with
JavaServer Pages (JSP) 2.1 and JavaServer Faces (JSF) 1.2.

This is easier said than done, because to use JSP and JSF, you need to know at least some
Java, HTML, XML, and SQL. Moreover, some knowledge of JavaScript and Cascading Style
Sheets (CSS) would also be useful, and you couldn't fully exploit the power of JSP/JSF without
knowing the JSP Expression Language (EL) and the XPath language.

To cover all this ground, we've decided to relegate most of the details to appendixes and
use the main body of the book to teach you key concepts and components with as little clutter
as possible.

Chapter 1 introduces you to JSP, describes the general structure of JSP applications, and
explains the full code of your first JSP application. At the end of the chapter, we also tell you
how to install the application in Tomcat. We knew that you would be eager to see something
working, and we didn't want to make you wait for it!

Chapter 2 is where we cover all aspects and components of JSP. After giving you a brief
summary of the Java syntax, we introduce the online bookshop application that we'll use as
an example in several chapters. We then explain how to use JSP variables, directives, and
standard actions, how to create your own custom actions, and how to use JSTL and EL.
Finally, we briefly describe how to write JSP documents in XML syntax.

Having quenched your thirst for getting into JSP as quickly as possible, we take a step
back in Chapter 3 and tell you about HTML. This is important, because HTML is the result
of executing JSP pages, and you must be familiar with it. After describing the HTTP request-
response mechanism, we explain the HTML components (text, objects, links, tables, and
forms), introduce CSS, and give you some examples of JavaScript.

In Chapter 4, we tell you how to access databases from JSP. It would make little sense to
talk about dynamic web pages without permanent data storage.

In Chapter 5, we introduce you to JSF and show you how it fits together with JSP.

Chapter 6 is dedicated to XML. After reading this chapter, you'll understand why developing a web application without XML is unthinkable!

In Chapter 7, we describe Tomcat.

Chapter 8, the last chapter of the book, is dedicated to the online bookshop application.
We bring together the pieces we've shown in the preceding chapters and give you the last
missing bits.

In Appendix A, we explain how to download and install all the packages you need: Java,
JSP, Tomcat, SQL, and so on.

Appendixes B, C, D, and E describe HTML character sets, HTML, JSP, and SQL, respectively. This is where you'll find the details we left out in the preceding chapters.

Appendix F provides a quick reference to JSF, Appendix G introduces you to the Eclipse integrated development environment (IDE), and Appendix H lists abbreviations and acronyms.

After reading this book, you'll have acquired a toolbox to develop good-quality web applications. Having the right idea and implementing the next killer application that will make you a millionaire/billionaire is entirely up to you!

CHAPTER 1

Introducing JavaServer Pages and Tomcat

What makes the Web really useful is its interactivity. By interacting with some remote server, you can find the information you need, do your banking, or buy online. And every time you type something into a web form, an application "out there" interprets your request and prepares a web page to respond. JavaServer Pages (JSP) is a technology that helps you create such dynamically generated pages.

Sun Microsystems introduced the Java servlet application programming interface (API) in June 1997 with the purpose of providing an efficient and easily portable mechanism to develop web pages with dynamic content. In a nutshell, the servlet package defines Java classes to represent requests sent to the server by the remote web browsers and responses traveling in the opposite direction. A servlet is nothing other than a Java object residing on a server that receives requests via the Internet, accesses resources (such as databases), implements the logic to prepare the responses, and sends the responses back to the network.

The Apache Software Foundation (ASF) developed the Apache Tomcat application server to provide an environment in which servlets can execute. Tomcat is also capable of converting JSP documents into servlets.

In this chapter, we'll introduce you to Java servlets and JSP, and we'll show you how they execute together within Tomcat to generate dynamic web pages. We'll barely scratch the surface of both JSP and Tomcat, and we won't even mention JSF. We'll show you how to develop applications with basic tools, rather than in an environment that takes care of most menial tasks and provides sophisticated checking and debugging capabilities. This will give you a better understanding of what modern tools can do for you.

We know that you're eager to jump into the thick of things. Therefore, after briefly describing how JSP-based web applications are structured, we'll show you at once a nontrivial example, without explaining everything beforehand.

We recommend that you first install the software packages as described in Appendix A. You'll then be able to execute the examples and get a feel for them, rather than just go through the code in print.

What Is JSP?

As we said, JSP is a technology that lets you add dynamic content to web pages. Without JSP, you always have to update the appearance or the content of plain static HTML pages by hand. Even if all you want to do is change a date or a picture, you must edit the HTML file and type in your modifications. Nobody is going to do it for you, whereas with JSP, you can make the content depend on many factors, including the time of the day, the information provided by the user, her history of interaction with your web site, and even her browser type. This capability is essential to provide online services in which each customer is treated differently depending on her preferences and requirements. A crucial aspect of providing meaningful online services is for the system to be able to *remember* data associated with the service and its users. That's why databases play an essential role in dynamic web pages. But let's take it one step at a time.

HISTORY

Sun Microsystems introduced JSP in 1999. Developers quickly realized that additional tags would be useful, and the JSP Standard Tag Library (JSTL) was born. JSTL is a collection of custom tag libraries that encapsulate the functionality of many JSP standard applications, thereby eliminating repetitions and making the applications more compact. Together with JSTL also came the JSP Expression Language (EL).

In 2003, with the introduction of JSP 2.0, EL was incorporated into the JSP specification, making it available for custom components and template text, not just for JSTL, as was the case in the previous versions. Additionally, JSP 2.0 made it possible to create custom tag files, thereby perfecting the extensibility of the language.

In parallel to the evolution of JSP, several frameworks to develop web applications became available. In 2004, one of them, JavaServer Faces (JSF), focused on building user interfaces (UIs) and used JSP by default as the underlying scripting language. It provided an API, JSP custom tag libraries, and an expression language.

The Java Community Process (JCP), formed in 1998, released in May 2006 the Java Specification Request (JSR) 245 titled *JavaServer Pages 2.1*, which effectively aligns JSP and JSF technologies. In particular, JSP 2.1 includes a Unified EL (UEL) that merges together the two versions of EL defined in JSP 2.0 and JSF 1.2 (itself specified as JSR 252). Sun Microsystems includes JSP 2.1 in its Java Platform, Enterprise Edition 5 (Java EE 5), finalized in May 2006 as JSR 244. The classes included in EE 5 rely on the general classes that form the Java Platform, Standard Edition 5 (Java SE 5), which is available as Java Runtime Environment (JRE) and Java Development Kit (JDK).

Meanwhile, the servlet technology has evolved, and Sun Microsystems released Servlet 2.5 in September 2005. The JCP formally specified Servlet 2.5 as an updated version of JSR 152 in May 2006.

In summary, Java EE 5 includes JSP 2.1, which in turn specifies a UEL consistent with JSF 1.2, while Java SE 5 provides the foundation classes, and Servlet 2.5 includes a library to handle HTTP requests.

Viewing a Web Page

To understand JSP, you first need to have a clear idea of what happens when you ask your browser to view a web page, either by typing a URL in the address field of your browser or by clicking on a hyperlink. Figure 1-1 shows you how it works.

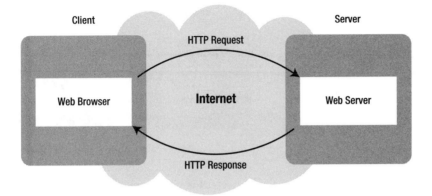

Figure 1-1. *Viewing a plain HTML page*

The following steps show what happens when you request your browser to view a web page:

1. When you type an address such as http://www.website.com/path/whatever.html into the address field, your browser first resolves www.website.com (i.e., the name of the web server) into the corresponding Internet Protocol (IP) address, usually by asking the domain name server provided by your Internet Service Provider (ISP). Then your browser sends an HTTP request to the newly found IP address to receive the content of the file identified by /path/whatever.html.

2. In reply, the web server sends an HTTP response containing a plain-text HTML page. Images and other nontextual components, such as applets and sounds, only appear in the page as references.

3. Your browser receives the response, interprets the HTML code contained in the page, requests the nontextual components from the server, and displays the lot.

Viewing a JSP Page

With JSP, the web page doesn't actually exist on the server. As you can see in Figure 1-2, the server creates it fresh when responding to each request.

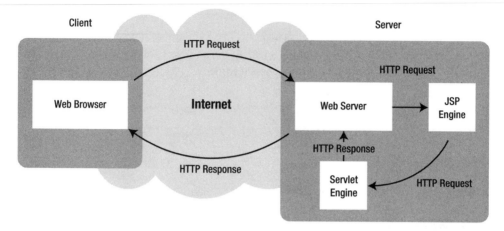

Figure 1-2. *Viewing a JSP page*

The following steps explain how the web server creates the web page:

1. As with a normal page, your browser sends an HTTP request to the web server. This doesn't change with JSP, although the URL probably ends in .jsp instead of .html.

2. The web server is not a normal server, but rather a Java server, with the extensions necessary to identify and handle Java servlets. The web server recognizes that the HTTP request is for a JSP page and forwards it to a JSP engine.

3. The JSP engine loads the JSP page from disk and converts it into a Java servlet. From this point on, this servlet is indistinguishable from any other servlet developed directly in Java rather than JSP, although the automatically generated Java code of a JSP servlet is difficult to read, and you should never modify it by hand.

4. The JSP engine compiles the servlet into an executable class and forwards the original request to a servlet engine. Note that the JSP engine only converts the JSP page to Java and recompiles the servlet if it finds that the JSP page has changed since the last request. This makes the process more efficient than with other scripting languages (such as PHP) and therefore faster.

5. A part of the web server called the *servlet engine* loads the Servlet class and executes it. During execution, the servlet produces an output in HTML format, which the servlet engine passes to the web server inside an HTTP response.

6. The web server forwards the HTTP response to your browser.

7. Your web browser handles the dynamically generated HTML page inside the HTTP response exactly as if it were a static page. In fact, static and dynamic web pages are in the same format.

You might ask, "Why do you say that with JSP, the page is created fresh for each request, if it is only recompiled when it has been updated?"

What reaches your browser is the *output* generated by the servlet (by the converted and compiled JSP page), not the JSP page itself. The same servlet produces different outputs depending on the parameters of the HTTP request and other factors. For example, suppose you're browsing the products offered by an online shop. When you click on the image of a product, your browser generates an HTTP request with the product code as a parameter. As a result, the servlet generates an HTML page with the description of that product. The server doesn't need to recompile the servlet for each product code.

The servlet queries a database containing the details of all the products, obtains the description of the product you're interested in, and formats an HTML page with that data. This is what dynamic HTML is all about!

Plain HTML is not capable of interrogating a database, but Java is, and JSP gives you the means of including snippets of Java inside an HTML page.

Hello World!

A small example of JSP will give you a more practical idea of how JSP works. Let's start once more from HTML. Listing 1-1 shows you a plain HTML page to display "Hello World!" in your browser's window.

Listing 1-1. *hello.html*

```
<html>
<head><title>Hello World static HTML</title></head>
<body>
Hello World!
</body>
</html>
```

Create this folder to store `hello.html`:

```
C:\Program Files\Apache Software Foundation\Tomcat 6.0\webapps\hello\
```

Type this URL to see the web page in the browser:

```
http://localhost:8080/hello/hello.html
```

Normally, to ask your browser to check that the syntax of the page conforms to the XHTML standard of the World Wide Web Consortium (W3C), you would have to start the page with the following three lines:

```
<?xml version="1.0" encoding="ISO-8859-1"?>
<!DOCTYPE html PUBLIC "-//W3C//DTD XHTML 1.0 Strict//EN"
  "http://www.w3.org/TR/xhtml1/DTD/xhtml1-strict.dtd">
```

You'd also have to replace this line:

```
<html>
```

with this line:

```
<html xmlns="http://www.w3.org/1999/xhtml" xml:lang="en" lang="en">
```

However, for this simple example, we prefer to keep the code to what's essential.
Figure 1-3 shows you how this page will appear in your browser.

Figure 1-3. *"Hello World!" in plain HTML*

If you view the page source through your browser, not surprisingly you'll see exactly
what's shown in Listing 1-1. To obtain exactly the same result with a JSP page, you only need
to insert a JSP directive before the first line, as shown in Listing 1-2, and change the file
extension from html to jsp.

Listing 1-2. *"Hello World!" in a Boring JSP Page*

```
<%@page language="java" contentType="text/html"%>
<html>
<head><title>Hello World not-so-dynamic HTML</title></head>
<body>
Hello World!
</body>
</html>
```

■**Note** Microsoft Internet Explorer 7 only interprets JSP pages that include the page contentType
directive.

Obviously, there isn't much point in using JSP for such a simple page. It only pays to use
JSP if you use it to include dynamic content. Check out Listing 1-3 for something more juicy.

Listing 1-3. *hello.jsp*

```
<%@page language="java" contentType="text/html"%>
<html>
<head><title>Hello World dynamic HTML</title></head>
<body>
Hello World!
<%
  out.println("<br/>Your IP address is " + request.getRemoteAddr());

  String userAgent = request.getHeader("user-agent");
  String browser = "unknown";

  out.print("<br/>and your browser is ");
  if (userAgent != null) {
    if (userAgent.indexOf("MSIE") > -1) {
      browser = "MS Internet Explorer";
      }
    else if (userAgent.indexOf("Firefox") > -1) {
      browser = "Mozilla Firefox";
      }
    }
  out.println(browser);
  %>
</body>
</html>
```

As with hello.html, you can view hello.jsp by placing it in the webapps\hello\ folder.

The code within the <% … %> pair is a scriptlet written in Java. When Tomcat's JSP engine interprets this module, it creates a Java servlet containing 92 lines of code, among which you can find those shown in Listing 1-4 (with some indentation and empty lines removed).

Listing 1-4. *Java Code from the "Hello World!" JSP Page*

```
out.write("\r\n");
out.write("<html>\r\n");
out.write("<head><title>Hello World dynamic HTML</title></head>\r\n");
out.write("<body>\r\n");
out.write("Hello World!\r\n");
out.write('\r');
out.write('\n');
out.println("<br/>Your IP address is " + request.getRemoteAddr());
String userAgent = request.getHeader("user-agent");
String browser = "unknown";
out.print("<br/>and your browser is ");
```

```
if (userAgent != null) {
  if (userAgent.indexOf("MSIE") > -1) {
    browser = "MS Internet Explorer";
    }
  else if (userAgent.indexOf("Firefox") > -1) {
    browser = "Mozilla Firefox";
    }
  }
out.println(browser);
out.write("\r\n");
out.write("</body>\r\n");
out.write("</html>\r\n");
```

As we said before, this servlet executes every time a browser sends a request to the server. However, before the code shown in Listing 1-4 executes, the variable out is bound to the content of the response. As a result, everything written to out ends up in the HTML page that you'll see in your browser. The scriptlet, shown in bold, is copied to the servlet. Everything else is written to the output. This should clarify how the mix of HTML and Java is achieved in a JSP page.

As the variable out is defined in each servlet, you can use it within any JSP module to insert something into the response. Another such "global" JSP variable is request (of type HttpServletRequest). The request contains the IP address from which the request was originated—that is, of the remote computer with the browser (remember that this code runs on the server). To extract the address from the request, you only need to execute its method getRemoteAddr(). The request also contains information about the browser. When some browsers send a request, they provide somewhat misleading information, and the format is complex. However, the code in Listing 1-4 shows you how to determine whether you're using Microsoft Internet Explorer or Mozilla Firefox. Figure 1-4 shows the generated page as it appears in a browser.

Figure 1-4. *"Hello World!" in JSP*

Notice that IP address 127.0.0.1 is consistent with the host localhost. And just in case you want to see that the HTML is indeed dynamic, check out Figure 1-5. Incidentally, the method you used in hello.jsp to identify the Internet Explorer from the user agent is the official one provided by Microsoft.

Figure 1-5. *"Hello World!" in JSP with Internet Explorer*

JSP Application Architectures

The insertion of Java code into HTML modules opens up the possibility of building dynamic web pages, but to say that it is possible doesn't mean that you can do it efficiently and effectively. If you start developing complex applications by means of scriptlets enclosed in <% ... %> pairs, you'll rapidly reach the point where the code will become difficult to maintain. The key problem with mixing Java and HTML, as in "Hello World!," is that the application logic and the way the information is presented in the browser are mixed. In general, the business application designers and the web page designers are different people with complementary and only partly overlapping skills. While application designers are experts in complex algorithms and databases, web designers focus on page composition and graphics. The architecture of your JSP-based applications should reflect this distinction. The last thing you want to do is blur the roles within the development team and end up with everybody doing what somebody else is better qualified to do.

The Model 1 Architecture

The first solution to this problem that developers found was to define the JSP Model 1 architecture, in which the application logic is implemented in Java classes (i.e., Java beans), which you can then use within JSP (see Figure 1-6).

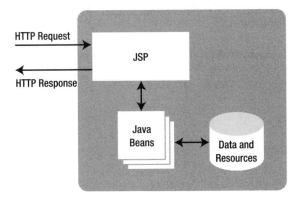

Figure 1-6. *The JSP Model 1 architecture*

Model 1 is acceptable for applications containing up to a few thousand lines of code, and especially for programmers, but the JSP pages still have to handle the HTTP requests, and this can cause headaches for the page designers.

The Model 2 Architecture

A better solution, also suitable for larger applications, is to separate application logic and page presentation. This solution comes in the form of the JSP Model 2 architecture, also known as the model-view-controller (MVC) design pattern (see Figure 1-7).

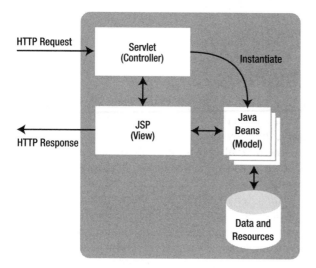

Figure 1-7. *JSP Model 2 architecture*

With this model, a servlet processes the request, handles the application logic, and instantiates the Java beans. JSP obtains data from the beans and can format the response without having to know anything about what's going on behind the scenes. To illustrate this model, we will describe a sample application called Ebookshop, a small application to sell books online. Ebookshop is not really functional, because the list of books is hard-coded in the application rather than stored in a database. Also, nothing happens once you confirm the order. However, this example serves the purpose of showing you how Model 2 lets you separate business logic and presentation.

Figure 1-8 shows the Ebookshop's home page, which you see when you type http://localhost:8080/ebookshop in your browser's address field.

Figure 1-8. *The Ebookshop home page*

You can select a book by clicking on the drop-down list, as shown in the picture, type in the number of copies you need, and then click the Add to Cart button. Every time you do so, the content of your shopping cart appears at the bottom of the window, as shown in Figure 1-9.

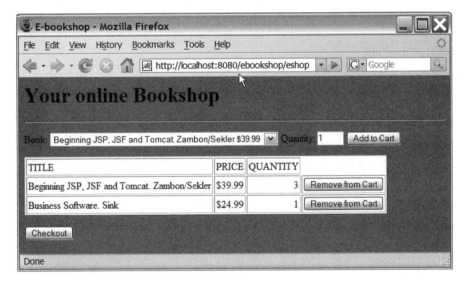

Figure 1-9. *The Ebookshop home page displaying the shopping cart*

You can remove an item from the shopping cart or go to the checkout. If you add additional copies of a book to the cart, the quantity in the cart will increase accordingly.

If you click on the Checkout button, you'll see the page shown in Figure 1-10.

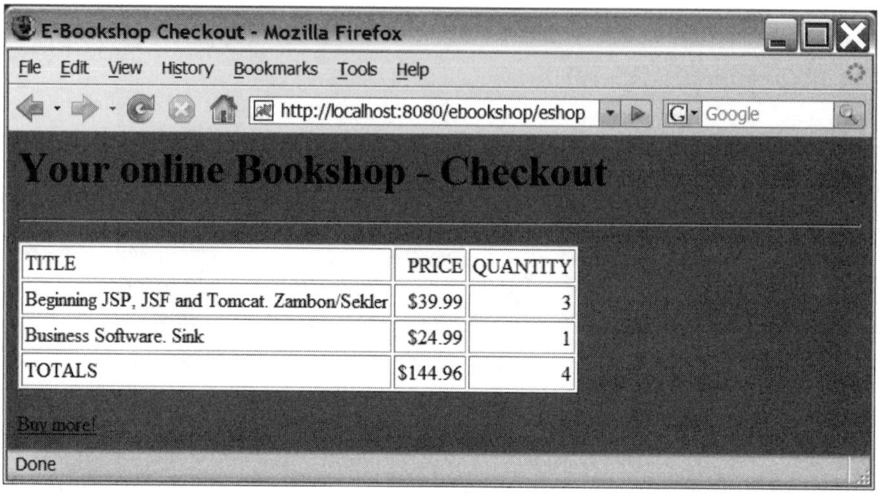

Figure 1-10. *The Ebookshop checkout page*

If you click on the Buy more! link, you'll go back to the home page with an empty shopping cart, ready for more shopping.

The Ebookshop Home Page

Listing 1-5 shows the home page http://localhost:8080/ebookshop/index.jsp. For your convenience, we've highlighted the JSP directives and scriptlets in bold.

Listing 1-5. *The Ebookshop Home Page index.jsp*

```
<%@page language="java" contentType="text/html"%>
<%@page session="true" import="java.util.*, ebookshop.Book"%>
<html>
<head>
  <title>E-bookshop</title>
  <style type="text/css">
    body {background-color:gray; font-size=10pt;}
    H1 {font-size:20pt;}
    table {background-color:white;}
    </style>
  </head>
<body>
  <H1>Your online Bookshop</H1>
  <hr/><p/>
<%  // Scriptlet 1: check whether the book list is ready
  Vector booklist = (Vector)session.getValue("ebookshop.list");
  if (booklist == null) {
    response.sendRedirect("/ebookshop/eshop");
    }
```

```jsp
    else {
    %>
      <form name="addForm" action="eshop" method="POST">
        <input type="hidden" name="do_this" value="add">
        Book:
        <select name=book>
<% // Scriptlet 2: copy the book list to the selection control
        for (int i = 0; i < booklist.size(); i++) {
            out.println("<option>" + (String)booklist.elementAt(i) + "</option>");
            }
    %>
        </select>
        Quantity: <input type="text" name="qty" size="3" value="1">
        <input type="submit" value="Add to Cart">
      </form>
      <p/>
<% // Scriptlet 3: check whether the shopping cart is empty
    Vector shoplist = (Vector)session.getValue("ebookshop.cart");
    if (shoplist != null  &&  shoplist.size() > 0) {
    %>
        <table border="1" cellpadding="2">
        <tr>
        <td>TITLE</td>
        <td>PRICE</td>
        <td>QUANTITY</td>
        <td></td>
        </tr>
<% // Scriptlet 4: display the books in the shopping cart
        for (int i = 0; i < shoplist.size(); i++) {
          Book aBook = (Book)shoplist.elementAt(i);
    %>
          <tr>
            <form name="removeForm" action="eshop" method="POST">
              <input type="hidden" name="position" value="<%=i%>">
              <input type="hidden" name="do_this" value="remove">
              <td><%=aBook.getTitle()%></td>
              <td align="right">$<%=aBook.getPrice()%></td>
              <td align="right"><%=aBook.getQuantity()%></td>
              <td><input type="submit" value="Remove from Cart"></td>
            </form>
          </tr>
<%
        } // for (int i..
    %>
        </table>
```

```
      <p/>
      <form name="checkoutForm" action="eshop" method="POST">
        <input type="hidden" name="do_this" value="checkout">
        <input type="submit" value="Checkout">
      </form>
<%
      } // if (shoplist..
    } // if (booklist..else..
  %>
  </body>
</html>
```

First, index.jsp (shown in Scriptlet 1) checks whether the list of books to be sold is available and, if it isn't, it passes the control to the servlet, which then must initialize the book list. In reality, the book list would be very long and kept in a database. Note that JSP doesn't *need to know* where the list is kept. This is the first hint at the fact that application logic and presentation are separate. You'll see later how the servlet fills in the book list and returns control to index.jsp. For now, let's proceed with the analysis of the home page.

If Scriptlet 1 discovers that the book list exists, it copies it into the select control one by one (as shown in Scriptlet 2). Notice how JSP simply creates each option by writing to the out stream. When the buyer clicks on the Add to Cart button after selecting a title and setting the number of copies, the home page posts a request to the servlet with the address eshop and with the hidden parameter do_this set to add. Once more, the servlet takes care of updating or creating the shopping cart by instantiating the class Book for each new book added to the cart. This is application logic, not presentation of information.

Scriptlet 3 checks whether a shopping cart exists. index.jsp, being completely data-driven, doesn't remember what has happened before, so it runs every time from the beginning. Therefore, it checks for the presence of a shopping cart even when the buyer sees the book list for the very first time.

Scriptlet 4 displays the items in the shopping cart, each one with its own form. If the buyer decides to delete an entry, index.jsp sends a request to the servlet with the hidden parameter do_this set to remove.

The sole purpose of the last two scriptlets is to close the curly brackets of ifs and fors. However, notice that the form to ask the servlet to do the checkout is only displayed to the buyer when the shopping cart isn't empty. If the buyer clicks on the Checkout button, index.jsp will send a request to the servlet with the hidden parameter do_this set to checkout.

Finally, notice that some elements enclosed within <%= and %> are mixed inside the normal HTML. They are <%=i%>, <%=aBook.getTitle()%>, <%=aBook.getPrice()%>, and <%=aBook.getQuantity()%>. These elements let you embed values resulting from JSP expressions in HTML without having to execute scriptlets. The first expression, <%=i%>, is the position of the book within the shopping cart. The other three are the execution of methods of an object of type Book, which the servlet instantiated for each new book added to the cart.

You've probably noticed that the address shown in the browser is http://localhost:8080/ebookshop/eshop. This is actually the address of the Java servlet that controls the application.

The Ebookshop Servlet

Listing 1-6 shows the source code of the servlet.

Listing 1-6. *ShoppingServlet.java*

```java
package ebookshop;
import java.util.*;
import java.io.*;
import javax.servlet.*;
import javax.servlet.http.*;
import ebookshop.Book;

public class ShoppingServlet extends HttpServlet {

  public void init(ServletConfig conf) throws ServletException  {
    super.init(conf);
    }

  public void doGet (HttpServletRequest req, HttpServletResponse res)
      throws ServletException, IOException {
    doPost(req, res);
    }

  public void doPost (HttpServletRequest req, HttpServletResponse res)
      throws ServletException, IOException {
    HttpSession session = req.getSession(true);
    Vector<Book> shoplist =
      (Vector<Book>)session.getAttribute("ebookshop.cart");
    String do_this = req.getParameter("do_this");
    if (do_this == null) {
      Vector<String> blist = new Vector<String>();
      blist.addElement("Beginning JSP, JSF and Tomcat. Zambon/Sekler $39.99");
      blist.addElement("Beginning JBoss Seam. Nusairat $39.99");
      blist.addElement("Founders at Work. Livingston $25.99");
      blist.addElement("Business Software. Sink $24.99");
      blist.addElement("Foundations of Security. Daswani/Kern/Kesavan $39.99");
      session.setAttribute("ebookshop.list", blist);
      ServletContext    sc = getServletContext();
      RequestDispatcher rd = sc.getRequestDispatcher("/");
      rd.forward(req, res);
      }
```

```java
      else {
        if (do_this.equals("checkout"))  {
          float dollars = 0;
          int   books = 0;
          for (int i = 0; i < shoplist.size(); i++) {
            Book  aBook = (Book)shoplist.elementAt(i);
            float price = aBook.getPrice();
            int   qty = aBook.getQuantity();
            dollars += price * qty;
            books += qty;
            }
          req.setAttribute("dollars", new Float(dollars).toString());
          req.setAttribute("books", new Integer(books).toString());
          ServletContext     sc = getServletContext();
          RequestDispatcher rd = sc.getRequestDispatcher("/Checkout.jsp");
          rd.forward(req, res);
          } // if (..checkout..
        else {
          if (do_this.equals("remove")) {
            String pos = req.getParameter("position");
            shoplist.removeElementAt((new Integer(pos)).intValue());
            }
          else if (do_this.equals("add")) {
            boolean found = false;
            Book aBook = getBook(req);
            if (shoplist == null) {  // the shopping cart is empty
              shoplist = new Vector<Book>();
              shoplist.addElement(aBook);
              }
            else {  // update the #copies if the book is already there
              for (int i = 0; i < shoplist.size() && !found; i++) {
                Book b = (Book)shoplist.elementAt(i);
                if (b.getTitle().equals(aBook.getTitle())) {
                  b.setQuantity(b.getQuantity() + aBook.getQuantity());
                  shoplist.setElementAt(b, i);
                  found = true;
                  }
                } // for (i..
              if (!found) {  // if it is a new book => Add it to the shoplist
                shoplist.addElement(aBook);
                }
              } // if (shoplist == null) .. else ..
            } // if (..add..
```

```
        session.setAttribute("ebookshop.cart", shoplist);
        ServletContext sc = getServletContext();
        RequestDispatcher rd = sc.getRequestDispatcher("/");
        rd.forward(req, res);
        } // if (..checkout..else
      } // if (do_this..
    } // doPost

  private Book getBook(HttpServletRequest req) {
    String myBook = req.getParameter("book");
    int    n = myBook.indexOf('$');
    String title = myBook.substring(0, n);
    String price = myBook.substring(n+1);
    String qty = req.getParameter("qty");
    return new Book(title, Float.parseFloat(price), Integer.parseInt(qty));
    } // getBook
  }
```

As you can see, the init() method only executes the standard servlet initialization, and the doGet() method simply executes doPost(), where all the work is done. If you were to remove the doGet() method, you would effectively forbid the direct call of the servlet. That is, if you typed http://localhost:8080/ebookshop/eshop in your browser, you would receive an error message that says the requested resource isn't available. As it is, you can type the URL with or without trailing eshop.

When you analyze index.jsp, you can see that it can pass control to the servlet on four occasions, as listed here from the point of view of the servlet:

1. **If no book list exists**: This happens when the buyer types http://localhost:8080/ ebookshop/. The servlet executes without any parameter, initializes the book list, and passes control straight back to index.jsp.

2. **When the buyer clicks on Add to Cart**: The servlet executes with do_this set to add and a parameter containing the book description. Normally, this would be done more elegantly with a reference to the book rather than the whole description, but we want to keep things as simple as possible. The servlet creates a cart if necessary and adds to it a new object of type Book or, if the same book is already in the cart, updates its quantity. After that, it passes the control back to index.jsp.

3. **When the buyer clicks on Remove from Cart**: The servlet executes with do_this set to remove and a parameter containing the position of the book within the cart. The servlet removes the book in the given position by deleting the object of type Book from the vector representing the cart. After that, it passes the control back to index.jsp.

4. **When the buyer clicks on Checkout**: The servlet executes with do_this set to checkout. The servlet calculates the total amount of money and the number of books ordered, adds them as attributes to the HTTP request, and passes the control to Checkout.jsp, which has the task of displaying the bill.

More on Ebookshop

By now, it should be clear to you how the servlet is in control of the application and how JSP is only used to present the data. To see the full picture, you only need to see Book.java, the Java bean used to represent a book, and Checkout.jsp, which displays the bill. Listing 1-7 shows the code for Book.java.

Listing 1-7. *Book.java*

```java
package ebookshop;
public class Book {
  String title;
  float  price;
  int    quantity;
  public Book(String t, float p, int q) {
    title   = t;
    price   = p;
    quantity = q;
    }
  public String getTitle()         { return title; }
  public void   setTitle(String t) { title = t; }
  public float  getPrice()         { return price; }
  public void   setPrice(float p)  { price = p; }
  public int    getQuantity()      { return quantity; }
  public void   setQuantity(int q) { quantity = q; }
  }
```

In a more realistic case, the class Book would contain much more information, which the buyer could use to select the book. Also, the class attribute title is a misnomer, as it also includes the author names, but you get the idea. Listing 1-8 shows the code for Checkout.jsp.

Listing 1-8. *Checkout.jsp*

```jsp
<%@page language="java" contentType="text/html"%>
<%@page session="true" import="java.util.*, ebookshop.Book" %>
<html>
<head>
  <title>E-Bookshop Checkout</title>
  <style type="text/css">
    body {background-color:gray; font-size=10pt;}
    H1 {font-size:20pt;}
    table {background-color:white;}
    </style>
  </head>
<body>
  <H1>Your online Bookshop - Checkout</H1>
  <hr/><p/>
  <table border="1" cellpadding="2">
```

```
    <tr>
      <td>TITLE</td>
      <td align="right">PRICE</td>
      <td align="right">QUANTITY</td>
    </tr>
<%
    Vector shoplist = (Vector)session.getValue("ebookshop.cart");
    for (int i = 0; i < shoplist.size(); i++) {
      Book anOrder = (Book)shoplist.elementAt(i);
 %>
    <tr>
      <td><%=anOrder.getTitle()%></td>
      <td align="right">$<%=anOrder.getPrice()%></td>
      <td align="right"><%=anOrder.getQuantity()%></td>
    </tr>
<%
    }
    session.invalidate();
 %>
    <tr>
      <td>TOTALS</td>
      <td align="right">$<%=(String)request.getAttribute("dollars")%></td>
      <td align="right"><%=(String)request.getAttribute("books")%></td>
    </tr>
    </table>
  <p/>
  <a href="/ebookshop/eshop">Buy more!</a>
  </body>
</html>
```

Checkout.jsp displays the shopping cart and the totals precalculated by the servlet, and it invalidates the session so that a new empty shopping cart will be created if the application is restarted from the same browser window.

Note that you could have included the checkout logic in index.jsp and made its execution dependent on the presence of the two totals. However, we wanted to show you a more structured application. It's also better design to keep different functions in different JSP modules. In fact, we could have also kept the shopping cart in a separate JSP file. In real life, we would have certainly done so. In addition, we would have saved the styles in a Cascading Style Sheets (CSS) file rather than repeating them in all JSP sources. Finally, there is close to no error checking and reporting. You could easily crash this application.

Before we move on, you'll certainly find it interesting to see the dynamic HTML page, which actually reaches the browser after adding one item to the shopping cart (see Listing 1-9, in which we've removed some empty lines).

Listing 1-9. *HTML Generated by index.jsp*

```
<html>
<head>
  <title>E-bookshop</title>
  <style type="text/css">
    body {background-color:gray; font-size=10pt;}
    H1 {font-size:20pt;}
    table {background-color:white;}
    </style>
  </head>
<body>
  <H1>Your online Bookshop</H1>
  <hr/><p/>
    <form name="addForm" action="eshop" method="POST">
      <input type="hidden" name="do_this" value="add">
      Book:
      <select name=book>
<option>Beginning JSP, JSF and Tomcat. Zambon/Sekler $39.99</option>
<option>Beginning JBoss Seam. Nusairat $39.99</option>
<option>Founders at Work. Livingston $25.99</option>
<option>Business Software. Sink $24.99</option>
<option>Foundations of Security. Daswani/Kern/Kesavan $39.99</option>
        </select>
      Quantity: <input type="text" name="qty" size="3" value="1">
      <input type="submit" value="Add to Cart">
      </form>
    <p/>
      <table border="1" cellpadding="2">
      <tr>
      <td>TITLE</td>
      <td>PRICE</td>
      <td>QUANTITY</td>
      <td></td>
      </tr>
        <tr>
          <form name="removeForm" action="eshop" method="POST">
            <input type="hidden" name="position" value="0">
            <input type="hidden" name="do_this" value="remove">
            <td>Beginning JSP, JSF and Tomcat. Zambon/Sekler </td>
            <td align="right">$39.99</td>
            <td align="right">3</td>
            <td><input type="submit" value="Remove from Cart"></td>
            </form>
          </tr>
      </table>
```

```
      <p/>
      <form name="checkoutForm" action="eshop" method="POST">
        <input type="hidden" name="do_this" value="checkout">
        <input type="submit" value="Checkout">
        </form>
  </body>
</html>
```

Neat, isn't it?

You now have in your hands the full code of a nontrivial Java/JSP application, but you still need to know how to make these four modules work together. For that, you need a web server that translates your JSP pages into Java, executes your servlet, and acts as an interface between your web application and the remote browsers. You guessed it: Tomcat.

What Role Does Tomcat Play in All This?

Tomcat is what makes the Ebookshop application accessible over the Internet. Its latest release (6.0) implements JSP 2.1 and EL 2.1. It obviously requires the Java SE 5 runtime environment, because older releases don't include the correct versions of JSP and EL. The beauty of Tomcat is that it also includes its own HTTP server, so you don't need anything else to handle client requests.

Rather than providing abstract and general explanations, we'll use the Ebookshop example to tell you what to do in practice. You have to organize the following files: index.jsp, Checkout.jsp, ShoppingServlet.java, and Book.java. First, create the folder structure shown in Figure 1-11 in C:\Program Files\Apache Software Foundation\Tomcat 6.0\webapps\, and place your four source files as indicated (see Appendix A for the installation procedure of Tomcat).

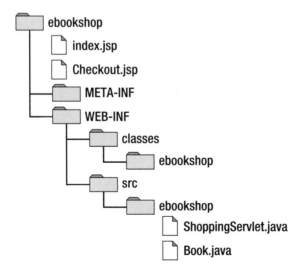

Figure 1-11. *The Ebookshop folder structure*

To get the application to work, you first need to compile the two Java modules. Assuming that you've already installed the appropriate JDK (again, see Appendix A for the instructions), it boils down to executing the Java compiler from the command line. You should write a small batch file rather than always open a DOS window, change the directory, and type the command. Listing 1-10 shows an example of a batch file you could use. Just place it inside the WEB-INF folder and double-click it.

Listing 1-10. *compile_it.bat*

```
@echo off
set aname=ebookshop
set /P fname=Please enter the java file name without extension:
set fil=%aname%\%fname%
echo *** compile_it.bat: compile src\%fil%.java
javac -verbose -deprecation -Xlint:unchecked -classpath classes src\%fil%.java
if %errorlevel% GTR 1 goto _PAUSE
echo *** compile_it.bat: move the class to the package directory
move /y src\%fil%.class classes\%fil%.class
:_PAUSE
pause
```

The batch file opens a DOS window automatically and asks you to type the name of a Java file (without the extension). It then compiles the file and moves the resulting class into the classes\ebookshop\ subfolder. This line invokes the Java compiler with the switches that maximize both the information you get and the checks on your sources:

```
javac -verbose -deprecation -Xlint:unchecked -classpath classes src\%fil%.java
```

Notice the classpath switch, which tells the compiler to look for classes in the local directory in addition to the usual places where the Java libraries are kept. This is necessary, because ShoppingServlet.java imports the class Book and without the classpath switch, the compiler wouldn't know where to find it. This also means that you have to compile Book.java *before* ShoppingServlet.java.

When executing your application, Tomcat looks for classes in the WEB-INF\classes\ folder immediately inside the root folder of your application (in this case ebookshop), which in turn is immediately inside webapps. The directory structure inside WEB-INF\classes must reflect what you write in the package statement at the beginning of the Java sources. In your Java sources, you have this statement:

```
package ebookshop;
```

If you had written this instead:

```
package myApplications.ebookshop;
```

you would have had to insert a myApplications folder below classes and above ebookshop. To avoid confusion, note that the package name has nothing to do with the name of the application. That is, you could have named the package (and, therefore, the folder below the classes)

qwertyuiop instead of ebookshop. In fact, you could have dispensed with the package statement altogether and placed your classes directly inside the classes folder. Finally, you could
have also created a JAR file.

Tomcat automatically converts your JSP files into Java classes the first time they're
needed, but before you're ready to go, you still need to write an additional file where you
describe the structure of your application to Tomcat. This file *must* be named web.xml and
placed in WEB-INF, as you can see in Listing 1-11.

Listing 1-11. *web.xml*

```
<?xml version="1.0" encoding="ISO-8859-1"?>
<web-app xmlns="http://java.sun.com/xml/ns/j2ee"
    xmlns:xsi="http://www.w3.org/2001/XMLSchema-instance"
    xsi:schemaLocation="~CCC
"http://java.sun.com/xml/ns/j2ee http://java.sun.com/xml/ns/j2ee/web-app_2_4.xsd"
    version="2.4">
  <display-name>Electronic Bookshop</display-name>
  <description>
    e-bookshop example for
    Beginning JSP, JSF and Tomcat: from Novice to Professional
    </description>
  <servlet>
    <servlet-name>EBookshopServlet</servlet-name>
    <servlet-class>ebookshop.ShoppingServlet</servlet-class>
    </servlet>
  <servlet-mapping>
    <servlet-name>EBookshopServlet</servlet-name>
    <url-pattern>/eshop</url-pattern>
    </servlet-mapping>
</web-app>
```

The two crucial lines are those highlighted in bold. The first one tells Tomcat that the
servlet is in classes\ebookshop\ShoppingServlet.class. The second one tells Tomcat that the
requests will refer to the servlet as /eshop. As the root folder of this application (i.e., the folder
immediately inside webapps) is ebookshop, Tomcat will then route to this servlet all the requests
it will receive for the URL http://servername:8080/ebookshop/eshop.
The element <servlet-name> in both <servlet> and <servlet-mapping> is only needed to make
the connection between the two. If you now open a browser and type http://localhost:8080/
ebookshop/, you should see the application's home page.

You might be wondering about the purpose of the META-INF folder. Place inside that folder
an empty file named MANIFEST.MF, zip the content of the whole application folder (webapps\
ebookshop\), taking care to include entries for the relative folder paths, and rename the file
ebookshop.war. By doing so, you've created a Web ARchive (WAR). To deploy your application
on a different server, just place the WAR file inside the webapps folder. Tomcat unpacks it for
you automatically *as soon as it realizes* that it's there. What could be easier than that?

Summary

In this chapter, we told you what happens on the server when you click a link in your browser to view a new page. We then introduced servlet and JSP technologies and explained what role they play in a web server.

We showed you a simple HTML page and how you can begin to add dynamic content to it with JSP. Next, we described how JSP-based applications are structured. Using the Ebookshop sample application, we showed a practical example of the MVC architecture. Finally, we introduced you to Tomcat and described how to install the Ebookshop application.

We covered a lot of ground in this chapter, showing you all the parts of a small working web application. Don't worry if you're finding it a bit difficult to absorb it all. Everything will become clear as we proceed through the next chapters in a more systematic fashion.

CHAPTER 2

■ ■ ■

JSP Explained

In the previous chapter, we placed JSP in the context of web applications, described JSP in generic terms, and showed a couple of examples. In this chapter, we'll briefly introduce all the JSP components and then jump into more interesting examples. For more details on the JSP components, please refer to Appendix D. At the end of this chapter, we'll show you an alternative syntax for JSP pages, which makes them 100% XML-compliant.

Introduction

In Chapter 1's simple `hello.jsp` example (shown in Listing 1-3), you saw that `request.getHeader("user-agent")` returns a string that describes the client's web browser. Despite the fact that the variable `request` isn't defined anywhere, this works because Tomcat defines several *implicit variables*: `application`, `config`, `out`, `pageContext`, `request`, `response`, and `session`. The most commonly used are `out` and `request`, followed by `application` and `session`.

This first line of `hello.jsp` is an example of a *directive* element, another component of JSP:

```
<%@page language="java" contentType="text/html"%>
```

Directives provide Tomcat with information it needs to translate the JSP page. As such, directives are independent of specific requests. Besides `page`, other available directives are `include` and `taglib`.

In Chapter 1, we didn't show you any example of a *standard action*, another component of JSP. The purpose of standard actions is to encapsulate activities that Tomcat performs when handling an HTTP request from a client. There are more than a dozen standard actions: `attribute`, `body`, `element`, `fallback`, `forward`, `getProperty`, `include`, `param`, `params`, `plugin`, `setProperty`, `text`, and `useBean`. For example, the following standard action includes in a JSP page the output of another JSP:

```
<jsp:include page="another.jsp"/>
```

The `hello.jsp` example also includes another JSP component, a *scripting element*, which is a scriptlet delimited by the pair <% and %>. All scripting elements consist of code delimited by particular sequences of characters.

EL is a JSP component that gives you easy access to external objects (i.e. Java beans).

JSP provides a mechanism that lets you define custom actions in which a prefix of your choice replaces the `jsp` of the standard actions. With the *tag extension mechanism*, you can create libraries of actions, which you can then use in all your applications. Several custom actions have become so widely used in the programming community that Sun Microsystems decided to standardize them. The result is JSTL.

Scripting Elements and Java

A JSP page consists of a page template, which is composed of HTML code, as well as JSP elements, such as directives, scripting elements, and standard actions. As we mentioned in Chapter 1, scriptlets, which are a type of scripting element, let you embed Java code in an HTML page.[1]

Every Java executable—whether it's a free-standing program running directly within a runtime environment, an applet executing inside a browser, or a servlet executing in a container such as Tomcat—boils down to instantiating classes into objects and executing their methods. This might not be so apparent with JSP, because Tomcat wraps every JSP page into a class of type `Servlet` behind the scenes, but it still applies.

Java methods consist of a sequence of operations to instantiate objects, allocate memory for variables, calculate expressions, perform assignments, or execute other methods.

In this section, we'll summarize the syntax of Java while keeping JSP in mind. This practical introduction will provide the essentials and point out some pitfalls.

Data Types and Variables

Java makes available primitive data types similar to the basic types of C/C++ (see Table 2-1). However, there is one important, if not so apparent, difference. The precision of the numeric types is implementation-dependent in C, but it is guaranteed to be constant across platforms in Java.

Table 2-1. *Java Data Types*

Name	Class	Description
byte	Byte	1-byte signed integer (−128 to +127)
short	Short	2-byte signed integer (−32,768 to +32,767)
int	Integer	4-byte signed integer (−2,147,483,648 to +2,147,483,647)
long	Long	8-byte signed integer (approximately -10^{19} to $+10^{19}$)
float	Float	32-bit signed floating-point (8-bit exponent, 23-bit precision)
double	Double	64-bit signed floating-point (11-bit exponent, 52-bit precision)
char	Character	16-bit unsigned Unicode
boolean	Boolean	Either true or false

---

1. *Beginning Java Objects: From Concepts to Code, Second Edition* by Jacquie Barker (Apress, 2005) covers object concepts, modeling, and Java programming.

The second column of Table 2-1 gives you the names of the so-called *wrapper classes* that Java makes available for each primitive type. These classes provide some useful static methods to manipulate numbers. For example, Integer.parseInt(String s, int radix) interprets a string as a number in the base set by the second argument and returns it as an int value (e.g., Integer.parseInt("12", 16) and Integer.parseInt("10010", 2) both return 18).

Programs in Java can be platform-independent, because all platform dependencies are "hidden" inside libraries. The wrapper classes are in the java.lang library, together with dozens of other general classes such as String and Math. You can find the full documentation of the Java 6.0 platform at http://java.sun.com/javase/6/docs/, and you can find a description of its classes at http://java.sun.com/javase/6/docs/api/.

Here are some examples of how you can declare variables and initialize them:

```
String aString = "abcdxyz";
int k = aString.length();  // k is then set to 7
char c = aString.charAt(4);  // c is set to 'x'
static final String NAME = "John Doe";
```

The final keyword in the last example of declarations makes the variable unchangeable. This is how you define constants in Java. The static keyword indicates that a variable is to be shared by all objects instantiated from the class within the same application.

The use of static variables in JSP requires some further comment. In JSP, you can declare variables in three ways:

```
<% int k = 0; %>
<%! int k = 0; %>
<% static int k = 0; %>
```

The first declaration means that a new variable is created for each incoming HTTP client request; the second one means that a new variable is created for each new instance of the servlet; and the third one means that the variable is shared among all instances of the servlet.

Tomcat converts each JSP page into a subclass of the HTTP servlet class (javax.servlet.http.HttpServlet). Normally, Tomcat instantiates each one of these classes only once and then creates a Java thread for each incoming request. The same servlet object is then executed within each thread. As there is a single servlet instance, the second and third declarations have identical results with Tomcat. However, this is no longer true if you direct Tomcat to create a new servlet instance for each incoming request. Then, only the third declaration will guarantee that the variable is shared among all requests.

You're free to name your variables as you like, though your case-sensitive string of characters must begin with a letter, a dollar, or an underscore and not contain a space. That said, be aware that the following keywords are reserved and will cause a compilation error: abstract, assert, boolean, break, byte, case, catch, char, class, const, continue, default, do, double, else, enum, extends, final, finally, float, for, goto, if, implements, import, instanceof, int, interface, long, native, new, package, private, protected, public, return, short, static, strictfp, super, switch, synchronized, this, throw, throws, transient, try, void, volatile, and while. Whenever possible, use capital letters for constants.

Hexadecimal numbers start with 0x and can contain 0-9, A-F, and a-f (e.g., 0x1A). Special characters are *escaped* with a backslash: backslash: \\, backspace: \b, carriage return: \r, double quote: \", form feed: \f, line feed: \n, single quote: \', and tab: \t. With \u followed by up to four hexadecimal digits, you can specify any Unicode character (e.g., \u1F3).

Objects and Arrays

To create an object of a certain type (i.e., to instantiate a class), use the keyword new, as in the following example:

```
Integer integerVar = new Integer(55);
```

This creates an object of type Integer with the value 55.

You can have arrays of any object type or primitive data type, as in the following examples of array declarations:

```
int[] intArray1;
int[] intArray2 = {10, 100, 1000};
String[] stringArray = {"a", "bb"};
```

intArray1 is null; intArray2 is an array of length 3 containing 10, 100, and 1000; and stringArray is an array of length 2 containing the strings "a" and "bb". Although arrays look like something special, they're actually just objects and treated like that. Therefore, you can initialize them with new. For example, this line of code declares an integer array with 10 elements, each initialized to zero:

```
int[] array = new int[10];
```

A two-dimensional table is an array in which each element object is itself an array. This is *not* like in C, where a single block of memory contains all elements of multidimensional tables. For example, this line of code represents a table of two rows, but the first row has three elements, while the second one has only two:

```
int[][] table1 = {{11, 12, 13}, {21, 22}};
```

If you define something like this:

```
int[][] table = new int[2][3];
```

you have a table with two rows and three columns, with all elements initialized to zero.

When declaring a table, you can leave the last dimension empty. For example, the following declaration results in a table of two rows, but the rows are undefined and remain set to null:

```
int[][] table = new int[2][];
```

Before being able to assign values to the individual elements of such a partially defined table, you'll have to declare its rows or assign already declared monodimensional arrays to them:

```
int[] anArray = {10, 100};
table[0] = anArray;
table[1] = new int[5];
```

Operators, Assignments, and Comparisons

There are no surprises with the binary operators—that is, the operators that require two operands. They include the expected addition, subtraction, multiplication, division, and modulus (i.e., the remainder of an integer division) operators. When applied to strings, the addition operator concatenates them.

Besides the normal assignment operator represented by the equal sign, there is also an assignment operator for each binary one. For example, this line of code means that you take the current value of the variable a, add to it b, and store it back into a:

```
a += b;  // same as a = a + b;
```

The most commonly used unary operators (i.e., operators that require a single operand) include a minus sign, which negates what follows, and the increment and decrement operators:

```
a = -b;
a++;  // same as a += 1;
a--;  // same as a -= 1;
```

You can assign the value of an expression of one type to a variable of another type, but with some restrictions. With numeric types, you can only assign values to variables that are of the same type or "larger." For example, you can assign an int value to a variable of type long, but to assign a long value to an int variable, you have to *typecast* (i.e., downcast) the value, as in int iVar = (int)1234567L;. Be careful with that!

You can assign objects to variables of other types, but only if the type of the variable is a superclass of the class from which the object was instantiated. As with primitive data types, you can typecast a value of a superclass into a variable of a subclass type.

Comparison operators are straightforward when applied to primitive data types. You have == to check for equality, != to check for inequality, > to check for "greater than," >= to check for "greater than or equal to," < to check for "less than," and <= to check for "less than or equal to." Nothing surprising there. However, you have to be careful when you make comparisons between objects, as the following example illustrates:

```
String s1 = "abc";
String s2 = "abc";
String s3 = "abcd".substring(0,3);
boolean b1 = (s1 == "abc");  // parentheses not needed but nice!
boolean b2 = (s1 == s2);
boolean b3 = (s1 == s3);
```

As perhaps you expected, b1 and b2 turn out to be true, but b3 is false, although s3 was set to "abc"! The problem is that comparison operators don't look inside the objects. They only check whether the objects are *the same instance* of a class, not whether they're identical. Therefore, as long as you shift around the "abc" string, the compiler keeps referring to the same instance of a literal string, and everything behaves as expected. However, when you create a different instance of "abc", the check for equality fails. The lesson to be learned is that if you want to compare the content of objects, you have to use the equals method. In this example, s1.equals(s3) would have returned true.

For objects, you also have the comparison operator instanceof, which isn't available for primitive data types such as int. For example, ("abc" instanceof String) calculates to true. Be aware that an object isn't only an instance of the class it was instantiated from, but it's also an instance of all its superclasses up to and including Object, which is the superclass of all classes.

With && for *logical and*, || for *logical or*, and ! for *logical not*, you can concatenate comparisons to form more complex conditions. For example, ((a1 == a2) && !(b1 || b2)) calculates to true only if a1 equals a2 and both boolean variables b1 and b2 are false.

Selections

This statement assigns to the string variable s a different string depending on a condition:

```
if (a == 1) {
  s = "yes";
  }
else {
  s = "no";
  }
```

You can omit the else part.

You could have achieved an identical result with a conditional expression and a single assignment:

```
s = (a == 1) ? "yes" : "no";
```

You could also achieve the same result with the following code:

```
switch(a) {
  case 1:
    s = "yes";
    break;
  default:
    s = "no";
    break;
  }
```

Obviously, the switch statement is only useful when there are more than just two alternatives. For example, instead of having a chain of if/else statements, as in the following example:

```
if (expression == 3) {...}
else if (expression == 10) {...}
else {...}
```

you would gain both clarity and conciseness with:

```
switch (expression) {
  case (3): ... break;
  case (10): ... break;
  default: ... break;
  }
```

At the very least, you'll calculate the expression only once. Note that if you omit a break, execution continues to the following case.

Iterations

This statement repeatedly executes the *statements* with increasing values of k, beginning from *initial-value*:

```
for (int k = initial-value; k < limit; k++) { statements; }
```

The general format is:

```
for (initial-assignment; end-condition; iteration-expression) { statements; }
```

The *initial-assignment* is executed only once, before entering the loop. The *statements* are then repeatedly executed as long as the *end-condition* is satisfied. They are not executed at all if the *end-condition* is false from the beginning. The *iteration-expression* is executed at the end of each iteration, before the *end-condition* is checked to see whether a new iteration is to be performed.

You can omit either the *initial-assignment* or the *iteration-expression*. If you omit both, you should replace the keyword for with the keyword while. The following two lines are equivalent:

```
while (end-condition) { statements; }
for (;end-condition;) { statements; }
```

The do-while statement is an alternative to the while loop:

```
do { statements; } while (end-condition);
```

The do-while statement checks the *end-condition* at the end of an iteration instead of at the beginning, like the for and while loops do. As a result, the statements inside a do-while loop are always executed at least once.

The iterations statements described so far are identical to those of C, but Java 5.0 introduced a variant of the for loop, tailored to make the handling of collections easier. Suppose you need a method that produces a concatenation of a set of strings. It might look like this:

```
String concatenate(Set<String> ss) {
  String conc = "";
  Iterator<String> iter = ss.iterator();
  while (iter.hasNext()) {
    conc += iter.next();
    }
  return conc;
  }
```

With the Java for-each loop, you can drop the definition of the iterator and write clearer code:

```
String concatenate(Set<String> ss) {
  String conc = "";
  for (String s : ss) {
    conc += s.next();
    }
  return conc;
  }
```

The Online Bookshop

We'll use the sample online bookshop application throughout the rest of the book. Taking an object-oriented (OO) approach, we'll specify the objects that the application is supposed to handle, the operations that are to be performed on the objects, and the roles of the people who perform those operations. Each role corresponds to an interface; in this case, we'll limit ourselves to the public interface that's available to customers buying from a catalogue. In other words, we won't discuss the administrator role and the corresponding interface to manage products, orders, customers, and so on.

Objects and Operations

In this sample application, we won't keep track of orders and customers, so once the customer goes to the checkout, enters her credit-card information, and checks out, we'll save the order for later use but won't do anything with it. In the real world, we'd have to process the purchase by charging a credit card and dispatching the order.

Product Categories

It's essential that you group your products into categories, especially if you sell a lot of individual ones. In this sample application, we define only one category, but in reality you'd need more. As our shop only sells books, our categories refer to broad subjects such as computing, narrative, and science.

For each category, we define a name and an identifier that's guaranteed to be unique, so we can refer to each category without ambiguity. For this application, we only need to obtain a category name given its ID. Updating categories would be a task for the administrator role, which, as we said, we won't be supporting.

Books

For each book, we define *title*, *author*, *price*, unique *identifier*, *category ID*, and an image of the *front cover*. Customers must be able to select books from a category, search for books, display the book details, and put books into a shopping cart.

Updating book attributes would be an administrator function, which we won't implement in this application.

Shopping Cart

At a minimum, a shopping cart is a list of items, each consisting of a book identifier and the number of copies. We have decided to duplicate the book title, description, and price in the shopping cart. Besides simplifying the application, this also protects the customer from book updates that might occur while he's still shopping. In a more sophisticated application, when some book attributes change, you might like to notify customers who've placed the book in their cart but haven't yet completed the checkout. You wouldn't be able to do so without saving the original information.

Customers must be able to change the number of copies of each book in the cart, remove a book altogether, and go to the checkout. They should also be able to display the shopping cart at any time.

Order

Although this sample application doesn't cover orders, we think it's useful to specify how you should structure it. You need two separate classes: one to represent the ordered items, and one with the customer's data.

For each ordered item, you should save the book data obtained from the shopping cart. The Order object should include all the customer data and define a unique order number.

The Customer Interface

Figure 2-1 shows the home page of the online bookshop. The top includes a link to the shopping cart, while the sidebar on the left features a search box and a list of categories. The other pages only differ in the central panel, which in the home page contains the welcoming string.

Figure 2-1. *Eshop's home page*

Figure 2-2 shows the panel containing the list of books in a category.

Figure 2-2. *A book category on Eshop*

Figure 2-3 shows the details of a book.

Figure 2-3. *A book's details on Eshop*

Figure 2-4 shows the shopping cart with a couple of items.

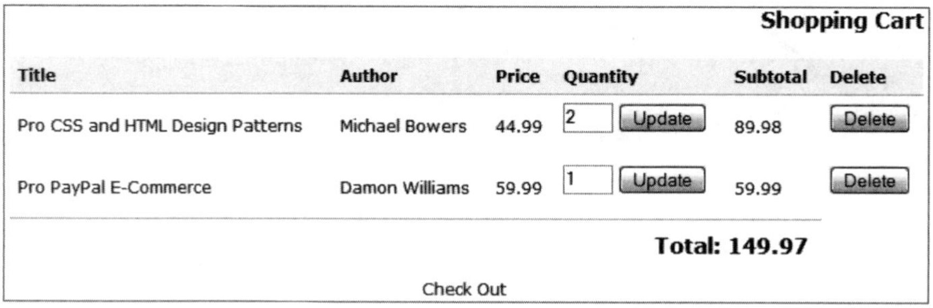

Figure 2-4. *Eshop's shopping cart*

Pretty straightforward, isn't it?

The Eshop Architecture

The design of the Eshop application uses an MVC architecture. The data and the business logic (the model) reside in a database and Java classes; the user interface (the view) is implemented in JSP; and the handler of client requests (the controller) is an HTTP Java servlet.

When the servlet receives a client HTTP request, it instantiates the model's central class and forwards the request to the appropriate JSP page. The JSP page obtains data from the model and generates the HTML response. The model isn't aware of what the JSP pages do with the data they obtain, and the JSP pages aren't aware of where and how the model keeps the data.

The Model

The central model class is called DataManager. Its purpose is to hide all database operations from the JSP pages. DataManager supports some methods that have to do with initialization and connecting to the database, which we'll look at in later chapters. For the time being, we're more interested in the methods that implement the business logic of the application. Table 2-2 lists these methods.

Table 2-2. *DataManager Methods*

Type	Method
String	getCategoryName(int categoryId)
Hashtable	getCategories()
ArrayList	getSearchResults(String keyword)
ArrayList	getBooksInCategory(String categoryId)
Book	getBookDetails(int bookId)
long	insertOrder(String contactName, String deliveryAddress, String ccName, String ccNumber, String ccExpiryDate, Hashtable shoppingCart)

Their purpose should be pretty clear. We have just two remarks concerning insertOrder. First, the value it returns is the order ID to be given back to the client. Second, in a more realistic case, all parameters, with the exception of the shopping cart, would be replaced by a customer ID, typically the customer's e-mail address. In this simple application, however, we aren't keeping track of the customers.

The Controller

The controller servlet extends javax.servlet.http.HttpServlet and is named ShopServlet.

Servlet Initialization

Tomcat executes the servlet method init immediately after instantiating the servlet (see Listing 2-1).

Listing 2-1. *ShopServlet.java - init Method*

```java
public void init(ServletConfig config) throws ServletException {
  System.out.println("*** initializing controller servlet.");
  super.init(config);

  DataManager dataManager = new DataManager();
  dataManager.setDbUrl(config.getInitParameter("dbUrl"));
  dataManager.setDbUserName(config.getInitParameter("dbUserName"));
  dataManager.setDbPassword(config.getInitParameter("dbPassword"));

  ServletContext context = config.getServletContext();
  context.setAttribute("base", config.getInitParameter("base"));
  context.setAttribute("imageUrl", config.getInitParameter("imageUrl"));
  context.setAttribute("dataManager", dataManager);

  try {  // load the database JDBC driver
    Class.forName(config.getInitParameter("jdbcDriver"));
    }
  catch (ClassNotFoundException e) {
    System.out.println(e.toString());
    }
  }
```

As you can see, the initialization consists of three main activities: instantiating and configuring the data manager, saving some parameters for later use by the JSP pages, and loading the driver necessary to access the database. (In the code, JDBC stands for Java Database Connectivity.)

Notice that all these activities are done by setting attributes to values obtained through this method:

```java
config.getInitParameter("init-parameter-name")
```

These values are stored in the WEB-INF\web.xml file, as shown in Listing 2-2.

Listing 2-2. *Extracted from web.xml*

```xml
<web-app ...>
  ...
  <servlet>
    ...
    <init-param>
      <param-name>dbUrl</param-name>
      <param-value>jdbc:mysql://localhost:3306/shop</param-value>
      </init-param>
    ...
    </servlet>
  ...
  </web-app>
```

By defining the critical initialization parameters in `web.xml`, you can change the parameters without having to modify the application code. Table 2-3 shows the initialization parameters defined for this application.

Table 2-3. *Servlet Initialization Parameters*

Name	Value
base	/eshop/shop
imageUrl	/eshop/images/
jdbcDriver	com.mysql.jdbc.Driver
dbUrl	jdbc:mysql://localhost:3306/shop
dbUserName	root
dbPassword	..

For ease of use, we didn't make the database password-protected, but this is obviously something you'd want to do in real life.

Tomcat makes available to JSP the same servlet context that `ShopServlet.java` obtains by executing the method `config.getServletContext()`. For example, the attribute stored with `context.setAttribute("imageUrl", ...)` from within the servlet is available to JSP pages as the value returned by the method `application.getAttribute("imageUrl")`.

Request Handling

When the servlet receives a request, it forwards it to a JSP page on the basis of the request parameter `action`, which in turn is set by the previous page, which depends on what the user does. For example, the page that shows the shopping cart also includes a button to check out. If the user clicks on it, the page will send to the servlet a request with the `action` parameter set to `"checkOut"`.

The View

Table 2-4 shows the list of all JSP pages in the application.

Table 2-4. *JSP Pages*

Name	Function	Mode of Access
index.jsp	The initial page welcoming a new user	Requested directly by the user
LeftMenu.jsp	Standard page sidebar	Included in all non-menu pages
TopMenu.jsp	Standard page header	Included in all non-menu pages
SelectCatalog.jsp	Lists books of a category	LeftMenu.jsp
SearchOutcome.jsp	Lists books selected through a search	LeftMenu.jsp

Continued

Table 2-4. *Continued*

Name	Function	Mode of Access
BookDetails.jsp	Shows the details of one book	SelectCatalog.jsp and SearchOutcome.jsp
ShoppingCart.jsp	Displays the shopping cart	TopMenu.jsp and ShoppingCart.jsp
Checkout.jsp	Requests a customer's payment data	ShoppingCart.jsp
OrderConfirmation.jsp	Confirms acceptance of an order	Checkout.jsp

Additionally, we have a style-sheet file named eshop.css.

A typical user session proceeds as follows:

1. The user starts by accessing http://your-web-site/eshop/shop and sees the welcoming page with a left-side menu containing a search box and a list of book categories.

2. The user either types a word in the search box and hits the Search button or selects a book category.

3. The user selects one of the books by clicking on the corresponding Details link. The application then shows the user a page with an image of the front cover of the book and all the information available in the database about the book.

4. The user adds the book to the shopping cart. The user is taken to the shopping cart automatically, where she can update the number of copies or delete the book entry.

5. The user repeats steps 2 through 4 until she is ready to complete the order. From the shopping cart page, she can then click on the Check Out link.

6. The checkout page asks the user to provide her personal and financial data. When the user clicks on the Check Out button, the page tells the application to memorize the order.

At any time, the user can add books through the left-side menu or go to the shopping cart through the top-side menu to modify the order.

Summary of JSP Features

In this section, we'll introduce JSP features and show you how we used them in the Eshop application. For further information on the JSP features, refer to Appendix D.

Implicit Variables

As mentioned earlier, Tomcat defines several implicit actions, but we'll only discuss out, request, and application in this chapter.

Implicit Variable: out

You use the out variable in JSP as you use the System.out object in Java: to write to the standard output. The standard output for a JSP page is the body of the HTML response sent back to the client. Therefore, the scriptlet <% out.print(*expression*); %> causes the result of the expression to be displayed in the client's browser. You can achieve the same result by simply typing <%=*expression*%>.

Keep in mind that whatever you write in a JSP page outside scriptlets and other JSP elements is sent to the output anyway. Therefore, the following three lines have exactly the same effect on the response:

```
<% out.print("abc"); %>
<%="abc"%>
abc
```

Clearly, it makes no sense to use the first two formats when you need to write constant values. To decide whether to use a scriptlet or an expression delimited by <%=..%>, you should look at the surrounding code and decide what makes it as easy as possible to read.

The most useful methods of the object out are print and println. The only difference between the two is that println appends a newline character to the output. As an argument, both methods accept a string or any other primitive type variable. In the following example, the int value stored in intVar is converted to a string automatically:

```
out.print("a string" + intVar + obj.methodReturningString() + ".");
```

Incidentally, you could use either of the following two methods to do the conversion manually:

```
String s = Integer.toString(intVar);
String s = "" + intVar;
```

Be aware that if you try to print an object or an array by sticking its name into a print statement, you *won't* see its content in the output. Instead, you'll see a mysterious string representing the reference to the object.

Everything within a JSP page that's outside JSP elements is sent to the output. This includes the newline characters at the end of each element. This causes a proliferation of empty lines in the output. For example, this code causes three empty lines in the output:

```
<% first element %>  here is a newline!
<% second element %>  here is a newline!
<% third element %>  here is a newline!
```

To remove the empty lines (or at least most of them), you have three options. First, you can "chain" the element delimiters, so that the newlines are *inside* the elements and don't show up in the output:

```
<% first element %><%
   second element %><%
   third element %>  here is a newline!
```

Second, you can put the newlines inside JSP comments:

```
<% first element %><%--
--%><% second element %><%--
--%><% third element %>  here is a newline!
```

Third, you can write the following directive at the beginning of your page:

```
<%@page trimDirectiveWhitespaces="true"%>
```

Implicit Variable: request

The request variable gives you access to a lot of information concerning the request itself (such as its parameters and headers) and the client that generated it. In this section, we'll only briefly describe some of the more than 50 methods available. As always, we encourage you to refer to Appendix D for some gory details.

Getting the Request Parameters

All applications have to read the request parameters. Eshop does this in the controller applet, but other simpler applications will probably do it within JSP. Typically, you first execute this code:

```
String myPar = request.getParameter("par-name");
```

You then do something with a parameter only if it exists—that is, if getParameter returns a non-null value:

```
if (par != null) { ...
```

Note that in the request generated by a URL like this:

```
http://localhost:8080/my_page.jsp?aaa&bbb=&ccc=3
```

the parameters aaa and bbb exist, although they're set to the empty string. Therefore, getParameter does *not* return null for them.

You need to be aware of the fact that the request could include more than one value associated with the same parameter. For example, this code generates a request with three values for the parameter aaa:

```
http://localhost:8080/my_page.jsp?aaa&aaa=4&aaa=7
```

If you execute getParameter, you only get the first value, which is the empty string in the example. If you want to get them all, you have to use a different method:

```
String[] par = request.getParameterValues("par-name");
```

This returns an array of strings. To check that the parameter has actually been set to something and only once, you might perform the following test:

```
if (par != null  &&  par.length == 1  &&  par[0].length() > 0) { ...
```

Getting Information on the Client

The getLocale method returns the client's preferred Locale. For example, this code is likely to set the variable clientLocale to the string "en_US":

```
String clientLocale = request.getLocale().toString();
```

If you had a multilingual site, the locale would tell you the working language of your user. You could check whether you support it and, if you do, set it as a default for the response.

The getRemoteHost method, which returns the client's host name (or that of his proxy server), could be useful in a similar way, because you could look at the string after the last dot to identify foreign domain names (e.g., it for Italy). Unfortunately, the remote address cannot be resolved to a name in many cases, and you end up getting only the client's IP address, exactly as if you had called the getRemoteAddress method. Services available on the Internet let you resolve an IP address to the country where the system resides, but they're quite expensive.

Implicit Variable: application

We mentioned the application variable when talking about the controller servlet initialization method. As we said, Tomcat makes available to JSP the servlet context as the implicit variable application. Therefore, the controller servlet can pass information to the JSP pages of Eshop. In general, application attributes are an efficient way to pass information between pages.

Implicit Variable: session

The term *session* refers to all the interactions that a user has with a server from the moment the user accesses the first page of an application to the moment he closes his browser (or the session expires, because the browser remained inactive for too long).

When Tomcat receives an HTTP request, it checks whether the request contains a cookie named JSESSIONID. If it doesn't find it, it creates the cookie with a unique value and attaches it to the response. This establishes the beginning of a session. If the client's browser accepts cookies, it sends that cookie together with all requests.

The session variable lets your JSP pages store information associated with each individual user. For example, following a user login, you can set a session attribute to the access level of that user, so that all the pages of your application can check it before performing their function. In its simplest form, you could set up such a mechanism like this:

```
session.setAttribute("MyAppOperator", "");
```

Then, you can use this code to check it:

```
boolean isOperator = (session.getAttribute("MyAppOperator")  != null);
if (isOperator) { ...
```

JSP Directives

JSP pages use JSP directives to pass data about themselves to Tomcat. This data influences the translation process from a script file to a Java servlet class. Directives only play a role when a JSP page is modified and needs to be recompiled, so they have no specific effect on the individual HTML responses.

There are three directives: page, include, and taglib. Their syntax is as follows:

```
<%@directive-name attribute-list%>
```

attribute-list is a sequence of one or more *attribute-name*="*attribute-value*" pairs.

Directive: page

The page directive is used in all JSP files and has more than a dozen attributes. Typically, a JSP file starts with the page directive:

```
<%@page language="java" contentType="text/html"%>
```

followed by one or more further page directives:

```
<%@page import="java.util.ArrayList"%>
<%@page import="java.util.Iterator"%>
<%@page import="eshop.beans.Book"%>
```

These directives tell the compiler which external classes are needed. It isn't good practice to import whole class libraries, as in this example:

```
<%@page import="java.util.*"%>
```

because any relaxation of control creates problems sooner or later. In any case, as you can see here, you don't need to write a separate directive for each class:

```
<%@page import="java.util.ArrayList, java.util.Iterator"%>
```

Directive: include

The include directive lets you insert the unprocessed content of an external file. For example, this line of code includes a file named some_jsp_code with the extension jspf:

```
<%@include file="some_jsp_code.jspf"%>
```

JSPF stands for *JSP Fragment*, although more recently, chunks of JSP code have been called *JSP Segments*, rather than Fragments. In fact, any text file with any extension will do.

Tomcat does the merging before any translation. Therefore, the raw content of the included file is pasted into the page without any check. Use this directive sparingly, because it can easily lead to unmaintainable code with bits and pieces spread all over the place.

Directive: taglib

You can create your own libraries of JSP tags, so that you can write statements like the following:

```
<my:oneOfMyTags> ... </my:oneOfMyTags>
```

Later in this chapter, in the "JSP's Tag Extension Mechanism" section, we'll explain the possible advantages of creating your own libraries of tags and how to do it. For the time being, simply know that you can use the `taglib` directory to tell Tomcat what libraries to load and where they are. Take this line, for example:

```
<%@taglib uri="http://mysite.com/mytags" prefix="my" %>
```

Many libraries are available for download from the Internet, some of which are standardized and widely used.

JSP Standard Actions

While Tomcat executes directive elements when translating a page, it executes action elements when processing a client's HTTP request. The purpose of JSP actions is to specify activities to be performed when a page is requested.

Actions can operate on objects and have an effect on each response. They normally take this form:

```
<jsp:action-name action-attribute-list/>
```

`action-attribute-list` is a sequence of one or more `attribute-name="attribute-value"` pairs. However, actions can also have a body, like in the following example:

```
<jsp:action-name attribute-list>
  <jsp:subaction-name subaction-attribute-list/>
  </jsp:action-name>
```

There are eight JSP standard actions (`element`, `forward`, `getProperty`, `include`, `plugin`, `setProperty`, `text`, and `useBean`) and five subactions that can only appear in the body of other actions (`attribute`, `body`, `fallback`, `param`, and `params`). In this chapter, however, we'll only introduce you to some of them. For a full description, please refer to Appendix D.

Actions: forward, include, and param

To terminate execution of the current page and forward the request to another page, use this code:

```
<jsp:forward page="myOtherPage.jsp">
  <jsp:param name="newParName" value="newParValue"/>
  </jsp:forward>
```

Use this code to execute another page and append its output to that of the current one:

```
<jsp:include page="myOtherPage.jsp"/>
```

In the previous example on jsp:forward, we've defined a new parameter, which the destination page can access with request.getParameter("newParName") like any other request parameter.

Tomcat clears the output buffer upon executing the forward action. Therefore, the HTML code generated up to that point by the forwarding page is lost. On the other hand, Tomcat doesn't clear the output buffer when it executes the include action.

With both forward and include, the destination page must be a well-formed and complete JSP page. The forward action must satisfy the additional requirement of generating a complete and valid HTML page, because the output of the destination page is what goes back to the client's browser in the HTML response. The destination page of an include might even generate only a single character, although in most cases it provides HTML code. For example, the top bar of the Eshop application is generated in the page TopMenu.jsp (see Listing 2-3) and included in seven JSP pages with this code:

```
<jsp:include page="TopMenu.jsp" flush="true"/>
```

The flush attribute ensures that the HTML generated so far by the including page is sent to the client before executing the included page.

Listing 2-3. *TopMenu.jsp*

```
<%@page language="java" contentType="text/html"%>
<%
  String base = (String)application.getAttribute("base");
  String imageUrl = (String)application.getAttribute("imageUrl");
  %>
<div class="header">
  <div class="logo">
    <p>e-Shopping Center</p>
    </div>
  <div class="cart">
    <a class="link2" href="<%=base%>?action=showCart">Show Cart
      <img src="<%=imageUrl%>/cart.gif" border="0"/></a>
    </div>
  </div>
```

TopMenu.jsp generates the HTML code, as shown in Listing 2-4 (the empty lines have been removed).

Listing 2-4. *HTML Generated by TopMenu.jsp*

```
<div class="header">
  <div class="logo">
    <p>e-Shopping Center</p>
    </div>
```

```
<div class="cart">
  <a class="link2" href="/eshop/shop?action=showCart">Show Cart
    <img src="/eshop/images//cart.gif" border="0"/></a>
  </div>
</div>
```

Notice that TopMenu.jsp uses styles (such as class="header") that aren't loaded or defined within the same file. If you're wondering how that's possible, you probably don't clearly understand the distinction between source JSP and output HTML. The JSP code in TopMenu.jsp is executed on the server, and it produces HTML code, which is then appended to the output buffer. JSP *doesn't need* style sheets. It is the generated HTML that needs them when it's interpreted by the client's browser.

Actions: useBean and setProperty

The useBean action declares a new JSP scripting variable and associates it with a Java object. For example, this code declares the variable dataManager of type eshop.model.DataManager:

```
<jsp:useBean id="dataManager" scope="application"
  class="eshop.model.DataManager"/>
```

This is the same data manager instantiated and configured in ShopServlet.java as you saw earlier in this chapter in Listing 2-1. JSP uses this variable to access the data without having to worry about its location and implementation. For example, when a user selects a book and clicks on the link to add it to the shopping cart, the controller servlet executes ShoppingCart.jsp with an argument set to the book identifier. Inside ShoppingCart.jsp, you only need to execute a method of the dataManager to obtain all the book details, which are actually stored in a MySQL database:

```
Book book = dataManager.getBookDetails(bookId);
```

The result is stored in an object of type book, from which you can obtain the book details by executing simple get methods such as book.getTitle() and book.getAuthor().

Possible values for the scope attribute of the useBean action are page, request, session, and application, with page as the default.

The useBean action can actually instantiate new objects, rather than just declare and make accessible objects that are already defined, such as the data manager. Appendix D describes all the possible attributes and what they do. Here we only want to show you how, after useBean has instantiated a class, the setProperty action can automatically set its attributes to the values of request parameters.

But before we do that, we have to explain that a bean property is nothing else than an attribute of the bean class for which the standard get and put methods have been defined. The standard methods must be named get and put, followed by the name of the attribute with the first letter capitalized. For example, if you define the attribute named myAttr, you must define getMyAttr and setMyAttr; otherwise, it won't be recognized as a bean property, and what we're about to say won't work.

The JSP module `OrderConfirmation.jsp` of the Eshop application has the following two elements:

```
<jsp:useBean id="customer" class="eshop.beans.Customer"/>
<jsp:setProperty property="*" name="customer"/>
```

The `useBean` action instantiates an object of type `Customer` and associates it with the variable named `customer`. By defining `property="*"`, the `setProperty` action states that all bean properties of the newly created object are to be set. What `setProperty` does *not* define is where the values of the properties should come from. This is because they come from request parameters named *exactly* as the properties. Check out the definition of the `Customer` class, shown in Listing 2-5.

Listing 2-5. *Customer.java*

```java
package eshop.beans;

public class Customer {
  private String contactName = "";
  private String deliveryAddress = "";
  private String ccName = "";
  private String ccNumber = "";
  private String ccExpiryDate = "";

  public String getContactName() {
    return contactName;
    }
  public void setContactName(String contactName) {
    this.contactName = contactName;
    }

  public String getDeliveryAddress() {
    return deliveryAddress;
    }
  public void setDeliveryAddress(String deliveryAddress) {
    this.deliveryAddress = deliveryAddress;
    }

  public String getCcName() {
    return ccName;
    }
  public void setCcName(String ccName) {
    this.ccName = ccName;
    }
```

```
public String getCcNumber() {
  return ccNumber;
  }
public void setCcNumber(String ccNumber) {
  this.ccNumber = ccNumber;
  }

public String getCcExpiryDate() {
  return ccExpiryDate;
  }
public void setCcExpiryDate(String ccExpiryDate) {
  this.ccExpiryDate = ccExpiryDate;
  }
}
```

As you can see, the Customer class defines private attributes and then the methods to access them.

The useBean action:

```
<jsp:useBean id="customer" class="eshop.beans.Customer"/>
```

is equivalent to:

```
Customer customer = new Customer();
```

So far, not so interesting. However, the setProperty action:

```
<jsp:setProperty property="*" name="customer"/>
```

is equivalent to the following:

```
customer.setContactName(request.getParameter("contactName"));
customer.setDeliveryAddress(request.getParameter("deliveryAddress"));
customer.setCcName(request.getParameter("ccName"));
customer.setCcNumber(request.getParameter("ccNumber"));
customer.setCcExpiryDate(request.getParameter("ccExpiryDate"));
```

Now you can see the convenience of using setProperty.

Comments and Escape Characters

The comment delimiters <%-- .. --%> have the same function as /* .. */ in Java. You can also use them to "switch off" JSP elements, as shown here:

```
<%-- <jsp:include page="whatever.jsp"/> --%>
```

This can span over several lines.

To include the sequence of characters <% and %> in template text, you have to "break" them with a backslash, like in <\% and %\>, so that the JSP engine doesn't interpret them as the beginning and end of scripting elements. Alternatively, you can replace the inequality signs with their HTML entities, as in <% and %>.

JSP's Tag Extension Mechanism

Wouldn't it be nice if you could define your own actions to replace lengthy scriptlets? By "hiding" functions behind custom tags, you could increase the modularity of your pages and increase their maintainability. Well, it's possible, and in this section we're going to tell you how to do it.

You can write a statement like this in a JSP page:

```
<prefix:actionTag attributeName="value"/>
```

But first, you need to follow these steps:

1. Define Java classes that provide the functionality of the actions you're defining, including the definition of their attributes (e.g., attributeName). These classes are called *tag handlers*.

2. Provide a formalized description of your action elements, so that Tomcat knows how to handle them. For example, you need to specify which actions can have a body and which attributes can be omitted. Such a description is called a tag library descriptor (TLD).

3. In the JSP pages, tell Tomcat that the pages need your *tag library* and specify the prefix that you want to identify those custom tags with.

We'll take you through these steps, beginning with bodyless actions, which are simpler to implement.

Bodyless Custom Actions

A bodyless action is an element that, not having an end tag, cannot enclose a body between start and end tags. Let's say you want to develop an action that prints the day of the week of any given date:

```
<wow:weekday date="date"/>
```

The date attribute accepts values in the form yyyy-mm-dd and defaults to the current date.

Step 1: Define the Tag Handler

A tag handler for a bodyless custom tag is a class that implements the interfaces java.io.Serializable and javax.servlet.jsp.tagext.Tag. Remember that to satisfy an interface, you have to implement all the methods it defines.

To satisfy Serializable, you only need to define a unique identifier, like this:

```
static final long serialVersionUID = 1L;
```

However, to satisfy the Tag interface, you have to define the methods listed in Table 2-5.

Table 2-5. *The Methods of the Tag Interface*

Method	Description
int doEndTag()	Processes the end tag
int doStartTag()	Processes the start tag
Tag getParent()	Provides a reference to the closest enclosing tag handler
void release()	Removes all the references to objects
void setPageContext(PageContext pc)	Sets the current page context

Fortunately, the javax.servlet.jsp.tagext.TagSupport class makes life easier by implementing the Tag interface with default methods and other useful methods. Therefore, you only need to extend TagSupport and overwrite the methods you need for the custom action. You certainly don't need getParent, because the action isn't going to be used in the body of other actions. You don't need doStartTag either, because the action is bodyless, and, as a consequence, you don't have separate start and end tags. In conclusion, you only need to overwrite doEndTag with a method containing all the functionality of the weekday tag.

Listing 2-6 shows you the code of the whole tag handler.

Listing 2-6. *WeekdayTag.java*

```java
package tags;

import javax.servlet.jsp.JspException;
import javax.servlet.jsp.tagext.TagSupport;
import java.util.Date;
import java.text.SimpleDateFormat;
import java.util.Calendar;
import java.util.GregorianCalendar;

public class WeekdayTag extends TagSupport {
  static final long serialVersionUID = 1L;
  static final String[] WD = {"","Sun","Mon","Tue","Wed","Thu","Fri","Sat"};
  private String date;

  public void setDate(String date) {
    this.date = date;
    }

  public int doEndTag() throws JspException {
    GregorianCalendar cal = new GregorianCalendar();
    SimpleDateFormat fmt = new SimpleDateFormat("yyyy-MM-dd");
    fmt.setLenient(true);
    if (date != null && date.length() > 0) {
      Date d = new Date();
```

```
      try {
        d = fmt.parse(date);
        }
      catch (Exception e) {
        throw new JspException("Date parsing failed: " + e.getMessage());
        }
      cal.setTime(d);
      }
    try {
      pageContext.getOut().print(WD[cal.get(Calendar.DAY_OF_WEEK)]);
      }
    catch (Exception e) {
      throw new JspException("Weekday writing failed: " + e.getMessage());
      }
    return EVAL_PAGE;
    }
  }
```

You need the setDate method because Tomcat uses it to pass the value of the action's date attribute to the tag handler. The corresponding getDate method isn't present, because it is never used and can be omitted. If the action is executed without the date attribute, the date variable defined in doEndTag remains set to null, and the calendar cal, which is used to determine the day of the week, remains set to the current date. On the other hand, if a date attribute is specified in the action, its value will be parsed and used to set the calendar.

Notice that the name of the tag handler is named like the tag but with the first letter capitalized and with the Tag suffix. This is a good practice to follow, but you can name your handlers as you like. You'll see in a moment how to make the association between a tag and its handler.

The return value EVAL_PAGE means that execution should continue with the page code following the custom action. Use SKIP_PAGE to abort the page.

In any case, you should place your handlers in the classes subdirectory of WEB-INF. For example, the handler WeekdayTag.class is in WEB-INF\classes\tags\, consistent with the fact that it's part of the package tags.

Step 2: Define the TLD

The TLD is an XML file that describes your tags so that Tomcat knows how to deal with them. Listing 2-7 shows the full TLD for the custom tag library.

Listing 2-7. *wow.tld*

```
<?xml version="1.0" encoding="ISO-8859-1"?>
<taglib xmlns="http://java.sun.com/xml/ns/javaee"
    xmlns:xsi="http://www.w3.org/2001/XMLSchema-instance"
    xsi:schemaLocation="http://java.sun.com/xml/ns/javaee ➥
http://java.sun.com/xml/ns/j2ee/web-jsptaglibrary_2_1.xsd"
    version="2.1">
```

```
<description>Example of a simple tag library</description>
<tlib-version>1.0</tlib-version>
<short-name>wow</short-name>
<tag>
  <description>Displays the day of the week</description>
  <display-name>weekday</display-name>
  <name>weekday</name>
  <tag-class>tags.WeekdayTag</tag-class>
  <body-content>empty</body-content>
  <attribute>
    <name>date</name>
    <type>java.lang.String</type>
    <rtexprvalue>true</rtexprvalue>
    </attribute>
  </tag>
</taglib>
```

As you can see, the outermost element is taglib, which contains a tag element for each custom action (in this case, only weekday). Apart from tag, all taglib subelements in the example are for information purposes or to be used by tools; you can omit them.

The tag element contains an attribute subelement for each action attribute (in this case, only date). Of the tag subelements in the example, you can omit description and display-name. name defines the custom action name, tag-class specifies the fully qualified class name of the tag handler, and body-content specifies the action to be bodyless.

The subelement tag-class is what gives you the freedom to name your tag handlers as you like. The subelement body-content is mandatory and can only have one the following three values: empty, scriptless, or tagdependent. The value scriptless is the default and means that the body cannot contain scripting elements, while EL expressions and JSP actions are accepted and processed normally. The value tagdependent means that the body content is passed to the tag handler as it is, without any processing. This is useful if the body contains character sequences, such as <%, that would confuse Tomcat.

Note that up to JSP 2.0, body-content was mandatory, and body-content="JSP" was valid. This is no longer the case with JSP 2.1.

The attribute element in the example has three subelements: name, which sets the action attribute name; type, which sets the class name of the attribute value; and rtexprvalue, which accepts values at request time. If you had used a type other than String, the value passed to the tag handler would have been of that type. For example, with an attribute defined like this:

```
<attribute>
  <name>num</name>
  <type>java.lang.Integer</type>
  </attribute>
```

you would have included the following code in the tag handler:

```
private int num;
public void setNum(Integer num) {
  this.num = num.intValue();
  }
```

When processing the start tag of the custom action, Tomcat would have parsed the string passed to the action (as in num="23") to obtain the Integer value for the tag handler.

By setting the subelement rtexprvalue to true, you specify that dynamic values defined at request time be accepted. If you had omitted the subelement or set it to false, you would have been forced to pass only constant values, such as date="2007-12-05", to the action instead of runtime values such as date="<%=aDate%>". (rtexpr stands for real-time expression.)

Inside WEB-INF, create a folder named tlds and place wow.tld there.

Step 3: Use the Custom Action

Listing 2-8 shows you a simple JSP page to test the weekday custom action.

Listing 2-8. *weekday.jsp*

```
1: <%@page language="java" contentType="text/html"%>
2: <%@taglib uri="/WEB-INF/tlds/wow.tld" prefix="wow"%>
3: <% String d = request.getParameter("d"); %>
4: <html><head><title>weekday tag</title></head><body>
5: weekday today: <wow:weekday/><br/>
6: weekday <%=d%>: <wow:weekday date="<%=d%>"/>
7: </body></html>
```

Line 2 contains the taglib directive, line 4 uses weekday without the date attribute, and line 6 passes the request parameter d to the action. It's as simple as that.

If you type http://localhost:8080/tags/weekdays.jsp?d=2007-12-25 in the browser, you get two lines, such as Today: Wed and 2007-12-25: Tue. If you type the URL without the query, the second line of the output becomes null: Wed. On the other hand, if you type a query with a bad date, such as d=2007-1225, Tomcat will show you an error page with a back trace, the first line of which is as follows:

```
org.apache.jasper.JasperException: javax.servlet.ServletException:
  javax.servlet.jsp.JspException:
    Date parsing failed: Unparseable date: "2007-1225"
```

Bodied Custom Actions

To show you the differences from the bodyless action, we'll implement a version of the weekday action that expects the date in its body instead of in an attribute:

```
<wow:weekdayBody>date</wow:weekdayBody>
```

Step 1: Define the Tag Handler

Similar to bodyless actions, the tag handlers for bodied actions need to implement an interface, only this time it's javax.servlet.jsp.tagex.BodyTag instead of Tag. Again, similar to bodyless actions, the API provides a convenient class that you can use as a basis: javax.servlet.jsp.tagext.BodyTagSupport. However, as opposed to what you did in the tag handler for a bodyless action, you cannot simply replace the doEndTag method, because the action body will have come and gone by the time you reach the end tag. You first have to override doAfterBody.

An additional complication concerns the default date: if you write the action with an empty body, as follows

```
<wow:weekdayBody></wow:weekdayBody>
```

the method doAfterBody won't be executed at all. How can you then print out the default day?

The answer is simple: you have to override the doEndTag method and write the default date from there in case there is no body. Listing 2-9 shows the end result.

Listing 2-9. *WeekdayBodyTag.java*

```java
package tags;

import javax.servlet.jsp.JspException;
import javax.servlet.jsp.tagext.BodyTagSupport;
import java.util.Date;
import java.text.SimpleDateFormat;
import java.util.Calendar;
import java.util.GregorianCalendar;

public class WeekdayBodyTag extends BodyTagSupport {
  static final long serialVersionUID = 1L;
  static final String[] WD = {"","Sun","Mon","Tue","Wed","Thu","Fri","Sat"};
  private boolean bodyless = true;  /* 1 */

  public int doAfterBody() throws JspException {
    String date = getBodyContent().getString();  /* 2 */
    GregorianCalendar cal = new GregorianCalendar();
    Date d = new Date();
    SimpleDateFormat fmt = new SimpleDateFormat("yyyy-MM-dd");
    fmt.setLenient(true);
    try {
      d = fmt.parse(date);
      }
    catch (Exception e) {
      throw new JspException("Date parsing failed: " + e.getMessage());
      }
    cal.setTime(d);
```

```
      try {
         getPreviousOut().print(WD[cal.get(Calendar.DAY_OF_WEEK)]);  /* 3 */
         }
      catch (Exception e) {
         throw new JspException("Weekday writing failed: " + e.getMessage());
         }
    bodyless = false;  /* 4 */
    return SKIP_BODY;
    }

  public int doEndTag() throws JspException {
    if (bodyless) {  /* 5 */
      GregorianCalendar cal = new GregorianCalendar();
      try {
        pageContext.getOut().print(WD[cal.get(Calendar.DAY_OF_WEEK)]);
        }
      catch (Exception e) {
        throw new JspException("Weekday writing failed: " + e.getMessage());
        }
      }
    return EVAL_PAGE;
    }
  }
```

Lines 1, 4, and 5 implement the mechanism to ensure that you write the default date but only when the body is empty. In line 1, you define a boolean instance variable called bodyless and set it to true. If there is a body to process, doAfterBody in line 4 sets it to false otherwise doEndTag in line 5 prints the default day of the week.

Line 2 shows you how to get the body content, and line 3 shows you how to get the method to print while processing the body. The method has been named getPreviousOut to remind you that there can be actions within actions, in which case you'll want to append the output of an inner action to that of an outer one.

Notice that you no longer need to check for null, because if doAfterBody is executed, you can be sure that there is a date to process.

Step 2: Define the TLD

To define the new action, you only need to add the <tag> shown in Listing 2-10 after the <tag> for the bodyless weekday action.

Listing 2-10. *The tag Element for weekdayBody*

```
<tag>
  <description>Displays the day of the week</description>
  <display-name>weekdayBody</display-name>
  <name>weekdayBody</name>
  <tag-class>tags.WeekdayBodyTag</tag-class>
  <body-content>scriptless</body-content>
  </tag>
```

Notice that you define the body-content subelement as scriptless even though it's the default. The purpose is to make the code more readable. It's just a matter of taste.

Step 3: Use the Custom Action

Listing 2-11 shows a couple more lines before the end body tag of weekday.jsp.

Listing 2-11. *weekday.jsp with Bodied Actions*

```
<%@page language="java" contentType="text/html"%>
<%@taglib uri="/WEB-INF/tlds/wow.tld" prefix="wow"%>
<html><head><title>weekday tag</title></head><body>
weekday today: <wow:weekday/><br/>
weekday ${param.d}: <wow:weekday date="${param.d}"/><br/>
weekdayBody today: <wow:weekdayBody></wow:weekdayBody><br/>
weekdayBody ${param.d}: <wow:weekdayBody>${param.d}</wow:weekdayBody><br/>
</body></html>
```

You also replace the request.getParameter("d") logic with the simpler and more elegant EL expression ${param.d}. You have to use an EL expression in any case, because scripting elements aren't allowed in the body of an action. Therefore, you couldn't have used <%=d%>.

■**Caution** Many tag libraries are available on the Internet. JSTL provides many actions that you can use and reuse, which we'll write about in the next section. It certainly pays, in terms of both quality and efficiency, to not start developing actions from scratch unless they give you clear and quantifiable benefits.

JSTL and EL

Many developers have implemented similar custom actions to remove or at least reduce the need for scripting elements. Eventually, a new effective standard known as JSTL was born.

However, JSTL is of little use without EL, which lets you access and manipulate objects in a compact and efficient way. We'll first introduce you to EL, so that you'll understand it when you need it in the JSTL examples.

JSP Expression Language

EL was introduced in JSP 2.0 as an alternative to the scripting elements. You can use EL expressions in standard and custom action attributes specified to be capable of accepting runtime expressions. You can also use EL in template text. You can represent EL expressions with two constructs: ${expr} and #{expr}.

EL Expressions

To explain when you can or should use the two EL representations (${} and #{}), we must clarify the distinction between lvalues and rvalues.

The *l* stands for *left*, and the *r* stands for *right*. These values refer to the fact that in most computer languages, the assigned value is on the right-hand side of an assignment statement, while the value to be assigned to is on the left-hand side. For example, this Java statement:

```
ka[k] = j*3;
```

means that the result of the evaluation of j*3 (an rvalue) is to be assigned to the value resulting from the evaluation of ka[k] (an lvalue). Clearly, an lvalue must be a reference to something you can assign values to (a variable or some attribute/property of an object), while there is no such restriction on rvalues.

Suppose that you have a page with a form. Wouldn't it be nice if you could specify *directly in the input elements of the form* the references to where the user's inputs should be stored? For example, it'd be nice to specify something like <input id="firstName" value="*lvalue*">, with the *lvalue* pointing to where you want to store the input typed by the user. Then, when the form is submitted, there should be a mechanism to automatically take the user's input and store it where you specified. Perhaps you could also define a new attribute of the input element to provide a validating method. Inside the input element, you would then already have everything you need to accept the user's input, validate it, and store it away.

This sounds great, but normally everything you write in a JSP page is evaluated at compile time. For example, if you set the value attribute of the input element to ${formBean.firstName}, this evaluates to an rvalue. At compile time, the value of the firstName attribute of formBean is assigned to the value attribute of the input element, and that's it. You need a way of *deferring* evaluation of the *lvalue* until you really need it—that is, once the form is submitted.

Well, you're in luck, because the following JSF code does exactly that:

```
<h:form>
  <h:inputText id="firstName"
    value="#{formBean.firstName}"
    validator="#{formBean.validateFirstName}"/>
</h:form>
```

The # before the EL braces tells Tomcat to defer evaluation and use its result as an lvalue. EL expressions with the dollar sign are evaluated at compile time like everything else. In any other aspect, parsing and evaluation of the two representations are identical.

Using EL Expressions

The expr in ${expr} can contain literals, operators, and references to objects and methods. Table 2-6 shows some examples and their results.

Table 2-6. *EL Expressions*

EL Expression	Result
${1 <= (1/2)}	false
${5.0 > 3}	true
${100.0 == 100}	true
${'a' < 'b'}	true
${'fluke' gt 'flute'}	false
${1.5E2 + 1.5}	151.5
${1 div 2}	0.5
${12 mod 5}	2
${empty param.a}	true if the request parameter a is null or an empty string
${sessionScope.cart.nItems}	The value of the nItems property of the session-scoped attribute named cart
${aBean.aProp}	The value of the aProp property of the aBean bean
${aMap[entryName]}	The value of the entry named entryName in the map named aMap

The operators behave in general like in Java, but with one important difference: the equality operator (==) applied to string variables compares their contents, not whether the variables refer to the same instance of a string. That is, it behaves like Java's String.equals() method.

In addition to EL operators identical to Java operators, you also have most of their literal equivalents: not for !, div for /, mod for %, lt for <, gt for >, le for <=, ge for >=, eq for ==, ne for !=, and for &&, and or for ||. You also have the unary operator empty, to be used as shown in one of the examples in Table 2-6.

The EL operators . (i.e., the dot) and [] (i.e., indexing) are more powerful and forgiving than the corresponding Java operators.

When applied to a bean, as in ${myBean.prop}, the dot operator is interpreted as an indication that the value of the property should be returned, as if you'd written myBean.getProp() in a scripting element. As a result, for example, this line of code:

```
${pageContext.servletContext.servletContextName}
```

is equivalent to this line:

```
<%=pageContext.getServletContext().getServletContextName()%>
```

Furthermore, ${first.second.third}, equivalent to <%=first.getSecond().getThird()%>, returns null when first.second evaluates to null, although in the expression, we try to dereference it with .third. The JSP scripting equivalent would throw a NullPointerException.

Array indexing allows you to try to access an element that doesn't exist, in which case it simply evaluates to null. For example, if you have an array of ten elements, the EL expression ${myArray[999]} returns null instead of throwing an ArrayIndexOutOfBoundsException, as JSP would have done.

You can use both the dot and indexing operator to access maps. For example, these two EL expressions both return the value associated with the key named myKey:

```
${myMap.myKey}
${myMap["myKey"]}
```

There is a tiny difference, though: you cannot use the dot operator if the name of the key contains a character that confuses EL. For example, ${header["user-agent"]} is OK, but ${header.user-agent} doesn't work, because the dash between user and agent in the second expression is interpreted as a minus sign. Unless you have a variable named agent, both header.user and agent evaluate to null and, according to the EL specification document, ${null - null} evaluates to zero. Therefore, the first expression would probably return a zero. You would encounter a different, but potentially more serious, problem if you had a map key containing a dot. For example, you could use ${param["my.par"]} without problems, but ${param.my.par} would probably result in a null. This would be bad, because null is a possible valid outcome. We suggest you use the bracketed form in all occasions and simply forget this issue.

Similar to JSP, EL contains implicit objects, listed in Table 2-7.

Table 2-7. *EL's Implicit Objects*

Object	Description
pageContext	The context of the JSP page. In particular, pageContext.servletContext gives you a reference to the same object referenced by the implicit variable application in JSP. Similarly, pageContext.session is equivalent to JSP's session, pageContext.request to JSP's request, and pageContext.response to JSP's response.
param	Maps a request parameter name to its first value.
paramValues	Maps a request parameter name to an array of its values.
header	Maps a request header name to its first value.
headerValues	Maps a request header name to an array of its values.
cookie	Maps a cookie name to a single cookie.
initParam	Maps the name of a context initialization parameter to its value.
pageScope	Maps page-scoped variable names to their values.
requestScope	Maps request-scoped variable names to their values.
sessionScope	Maps session-scoped variable names to their values.
applicationScope	Maps application-scoped variable names to their values.

■**Caution**   JSP scripting variables are *not* valid within EL expressions.

You've probably noticed that EL doesn't include any way of declaring variables. Within EL expressions, you can use variables set with the `c:set` JSTL core action (which we'll describe in the next section) or scoped attributes. For example, all of these definitions let you use the EL expression `${xyz}`:

```
<c:set var="xyz" value="33"/>
<% session.setAttribute("xyz", "44"); %>
<% pageContext.setAttribute("xyz", "22"); %>
```

However, you have to pay attention to scope precedence. The variable set with `c:set` and the attribute in `pageContext` *are the same variable*. That is, `c:set` defines an attribute in the page context. The attribute in `sessionContext` is a different variable, and you cannot access it with `${xyz}` because it is "hidden" behind the attribute with the same name in the page context. To access a session attribute, you have to prefix its name with `sessionScope`, as in `${sessionScope.xyz}`. If you don't specify a scope, EL looks first in the page, then in the request, then in the session, and finally in the application scope.

■**Caution** EL expressions cannot be nested. Expressions such as `${expr1[${expr2}]}` are illegal.

You can make composite expressions consisting of several EL expressions and additional text, as in the following example:

```
<c:set var="varName" value="Welcome ${firstName} ${lastName}!"/>
```

However, you cannot mix the `${}` and `#{}` forms.

JSP Standard Tag Library

JSTL consists of five tag libraries, as shown in Table 2-8. (i18n stands for *internationalization— i + 18 omitted letters + n*.)

Table 2-8. *JSTL Tag Libraries*

Area	Functionality
Core	Variable support, flow control, URL management, and miscellaneous
i18n	Locale, message formatting, and number and date formatting
Functions	Collection length and string manipulation
Database	SQL
XML	XML core, flow control, and transformation

We'll tell you how to load the libraries, give you the list of tags, and show you some examples.

Table 2-9 contains a list of all the tags defined in the five libraries.

Table 2-9. *The JSTL Tags*

Core	i18n	Functions	Database	XML
c:catch	fmt:bundle	fn:contains	sql:dateParam	x:choose
c:choose	fmt:formatDate	fn:containsIgnoreCase	sql:param	x:forEach
c:forEach	fmt:formatNumber	fn:endsWith	sql:query	x:if
c:forTokens	fmt:message	fn:escapeXml	sql:setDataSource	x:otherwise
c:if	fmt:param	fn:indexOf	sql:transaction	x:out
c:import	fmt:parseDate	fn:join	sql:update	x:param
c:otherwise	fmt:parseNumber	fn:length		x:parse
c:out	fmt:requestEncoding	fn:replace		x:set
c:param	fmt:setBundle	fn:split		x:transform
c:redirect	fmt:setLocale	fn:startsWith		x:when
c:remove	fmt:setTimeZone	fn:substring		
c:set	fmt:timeZone	fn:substringAfter		
c:url		fn:substringBefore		
c:when		fn:toLowerCase		
		fn:toUpperCase		
		fn:trim		

To use the JSTL libraries in JSP pages, you must declare them in `taglib` directives as follows:

```
<%@taglib prefix="c" uri="http://java.sun.com/jsp/jstl/core"%>
<%@taglib prefix="fmt" uri="http://java.sun.com/jsp/jstl/fmt"%>
<%@taglib prefix="fn" uri="http://java.sun.com/jsp/jstl/functions"%>
<%@taglib prefix="sql" uri="http://java.sun.com/jsp/jstl/sql"%>
<%@taglib prefix="x" uri="http://java.sun.com/jsp/jstl/xml"%>
```

In the following sections of this chapter, we'll show you examples of all libraries with the exception of JSTL-SQL.

The Core Library: Listing the Parameters

If you want to list all the parameters in a request without using JSTL, you'll have to do something like what's shown in Listing 2-12.

Listing 2-12. *req_params.jsp*

```
01: <%@page language="java" contentType="text/html"%>
02: <%@page import="java.util.*, java.io.*"%>
03: <%
04:    Map       map = request.getParameterMap();
05:    Object[] keys = map.keySet().toArray();
06:    %>
07: <html><head><title>Request Parameters</title></head><body>
08:    Map size = <%=map.size()%>
09:    <table border="1">
10:       <tr><td>Map element</td><td>Par name</td><td>Par value[s]</td></tr>
11: <%
12:       for (int k = 0; k < keys.length; k++) {
13:         String[] pars = request.getParameterValues((String)keys[k]);
14:         out.print("<tr><td>" + k + "</td><td>'" + keys[k] + "'</td><td>");
15:         for (int j = 0; j < pars.length; j++) {
16:           if (j > 0) out.print(", ");
17:           out.print("'" + pars[j] + "'");
18:           }
19:         out.println("</td></tr>");
20:         }
21:    %>
22:       </table>
23: </body></html>
```

Appendix D includes a detailed explanation of req_params.jsp in Listing D-14. Here you use it only to develop a JSTL-based equivalent. In any case, req_params.jsp is conceptually simple: you get the map of the request parameters (in line 4), loop through the parameters, and print them out (in lines 12-20). Each parameter can have more than one value, so you have a small loop inside the main loop to go through all the values of each parameter (lines 15-18).

The idea is simple, but the code isn't easy to read. You can improve it by writing some of the HTML tags from within the JSP loop, rather than mixing them with several small script elements, but it still doesn't look very readable. Listing 2-13 shows you the same functionality of req_params.jsp but implemented with core JSTL and without scripting elements.

Listing 2-13. *req_params_jstl.jsp*

```
01: <%@page language="java" contentType="text/html"%>
02: <%@taglib prefix="c" uri="http://java.sun.com/jsp/jstl/core"%>
03: <%@taglib prefix="fn" uri="http://java.sun.com/jsp/jstl/functions"%>
04: <html><head><title>Request Parameters with JSTL</title></head><body>
05:    Map size = <c:out value="${fn:length(paramValues)}"/>
06:    <table border="1">
07:       <tr><td>Map element</td><td>Par name</td><td>Par value[s]</td></tr>
```

```
08:     <c:set var="k" value="0"/>
09:     <c:forEach var="par" items="${paramValues}"><tr>
10:       <td><c:out value="${k}"/></td>
11:       <td><c:out value="${par.key}"/></td>
12:       <td><c:forEach var="val" items="${par.value}">
13:         <c:out value="'${val}'"/>
14:       </c:forEach></td>
15:       <c:set var="k" value="${k+1}"/>
16:     </tr></c:forEach>
17:   </table>
18: </body></html>
```

The lines in bold have replaced the lines of req_params.jsp. Gone is the importing of
Java libraries, and gone are the script elements. Lines 2 and 3 show the taglib directives
for the JSTL core and functions. In Line 5, you can see how to use the fn:length function
to determine the size of the EL implicit object paramValues. You use the c:out action to
print the value of the EL expression to the output. You could have just written the naked
EL expression, but c:out automatically converts characters that have special HTML meaning to the corresponding HTTP entities. For example, it writes & instead of &. Therefore,
it's better to use c:out.

In lines 8 and 15, you use c:set to initialize and increment an index; in lines 9 and 12, you
use c:forEach, which lets you go through the elements of maps and arrays.

If you execute this line of code:

`http://localhost:8080/tests/req_params_jstl.jsp?a=3&b=5&a=3&c=7&b=1&d`

you'll get the output shown in Figure 2-5.

Map size = 4

Map element	Par name	Par value[s]
0	d	"
1	b	'5' '1'
2	c	'7'
3	a	'3' '3'

Figure 2-5. *The table generated by req_params_jstl.jsp*

Other Core Tags

The JSTL versions of the Java if and switch tags are particularly useful tags. For example, this
body is executed only if the EL expression calculates to true:

`<c:if test="EL-expression"> ... </c:if>`

Unfortunately, there is no c:else, but the JSTL version of switch (c:choose) is much more
powerful than the original. In fact, it's more like a chain of if .. else if .. else:

```
<c:choose>
  <c:when test="EL-expression-1"> ... </c:when>
  <c:when test="EL-expression-2"> ... </c:when>
  ...
  <c:otherwise> ... </c:otherwise>
</c:choose>
```

The i18n Library: Writing Multilingual Applications

You can take one of two approaches to internationalizing a web application: you can either provide a different version of the JSP pages for each locale and select them via a servlet to process each request, or you can save locale-specific data in separate resource bundles and access them via i18n actions. The JSTL internationalization actions support both, but we'll concentrate on the second approach, where the work of switching between languages is actually done in JSP.

For example, suppose that you want to support English and Italian. The first thing that you have to do is identify all the strings that are going to be different in the two languages and then define two bundles. Listing 2-14 shows the English bundle.

Listing 2-14. *MyBundle_en.java*

```
package myPkg.i18n;
import java.util.*;
public class MyBundle_en extends ListResourceBundle {
  public Object[][] getContents() {return contents;}
  static final Object[][] contents = {
    {"login.loginmess","Please login with ID and password"},
    {"login.submit","Submit"},
    {"login.choose","Choose the language"},
    {"login.english","English"},
    {"login.italian","Italian"}
    };
  }
```

Listing 2-15 shows the Italian bundle.

Listing 2-15. *MyBundle_it.java*

```
package myPkg.i18n;
import java.util.*;
public class MyBundle_it extends ListResourceBundle {
  public Object[][] getContents() {return contents;}
  static final Object[][] contents = {
    {"login.loginmess","Loggati con ID e parola d'ordine"},
    {"login.submit","Invia"},
    {"login.choose","Scegli la lingua"},
```

```
      {"login.english","Inglese"},
      {"login.italian","Italiano"}
      };
  }
```

As you can see, a bundle is nothing other than a Java class that extends the class
`java.util.ListResourceBundle`. In this example, you're limiting yourself to a simple login
page, but in reality, you'll have to include all the language-specific messages of your application. We used the prefix `login` to show you that it's possible to group messages within
a bundle. You can compile the Java files from the command line with `javac` to obtain the
two files `MyBundle_en.class` and `MyBundle_it.class`. Place both files inside the `WEB-INF\`
`classes\myPkg\i18n\` folder of your application's root directory, as you would do with
any other custom class.

Listing 2-16 shows you the login page.

Listing 2-16. *index.jsp*

```
01: <%@page language="java" contentType="text/html"%>
02: <%@taglib prefix="c" uri="http://java.sun.com/jsp/jstl/core"%>
03: <%@taglib prefix="fmt" uri="http://java.sun.com/jsp/jstl/fmt"%>
04: <c:set var="langExt" value="en"/>
05: <c:if test="${param.lang!=null}">
06:   <c:set var="langExt" value="${param.lang}"/>
07:   </c:if>
08: <fmt:setLocale value="${langExt}"/>
09: <fmt:setBundle basename="myPkg.i18n.MyBundle"
10:   var="lang" scope="session"/>
11: <html><head><title>i18n</title></head><body>
12: <h1><fmt:message key="login.loginmess" bundle="${lang}"/></h1>
13: <form method="post" action="home.jsp">
14:   <input name=id>
15:   <input name=passwd>
16:   <input type="submit"
17:     value="<fmt:message key="login.submit" bundle="${lang}"/>"
18:     >
19: <h2><fmt:message key="login.choose" bundle="${lang}"/></h2>
20: <a href="index.jsp?lang=en">
21:   <fmt:message key="login.english" bundle="${lang}"/>
22:   </a>
23:  
24: <a href="index.jsp?lang=it">
25:   <fmt:message key="login.italian" bundle="${lang}"/>
26:   </a>
27: </body></html>
```

Lines 4-7 ensure that the page variable `langExt` is not `null` by setting it to `en` when the
page is requested the first time. Line 8 sets the locale to the requested language code. The list
of valid language codes is defined in the International Organization for Standardization (ISO)

639 standard. They're in lowercase (e.g., it for Italian), so you can't confuse them with the country codes, as defined in the ISO 3166 standard, which are in uppercase (e.g., IT for Italy).

In line 9, you set the bundle. Notice that it looks like the fully qualified class name of the two bundle classes but without the trailing underscore and language code. This is exactly how it should be done; otherwise, JSTL won't find your messages. After executing fmt:setBundle, the session variable lang points to the bundle in the correct language, thanks to the locale and the basename attribute.

After that, you only need to type this code to insert the message corresponding to the given key name:

```
<fmt:message key="keyName" bundle="${lang}"/>
```

Notice how the double quotes are nested in line 17 without causing any problem. This is because the actions are processed first. By the time Tomcat arrives to process the HTML, only the outer double quotes remain.

Figure 2-6 shows what the page looks like the first time you view it.

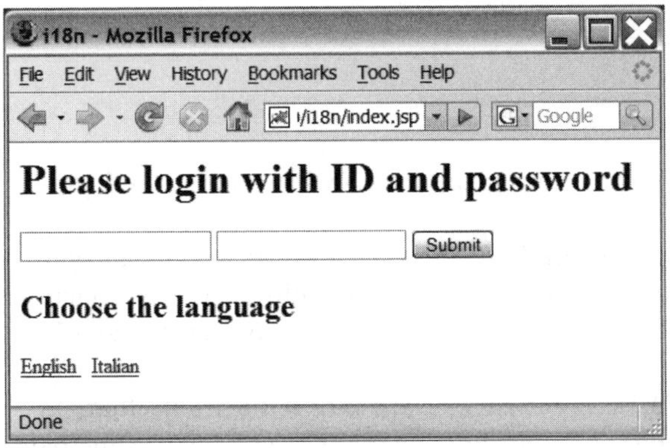

Figure 2-6. *The first time you view index.jsp*

Figure 2-7 shows how the page looks when you choose Italian by clicking on one of the bottom links.

Figure 2-7. *The Italian version of index.jsp*

If Tomcat cannot find the bundles, it will display the key name preceded and followed by three question marks, as shown in Figure 2-8. This indicates that you must have made a mistake in the directory names.

Figure 2-8. *index.jsp cannot find the messages.*

XML Tags

The XML actions specified in JSTL are meant to address the basic XML needs that a JSP programmer is likely to encounter.

To make XML file contents easier to access, the W3C specified the XML Path Language (XPath), where it chose the name XPath to indicate that it describes paths within XML documents (see http://www.w3.org/TR/xpath). The XML actions rely on that language to identify XML components.

To avoid confusion between EL expressions and XPath expressions, the actions that require an XPath expression always use the select attribute. In this way, you can be sure that all expressions outside select are EL expressions. The actions that require a select attribute are x:forEach, x:if, x:out, x:set, and x:when.

Introduction to XPath

XPath expressions generally identify a set of XML nodes through patterns. Extensible Stylesheet Language Transformations (XSLT) templates then use those patterns when they apply transformations. Possible XPath nodes can be any of the following: attribute, comment, element, namespace, processing instruction, root, and text.

As with URLs, XPath uses a slash as a separator. Absolute paths start with a slash, while all other paths are relative. Similar to file directories, a period indicates the current node, while a double period indicates the parent node.

Several nodes with the same name are distinguished by indexing them, as Java does with array elements. For example, let's say you have the following XML code:

```
<a> <b>whatever</b> <b>never</b> </a>
<c> <non_b>no</non_b> <b>verywell</b> </c>
<a> <b attr="zz">nice</b> <b attr="xxx">ok</b> </a>
```

The pattern /a/b selects the four <b> elements, which contain whatever, never, nice, and ok. The <b> element with verywell isn't selected, because it's inside <c> instead of <a>. The pattern /a[1]/b[0] selects the <b> element with nice. Attribute names are prefixed by an @. For example, /a[1]/b[1]/@attr refers to the attribute that has the value xxx in the example.

A clever thing in XPath: you can use conditions as indices. For example, /a/b[@attr="zz"] selects the same <b> element selected by /a[1]/b[0], while /a[b] selects all <a> elements that have <b> as a child (in the example, both), and /a[b="never"] selects the first <a> element. A final example: /a/b[@attr][0] selects the first element that has the attribute attr (i.e., /a[1]/b[0] once again).

XPath defines the wildcards *, which matches any element, and @*, which matches any attribute. It also defines several operators and functions related to node sets, positions, or namespaces, and it defines string, numeric, boolean, and conversion operations.

Within XPath, you have access to the implicit JSP objects you're familiar with. Table 2-10 lists the mappings.

Table 2-10. *XPath Mappings of Implicit JSP Objects*

JSP	XPath
pageContext.findAttribute("attrName")	$attrName
request.getParameter("parName")	$param:paramName
request.getHeader("headerName")	$header:headerName
cookie's value for name foo	$cookie:foo
application.getInitParameter("initParName")	$initParam:initParName
pageContext.getAttribute("attrName", PageContext.PAGE_SCOPE)	$pageScope:attrName
pageContext.getAttribute("attrName", PageContext.REQUEST_SCOPE)	$requestScope:attrName
pageContext.getAttribute("attrName", PageContext.SESSION_SCOPE)	$sessionScope:attrName
pageContext.getAttribute("attrName", PageContext.APPLICATION_SCOPE)	$applicationScope: attrName

A Practical Example

So far, everything has been pretty dry and abstract. To spice things up a bit, we're going to write a JSP page that parses an XML file and selects its elements and attributes. Listing 2-17 shows the XML file we'll play with, starfleet.xml.

Listing 2-17. *starfleet.xml*

```
<?xml version="1.0" encoding="ISO-8859-1"?>
<starfleet>
  <starship name="Enterprise" sn="NX-01">
    <class commissioned="2151">NX</class>
    <captain>Jonathan Archer</captain>
    </starship>
```

```
<starship name="USS Enterprise" sn="NCC-1701">
  <class commissioned="2245">Constitution</class>
  <captain>James Tiberius Kirk</captain>
  </starship>
<starship name="USS Enterprise" sn="NCC-1701-A">
  <class commissioned="2286">Constitution</class>
  <captain>James T. Kirk</captain>
  </starship>
<starship name="USS Enterprise" sn="NCC-1701-B">
  <class commissioned="2293">Excelsior</class>
  <captain>John Harriman</captain>
  </starship>
<starship name="USS Enterprise" sn="NCC-1701-C">
  <class commissioned="2332">Ambassador</class>
  <captain>Rachel Garrett</captain>
  </starship>
<starship name="USS Enterprise" sn="NCC-1701-D">
  <class commissioned="2363">Galaxy</class>
  <captain>Jean-Luc Picard</captain>
  </starship>
<starship name="USS Enterprise" sn="NCC-1701-E">
  <class commissioned="2372">Sovereign</class>
  <captain>Jean-Luc Picard</captain>
  </starship>
</starfleet>
```

In this example, you'll display the information available in a table, like that shown in Figure 2-9.

Name	S/N	Class	Year	Captain
Enterprise	NX-01	NX	2151	Jonathan Archer
USS Enterprise	NCC-1701	Constitution	2245	James Tiberius Kirk
USS Enterprise	NCC-1701-A	Constitution	2286	James T. Kirk
USS Enterprise	NCC-1701-B	Excelsior	2293	John Harriman
USS Enterprise	NCC-1701-C	Ambassador	2332	Rachel Garrett
USS Enterprise	NCC-1701-D	Galaxy	2363	Jean-Luc Picard
USS Enterprise	NCC-1701-E	Sovereign	2372	Jean-Luc Picard

Figure 2-9. *Starfleet information*

Nothing could be simpler. See Listing 2-18.

Listing 2-18. *starfleet.jsp*

```
01: <%@page language="java" contentType="text/html"%>
02: <%@taglib uri="http://java.sun.com/jsp/jstl/core" prefix="c"%>
03: <%@taglib uri="http://java.sun.com/jsp/jstl/xml" prefix="x"%>
04: <c:import url="starfleet.xml" var="sf"/>
05: <x:parse doc="${sf}" varDom="dom"/>
06: <html><head>
07:   <title>Parsing starfleet.xml</title>
08:   <style>th {text-align:left}</style>
09:   </head>
10: <body>
11: <table border="1">
12:   <tr><th>Name</th><th>S/N</th><th>Class</th><th>Year</th><th>Captain</th></tr>
13:   <x:forEach var="tag" select="$dom//starship">
14:     <tr>
15:       <td><x:out select="$tag/@name"/></td>
16:       <td><x:out select="$tag/@sn"/></td>
17:       <td><x:out select="$tag/class"/></td>
18:       <td><x:out select="$tag/class/@commissioned"/></td>
19:       <td><x:out select="$tag/captain"/></td>
20:     </tr>
21:   </x:forEach>
22:   </table>
23: </body>
24: </html>
```

In line 4, you load the XML file in memory, and in line 5, you parse it into an object of type org.apache.xerces.dom.DeferredDocumentImpl, which implements the standard interface org.w3c.dom.Document of a Document Object Model (DOM). In lines 13-21, you loop through all the starship tags of the DOM, regardless of how "deep" they are in the structure. You can achieve this with the double slash. In fact, all the starship tags are direct children of the root tag starfleet, so you also could have selected $tag/starfleet/tag. Inside the x:forEach loop, the variable tag refers in turn to each starship tag, and you can print the information contained in attributes and subelements. Notice that the select paths inside the loop always start with the slash. This is because the root element in each loop iteration is a starship tag, not starfleet.

XML Syntax

JSP pages with scripting elements aren't XML files. This implies that you cannot use XML tools when developing JSP pages. However, it is possible to write JSP in a way to make it correct XML. The trick is to use standard JSP actions, JSTL with EL, and possibly non-JSTL custom actions. Actually, some "special standard" (pun intended!) JSP actions have been defined to support the XML syntax (jsp:root, jsp:output, and jsp:directive). In any case, such XML modules are called *JSP documents*, as opposed to the *JSP pages* written in the traditional non XML–compliant way.

Listing 1-3 showed you how to convert the JSP page hello.jsp to a JSP document. Listing 2-19 shows the same code, using line numbers.

Listing 2-19. *hello.jsp*

```
01: <%@page language="java" contentType="text/html"%>
02: <html>
03: <head><title>Hello World dynamic HTML</title></head>
04: <body>
05: Hello World!
06: <%
07:    out.println("<br/>Your IP address is " + request.getRemoteAddr());
08:
09:    String userAgent = request.getHeader("user-agent");
10:    String browser = "unknown";
11:
12:    out.print("<br/>and your browser is ");
13:    if (userAgent != null) {
14:      if (userAgent.indexOf("MSIE") > -1) {
15:        browser = "MS Internet Explorer";
16:      }
17:      else if (userAgent.indexOf("Firefox") > -1) {
18:        browser = "Mozilla Firefox";
19:      }
20:    }
21:    out.println(browser);
22:    %>
23: </body>
24: </html>
```

Listing 2-20 shows an XML document that only writes "Hello World!". You'll convert the scriptlet that displays the dynamic information later.

Listing 2-20. *Partial hello.jspx*

```
01: <?xml version="1.0" encoding="ISO-8859-1"?>
02: <jsp:root
03:    xmlns:jsp="http://java.sun.com/JSP/Page"
04:    xmlns:c="http://java.sun.com/jsp/jstl/core"
05:    version="2.1"
06:    >
07: <jsp:directive.page
08:    language="java"
09:    contentType="ISO-8859-1"
10:    pageEncoding="ISO-8859-1"
```

```
11:    />
12: <html>
13:    <head><title>Hello World in XHTML</title></head>
14:    <body>Hello World!</body>
15:    </html>
16: </jsp:root>
```

Line 1 states that the file is XML-compliant. The root element in lines 2-6 has several purposes. For example, it lets you use the jsp extension instead of the recommended jspx. It's also a convenient place where you can group namespace declarations (xmlns). The namespace declaration for the JSTL core tag library is the XML equivalent of the taglib directive in JSP pages. You don't need to specify the JSP namespace in JSP pages, but you cannot omit it in a JSP document; otherwise, the jsp: tags won't be recognized.

Lines 7-10 are the XML equivalent of the page directive of JSP pages. Also, the <jsp:directive.include file="relativeURL"/> element is equivalent to the include directive. Lines 12-15 are the output HTML document. You only need to write it in XHTML to make it XML-compliant.

To be consistent and support the full validation of our code, you could also include the proper !DOCTYPE in the generated HTML document. The best way to do this is to use the attributes of the jsp:output action specifically designed for this purpose. You only need to replace the <html> tag in line 12 with the following lines:

```
<jsp:output
  doctype-root-element="html"
  doctype-public="-//W3C//DTD XHTML 1.0 Strict//EN"
  doctype-system="http://www.w3.org/TR/xhtml1/DTD/xhtml1-strict.dtd"
  />
<html xmlns="http://www.w3.org/1999/xhtml">
```

Yes, it's quite a bit of work just to write "Hello World!", but this overhead is going to stay the same for JSP documents of any size.

If you look at the generated HTML, you'll see that it consists of only two lines: the first one with the !DOCTYPE, and the second one with all the rest. If you want to have newlines between elements in the output, you have to write them. You can actually do this with the jsp:text action. For example, all the jsp:text elements in the following code fragment contain a newline followed by two spaces:

```
<html xmlns="http://www.w3.org/1999/xhtml"><jsp:text>
  </jsp:text><head><title>Hello World in XHTML</title></head><jsp:text>
  </jsp:text><body>Hello World!</body><jsp:text>
  </jsp:text></html>
```

As the jsp:text content is sent to the output, the HTML generated will be written over several lines and indented:

```
<html xmlns="http://www.w3.org/1999/xhtml">
  <head><title>Hello World in XHTML</title></head>
  <body>Hello World!</body>
  </html>
```

The other possibility is to use a CDATA section to enclose the whole HTML:

```
<![CDATA[<html xmlns="http://www.w3.org/1999/xhtml">
  <head><title>Hello World in XHTML</title></head>
  <body>Hello World!</body>
  </html>]]>
```

This way, the whole block will be sent to the client as it is, uninterpreted. However, it seems an admission of defeat to send off code that could have been validated for XML compliance at the source. Don't you think?

Now you're finally ready to tackle the conversion to XML of the hello.jsp scriptlet that displays the IP address and the browser type of the client, as shown in lines 6–22 of Listing 2-19.

Summary

In this chapter, we introduced you to all aspects of JSP. First, we explained the Java syntax used in scriptlets. We then described an online bookshop to show you how you can informally but effectively specify and design a web application with an MVC architecture. This Eshop application also provided a framework for more complex examples of JSP.

After discussing JSP's implicit variables, directives, and standard actions, we explained how to create your own custom actions, and we described JSTL and EL. Finally, we told you how to write JSP modules in XML syntax.

You now have much of the information you need to write JSP-based applications.

However, JSP can only take you so far without a solid knowledge of HTTP and HTML. Therefore, in the next chapter, we'll take a step back and examine HTTP and HTML in some detail.

■ ■ ■

CHAPTER 3

The Web Page

You'll find a lot of material on how to write web pages both on the Internet and in print. But a book on JSP wouldn't be complete without a chapter explaining what makes the World Wide Web work as it does. We'll explain the key concepts while covering as much ground as possible.

Web Pages in General

For your browser to render a web page correctly, it must be able to do the following:

- **Communicate with the server, or servers, where the page content is stored**: This means the browser must support the necessary protocols, and it must be configured correctly and include the proper addressing.

- **Interpret the page syntax correctly and act on it as expected by the page designer**: This means using the same standards that are used on the server and conforming to them.

- **Include the plug-ins and have access to the facilities needed to process all components of the page**: For example, the browser must be able to render Adobe Shockwave animations or whatever else the page designer has included on the page.

Before going into the details of how you structure and develop web pages, we'll provide some background information to put everything into the right perspective.

The Protocols

A data-communication protocol is a standardized set of rules that computers must follow to be able to communicate with each other. The protocol rules define the format of the *data packets* being transferred and the way in which the exchange takes place.

To make this complex process more manageable, the functionality necessary to move data across networks is broken down into layers organized into *protocol stacks*, or *protocol suites*. Higher layers can perform more general and complex tasks by relying on the services of the lower layers. Computers communicate across the Internet by means of the Internet protocol stack, which consists of five layers. Starting from the top, these layers are *application, transport, network, link,* and *physical*.

To get an idea of the complexity of the whole Internet protocol suite, consider that the list of Internet standards has become a standard itself: Request for Comments (RFC) 2700. It includes 59 protocol specifications, 66 draft standards, 520 proposed standards, 146 experimental protocols, and 60 historic protocols, and, yes, it lists itself in the top spot.

The operating system of every computer connected to the Internet includes an implementation of the Internet protocol stack. However, this chapter focuses on web applications, so we're not going to discuss the two lowest layers (physical and link), which are local to your setup (for example, Ethernet and wireless LAN).

The first layer of interest is the network layer (IP), which is the lowest one operating end to end. Each computer connected to the Internet is identified via its IP address, which the ISP normally assigns every time the computer connects to the network. To find out the IP address of your PC, open a DOS window and type `ipconfig`. You'll get several lines of information, including one that shows your IP address as a string of four numbers separated by dots—something like `84.74.96.111`. To get the IP address of a server, type the command `nslookup`. When you get a greater-than sign as a prompt, type the name of the server and hit `Enter`. For example, if you type `www.yahoo.com`, you'll get the string `87.248.113.14`, which is Yahoo's IP address. If you then open a browser and type Yahoo's IP address where you'd normally type a URL, you'll see Yahoo's home page.

The next layer up, the transport layer, uses the Transmission Control Protocol (TCP) to ensure that information packets reach their destination reliably. TCP associates so-called ports with the applications running on a computer, thereby ensuring separate and concurrent data communication for, say, your e-mail and your Skype calls. You might have heard of the User Datagram Protocol (UDP). Like TCP, UDP belongs to the transport layer and assigns ports to applications, but unlike TCP, it doesn't guarantee reliable delivery of packets. It isn't relevant to us in this book.

The top layer is the application layer. Each application running on one computer *attaches* itself to its TCP/UDP port or ports. The protocol for web pages is HTTP, or HTTPS for encrypted pages. Your web browser is actually able to handle several ports, depending on the protocol you specify in the URL. For example, pages with URLs beginning with `http://` go through port 80, while those with `https://` use port 443, and those with `ftp://` use ports 20 and 21. Note that the browser will use additional ports if necessary. For example, a video stream in Windows Media format will go through port 1755. This is important to know if a firewall exists between client and server. The Internet Assigned Numbers Authority (IANA) is in charge of keeping official port assignments. You'll find the list at `http://www.iana.org/assignments/port-numbers`.

The URL `http://localhost:8080/ebookshop/` that you saw in the previous chapters specifies that on the host side, the port number for HTTP is 8080 (IANA identifies it as *HTTP Alternate*) instead of 80, which is the standard port for HTTP. This is because Tomcat expects and routes HTTP traffic through port 8080. In Chapter 7, you'll see how you can change it to the default port 80.

Figure 3-1 shows you what happens when you send a request from your PC to a web page.

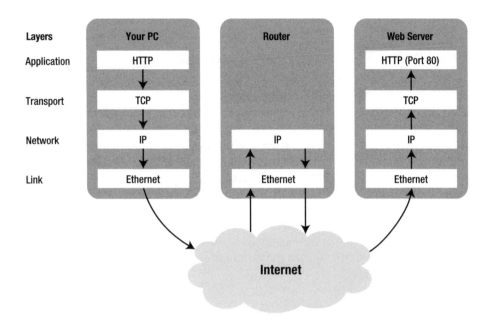

Figure 3-1. *Following an HTTP request through the Internet protocol stacks*

The web browser sends the request to the Internet protocol stack that is implemented on your PC. Each of the layers attaches information to your request in the form of a header, so the same layer on the server knows what to do with the packet. The packet grows as it descends the protocol stack, and it might end up fragmented into several parts before reaching the bottom. For example, the IP header contains, among other fields, the source IP address (i.e., the IP address of your PC, which you can see with the DOS command ipconfig) and the destination IP address (i.e., the address of the server, which you can obtain from the name server of your ISP). Instead of Ethernet, you might have a wireless LAN layer, but ultimately your request will end up encapsulated in data packets traveling through the Internet. On their way to the server, the data packets encounter routers that forward them toward the server on the basis of the destination IP address. Depending on your location relative to that of the server, the packets might "hop" on a dozen or more routers. Finally, your packets reach the server. The process that occurred on your PC is reversed, and your request is put back together. The destination port tells the protocol stack what application should handle it (i.e., a web server such as the Apache web server or the Apache Tomcat Java web server). The response follows a similar logical path in the reverse direction.

The Formatting

The importance of page composition was universally known well before the introduction of document-formatting programs such as Microsoft Word and desktop-publishing programs such as QuarkXPress and Microsoft Office Publisher. In the late 1970s, Donald Knuth, dissatisfied with the quality of typesetting, began developing TeX, which became the language of choice for typesetting scientific papers.

■**Note** Donald Knuth is a scientist who, more than anybody else, is responsible for the systematization of computer science, the theory of compiling, and the algorithm theory. His encyclopedic book, *The Art of Computer Programming* (Volume 4, Fascicle 4, Addison-Wesley Professional, 2006), remains, after many years, *the* repository of knowledge for computer scientists around the world.

TeX and HTML are both markup languages: you embed standardized keywords into the text that specify how you want the output to appear. Both TeX and HTML descend from Standard Generalized Markup Language (SGML), which is the first functional and extensible markup language. During the past decade, the W3C has simplified SGML into XML and has redefined HTML as XHTML to make it conform to XML instead of SGML.

HTML, XML, and, more recently, XHTML have become the standard markup languages to define web pages. As this evolution was taking place, the idea of defining presentation styles separately from the page structure led the W3C to specify CSS, which lets you define document styles in separate files.

More Bits and Pieces

A web page can be more than just text and pictures. It can include richer and active content, such as video/audio clips and streams, Java applets, and Adobe Flash components. It can also interact locally with the viewer through client-side scripting languages, such as JavaScript.

For these components to work, you must extend your browser by downloading the necessary plug-ins and configuring it to allow the execution of applets and JavaScript. This obviously increases the risk of some malicious component exploiting unknown security holes in your browser to gain access to your data. Fortunately, an evolution toward safer Adobe Flash components and away from more dangerous ActiveX components is taking place among developers.

JavaScript deserves a particular mention. With JavaScript, you can introduce local interactivity on the client side. That is, your browser can perform checks and respond to your input without having to communicate with the server that provided the web page. For example, you could use JavaScript to check the syntax of the viewer's input into a form. The response to input errors would then be quicker than if the page had to go back to the server for checking. However, keep in mind that you'll have to repeat the checks on the server, because the browser might have been configured to disable JavaScript, or the viewer might have found a way of tricking your JavaScript checks into letting his wrong inputs through. As a result, you would have the same checks in two different places. However, checks that should stay identical have a bad tendency of getting out of sync, resulting in inconsistencies. All in all, especially with the steady increase of bandwidth available, you'll probably be better off doing your checks on the server side and only using JavaScript in a limited way or for nonessential checks.

URLs

URLs tell your browser where to find web pages, files, File Transfer Protocol (FTP) sites, and more. To be precise, a URL doesn't really tell where a resource is; it only provides the information necessary to be able to address the resource locally or across a network and establish communication with it. We're not talking about physical locations here.

A URL consists of several parts. For example, `http://localhost:8080/ebookshop/` can be broken down as follows:

- `http` is the protocol.

- `localhost` is the host name.

- `8080` is the port number on the host.

- `/ebookshop/` is the path.

In fact, although everybody speaks of URLs, the more general term is Uniform Resource Identifier (URI), which lets you define even a *fragment* within a resource. The Internet Society (ISOC) defines the URI format in the standard RFC 3986.

Let's break down this fictitious URI:

`http://good.at.it:8080/first/second_one/page.html?answer=no#exactly_here`

- `http` is the protocol (the standard name for this part of the URI is *scheme*).

- `//` is called the *hier-part* and determines what format is acceptable for the part of the URI that follows it.

- `good.at.it:8080` is referred to as the *authority*.

- `/first/second_one/page.html` is the path.

- `answer=no` is the query.

- `exactly_here` is the fragment.

The purpose of the RFC 3986 standard is to define a method of identification for all possible resources and to include particular cases of what has already become common use. However, we're only concerned with HTTP and web pages in this chapter, so we won't spend any more time on the most general formats.

There is just one more scheme that you might find useful in your web pages: `mailto`. By including a link to the URI `mailto:John.Doe@nowhere.com` within a web page, you can allow the viewer to start her e-mail program and create a new e-mail with the correct address already set. However, you might not like to do that, because many programs are capable of scanning web pages and extracting e-mail addresses from them for the sole purpose of sending junk mail. The elegant solution here is to display an e-mail address, `John.Doe(at)nowhere.com`, and create a JavaScript that converts the `(at)` into @ before returning the link. In this way, page scanners won't see the full address, although they might be able to recognize `(at)` and steal the address anyway.

Hosts and Paths

Host names are case-insensitive, meaning that you can write `WwW.GOOgle.cOM` if you prefer. You'll still land on the same web site. Incidentally, the same applies to e-mail addresses. It's irrelevant whether you capitalize names, such as in `John.Doe@nowhere.com`.

The same is not true for the paths. Even though you're running Tomcat under Windows, which has case-insensitive file and folder names, you can type `http://LOCALHOST:8080/ebookshop/` to execute your application, but if you type `http://localhost:8080/Ebookshop/`, you'll get an error page like that shown in Figure 3-2.

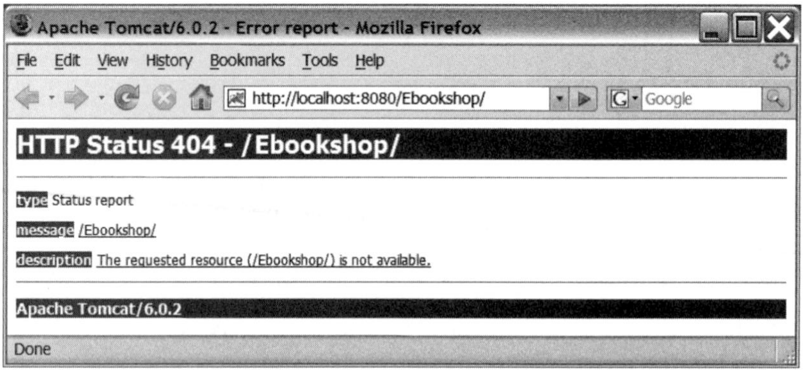

Figure 3-2. *Resource not available*

Originally, domain and host names could only be made out of the 26 letters of the English alphabet, the 10 decimal digits, and dashes. In July 2003, it became possible to register `.jp` domains containing Japanese characters, and in March 2004, `.de` domains with diacritical characters, such as in Lösung and Müller, sprung up. Spaces and other special characters are still not allowed.

The situation is different for paths and queries. They can include any character of the ISO 8859-1 (ISO Latin1) character set, which is a superset of the well-known ASCII standard. But of all 256 ISO Latin1 characters, all the non-ASCII characters, the non-printing ASCII characters, and even some of the printing ASCII characters need to be encoded in hexadecimal format.

For example, the path `/my preferred physicists/Erwin Schrödinger.html` must be encoded as follows:

`/my%20preferred%20phycisists/Erwin%20Schr%F6dinger.html`

where `%20` is ISO Latin1-32 (the space) and `%F6` is ISO Latin1-246 (the o-umlaut, ö).

In some cases, it is necessary to encode characters to prevent the browser from interpreting them as URL separator characters. For example, suppose you want to execute a JSP page with a parameter set to the ampersand. If you type this URL

`http://myServer.com/myPage.jsp?myPar=&`

your browser will send to the server a request with the parameter `myPar` set to the empty string. This is because the ampersand is normally used to indicate that another parameter follows, but it is legal not to write any further parameter after it. As a result, the browser behaves exactly as if you had ended the URL at the equal sign. To send the correct query, you have to replace the ampersand with %26.

Listing 3-1 shows you a JSP module that echoes back the HTTP request parameters. Just place it in Tomcat's ROOT directory and try it out.

Listing 3-1. *show_req.jsp*

```
<%@page import="java.io.*, java.util.*"%>
<%
  out.println("Method: " + request.getMethod() + "</br>");
  Enumeration  pars = request.getParameterNames();
  while (pars.hasMoreElements()) {
    String   parName = (String)pars.nextElement();
    String[] parValues = request.getParameterValues(parName);
    out.print(parName + " =");
    for (int k = 0; k < parValues.length; k++) {
      out.print(" '" + parValues[k] + "'");
      }
    out.println("</br>");
    }
%>
```

Figure 3-3 shows the results of Listing 3-1.

Figure 3-3. *The result of show_req.jsp*

In any case, ampersands can be used only as separators within the query, but they can appear in file and folder names. Conversely, some characters, such as colons and question marks, are OK in the query but not in the path.

All in all, be careful when using special characters. In Appendix B, you'll find the full list of the ISO Latin1 character set and each character's hex equivalent.

GET and POST Requests

When you type a URL in your browser and hit Enter, the browser sends an HTTP GET request to the server. This is the standard method for HTTP clients to request a document from a server. To request dynamic pages and to provide a meaningful response when the server needs additional information, you can also include at the end of the URL a query consisting of parameter-name/parameter-value pairs. Figure 3-3 demonstrates this, where the first line of the response is:

```
Method: GET
```

The maximum length of a URL has not been standardized and is not the same across browsers. Nevertheless, you can count on a couple of thousand characters. Definitely more than what you'll be wanting to type!

However, when a request is generated programmatically within JSP or HTML, a `GET` doesn't cut it. First of all, your query, including the hidden parameters, would be fully displayed in the browser's address window. This would be at the very least confusing. Second, the amount of data might exceed the maximum URL length. Third, you'll probably need to forward the request to another JSP or to a servlet. For each and all of these reasons, always use the `POST` method when making requests from within a web page.

HTML Elements and Tags

HTML documents are organized as a hierarchy of elements that normally consist of content enclosed between a pair of start and end tags. For example, the tags `<html>` and `</html>` delimit the whole HTML document.

The start tag can include element attributes, such as `<table border="1">`. Some elements are empty, in which case you can replace the end tag with a slash immediately before the closing bracket of the start tag, as in `<img src="mypict.gif"/>`. Unfortunately, this isn't always possible. For example, the form `<script ... />` isn't valid, and you have to keep both `<script>` and `</script>` tags even when there is nothing between them. We aren't aware of any other exception, but you never know!

Elements can be nested and, in fact, without nesting, no HTML page would be possible. Refer to Appendix C for brief descriptions of all HTML elements. In this section, we'll present only the general concepts and some examples of the most widely used HTML elements.

Validation

To validate the correctness of HTML code, you must include at the beginning of your HTML file the special element `<!DOCTYPE>`, which specifies the standard you intend to conform to. There are two possibilities that you should consider: HTML 4.01 (see `http://www.w3.org/TR/html4/cover.html`) and XHTML 1.0 (see `http://www.w3.org/TR/xhtml1/`).

The document type declaration for HTML 4.01 is as follows:

```
<!DOCTYPE html PUBLIC "-//W3C//DTD HTML 4.01//EN"
  "http://www.w3.org/TR/html4/strict.dtd">
```

The `DOCTYPE` for strict validation of XHTML 1.0 is:

```
<!DOCTYPE html PUBLIC "-//W3C//DTD XHTML 1.0 Strict//EN"
  "http://www.w3.org/TR/xhtml1/DTD/xhtml1-strict.dtd">
```

You can also decide to conform to the XHTML standard but without applying a strict validation. This allows you to use tags such as <center>, <u>, <strike>, and <applet>, which have been deprecated in XHTML 1.0. To do so, use the following transitional DOCTYPE:

```
<!DOCTYPE html PUBLIC "-//W3C//DTD XHTML 1.0 Transitional//EN"
  "http://www.w3.org/TR/xhtml1/DTD/xhtml1-transitional.dtd">
```

All these DOCTYPEs refer to Document Type Definitions (DTDs) made available by the W3C, which defines the tags and how you can use them. We recommend that you apply strict XHTML validation for all new modules you develop.

In any case, the differences between HTML and XHTML are as follows:

- **All XHTML elements must be properly nested**: For example, in HTML, you can write whatever. In XHTML, you must write whatever.

- **All XHTML elements must be closed**: For example, in HTML, you can write <p> without a corresponding </p>, and you can write <hr> and <br> without a slash before the closing bracket. In XHTML, you must either match each <p> with a </p>, or you must write <p/>, and you must write the slash, as in <hr/> and <br/>.

- **All XHTML elements must be in lowercase**: XHTML doesn't allow you to write elements in uppercase, such as <HTML> and <BODY>.

- **All XHTML elements must be nested inside the <html> element**: This was not enforced in HTML.

Following these rules will help you take pride in writing good-quality, clean code. If this sounds complicated, brace yourself, because we're not done yet with validation. If you want to use HTML frames within your XHTML page, you have to use the following DOCTYPE:

```
<!DOCTYPE html PUBLIC "-//W3C//DTD XHTML 1.0 Frameset//EN"
  "http://www.w3.org/TR/xhtml1/DTD/xhtml1-frameset.dtd">
```

This performs the exact same validation as the transitional DOCTYPE, but with the addition of <frameset>, which can replace <body>. In other words, the pages with frames aren't strictly validated, although obviously this doesn't prevent you from conforming to the strict validation rules when using frames. Before deciding to use frames, keep in mind that their use is somewhat controversial. Some people don't like them and simply disable them in their browsers. Others might use audio browsers and simply be unable to access frames. If you want to reach the widest audience, you should develop a second version of your pages without frames. Actually, to be sure that everything will work, you should design frameless pages first and only add the frames later. You might wonder why you should develop framed versions at all, and you'd be right. Follow our advice: forget the frames and apply strict XHTML validation. The time will certainly come when you'll be happy to have made this choice.

Document Structure and Basic Elements

Listing 3-2 shows the simplest possible HTML page you can write while still applying strict XHTML validation.

Listing 3-2. *basic.html*

```
<!DOCTYPE html PUBLIC "-//W3C//DTD XHTML 1.0 Strict//EN"
  "http://www.w3.org/TR/xhtml1/DTD/xhtml1-strict.dtd">
<html>
<head><title>This is the page title</title></head>
<p>This shouldn't be displayed, but it is!</p>
<body>
Here is where you put your page content.<br/>
Of the following 11 spaces >            < only one is displayed.
</body>
</html>
```

Figure 3-4 shows the outcome of Listing 3-2.

Figure 3-4. *A basic HTML page*

Place your content between <body> and </body> to have it displayed in the main browser window. The browser also displays the page title, but most of the rest of Listing 3-2 remains hidden. Furthermore, any sequence of spaces, tabs, and newlines is normally rendered as a single space, and in several cases, even that single remaining space is omitted—for example, when it immediately follows the start paragraph tag (<p>) or the break tag (<br/>). This gives you plenty of flexibility to format the page source as you like, and you should use it to make the code more maintainable through proper indentation and spacing.

Content: Text, Objects, and Links

Essentially, an HTML document consists of text, images, audio and video clips, active components such as scripts and executables, and hyperlinks. A browser then interprets and renders the components in sequence, mostly without inserting any empty space or newline between them.

A browser renders every component according to a series of defaults specified in the HTML/XHTML standard. You can change the defaults regarding fonts and font sizes of normal text by setting the appropriate browser options. In general, and more importantly, you can override the defaults when writing your HTML pages by defining the corresponding attributes of the enclosing tags or by defining a style. For example, you can underline text:

```
<p style="text-decoration: underline">this is underlined</p>
```

or you can choose a background color for your page:

```
<body style="background-color: yellow">
```

■**Tip** To shrink an image, reduce the original image on the server rather than change its height and width with the corresponding attributes of the `<img>` element. Your page will load faster.

You can use the `<object>` element to include any component. For example, this code displays a short video clip in Flash format:

```
<object type="application/x-shockwave-flash"
    data="myClip.swf" width="400" height="300">
  <param name="movie" value="myClip.swf"/>
  <p>This is a Flashy movie</p>
  </object>
```

This code lets you download an MPEG movie file:

```
<object type="video/mpeg"
     data=myClip.mpeg height="120" width="180">
  <p>Click <a href=MyMovie.mpeg>here</a> to download</p>
  </object>
```

This code lets you display a JPEG image:

```
<object type="image/jpeg"
    data="myImage.jpg"
    style="border-style: solid; border-width: 1px"/>
```

In any case, you might prefer to use the `<img>` element for images, because it allows you to define the short description text that appears when you hover with your mouse over the image:

```
<img src="myImage.jpg" alt="whatever it is"/>
```

■**Caution** To show long Flash movies or Flash streams, you have to do something more complicated than what we show in our example; otherwise, it won't work with Internet Explorer. For more information on this issue, see `http://thinkthanks.be/demo/flash-embedding-techniques/`, which provides a comparison of several methods for embedding Flash in web pages.

Once more, Appendix C tells you all you need to know about the HTML elements and their use.

Tables

Use the `<table>` element to display tabular data. `<tr>` and `<td>` let you define rows and data elements within the rows. Listing 3-3 shows the code you need to generate a sample table.

Listing 3-3. *HTML Code for a Table*

```
<table border="1"><tr style="background-color: #c0c0c0"><th>abc</th><th
align="center" colspan="2">a 2-column span</th></tr><tr><td>a1</td><td>
a2</td><td>a3</td></tr><tr><td rowspan="2">2-row<br/>span</td><td>b2
</td><td>b3</td></tr><tr><td>c2</td><td>c3</td></tr></table>
```

Figure 3-5 shows the results of the code in Listing 3-3.

Figure 3-5. *An HTML-generated table*

We've purposely packed the code to show you how difficult it is to interpret without proper indentation. You should find Listing 3-4 more readable.

Listing 3-4. *table.html*

```
<!DOCTYPE html PUBLIC "-//W3C//DTD XHTML 1.0 Strict//EN"
  "http//www.w3.org/TR/xhtml1/DTD/xhtml1-strict.dtd">
<html xmlns="http//www.w3.org/1999/xhtml" xmllang="en" lang="en">
<head><title>Table</title></head>
<body>
<table border="1">
  <tr style="background-color: #c0c0c0">
    <th>abc</th>
    <th align="center" colspan="2">a 2-column span</th>
    <!-- item merged into item on the left -->
    </tr>
  <tr>
    <td>a1</td>
    <td>a2</td>
    <td>a3</td>
    </tr>
```

```
  <tr>
    <td rowspan="2">2-row<br/>span</td>
    <td>b2</td>
    <td>b3</td>
    </tr>
  <tr>
    <!-- item merged into item above -->
    <td>c2</td>
    <td>c3</td>
    </tr>
  </table>
</body>
</html>
```

This code should be pretty self-explanatory. Notice how the browser sets the size of the different cells to the minimum necessary. You can change that by defining styles to set cell dimensions.

Some developers use tables to form clickable images in which all the areas are rectangular. For example, look at the portion of Listing 3-5 that we've highlighted in bold.

Listing 3-5. *penguin_tbl.html*

```
<!DOCTYPE html PUBLIC "-//W3C//DTD XHTML 1.0 Strict//EN"
  "http//www.w3.org/TR/xhtml1/DTD/xhtml1-strict.dtd">
<html xmlns="http//www.w3.org/1999/xhtml" xmllang="en" lang="en">
<head>
  <title>Penguin</title>
  <style type="text/css">img {border-width: 0px}</style>
  </head>
<body>
<table border="1" rules="none" cellpadding="0" cellspacing="0">
  <tr>
    <td><a href="top_left.html"><img src="penguin_tl.gif"/></a></td>
    <td><a href="top_right.html"><img src="penguin_tr.gif"/></a></td>
    </tr>
  <tr>
    <td><a href="bottom_left.html"><img src="penguin_bl.gif"/></a></td>
    <td><a href="bottom_right.html"><img src="penguin_br.gif"/></a></td>
    </tr>
  </table>
</body>
</html>
```

As you can see, this code defines a table with two rows and two columns, where each cell contains a hyperlinked image. We've styled the images to be rendered without borders, and we've defined the table to show no cell padding or spacing. The intention is to have the browser compose a large image by placing the four partial images adjacent to each other. Figure 3-6 shows the result.

Figure 3-6. *The Linux penguin sawed in half*

Firefox displays a five-pixel white band below each row of images. The same happens with Opera, while Internet Explorer displays the images as expected, without any band. Furthermore, the strict validation of HTML 4.0.1 causes the band to appear. Firefox removes the band if you change the XHTML validation from strict to transitional. The bottom line is that you're better off using a proper image map, as shown in Listing 3-6.

Listing 3-6. *penguin.html*

```
<!DOCTYPE html PUBLIC "-//W3C//DTD XHTML 1.0 Strict//EN"
   "http//www.w3.org/TR/xhtml1/DTD/xhtml1-strict.dtd">
<html xmlns="http//www.w3.org/1999/xhtml" xmllang="en" lang="en">
<head><title>Penguin</title></head>
<body>
<img src="penguin.gif" usemap="#map" width="257" height="303"/>
<map name="map" id="map"><table><tr>
  <td><a href="top_left.html" shape="rect" coords="0,0,113,119"
    title="top left"/></td>
  <td><a href="top_right.html" shape="rect" coords="114,0,257,119"
    title="top right"/></td>
  <td><a href="bottom_left.html" shape="rect" coords="0,120,113,303"
    title="bottom left"/></td>
  <td><a href="bottom_right.html" shape="rect" coords="114,120,257,303"
    title="bottom right"/></td>
  </tr></table></map>
</body>
</html>
```

Forms

To turn your web pages into an interactive experience, you have to give users the ability to make choices and type or upload information. To achieve this, you use the <form> element, which accepts data from the user and sends it to the server. Inside the <form> element, you define control elements of different types, as shown in Figure 3-7.

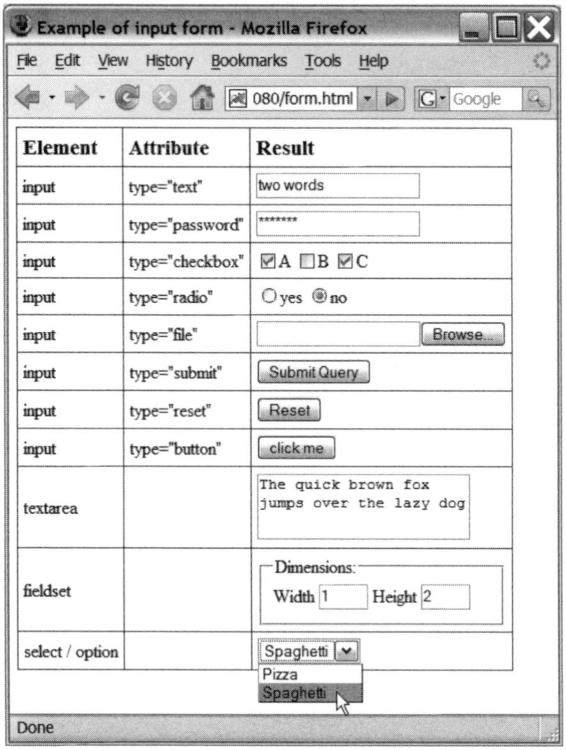

Figure 3-7. *An HTML form with examples of all input elements*

The various types of the <input> element let the user enter a string of text or a password, check one or more check boxes, choose one of several radio buttons, upload a file, submit a form, reset a form's fields, or trigger a JavaScript action by clicking a button. The <textarea> element lets the user enter several lines of text, while the <fieldset> element lets you group several input fields under one or more headings. To present multiple choices, you use the <select> element, which contains one <option> element for each alternative. Listing 3-7 shows the source code of Figure 3-7.

Listing 3-7. *form.html*

```
<!DOCTYPE html PUBLIC "-//W3C//DTD XHTML 1.0 Strict//EN"
  "http//www.w3.org/TR/xhtml1/DTD/xhtml1-strict.dtd">
<html xmlns="http//www.w3.org/1999/xhtml" xmllang="en" lang="en">
<head>
  <title>Example of input form</title>
  <style type="text/css">
    td.h {font-size: 120%; font-weight: bold}
    </style>
  </head>
<body>
<form action="">
  <input type="hidden" name="agent" value="007"/>
  <table  cellpadding="5" border="1" rules="all">
    <tr>
      <td class="h">Element</td><td class="h">Attribute</td>
      <td class="h">Result</td></tr>
    <tr>
      <td>input</td><td>type="text"</td>
      <td><input type="text" name="t"/></td>
      </tr>
    <tr>
      <td>input</td><td>type="password"</td>
      <td><input type="password" name="p"/></td>
      </tr>
    <tr>
      <td>input</td><td>type="checkbox"</td>
      <td>
        <input type="checkbox" value="a" name="abc">A</input>
        <input type="checkbox" value="b" name="abc">B</input>
        <input type="checkbox" value="c" name="abc">C</input>
        </td>
      </tr>
    <tr>
      <td>input</td><td>type="radio"</td>
      <td>
        <input type="radio" name="yn" value="y">yes</input>
        <input type="radio" name="yn" value="n">no</input>
        </td>
      </tr>
    <tr>
      <td>input</td><td>type="file"</td>
      <td><input type="file" name="f"/></td>
      </tr>
```

```
    <tr>
      <td>input</td><td>type="submit"</td>
      <td><input type="submit"/></td>
      </tr>
    <tr>
      <td>input</td><td>type="reset"</td>
      <td><input type="reset"/></td>
      </tr>
    <tr>
      <td>input</td><td>type="button"</td>
      <td><input type="button" value="click me" name="b"/></td>
      </tr>
    <tr>
      <td>textarea</td><td></td>
      <td><textarea name="ta">Default text</textarea></td>
      </tr>
    <tr>
      <td>fieldset</td><td></td>
      <td><fieldset>
        <legend>Dimensions:</legend>
        Width <input type="text" size="3" name="w"/>
        Height <input type="text" size="3" name="h"/>
        </fieldset></td>
      </tr>
    <tr>
      <td>select / option</td><td></td>
      <td><select name="food">
        <option value="pizza">Pizza</option>
        <option value="spaghetti" selected>Spaghetti</option>
        </select></td>
      </tr>
    </table>
  </form>
</body>
</html>
```

We've highlighted two lines in bold for you. The first line, which contains the `<form>` element, shows that the `action` attribute is set to the empty string. The `action` attribute defines the URL of the page that must handle the request form. An empty string means that the same page displaying the form will also handle it. The second highlighted line shows how you can use the `<input>` element to set parameters without the user being aware of it (unless she peeks at the source, that is).

If you fill in the form as shown in Figure 3-7 and click on the Submit Query button (or hit the Enter key), you'll see in the address field of your browser that the following string appears at the end of the URL (we've added the newlines for readability):

```
?agent=007
&t=two+words
&p=a++b++c
&abc=a
&abc=c
&yn=n
&f=
&ta=The+quick+brown+fox+jumps+over+the+lazy+dog
&w=1
&h=2
&food=spaghetti
```

The browser has translated each element inside the <form> element into a string of the type *parameter-name=parameter-value*. Notice that each space in the text fields has been replaced by a plus sign, including the spaces within the password. Also notice that the parameter abc appears twice, because we checked two of the three available check boxes.

We recommend that you always add two attributes to the <form> element: name="*your_form_name*" and method="post". You'll find the name attribute useful to add JavaScript to your page. Also, you can set the request method to POST, as we mentioned earlier in this chapter.

If this page had been a JSP instead of a static HTML document, the server would have processed the request parameters and set the fields in the response page to the corresponding values. Listing 3-8 shows an example of how such a JSP page would look like. Although this chapter is about HTML, you'll probably find this useful.

Listing 3-8. *form.jsp*

```jsp
<%@page language="java" contentType="text/html"%>
<%
  String   t_ = request.getParameter("t");
  if (t_ == null) t_ = "";
  String   p_ = request.getParameter("p");
  if (p_ == null) p_ = "";
  String[] abc_ = request.getParameterValues("abc");
  boolean  abc_a = false;
  boolean  abc_b = false;
  boolean  abc_c = false;
  if (abc_ != null) {
    for (int k = 0; k < abc_.length; k++) {
      if (abc_[k].length() == 1) {
        switch (abc_[k].charAt(0)) {
          case 'a': abc_a = true;
                    break;
          case 'b': abc_b = true;
                    break;
          case 'c': abc_c = true;
                    break;
```

```
            }
          }
        }
      }
    String    yn_ = request.getParameter("yn");
    boolean   yn_y = false;
    boolean   yn_n = false;
    if (yn_ != null) {
        yn_y = (yn_.equals("y"));
        yn_n = (yn_.equals("n"));
    }
    String    ta_ = request.getParameter("ta");
    if (ta_ == null) ta_ = "Default text";
    String    w_ = request.getParameter("w");
    if (w_ == null) w_ = "";
    String    h_ = request.getParameter("h");
    if (h_ == null) h_ = "";
    String    food_ = request.getParameter("food");
    if (food_ == null) food_ = "spaghetti";
    /*
     *  Here process the input
     */
    %>
<html>
<head>
  <title>Example of input form</title>
  <style type="text/css">
    td.h {font-size: 120%; font-weight: bold}
    </style>
  </head>
<body>
<form action="">
  <input type="hidden" name="agent" value="007"/>
  <table  cellpadding="5" border="1" rules="all">
    <tr>
      <td class="h">Element</td><td class="h">Attribute</td>
      <td class="h">Result</td></tr>
    <tr>
      <td>input</td><td>type="text"</td>
      <td><input type="text" name="t" value="<%=t_%>"/></td>
      </tr>
    <tr>
      <td>input</td><td>type="password"</td>
      <td><input type="password" name="p" value="<%=p_%>"/></td>
      </tr>
```

```
<tr>
  <td>input</td><td>type="checkbox"</td>
  <td>
    <input type="checkbox" value="a" name="abc"
      <%=(abc_a)?"checked":""%>
      >A</input>
    <input type="checkbox" value="b" name="abc"
      <%=(abc_b)?"checked":""%>
      >B</input>
    <input type="checkbox" value="c" name="abc"
      <%=(abc_c)?"checked":""%>
      >C</input>
  </td>
</tr>
<tr>
  <td>input</td><td>type="radio"</td>
  <td>
    <input type="radio" name="yn" value="y"
      <%=(yn_y)?"checked":""%>
      >yes</input>
    <input type="radio" name="yn" value="n"
      <%=(yn_n)?"checked":""%>
      >no</input>
  </td>
</tr>
<tr>
  <td>input</td><td>type="file"</td>
  <td><input type="file" name="f"/></td>
</tr>
<tr>
  <td>input</td><td>type="submit"</td>
  <td><input type="submit"/></td>
</tr>
<tr>
  <td>input</td><td>type="reset"</td>
  <td><input type="reset"/></td>
</tr>
<tr>
  <td>input</td><td>type="button"</td>
  <td><input type="button" value="click me" name="b"/></td>
</tr>
<tr>
  <td>textarea</td><td></td>
  <td><textarea name="ta"><%=ta_%></textarea></td>
</tr>
```

```
    <tr>
      <td>fieldset</td><td></td>
      <td><fieldset>
        <legend>Dimensions:</legend>
        Width <input type="text" size="3" name="w" value="<%=w_%>"/>
        Height <input type="text" size="3" name="h" value="<%=h_%>"/>
        </fieldset></td>
      </tr>
    <tr>
      <td>select / option</td><td></td>
      <td><select name="food">
        <option value="pizza"
          <%=(food_.equals("pizza"))?"selected":""%>
          >Pizza</option>
        <option value="spaghetti"
          <%=(food_.equals("spaghetti"))?"selected":""%>
          >Spaghetti</option>
        </select></td>
      </tr>
    </table>
  </form>
</body>
</html>
```

Cascading Style Sheets

The concept of *style sheets* has its origins in desktop publishing. Style sheets are used to separate presentation from content. The term *cascading* refers to the fact that you can write a series of style sheets, whereby each one builds upon and refines the styles defined in the more general ones.

The W3C has generated two standards that are relevant when talking about style sheets associated with HTML pages: Cascading Style Sheets, level 1 (CSS1), and Cascading Style Sheets, level 2 (CSS2). (See http://www.w3.org/TR/REC-CSS1 and http://www.w3.org/TR/ REC-CSS2, respectively.) In the abstract for CSS1, the W3C states:

> *CSS1 is a simple style sheet mechanism that allows authors and readers to attach style (e.g. fonts, colors and spacing) to HTML documents.*

The W3C states the following in the abstract for CSS2:

CSS2 builds on CSS1 and, with very few exceptions, all valid CSS1 style sheets are valid CSS2 style sheets. CSS2 supports media-specific style sheets so that authors may tailor the presentation of their documents to visual browsers, aural devices, printers, braille devices, handheld devices, etc. This specification also supports content positioning, downloadable fonts, table layout, features for internationalization, automatic counters and numbering, and some properties related to user interface.

As you can see, CSS2 exceeds the scope of the general introduction to CSS that is appropriate for this book.

Style Syntax

You need the following three components to define styles:

```
selector {property: value}
```

The selector is the HTML element you want to define, the property is the name of one of the element's attributes, and the value is the attribute value. You can define several attributes for the same element by separating them with a semicolon, and you can define several elements with a single definition by separating them with a comma. For example, this is a valid style definition:

```
h1, h2, h3 {
  font-family: "sans serif";
  color: red
  }
```

Note that you can freely insert spaces and newlines to make the styles more readable.

To define more than one style for the same element, you can associate a class name to each separate style. Listing 3-9 shows how you can define several paragraph styles and use them separately or together.

Listing 3-9. *p_styles.html*

```
<!DOCTYPE html PUBLIC "-//W3C//DTD XHTML 1.0 Strict//EN"
  "http://www.w3.org/TR/xhtml1/DTD/xhtml1-strict.dtd">
<html>
<head>
  <title>Styled paragraphs</title>
  <style type="text/css">
    p {font-size: 130%}
    p.bold {font-weight: bold}
    p.italic {font-style: italic}
    p.p123 {font-size: 100%; font-weight: normal; font-style: normal}
  </style>
</head>
```

```
<body>
<p>This is a default paragraph</p>
<p class="bold">This is a bold paragraph</p>
<p class="bold italic">This is a bold italic paragraph</p>
<p class="bold p123 italic">This is a normal paragraph</p>
</body>
</html>
```

Notice that to assign a paragraph (or any element) to more than one style class, you only need to list the names of the classes. Also, notice how you can use the class p.p123 to override the font size, weight, and style as defined in the preceding styles. p.p123 takes precedence over all others, because you defined it last within the element <style>. The order in which the class names appear in the class attribute of the paragraphs is irrelevant. Figure 3-8 shows the output of p_styles.html.

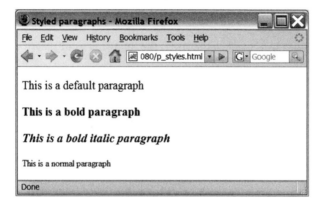

Figure 3-8. *Styled paragraphs*

If you omit the element name when defining a class, the style will apply to all the elements. For example, you can use this class with all elements rendering text:

```
.bold {font-weight: bold}
```

■**Caution** Firefox doesn't support class names that start with a number.

The complete list of properties covered by CSS1 is as follows: background, background-attachment, background-color, background-image, background-position, background-repeat, border, border-bottom, border-bottom-width, border-color, border-left, border-left-width, border-right, border-right-width, border-style, border-top, border-top-width, border-width, clear, color, display, float, font, font-family, font-size, font-style, font-variant, font-weight, height, letter-spacing, line-height, line-height, list-style, list-style-image, list-style-position, list-style-type, margin, margin-bottom, margin-left, margin-right, margin-top, padding, padding-bottom, padding-left, padding-right, padding-top, text-align, text-decoration, text-indent, text-shadow, text-transform, vertical-align, white-space, width, and word-spacing.

Additionally, there are some so-called pseudo-classes and pseudo-elements: active, first-letter, first-line, hover, link, and visited.

Now that you know the syntax of a style definition and have seen a couple of examples, you shouldn't have any problem using other properties. They're clearly described in the standard, and several web sites can help you. We found the W3 Schools site (http://www.w3schools.com/css/) to be quite good.

Placing Styles

You can define styles in three places: inline (as attributes within element start tags), internally (in the <style> element inside the <head>), and externally (in separate style-sheet files). Note that inline styles override internal styles, and internal styles override external styles.

Styles in Start Tags

You can define a style attribute in the start tag of most elements, as the following example shows:

```
<p style="color: red; font-weight: bold">bold and red</p>
```

This is appropriate when you want to use a style only once or for testing purposes. It wouldn't make sense to repeat the same style over and over again in several elements.

Styles Inside the <head> Element

Styles defined in the <head> of an HTML document by means of the <style> element, as we showed you in Listing 3-9, apply to the whole document. This makes sense for styles that you want to use exclusively in a single document. However, if you intend to reuse the styles in more than one document, you should define them in a separate file.

Styles in Separate Files

This solution gives you most flexibility and maintainability. Style-sheet files should have the extension css. To include a style-sheet file in an HTML document, you only need to place a line like this inside the <head> element:

```
<link rel="stylesheet" type="text/css" href="filename.css"/>
```

Note that the browser loads all style definitions one after the other in the order in which it encounters them. Therefore, if you include more than one file and/or if you mix in the <head> file inclusions and <style> elements, you can easily end up with conflicting styles.

Putting It All Together in an Example

As shown in Figure 3-9, today's web sites often use tabs so you can select different subjects. We'll show you how to implement these tabs with style sheets simply and elegantly.

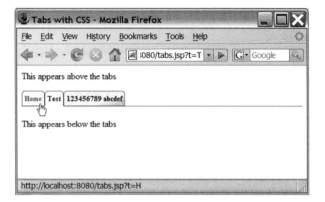

Figure 3-9. *Stylish tabs*

We'll start with the JSP document that generates the HTML page, as shown in Listing 3-10.

Listing 3-10. *tabs.jsp*

```jsp
<%@page language="java" contentType="text/html"%>
<%
  final char HOME = 'H', TEST = 'T', NUM = '1';
  String     s = request.getParameter("t");
  char       p = (s != null && s.length() > 0) ? s.charAt(0) : HOME;
  %>
<html>
<head>
  <title>Tabs with CSS</title>
  <link rel="stylesheet" type="text/css" href="tabs.css"/>
  </head>
<body>
<p>This appears above the tabs</p>
<div class="tabs">
  <ul>
    <li <% if (p == HOME) out.print("id=\"on\""); %>>
      <a href="tabs.jsp?t=<%=HOME%>"><span>Home</span></a>
      </li>
    <li <% if (p == TEST) out.print("id=\"on\""); %>>
      <a href="tabs.jsp?t=<%=TEST%>"><span>Test</span></a>
      </li>
    <li <% if (p == NUM) out.print("id=\"on\""); %>>
      <a href="tabs.jsp?t=<%=NUM%>"><span>123456789 abcdef</span></a>
      </li>
    </ul>
  </div>
```

```
<p>
   <br/>
  This appears below the tabs
  </p>
</body>
</html>
```

You should use a JSP module instead of a static HTML page, because with plain HTML, the tabs are not selectable. Also, it's a good opportunity to show you some more JSP.

The first section highlighted in bold is a scriptlet that sets the character variable p to the first character found in the input parameter t. If the input parameter is missing or empty, p is set to 'H'.

Each tab is implemented as an item of an unnumbered list. We've highlighted the item corresponding to the Test tab. This scriptlet writes id="on" to the output when the first character of the input parameter matches the character designated to identify the tab:

```
<% if (p == TEST) out.print("id=\"on\""); %>
```

Tags are formatted differently when the selector "on" is specified as a value of the id attribute. In this way, you can distinguish the current tab and draw it differently. Notice that in Figure 3-9, the Test tab is indeed *on*.

The content of the unnumbered item is

```
<a href="tabs.jsp?t=<%=TEST%>"><span>Test</span></a>
```

The hyperlink points to the URI tabs.jsp?t=T, which the browser loads when the user clicks on the tab. Listing 3-11 shows the style-sheet file.

Listing 3-11. *tabs.css*

```
div.tabs {
  float              : left;
  width              : 100%;
  background         : white url(tab_pixel.gif) repeat-x bottom;
  }
div.tabs ul {
  list-style         : none;
  margin             : 0px;
  padding            : 0px;
  }
div.tabs li {
  display            : inline;
  margin             : 0px;
  padding            : 0px;
  }
div.tabs a {
  float              : left;
  background         : url(tab_right.gif) no-repeat right top;
  border-bottom      : 1px solid black;
```

```
   font-size          : small;
   font-weight        : bold;
   text-decoration    : none;
   }
div.tabs li#on a {
   border-bottom      : 1px solid white;
   background-position: 100% 100%;
   }
div.tabs a:link, div.tabs a:active, div.tabs a:visited {
   color              : black;
   }
div.tabs a:hover {
   color              : #808080;
   background-position: 100% 100%;
   }
div.tabs span {
   float              : left;
   background         : url(tab_left.gif) no-repeat left top;
   padding            : 5px;
   white-space        : nowrap;
   }
```

All entries refer to div.tabs, which means that the styles are only to be applied to elements enclosed between <div class="tabs"> and </div>. In this way, you can define the properties that apply to all the tab elements by default. In particular, you can specify that the tabs are to build up from left to right as you defined them in the HTML document one by one. It also helps you define the gray line at the bottom of the line of tabs by repeating a single gray pixel (tab_pixel.gif) to span horizontally across the whole window.

You use list-style:none to specify that the unnumbered lists (element <ul>) should not be displayed with bullets. You need this style, because you want to display the items as tabs, and the default bullets would get in the way. Similarly, you need display:inline for the list item elements (<li>) to ensure that no line breaks are displayed before or after each item.

Next, you define how hyperlinks (element <a>) are to be rendered. First, you specify how you want to have the tab labels written, and you state that the image tab_right.gif is to be used as a background image aligned top-right. Figure 3-10 shows the image doubled in size for clarity. When you use it as a tab background top-right justified, only the upper half is visible, and its width is adjusted to match the width of the tab. The longer the text inside the tab, the more the image will be stretched horizontally, ensuring that the shading is applied to the whole tab. Its height is exactly twice the height of the tabs appropriate for the font size we've chosen.

Figure 3-10. *tab_right.gif*

The lower half of the picture, without shading, only becomes visible when you display it *bottom-right* justified, and this is exactly what you do when the tab is selected. This code shows how you operate the magic:

```
div.tabs li#on a {
  border-bottom      : 1px solid white;
  background-position: 100% 100%;
  }
```

When the id attribute of a <li> element is set to "on", the position of the background is shifted to 100% of the width and 100% of the height, bringing the lower half into view. At the same time, you overwrite the bottom gray line with a white one. Obviously, you could have simply defined a separate image with the bottom half and specified

```
background: url(tab_right_on.gif) no-repeat right top;
```

instead of using the shifting trick, but we wanted to show you something clever. By keeping the two halves together, you can ensure that they remain consistent if you need to modify one of them.

Now, let's take a look at the second-to-last definition:

```
div.tabs a:hover {
  color              : #808080;
  background-position: 100% 100%;
  }
```

This definition has the effect of removing the shaded background and turning the text to gray when you pass over a tab with your cursor, as you might have noticed in Figure 3-9.

To complete the tabs, you only need to display the left border of the tabs, and you can do this by attaching it as a left-justified, non-repeating background image to the <span> element.

In conclusion, CSS is a powerful tool that can do much more than just set a font size or a background color.

JavaScript

JavaScript is the most widely used client-side scripting language on the Web. By adding it to your web pages, you can make your pages *do things*, such as pre-validate forms or immediately react to a user's actions.

The syntax of JavaScript was modeled on that of Java. Therefore, if you know Java, you should find JavaScript easy to learn. One noteworthy difference from Java is that you can omit variable declarations in the top-level code. Moreover, JavaScript lacks Java's static typing and strong type checking. This gives you more freedom, but it comes with the risk of messing things up big way. JavaScript relies on built-in objects, but it doesn't support classes or inheritance. It's an interpreted language, and object binding is done at runtime.

At the end of 1995, Netscape introduced JavaScript in its Netscape Navigator web browser. Microsoft reverse-engineered JavaScript, added its own extensions (as Microsoft always does), and renamed it JScript. Some years later, Ecma International merged the two languages into the standard ECMA-262 and named the scripting language ECMAScript. Today, most browsers (including Firefox, Internet Explorer, and Opera) conform to the ECMA-262 third edition, which has been adopted as the ISO/IEC standard 16262. Everybody keeps referring to Java-Script, while they should really be saying ECMAScript. However, we've decided to stick to JavaScript so that you know what we are talking about.

Placing JavaScript Inside a Web Page

Before discussing some of the things you can actually do with JavaScript, let's see how you can include it in your web pages. You have two possibilities: you can either keep the script inside your HTML document:

```
<script type="text/javascript">
  /* Place your script here */
  </script>.
```

or save it in a separate file:

```
<script type="text/javascript" src="myScript.js"></script>
```

■**Caution** In both cases, you have to keep the end tag </script>, because the form <script ... /> is invalid.

In either case, you can decide to place your script in the <head> or within the <body>. If you want the script to execute in response to some event (e.g., when you pass your cursor over a button), place it in the <head>. If you place it in the <body>, the browser will execute it upon loading the page.

Responding to Events

You can place the onload and onunload events, which are associated with the whole window, in the <body> and <frameset> elements. For example, you can execute a JavaScript function when your page is loaded as follows:

```
<body onload="functionName">
```

In most tags, you can include a series of events, which are generated directly by a keyboard or a mouse. They are onclick, ondblclick, onkeydown, onkeypress, onkeyup, onmousedown, onmousemove, onmouseout, onmouseover, and onmouseup. In particular, onmouseover allows you to change the appearance of an element when you pass the cursor over it without clicking. The only tags that are excluded are base, bdo, br, frame, frameset, head, html, iframe, meta, param, script, style, and title, because it doesn't make any sense to associate events to those elements.

Finally, some events are associated with the status of form-related elements and are therefore only valid within forms. These events are onblur, onchange, onfocus, onreset, onselect, and onsubmit. The events onsubmit and onreset refer to the whole form, while the others refer to individual elements. In particular, onfocus is triggered when an element is clicked on or tabbed to and therefore becomes ready to accept input, while onblur is triggered when an element loses focus. You can check the form input by using either onchange to trigger a testing function specifically designed for an element or onsubmit to perform several checks bundled inside a single function. You should ensure that input errors are detected as soon as possible. You don't want your user to keep typing only to be told upon submitting the form that he did something wrong at the very beginning. In general, a combination of checks on individual elements plus a consistency check when the form is submitted is a good way to go.

Checking and Correcting Dates

As we already said, checking user inputs with JavaScript before the data leaves the browser makes for a quicker response, but it doesn't necessarily reduce the checks you have to do on the server side, because you cannot entirely depend on what happens on the client side. The user might have disabled JavaScript or maliciously altered your page to bypass the checks.

Nevertheless, security issues aside, client-side checks make for a better user experience. In this section, we'll give you an example of how to prevent a user from entering incorrectly formatted dates and how to work with dates. We'll use JSP instead of straight HTML, because it's much easier to use a JSP loop to prepare a <select> on days and months, rather than type them all by hand in plain HTML. Figure 3-11 shows you what you want to achieve.

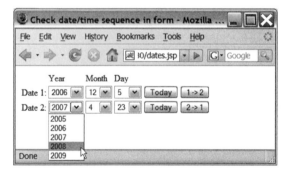

Figure 3-11. *Setting and copying dates*

You want to be able to set any valid date within a certain number of years, set a date to today, or copy a date at the press of a button. In particular, you need to ensure that when you select a month, the number of days changes automatically. Listing 3-12 shows the JSP module, where we've highlighted the JavaScript code in bold. Study this code first before passing to the file that contains the JavaScript functions.

Listing 3-12. *dates.jsp*

```
01:  <%@page language="java" contentType="text/html"%>
02:  <html>
03:  <head>
04:    <title>Check date/time sequence in form</title>
05:    <script type="text/javascript">
06:      var now = new Date();
07:      var thisDay   = now.getDate() - 1;
```

```
08:        var thisMonth = now.getMonth();
09:        var thisYear  = now.getYear();
10:        if (thisYear < 2000) thisYear += 1900; //for some browsers
11:        var firstYear = thisYear - 2;
12:        var lastYear = thisYear + 2;
13:        </script>
14:     <script type="text/javascript" src="dates.js"></script>
15:     </head>
16:  <body>
17:  <form name="f" action="">
18:     <table border="0">
19:        <tr><td> </td>
20:          <td>Year</td><td>Month</td><td>Day</td>
21:          <td> </td>
22:        </tr>
23:  <%  for (int k = 1, kMax = 2; k <= kMax; k++) { %>
24:  <%     String upd = "updateMonthDays('f', '"+k+"')"; %>
25:        <tr>
26:          <td>Date <%=k%>:</td>
27:          <td>
28:            <select name="yy<%=k%>" onchange="<%=upd%>">
29:              <script type="text/javascript">
30:                for (var jy = firstYear; jy <= lastYear; jy++) {
31:                  document.writeln("<option>" + jy + "</option>");
32:                  }
33:              </script>
34:            </select>
35:          </td>
36:          <td>
37:            <select name="mm<%=k%>" onchange="<%=upd%>">
38:  <%          for (int jm = 1; jm <= 12; jm++) { %>
39:              <option><%=jm%></option>
40:  <%          } %>
41:            </select>
42:          </td>
43:          <td>
44:            <select name="dd<%=k%>">
45:  <%          for (int jd = 1; jd <= 31; jd++) { %>
46:              <option><%=jd%></option>
47:  <%          } %>
48:            </select>
49:          </td>
50:          <td>
51:            <input type="button" name="today<%=k%>"
52:              value="Today" onclick="selectToday('f', '<%=k%>')"/>
53:  <%          int k1 = k; int k2 = k + 1; if (k2 > kMax) k2 = 1; %>
```

```
54:                    <input type="button" name="same_day"
55:                        value="<%=k1%> -> <%=k2%>"
56:                        onclick="copyDay('f', '<%=k1%>', '<%=k2%>')"/>
57:                    </td>
58:                </tr>
59:            <script type="text/javascript">
60:                selectToday('f', '<%=k%>')
61:            </script>
62: <%    } /* for (int k.. */ %>
63:        </table>
64:    </form>
65: </body>
66: </html>
```

Lines 5–12 set up some JavaScript variables that you'll use in several places. You could have used the Calendar class in JSP, but it would have provided the time of the server, not of the client. Even if your target users are within the United States, you'll have to take the several time zones into account. You might be wondering why you subtract 1 when calculating thisDay, while you don't subtract anything when calculating thisMonth. This is because getDate returns the day of the month (i.e., 1, 2, and so on), while getMonth returns 0 for January, 1 for February, and so on. We prefer to have all indices starting with the same value.

Lines 11 and 12 reflect our decision of making available two years in the past and two years in the future. In the real world, this decision will depend on your application. You use the year limits to define the options for the year selection in lines 29 and 30. Notice that you use JavaScript to write the <option> elements to the web page.

Line 60 shows a call to the function selectToday, which is a script that you insert directly into the page. It means that after rendering one row of the table of dates, the browser will set the date to today (the user's today, not the server's today).

Other bits of JavaScript are linked to the event onclick of each button and to the event onchange of the year and month selectors.

The onclick attributes in line 52:

```
onclick="selectToday('f', '<%=k%>')"
```

and in line 56:

```
onclick="copyDay('f', '<%=k1%>', '<%=k2%>')"
```

have the effect of executing the respective functions selectToday and copyDay with the argument list ('f', '1') if you click on a button of the first date, and with the argument list ('f', '2') if you click on a button of the second date.

We'll explain the functions when we look at the JavaScript file dates.js in Listing 3-13, but you can already see that you always pass the name of the <form> element as first argument of the call. You do this because you won't want to hard-code the form name inside a separate file.

The onchange="<%=upd%>" attribute, which you see in line 37, is expanded by JSP to onchange="updateMonthDays('f', '1')" for the first date and to onchange="updateMonthDays('f', '2')" for the second date. Its purpose is to ensure that when the user changes the month selection, the number of days changes accordingly. Remember that this happens on the client side and doesn't involve the server. The identical attribute also appears in line 28, to take into account that the user could select a leap year. In this case, you need to ensure that you display February with 29 days.

Now you can see why it's better to use JSP instead of plain HTML: you only need to write the code for one date, and the big loop between lines 23 and 62 repeats it for you for as many dates as you like. You only need to increase kMax to see more than two dates.

Listing 3-13 shows the JavaScript functions hidden in dates.js. We've highlighted the function headers.

Listing 3-13. *dates.js*

```
01:  /*
02:  **  Determine the number of days in the given month of the given year
03:  */
04:  function daysInMonth(m, y) {
05:    var daysInMonth = 31;
06:    if (m == 4  ||  m == 6  ||  m == 9  ||  m == 11) daysInMonth = 30;
07:    if (m == 2) {
08:      daysInMonth = ((y%4) == 0)
09:                        ? (((y%100) == 0)
10:                                   ? (((y%400) == 0) ? 29 : 28)
11:                                   : 29
12:                          )
13:                        :28
14:                        ;
15:    }
16:    return daysInMonth;
17:  }
18:  /*
19:  **  Adjust the days to the requested month and year
20:  */
21:  function updateMonthDays(formName, kDate) {
22:    var ddObj = eval("document." + formName + ".dd" + kDate);
23:    var mmObj = eval("document." + formName + ".mm" + kDate);
24:    var yyObj = eval("document." + formName + ".yy" + kDate);
25:    var mm = mmObj[mmObj.selectedIndex].text;
26:    var yy = yyObj[yyObj.selectedIndex].text;
27:    var wantedDays  = daysInMonth(mm, yy);
28:    var currentDays = ddObj.length;
29:    /*
30:     *  REMOVE days from the end if we have too many
31:     */
32:    while (wantedDays < currentDays) {
33:      ddObj.options[ddObj.length - 1] = null;
34:      currentDays--;
35:    }
36:    /*
37:     *  ADD days at the end if we are missing some
```

```
38:      */
39:      while (wantedDays > currentDays) {
40:        currentDays++;
41:        ddObj.appendChild(new Option(currentDays));
42:        }
43:      //
44:      if (ddObj.selectedIndex < 0) ddObj.selectedIndex = 0;
45:      }
46:    /*
47:    **  Select today
48:    */
49:    function selectToday(formName, kDate) {
50:      var ddObj = eval("document." + formName + ".dd" + kDate);
51:      var mmObj = eval("document." + formName + ".mm" + kDate);
52:      var yyObj = eval("document." + formName + ".yy" + kDate);
53:      yyObj[thisYear - firstYear].selected = true;
54:      mmObj[thisMonth].selected = true;
55:      updateMonthDays(formName, kDate);
56:      ddObj[thisDay].selected = true;
57:      }
58:    /*
59:    **  Copy a day to another
60:    */
61:    function copyDay(formName, kFrom, kTo) {
62:      var ddFromObj = eval("document." + formName + ".dd" + kFrom);
63:      var mmFromObj = eval("document." + formName + ".mm" + kFrom);
64:      var yyFromObj = eval("document." + formName + ".yy" + kFrom);
65:      var ddToObj = eval("document." + formName + ".dd" + kTo);
66:      var mmToObj = eval("document." + formName + ".mm" + kTo);
67:      var yyToObj = eval("document." + formName + ".yy" + kTo);
68:      yyToObj[yyFromObj.selectedIndex].selected = true;
69:      mmToObj[mmFromObj.selectedIndex].selected = true;
70:      updateMonthDays(formName, kTo);
71:      ddToObj[ddFromObj.selectedIndex].selected = true;
72:      }
```

The function daysInMonth is pretty straightforward. It accepts the month and year as arguments and returns the number of days in that month. Lines 8–14 express the fact that the leap years are divisible by 4, but not if they're also divisible by 100, but yes if they're also divisible by 400. That's why the year 2000 was a leap year, but the year 1900 was not, and the year 2100 will not be.

updateMonthDays ensures that you display the correct number of days for each month. Remember that the days are <option> elements within a <select> control element. In lines 23–27, you extract the selected text from the <select> elements for month and year and use daysInMonth to obtain the number of days you need. In line 28, you obtain the number of days displayed before changing either the year or month, thereby forcing the execution of updateMonthDays. The length of the <select> element is nothing other than the length of the array of <option> elements, which the <select> element contains. Therefore, you can use ddObj.length instead of ddObj.options.length. Each iteration of the while loop in lines 32–35 deletes the last <option> (i.e., the last day) by setting it to null and decreases the number of current days accordingly:

```
while (wantedDays < currentDays) {
  ddObj.options[ddObj.length - 1] = null;
  currentDays--;
  }
```

The iterations continue until the number of current days has been reduced to the number of days you need for the current month. Similarly, each iteration of the while loop in lines 39–42 increases the number of current days, creates a new option with the increased number, and appends it to the <select> element:

```
while (wantedDays > currentDays) {
  currentDays++;
  ddObj.appendChild(new Option(currentDays));
  }
```

The iterations continue until the number of current days has been increased to the number of days you need for the current month. The last line of updateMonthDays (line 44) is necessary in case the previously selected day has been removed. For example, if you selected March 31st and then changed the month to April, the day would be set to the 1st, because the 31st would no longer be there.

selectToday sets a date to the client's today. All the work is done in lines 54–56. Line 54 selects the month, line 55 adjusts the number of days of the month, and line 56 selects the day.

copyDay copies the day, month, and year from one date to another. All the work is done in the lines 68–71. Line 68 selects in the destination year the same index selected in the source year, line 69 does the same for the month, line 70 adjusts the number of days of the month, and line 71 selects in the destination day the same index selected in the source day.

Animation: Bouncing Balls

You can use JavaScript to animate your pages. Figure 3-12 shows you a page with a text field containing a couple of numbers, a button, and a square full of dots. This isn't so interesting, but that's only because it's a snapshot of a window. In reality, the dots bounce around within the square in all possible directions and at different speeds.

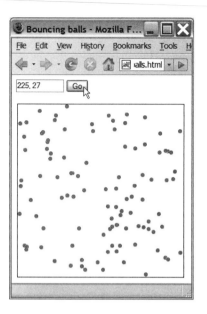

Figure 3-12. *A square full of bouncing balls*

Let's go through the code, starting with the style definitions and the HTML code, as shown in Listing 3-14.

Listing 3-14. *balls_no_js.html*

```
<!DOCTYPE html PUBLIC "-//W3C//DTD XHTML 1.0 Strict//EN"
  "http://www.w3.org/TR/xhtml1/DTD/xhtml1-strict.dtd">
<html>
<head>
  <title>Bouncing balls</title>
  <style>
    #square {
      position: absolute;
      border: thin solid;
      }
    div.ball img {
      position: absolute;
      }
    </style>
</head>
<body>
  <form name="f">
    <input type="text" name="t" size="10"/>
    <input type=button id="stop_go" onclick="stop()" value="Stop"/>
    </form>
```

```
      <div id="square"></div>
      <div id="ball" class="ball"><img src="ball.gif" alt=""/></div>
      </body>
</html>
```

The first style defines an object with a thin solid border identified as square, and the second style only states that all images within a division of class ball have absolute coordinates.

The HTML <body> includes a small form with the text field, the button, and two divisions: one identified as square and one of class ball. Figure 3-13 shows how a browser would render such a page.

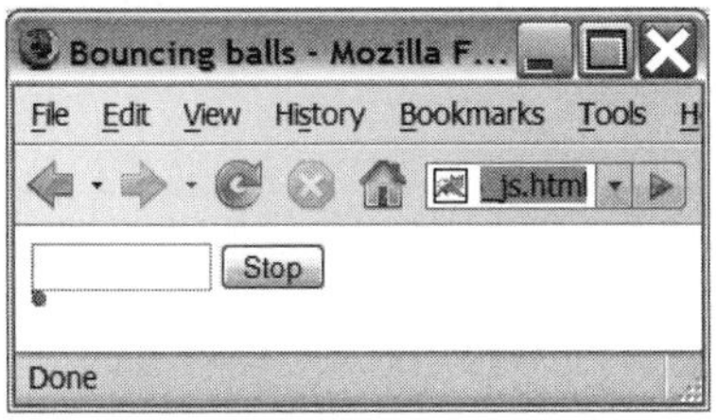

Figure 3-13. *No square and one ball at rest*

Boring. Listing 3-15 shows the full code of the page after you add the JavaScript part. We've highlighted the JavaScript variable definitions and the function names.

Listing 3-15. *balls.html*

```
01: <!DOCTYPE html PUBLIC "-//W3C//DTD XHTML 1.0 Strict//EN"
02:    "http://www.w3.org/TR/xhtml1/DTD/xhtml1-strict.dtd">
03: <html>
04: <head>
05:   <title>Bouncing balls</title>
06:   <style>
07:     #square {
08:       position: absolute;
09:       border: thin solid;
10:       }
11:     div.ball img {
12:       position: absolute;
13:       }
14:     </style>
15: <script type="text/javascript">
16: var MIN_X = 10;
17: var MIN_Y = 50;
18: var MAX_X = 310;
19: var MAX_Y = 350;
20: var DIAM = 7;
```

```
21:   var balls = [];
22:   var timer = null;
23:   //----------------------------
24:   function speed() {
25:      return DIAM*(0.5+1.5*Math.random())*((Math.random()>0.5)?1:-1);
26:      }
27:   function initBall(ball, xx, yy) {
28:      ball.xx = xx;
29:      ball.yy = yy;
30:      ball.sX = speed();
31:      ball.sY = speed();
32:      }
33:   function mouseDown(e) {
34:      var xx = e.clientX;
35:      var yy = e.clientY;
36:      document.f.t.value = xx + ", " + yy;
37:      if (xx > MIN_X && xx < MAX_X && yy > MIN_Y && yy < MAX_Y) {
38:         document.getElementById("ball").appendChild(balls[0].cloneNode(true));
39:         initBall(balls[balls.length-1], xx, yy);
40:         }
41:      }
42:   function moveBall(b) {
43:      b.xx += b.sX;
44:      b.yy += b.sY;
45:      b.style.left = b.xx + "px";
46:      b.style.top = b.yy + "px";
47:      if ((b.xx + b.sX + DIAM >= MAX_X) || (b.xx + b.sX <= MIN_X)) b.sX *= -1;
48:      if ((b.yy + b.sY + DIAM >= MAX_Y) || (b.yy + b.sY <= MIN_Y)) b.sY *= -1;
49:      }
50:   function moveBalls() {
51:      for (var k = 0; k < balls.length; k++) {
52:         moveBall(balls[k]);
53:         }
54:      }
55:   function go() {
56:      if (!timer) timer = setInterval(moveBalls, 20);
57:      var but = document.getElementById("stop_go");
58:      but.onclick = stop;
59:      but.value = "Stop";
60:      }
61:   function stop() {
62:      if (timer) {
63:         clearInterval(timer);
64:         timer = null;
65:         var but = document.getElementById("stop_go");
66:         but.onclick = go;
67:         but.value = "Go";
```

```
68:       }
69:     }
70:  function init() {
71:     var field = document.getElementById("square");
72:     field.style.left = MIN_X + "px";
73:     field.style.top = MIN_Y + "px";
74:     field.style.width = MAX_X - MIN_X + "px";
75:     field.style.height = MAX_Y - MIN_Y + "px";
76:     balls = document.getElementById("ball").getElementsByTagName("img");
77:     initBall(
78:       balls[0],
79:       (MAX_X - MIN_X)*Math.random(),
80:       (MAX_Y - MIN_Y)*Math.random()
81:       );
82:     balls[0].style.width = DIAM + "px";
83:     balls[0].style.height = DIAM + "px";
84:     document.onmousedown = mouseDown;
85:     go();
86:     }
87:  window.onload = init;
88:  </script>
89:  </head>
90:  <body>
91:    <form name="f">
92:      <input type="text" name="t" size="10"/>
93:      <input type=button id="stop_go" onclick="stop()" value="Stop"/>
94:      </form>
95:    <div id="square"></div>
96:    <div id="ball" class="ball"><img src="ball.gif" alt=""/></div>
97:    </body>
98:  </html>
```

(MIN_X, MIN_Y) and (MAX_X, MAX_Y), respectively, define the coordinates of the top-left and bottom-right corners of the rectangular area within which you want the balls to bounce. DIAM is the diameter of the balls. All dimensions are measured in pixels.

Line 87 directs the browser to execute the function init upon loading the HTML page. init uses MIN_X, MIN_Y, MAX_X, and MAX_Y to set the position and dimensions of the <DIV> square (see lines 71–75). Instead of doing this, you could have simply added the following four lines to the #square style (see lines 07–10):

```
left: 10px;
top: 50px;
width: 300px;
height: 300px;
```

However, it's never good practice to duplicate definitions, because sooner or later they will diverge and cause problems. It would have been worse if the style sheet had been in a separate file, but even in this case, we want to do it right, don't we?

After defining the square to be used as the field for the bouncing balls, init points the variable balls (which you've defined as an array) to the list of <img> elements inside the <div> ball (see line 76). As the HTML page contains a single image within the division ball (see line 96), that image is then accessible as balls[0]. To set the initial coordinates and the speed of the ball, init executes the function initBall. init calculates the initial coordinates as a random point within the square (see lines 79-80), while initBall calculates the horizontal and vertical components of the speed (see lines 30-31) by means of the function speed (see line 25). You measure the speed along each axis as the number of pixels covered by a ball in a given period of time (a 50th of a second, as you'll see in a moment). Notice how simply JavaScript lets you define new element attributes. The variable ball used inside initBall, like balls[0], points to an object that is the <img> element defined in line 96; when you write ball.xx = xx, JavaScript creates the attribute named xx and assigns to it the value of the xx parameter. Once initBall returns, init sets the dimensions of the ball image by updating its style (see lines 82-83) and assigns the JavaScript function mouseDown to the event document.mousedown (see line 84). This means that the function mouseDown will be executed every time the user presses a mouse button. We intend to create a new bouncing ball whenever this happens. The last action of init is to execute the function go, which starts the animation.

The first action of go (see line 56) is to start a time interval of 20ms (the 50th of a second we already mentioned). Every 20ms, the browser executes the function moveBalls. Notice that you only do this after checking that no timer is already running. This is a safety measure that isn't really necessary, because immediately after dealing with the timer, go sets the button to execute the function stop. Therefore, there is theoretically no way to execute go more than once. However, as you've learned, some defensive code usually results in more stable programs without significantly penalizing performance.

After go has completed, the name of the button is Stop, as shown in Figure 3-13. When the user clicks on it, the function stop removes the timer, thereby halting the animation. It then associates the button to the function go and renames it as Go. Similar to what you did concerning go, you check that a timer is running before attempting to stop it. Again, this isn't really necessary, but it makes us feel better!

When the animation is running, every 20ms the browser executes moveBalls, which just executes moveBall for each element in the array balls[]. moveBall increments the coordinates by their corresponding speed components (see lines 43-44) and updates the position stored in the style (see lines 45-46), which is what actually causes the image on the screen to move. After moving a ball, moveBall checks whether the ball has reached one of the sides of the rectangular field. If it has, moveBall inverts the corresponding speed component, so that when it executes the next time, the ball will "bounce off" the wall. You haven't really ensured that the ball bounces when it touches the border rather than when it overlaps with it or when it is one pixel away from it. It all depends on using the appropriate operations (<, <=, >=, and >) and adding or not adding a +1 when calculating the dimensions as differences between coordinates. However, we didn't think this was worth spending time on. We leave it up to you to ensure that the ball bounces back when it touches one side—not one pixel before and not one pixel after!

When you press the mouse button within the main browser window, the function mouseDown is executed. The first two lines (34 and 35) have the purpose of saving in two variables the horizontal and vertical coordinates of the cursor (incidentally, the e stands for *event*). This makes the code shorter and more readable. Line 36 writes the coordinates in the text field (see Figure 3-12). We did this to show you how to do it, although it's irrelevant for bouncing the balls. Notice how you use the names to identify the form and its text element, as opposed to defining an ID and using getElementById as you do elsewhere. The two important lines are 38 and 39, which you execute only when you click the mouse inside the rectangular field. You want to create a new bouncing ball that starts with random speed from the position where you click the mouse.

The purpose of line 38 is to display a new ball in the web page. If you study the code carefully, you'll see that line 38 is equivalent to the following three lines:

```
var ballDivObject = document.getElementById("ball");
var newBallObject = balls[0].cloneNode(true);
ballDivObject.appendChild(newBallObject);
```

The first line gets a pointer to the <div> element with the identifier set to ball. The second line makes a copy of the first ball. Remember that you defined it when the page was loaded. Therefore, when you click with the mouse, balls[0] certainly exists and points to a properly initialized ball—that is, to an <img> element with the additional attributes xx, yy, sX, and sY. The third line takes the new ball and attaches it to the ball <div> as a new child.

As a result, it is as if you had added a second image to the <div> defined in line 96:

```
<div id="ball" class="ball">
  <img src="ball.gif" alt=""/>
  <img src="ball.gif" alt=""/>
</div>
```

Now, however, the images also have the coordinate and speed attributes, which aren't part of the initial HTML code.

The new ball has the same coordinates and speed that the first ball had when you clicked the mouse. With line 39, you set the coordinates to those of the event (i.e., xx and yy), and initBall replaces the speed components with two new random values. Notice that after executing line 38, as you had set the array balls to point to the list of <img> objects within the ball <div>, the last element of balls points to the new ball you've just created by cloning.

■Tip Remember that the identifiers are supposed to be unique within the document. Make sure this is so!

An interesting extension would be to have the balls bounce against each other, but this would require a bit of math. At each wake-up, you'd have to check each ball against all the others to identify the pairs that come into contact. Then, for each one of those pairs, you'd have to calculate the total momentum, find the components of the two velocities perpendicular to the direction of the momentum, and invert those components. The assumption that all the balls have the same mass would reduce the problem to be purely geometrical, but probably not trivial for many. Anyhow, for those interested in physics, with several balls and after enough cycles, the exchange of momentum between the balls would model a *gas* of balls regardless of the initial conditions.

Animation: Ticker Tape

If you understood how `balls.html` works, you should be able to devise your own ticker tape.
In principle, the idea is simple: you write a message in a text field, and then, at regular intervals, you remove the first character of the message and stick it to the end. The message
appears to scroll from right to left (see Figure 3-14). Nevertheless, to do a good ticker tape,
there is more than meets the eye.

Figure 3-14. *The simplest possible ticker tape*

Listing 3-16 shows you how to create a simple ticker tape.

Listing 3-16. *ticker0.html*

```
<!DOCTYPE html PUBLIC "-//W3C//DTD XHTML 1.0 Strict//EN"
  "http://www.w3.org/TR/xhtml1/DTD/xhtml1-strict.dtd">
<html>
<head>
  <title>Ticker Tape 0</title>
  <script type="text/javascript">
    var msg = " This is a ticker tape message!          ";
    function tick_it() {
      msg = msg.substring(1) + msg.charAt(0);
      document.f.t.value = msg;
      window.setTimeout("tick_it()", 150);
      }
  </script>
</head>
<body>
  <form name="f"><input name="t" size="30" value=""/></form>
  <script type="text/javascript">tick_it();</script>
  </body>
</html>
```

This code may look straightforward, but it's not necessarily that simple. Notice that the
message you defined in the example, including an initial space, is 31 characters long. And yet,
you've still appended a dozen spaces to display it in a text element of size 30. This is because
the size attribute of a text element doesn't really reflect the correct number of characters it
can contain. If you hadn't added the extra spaces, a portion of the text field would have

remained blank. In other words, the scrolling text would have not scrolled through the whole text field. Ugly. You can usually resolve this issue by appending a large number of spaces or copies of the message itself to the end of the message. This solution is effective, but it would be nice to have a more elegant solution.

The crux of the problem lies in the fact that the length of a string depends on its font type and size. Developing software for the Macintosh decades ago, it was easily possible to determine the number of pixels needed to display a string. Java lets you do it now with the Graphics and FontMetrics classes. However, in HTML, it is not *officially* possible to know how long a piece of string is. In other words, the W3C hasn't standardized a way of obtaining the size of an element in pixels. However, Microsoft did it in Internet Explorer, and then both Opera and Firefox adopted the Microsoft extension to the standard. As a result, there is now an *unofficial* way of getting the length of a string in pixels. Have a look at Listing 3-17.

Listing 3-17. *ticker.html*

```
01:  <!DOCTYPE html PUBLIC "-//W3C//DTD XHTML 1.0 Strict//EN"
02:    "http://www.w3.org/TR/xhtml1/DTD/xhtml1-strict.dtd">
03:  <html>
04:  <head>
05:    <title>Ticker Tape</title>
06:    <script type="text/javascript">
07:      var msg = " This is a ticker tape message!";
08:      var TAPE_SIZE = 300; // in pixels
09:      function start_ticker() {
10:        document.f.t.style.width = TAPE_SIZE + "px";
11:        var xx = document.getElementById("x");
12:        var space_size = xx.offsetWidth - 1;
13:        xx.innerHTML = msg;
14:        var msg_size = xx.offsetWidth;
15:        var nSpaces = Math.ceil((TAPE_SIZE - msg_size) / space_size);
16:        for (var k = nSpaces; k > 0; k--) msg += " ";
18:        document.f.t.value = msg;
19:        tick_it();
20:        }
21:      function tick_it() {
22:        msg = msg.substring(1) + msg.charAt(0);
23:        document.f.t.value = msg;
24:        window.setTimeout("tick_it()", 150);
25:        }
26:    </script>
27:    </head>
28:  <body>
29:    <span id="x" style="visibility:hidden"> </span>
30:    <form name="f"><input name="t" value=""/></form>
31:    <script type="text/javascript">start_ticker();</script>
32:    </body>
33:  </html>
```

We've highlighted the differences between this version and `ticker0.html`, shown in Listing 3-16. Note that in line 7, we removed the dozen trailing spaces from the message. We did this because we intend to extend the message with enough spaces to bring its length to be just about the same as that of the text element.

All the work is done in the `start_ticker` function. In line 10, you set the size of the text element in pixels, rather than use the `size` attribute expressed in characters. In line 29, you define an invisible `<span>` element containing a single space, and in line 12, you determine the size of the element (i.e., the pixels occupied by the space in the horizontal direction) via the read-only property `offsetWidth`. This is one of the properties originally introduced by Microsoft and not included in any W3C specification.

In line 13, you replace the content of the `<span>` with the message using `innerHTML`, another Microsoft-originated property. This lets you obtain the length of the message string in pixels with `offsetWidth` (see line 14).

You now have all the information you need to calculate the number of spaces you have to append to your message in order to fill the whole text field. Everything works just fine, even when the message without any additional space already needs more space than what is available in the text field. In that case, `nSpace` becomes negative, and the `for` loop in line 16 terminates without adding any space. Incidentally, this is one of the reasons for adding a hard-coded space at the beginning of any message: you want to be sure that you display at least one empty space between repetitions of the message. It's better to insert the space at the beginning, because it makes the initial display of the message more readable.

Opera and Internet Explorer report that the length of the string is 181 pixels, while Firefox only counts 177 pixels. Odd, but inconsequential. If you want to check it for yourself, you can insert the following line toward the end of `start_ticker`:

```
alert("space: " + space_size + "; msg: " + msg_size);
```

What's Ajax?

Asynchronous JavaScript and XML (Ajax) is a mechanism for letting JavaScript communicate with the server *asynchronously*—that is, without reloading the page. This is possible by means of the new JavaScript built-in object `XMLHttpRequest`.

It seems easy, doesn't it? You create an `XMLHttpRequest` object within JavaScript, use it to send a request to the server, get the response, and, presto, you have fresh data for your web page without having to reload it. Well, conceptually it *is* easy, but it's not obvious how to do it, and it's even more tricky to maintain. We'll present a simple example of a page that displays the server time. First, you need to write a JSP page to return the time (see Listing 3-18).

Listing 3-18. *time.jsp*

```
<%@page language="java" contentType="text/html"
  %><%@page import="java.util.*"
  %><% out.print(new GregorianCalendar().getTime()); %>
```

We've removed all the spaces and newlines before and after the print statement, including a newline at the end. This ensures that only the time is returned. If you type the URL of this script in the address field of your browser, you'll get something like this:

```
Mon Apr 16 12:54:58 CEST 2007
```

CEST stands for Central European Summer Time; the server we're currently using is somewhere in Switzerland. You'll probably see some other time zone, but the format will be identical. A good place to check out the abbreviation for your time zone is http://www.timeanddate.com/library/abbreviations/timezones/.

Now that you have a way of getting the server time, you can write the HTML page to display with Ajax, as shown in Listing 3-19.

Listing 3-19. *ajax.html*

```
<!DOCTYPE html PUBLIC "-//W3C//DTD XHTML 1.0 Strict//EN"
  "http//www.w3.org/TR/xhtml1/DTD/xhtml1-strict.dtd">
<html xmlns="http//www.w3.org/1999/xhtml" xmllang="en" lang="en">
<head>
  <title>Example of Ajax</title>
  <script type="text/javascript" src="ajax.js"></script>
  </head>
<body>
  <form name="tForm">
    The time on the server is:
    <input type="text" name="tElement" readonly="readonly" size="30"/>
    <input type="button" value="Update" name="b"
      onClick="ajaxFun('tForm', 'tElement');"
      />
    </form>
  </body>
</html>
```

As you can see, we've highlighted two lines. The first is where you load the file ajax.js, which contains the JavaScript code to support the Ajax operation. The second line is where you execute the ajaxFun function whenever the user clicks the Update button. Notice that you pass to ajaxFun the names of the form and of the input element to be updated. You could have hard-coded the string "tForm.tElement" within the JavaScript module, but it would have been bad programming practice to use within ajax.js identifiers defined elsewhere. Global variables invariably lead to code that's difficult to maintain and should be avoided whenever possible.

To complete this brief introduction to Ajax, we still need to show you the JavaScript code. However, before we do that, check out Figure 3-15 to see how the browser renders the page.

Figure 3-15. *Server time with Ajax*

■**Tip** For the Ajax example to work with Internet Explorer 7.0, go to Tools ➤ Internet Options. On the General tab, click on the Settings button of the Browsing history, and select Every time I visit the webpage among the alternatives available for Check for newer versions of viewed pages. If you leave the setting on Automatic, Internet Explorer will update the time field only the first time you click on the Update button. Other versions of Internet Explorer have slightly different menus, such as Temporary Internet files instead of Browsing history.

Listing 3-20 shows the JavaScript code.

Listing 3-20. *ajax.js*

```
function ajaxFun(tf, te) {
  var tElem = eval("document." + tf + "." + te)
  var ajaxReq;
  try { // Firefox, Opera
    ajaxReq = new XMLHttpRequest();
    }
  catch (e) { // IE
    try{
    ajaxReq = new ActiveXObject("Msxml2.XMLHTTP");
    }
  catch (e) {
    try{ // IE second attempt
      ajaxReq = new ActiveXObject("Microsoft.XMLHTTP");
      }
    catch (e) {
      alert("Your browser does not support Ajax!");
      return false;
      }
    }
  }
  ajaxReq.open("GET", "time.jsp");
  ajaxReq.send(null);
  ajaxReq.onreadystatechange = function() {
    if(ajaxReq.readyState == 4) {
      tElem.value = ajaxReq.responseText;
      }
    }
  } // ajaxFun
```

You need the bulk of ajaxFun to instantiate XMLHttpRequest. As is often the case, Internet Explorer requires a special treatment. Once you've managed to store a valid XMLHttpRequest object in the variable ajaxReq, you set up the HTML request method (e.g., GET) and the target URL (in this case, the JSP module time.jsp). At this point, you can send off the request.

The control comes immediately back to JavaScript (the first letter of Ajax stands for *asynchronous*, remember?). In general, you don't want the browser to wait for the response, and you want your page to be able to do other things. This asynchronicity makes Ajax more useful than if its operations had to be done in sequence. When the state of the request changes, the browser executes the function `ajaxReq.onreadystatechange`. In that function, you need to check that the request has been completed, in which case you can then display the content of the response in the time field. Cool! See Table 3-1 for the list of possible status codes.

Table 3-1. *List of ajaxReq.readyState Codes*

Code	Meaning
0	Uninitiated
1	Loading
2	Loaded
3	Interactive
4	Complete

We've taken a minimalist approach for this example. The idea is for your server to send back an XML document, which you can then parse on the client side. You can find the latest version of the Ajax standard at the following URL: `http://www.w3.org/TR/XMLHttpRequest/`.

You can write an extension to the ticker-tape example to get a new message from the server at regular intervals. Effectively, you would only need to modify `ajaxFun` to open `next_message.jsp` instead of `time.jsp`. `next_message.jsp` would then obtain the message from a list or from a database, which could be updated asynchronously.

Summary

In this chapter, we described HTTP requests and responses and introduced you to the protocols that allow you to view a web page. After describing the structure of an HTML page and its main components, including text, objects, links, tables, and forms, we talked about CSS and how it can bring more "pep" into your pages. Finally, we showed you some examples of what you can do with JavaScript, and we introduced you to Ajax.

In this chapter, we talked about how a web page is displayed. In the next chapter, we'll move to "the back end" of web applications and talk about databases.

CHAPTER 4

Databases

In many cases, a web application is nothing more than a front end for a database (DB). In fact, what makes web pages dynamic is precisely the fact that there is a significant amount of data behind them.

A database consists of organized data—that is, the data itself and a *schema* that provides data structures. Nowadays, most databases are organized in *tables*. You can define the table characteristics independently of the actual data you're going to store into it. In fact, this is another instance of the separation of content and formatting, which you've already encountered when we discussed web applications.

A database management system (DBMS), such as MySQL or PostgreSQL, is a software package that lets you create, retrieve, update, and delete (CRUD) both items of data and elements of the schema.

Therefore, when talking about a database, you need to distinguish between three aspects:

- The data it contains

- The structure you impose on the data in order to CRUD it efficiently

- The software that allows you to manipulate both the data itself and the database structure (the DBMS)

Working with a database means that you're interacting with its DBMS. You can do that through a command line interface (CLI), through graphical user interfaces (GUIs) provided by the DBMS vendor and third parties, or programmatically through an API. In general, you use all three methods, each for a different purpose. The CLI is best suited for setting up the initial data structure and for testing, the API is for your web application to interact with the database to perform its tasks, and the GUI is what you use to check individual data items or fix one-off problems.

In this chapter's examples, we'll use MySQL as the DBMS of choice, because, first, it's available for free, and second, it's the most widely used of the freely available DBMSs, so it has been proven to work reliably in all sorts of environments. At the end of this chapter, we'll briefly talk about possible alternatives to MySQL.

Database Basics

In some cases, a DB might contain a small amount of data, have a simple structure, and reside together with the application software on a home PC. In other cases, at the higher end of the scale, it might hold millions of records, have a data structure of great complexity, and run on a cluster of powerful servers.

In any case, regardless of size, environment, and complexity, the DBMS is organized around the client/server architecture. The system on which your DB resides is the *server*, and the system from which you access your DB is the *client*, even when they're one and the same PC. Therefore, in order to be able to work with data and a data structure, you first have to establish a connection from the client to the database on the server. To be able to do so, you need the following three pieces of information:

- The URL of your server

- A user ID that allows you to access the DB

- The password that goes together with the user ID

Once you establish the connection, you can then begin to manipulate the DB structure and its content via SQL statements. Be aware that although you need to provide a user ID and password when you connect to the server, this doesn't automatically mean that a user has access to all databases on the same server. You can (and, in most cases, should) allow access to specific databases to some users and not others. In fact, you can define one or more new users for each new database you create. This ensures total confidentiality of data when several users share a database server. It's good practice to define different users for different applications so that you don't risk "cross-polluting" data.

In 1986, the American National Standards Institute (ANSI) adopted SQL as a standard, and ISO followed suit one year later. The current standard is ISO/IEC 9075, but, unfortunately, it's not freely available. If you want to have it, you have to buy it from ANSI or ISO. The SQL standard has been widely adopted, and, as a result, most of what we're going to say concerning SQL actually applies to all DBMSs. Unfortunately, there are still proprietary additions and variations that, in some cases, make SQL less portable than what it could and should be, but it won't affect us.

The SQL standard specifies at least 27 basic statements with numerous variants. They are alter, based on, begin, close, commit, connect, create, declare, delete, describe, disconnect, drop, end, event, execute, fetch, grant, insert, open, prepare, revoke, rollback, select, set, show, update, and whenever. In total, at the last count, 231 words were reserved by SQL as keywords. Therefore, it should be clear that in this chapter, we couldn't possibly give you more than a small introduction to SQL. Appendix E provides a more detailed SQL reference to help you along.

The basic structural elements of a DB are rows, columns, tables, and indices. In non-SQL terms, rows are data records, columns identify the record fields, tables are collections of records, and indices are ordered lists of records.

To design a database for a web application, you basically associate a table to each Java class that represents the data you need to store permanently. Each attribute of your class then becomes a column of your table. In a sense, to express it in OO terminology, each row corresponds to an instantiation of your class containing different data. For example, in the Eshop application, book categories are modeled with the Java class, as shown in Listing 4-1.

Listing 4-1. *Category.java*

```java
package eshop.beans;

public class Category {
  private int id;
  private String name;

  public Category(int id, String name) {
    this.id = id;
    this.name = name;
    }

  public int getId() { return id; }
  public void setId(int id) { this.id = id; }

  public String getName() { return name; }
  public void setName(String name) { this.name = name; }
  }
```

Accordingly, to store categories in the shop database, you can use the following SQL statement to create a table named categories:

```sql
create table shop.categories (
  category_id integer not null auto_increment unique,
  category_name varchar(70),
  primary key (category_id)
  );
```

Each SQL statement consists of a verb that defines the operation to be done (create table in this example), the identifier of the object operated on (shop.categories in this example), and one or more operation parameters, often enclosed in parentheses. When more than one object or parameter is needed, they're usually comma-separated. In the example, the first two parameters define the DB columns category_id and category_name. Notice how the attributes specified in the SQL statement match those defined in the Java class. When creating this table, we also told MySQL to create an index of category_id by declaring the column to contain unique values and designating it as the primary key of the table. The purpose is to speed up DB operations, although in this case, given the small size of the table, it obviously won't make any practical difference.

Use this code, which creates three new rows, to store new records in a DB:

```sql
insert into categories (category_id, category_name)
  values (1,'Web Development'), (2,'SF'), (3,'Action Novels');
```

Incidentally, be aware of the fact that SQL, contrary to Java, is not case-sensitive.

Use the powerful select SQL statement to read data. It lets you create complex queries that include sorting the data. Here's a simple example:

```sql
select category_id, category_name from categories where category_id = '2';
```

To retrieve all columns of a table, you replace the comma-separated list of columns with an asterisk. The where clause can consist of several conditions composed by means of logical operators.

You use the update statement to modify row contents:

```
update categories set category_name = 'SF' where category_id = '2';
```

Using delete lets you remove rows:

```
delete from categories where category_id > '3';
```

You can also operate on the data structure. To do so, you use the alter statement, as in the following example:

```
alter table categories add new_column_name column-definition;
```

This lets you add a column to an existing table. If you replace add with modify or drop, the alter statement will let you redefine a column or remove it.

In general, the SQL statements are grouped depending on their purposes. Table 4-1 gives you a summary of their classification.

Table 4-1. *Classification of SQL Statements*

Group	Description
Data Definition Language (DDL)	Statements used to define the DB structure (e.g., create, alter, drop, and rename)
Data Manipulation Language (DML)	Statements used to manage data (e.g., select, insert, update, and delete)
Data Control Language (DCL)	Statements used to control access to the data (e.g., grant, used to give access rights to a user, and revoke, used to withdraw them)
Transaction ControL (TCL)	Statements used to group together DML statements into logical transactions (e.g., commit and rollback)

In this chapter, we'll explain how to execute any SQL statement, but we'll concentrate mainly on DML.

SQL Scripts

As we said, a CLI is useful to initialize a database. As a CLI, MySQL makes available the program "MySQL Command Line Client," which starts in a DOS window and attempts at once to establish a connection as the default user ID to the default server. If you've set up MySQL as we suggest in Appendix A, the default user will be root and the default host will be localhost. After providing the correct password, you get a mysql> prompt and can start executing SQL statements.

You can play around with the commands, but the best way to use the CLI is with SQL scripts. These are plain-text files containing the statements you want to execute. At the mysql prompt, you only need to type backslash-period-space (\.) followed by the script file name, and off you go. In fact, you must use scripts if you want to ensure that your steps are repeatable and correctable. To create and populate the small database for the Eshop application, you can execute the script shown in Listing 4-2.

Listing 4-2. *shop.sql*

```
drop database shop;
create database shop;
create table shop.categories (
  category_id integer not null auto_increment unique,
  category_name varchar(70),
  primary key (category_id)
  );
create table shop.order_details (
  id double precision not null auto_increment unique,
  book_id integer,
  title varchar(70),
  author varchar(70),
  quantity integer,
  price double precision,
  order_id double precision,
  primary key (id)
  );
create table shop.orders (
  order_id double precision not null auto_increment unique,
  delivery_name varchar(70),
  delivery_address varchar(70),
  cc_name varchar(70),
  cc_number varchar(32),
  cc_expiry varchar(20),
  primary key (order_id)
  );
create table shop.books (
  book_id integer not null auto_increment unique,
  title varchar(70),
  author varchar(70),
  price double precision,
  category_id integer,
  primary key (book_id)
  );
create index category_id_key on shop.categories (category_id);
create index order_details_id_key on shop.order_details (id);
alter table shop.order_details add index order_id (order_id),
  add constraint order_id foreign key (order_id)
  references shop.orders (order_id)
  ;
```

```
create index order_id_key on shop.orders (order_id);
create index book_id_key on shop.books (book_id);
alter table shop.books add index category_id (category_id),
  add constraint category_id foreign key (category_id)
  references shop.categories (category_id)
  ;

/*------------------- Populate -------------------*/
USE shop;
INSERT INTO categories (
    category_id
  , category_name
  )
  VALUES
    (1,'Web Development')
  , (2,'SF')
  , (3,'Action Novels')
  ;
INSERT INTO books (
    book_id
  , title
  , author
  , price
  , category_id
  )
  VALUES
    (1,'Pro CSS and HTML Design Patterns','Michael Bowers',44.99,1)
  , (2,'Pro PayPal E-Commerce','Damon Williams',59.99,1)
  , (3,'The Complete Robot','Isaac Asimov',8.95,2)
  , (4,'Foundation','Isaac Asimov',8.95,2)
  , (5,'Area 7','Matthew Reilly',5.99,3)
  , (6,'Term Limits','Vince Flynn',6.99,3)
  ;
```

As you can see, the first part creates the DB, and the second part populates it, although normally you would keep the two parts in separate files. The first statement of the script tells MySQL to delete the whole DB. This isn't something you would normally do in a non-test environment. Also, notice the USE shop statement immediately before populating the tables. This is how you tell the CLI on which DB you want to operate. Finally, notice that comments are delimited by non-nested pairs of /* and */, like Java's block comments.

Java API

As you've already seen, you operate on databases by executing SQL statements. To do so from within Java/JSP, you need an API consisting of several interfaces, classes, and method definitions. Additionally, you also need a driver that implements that API for the specific DBMS (i.e.,

MySQL) in the native code of your system (i.e., an Intel/Windows PC). The API is called JDBC, and its most recent definition, version 4, is included in the class libraries `java.sql` and `javax.sql` of JDK version 6. To work with MySQL, you can use its implementation of JDBC, MySQL Connector/J version 5, which is a type 4 JDBC driver.

JDBC DRIVERS

The JDBC API lets you access databases from Java. There are four types of JDBC implementations (i.e., drivers).

JDBC drivers of type 1 are actually JDBC-ODBC bridges, because they access databases via an Open Database Connectivity (ODBC) driver. At the end of this chapter, we'll show you how to use the bridge provided by Sun Microsystems with the Java Virtual Machine (JVM).

JDBC drivers of type 2 use vendor-specific, native, client-side libraries. In other words, they interface to non-Java functions provided by the DBMS vendor, which in turn interfaces to the databases. These drivers are more efficient compared to those of type 1, but you can only use them locally. For example, to use the Oracle Call Interface (OCI) driver, you need to install an Oracle SQL client.

JDBC drivers of type 3 are written in Java, but instead of communicating directly with the databases, they rely on a middleware package that sits on an application server. An example of this type of driver is Oracle's JDBC thin driver.

JDBC drivers of type 4 are written entirely in Java and communicate directly with the DBMS server. This is the type you want!

Getting Started

The first step is to load the driver, without which nothing will work. To do so, you execute the method `Class.forName("com.mysql.jdbc.Driver")`. In the Eshop example, you do this in the `init` method of the servlet.

To be able to switch from MySQL to other DBMSs without much effort, store the driver name in an `init` parameter defined in `WEB-INF\web.xml` as follows:

```
<init-param>
  <param-name>jdbcDriver</param-name>
  <param-value>com.mysql.jdbc.Driver</param-value>
</init-param>
```

This way, you can load it as follows when initializing the servlet:

```
java.lang.Class.forName(config.getInitParameter("jdbcDriver"));
```

Once you load the driver, you also need to connect to the database before you can access its content. In the Eshop application, you do this by executing a data manager method, as shown in the following line of code:

```
java.sql.Connection connection = dataManager.getConnection();
```

The data manager's getConnection method in turn obtains the connection from the JDBC driver by executing this method:

```
java.sql.DriverManager.getConnection(dbURL, dbUserName, dbPassword);
```

To be able to change the database, the user ID, or the password without having to rebuild the application, you define them in servlet initialization parameters as you did for the name of the JDBC driver:

```
dbURL: jdbc:mysql://localhost:3306/shop
dbUserName: root
dbPassword: none
```

Port 3306 is the default for MySQL and can be configured differently. Obviously, in real life, you would use a different user and, most importantly, define a password. In any case, once you finish working with a database, you should always close the connection by executing connection.close().

Before you can start hacking at your database, you still need to create an object of type java.sql.Statement, as it is through the methods of that object that you execute SQL statements. Use this code to create a statement:

```
Statement stmt = connection.createStatement();
```

Once you're done with one statement, you should release it immediately with stmt.close(), because it takes a non-negligible amount of space, and you want to be sure that it doesn't hang around while your page does other things.

Accessing Data

The Statement class has 40 methods, plus some more inherited ones. Nevertheless, two methods are likely to satisfy most of your needs: executeQuery and executeUpdate.

The executeQuery Method

You use the executeQuery method to execute a select SQL statement, like this:

```
String sql = "select book_id, title, author from books where category_id=1"
    + " order by author, title";
ResultSet rs = stmt.executeQuery(sql);
```

In the example, the method returns in the variable rs of type java.sql.ResultSet all the books in category 1, sorted by author name and title. The rows in the result set only contain the columns specified in the select statement, which in this example are book_id, title, and author.

At any given time, you can only access the row of the result set pointed to by the so-called *cursor*, and by default you're constrained to move the cursor only forward. The usual way of accessing the rows of the result set is to start from the first one and "go down" in sequence. For example, with the test database for the online bookshop, the following code:

```
while (rs.next()) {
  out.println(rs.getString(3) + ", " + rs.getString(2) + "<br/>");
  }
```

would produce the following output:

```
Damon Williams, Pro PayPal E-Commerce
Michael Bowers, Pro CSS and HTML Design Patterns
```

The next method moves the cursor down one row. After the cursor goes past the last row, next() returns false, and the while loop terminates. Initially, the cursor is positioned *before* the first row. Therefore, you have to execute next() once in order to access the very first row.

Besides next(), there are other methods that let you reposition your cursor. Five of them return a boolean such as next(), which returns true if the cursor points to a row. They are absolute(*row-position*), first(), last(), previous(), and relative(*number-of-rows*). The beforeFirst() and afterLast()methods also move the cursor but are of type void, because they always succeed. The isBeforeFirst(), isFirst(), isLast(), and isAfterLast() methods check whether the cursor is in the corresponding positions, while getRow() returns the position of the row currently pointed to by the cursor.

Keep in mind that in order to be able to move the cursor around, you have to specify a couple of attributes when you create the statement—that is, *before* you actually execute the query. This is how you do it:

```
Statement stmt = connection.createStatement(
    ResultSet.TYPE_SCROLL_INSENSITIVE,
    ResultSet.CONCUR_READ_ONLY);
```

ResultSet.TYPE_SCROLL_INSENSITIVE is what allows you to move the cursor forth and back within the result set. This parameter can only have one of the following two other values: ResultSet.TYPE_FORWARD_ONLY (the default) or ResultSet.TYPE_SCROLL_SENSITIVE. The difference between SENSITIVE and INSENSITIVE is that with INSENSITIVE, you're not affected by changes made to the result set while you're working with it (more about this in a moment). This is probably what you want.

ResultSet.CONCUR_READ_ONLY states that you don't want to modify the result set. This is the default, and it makes sense in most cases. The alternative is to specify ResultSet.CONCUR_UPDATABLE, which allows you to insert, delete, and modify result rows. Now you can see why you might like to use ResultSet.TYPE_SCROLL_SENSITIVE as the first parameter: it lets you see the modifications made to the result set, rather than showing it how it was before the changes. On the other hand, in a complex application with several threads operating on the same result set, you'll probably prefer to ignore in each thread the changes made by the other threads. In such a situation, it would have to be 100% clear which thread would be allowed to modify which rows; otherwise, you'd end up with a mess.

ResultSet provides several methods for retrieving a column value in different formats, given a column position or its label. For example, the following two methods will return the same value:

```
long bookID = rs.getLong(1);
long bookID = rs.getLong("book_id");
```

The column position refers to the columns specified in the `select` statement. Notice that the column numbering begins with 1, not with 0 as is customary in Java. The types available are `Array`, `BigDecimal`, `Blob`, `boolean`, `byte`, `byte[]`, `Clob`, `Date`, `double`, `float`, `InputStream`, `int`, `long`, `NClob`, `Object`, `Reader`, `Ref`, `RowId`, `short`, `SQLXML`, `String`, `Time`, `Timestamp`, and `URL`. For most of these types exists a corresponding update method, which lets you modify a column. For example, this code writes "Joe Bloke" in the `author` column of the current row of the result set:

```
rs.updateString("author", "Joe Bloke");
```

There are no update methods for the types `InputStream`, `Reader`, and `URL`, but there are for `AsciiStream`, `BinaryStream`, `CharacterStream`, `NCharacterStream`, and `NString`. You can also set a column to `null` with the methods `updateNull(`*column-index*`)` and `updateNull(`*column-label*`)`.

ResultSet provides more than two dozen additional methods that let you do things such as transfer changes from an updated result set to the actual database or refresh a row that somebody else might have modified in the actual database after you performed the query. One method that you might find useful returns the column position in your result set given its name:

```
int findColumn(column-label)
```

The result set is automatically disposed of when the corresponding statement is closed. Therefore, you don't really need to execute `rs.close()`, at least if you close the statement as soon as you don't need it anymore.

The executeUpdate Method

You can use the `executeUpdate` method to execute the SQL statements `insert`, `update`, and `delete`. For example, if you want to add a new book category to the online bookshop example, you do something like this:

```
String sql = "insert into categories (category_id, category_name)"
    + " values (4, 'Comic Books')";
stmt.executeUpdate(sql);
```

You don't need to define all the columns, because the undefined fields are set automatically to their corresponding default values. That said, as you haven't specified any default in the definition of the `categories` table, the following statement would result in the field `category_name` being set to `null`:

```
stmt.executeUpdate("insert into categories (category_id) values (4)");
```

To avoid this occurrence, you could have defined the `category_name` column with a default:

```
category_name varchar(70) default 'Miscellanea'
```

Transactions

In the online bookshop, we've defined two separate tables for data associated with a book order: one for the customer data, and one for the individual books ordered (see the definitions of `orders` and `order_details` in Listing 4-2). It would be bad if you completely lost an order, but perhaps it would be even worse if you lost some items and only processed a partial order. It also would be a problem if you saved the order details in the database but failed to save the customer data. That would leave some "orphaned" book items with no information concerning the buyer. Fortunately, you don't need to worry about this, because you save the customer data first. Therefore, by the time you start saving the order details, the customer record is already on disk. But how do you ensure that the database only contains complete orders?

Normally, when you execute an SQL `insert`, the data is immediately stored into the database. To ensure the completion of orders, you could keep track of the updates you've already successfully executed and reverse them if you cannot complete the whole order. However, this would be very complicated and have no guarantee of success. Moreover, in a more complex application, there might be several operations proceeding in parallel and causing the same database records to be accessed concurrently. The solution must be a built-in, foolproof mechanism capable of ensuring that some complex transactions are done "in one shot" or not at all.

This mechanism obviously exists and is actually quite simple. It works like this:

1. Immediately after connecting to the DB with `conn = DriverManager.getConnection(...)`, execute `conn.setAutoCommit(false)`. This tells MySQL not to make permanent changes to the database until you confirm them.

2. Perform all the updates that form your complex transaction. Be sure that you place them inside a `try` block as part of a `try/catch` construct.

3. In the `catch` block, include the statement `conn.rollback()`. If one of the updates fails, an `SQLException` will be thrown, and when the `catch` block is executed, the `rollback` will cause MySQL to "forget" the uncommitted updates.

4. After the `try/catch`, when all the updates have completed without being interrupted by any exception, execute `conn.commit()` to tell MySQL that it can finalize the updates.

DB Access in Eshop

As we mentioned in Chapter 2, we're concentrating all database operations in the data model of an MVC architecture. JSP modules interact with the database by executing methods of the `DataManager` class, which accept and/or return data in the form of Java beans. By mediating DB access via the data manager and Java beans, you ensure that the view and the model can be developed independently.

Figure 4-1 shows the structure of the model.

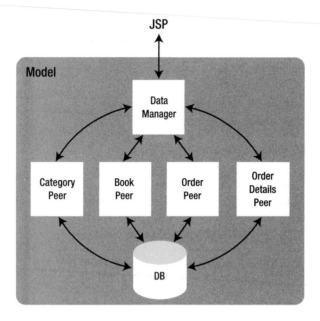

Figure 4-1. *The data model structure*

The DataManager class sets up and closes connections to the database; however, concerning table access, it only acts as a clearinghouse. Specific classes perform the actual operations on individual tables. In this way, you ensure that changes to individual tables have the minimum impact on the application.

For example, the JSP page that displays the book details obtains the information concerning the requested book by executing the following method of the data manager:

```
public Book getBookDetails(int bookID) {
  return BookPeer.getBookById(this, bookID);
  }
```

However, the getBookByID method in BookPeer.java performs the actual database access, as shown in Listing 4-3.

Listing 4-3. *The BookPeer.getBookID Method*

```
01: public static Book getBookById(DataManager dataManager, int bookID) {
02:   Book book = null;
03:   Connection connection = dataManager.getConnection();
04:   if (connection != null) {
05:     try {
06:       Statement s = connection.createStatement();
07:       String sql = "select book_id, title, author, price from books"
08:           + " where book_id=" + bookID;
09:       try {
```

```
10:            ResultSet rs = s.executeQuery(sql);
11:            if (rs.next()) {
12:              book = new Book();
13:              book.setId(rs.getString(1));
14:              book.setTitle(rs.getString(2));
15:              book.setAuthor(rs.getString(3));
16:              book.setPrice(rs.getDouble(4));
17:              }
18:            }
19:          finally { s.close(); }
20:          }
21:        catch (SQLException e) {
22:          System.out.println("Could not get book: " + e.getMessage());
23:          }
24:        finally {
25:          dataManager.putConnection(connection);
26:          }
27:      }  return book;
28:    }
```

In line 3, you open the database connection by invoking a method of the data manager that also reports an error in case of failure. Then you start a `try` block where you do the actual work. In the corresponding `catch` block, you display an error message (line 22), and in the `finally` block (line 25), you close the DB connection. Remember that the `finally` block is executed whether the `try` succeeds or not. In this way, you ensure that the connection is closed in case of failure.

Inside the outermost `try` (lines 5-20), you create a statement and set up the query string before starting a second `try` block (lines 9-17). Similar to what you did concerning the connection, you use the `finally` block to close the statement (line 19).

This is a technique of general applicability: every time you do something that needs to be undone, take care of it immediately inside a `try` block by placing the "undoing" statement in the corresponding `finally`. In this way, you'll be sure not to leave any "ghosts" behind you. It's true that Java's garbage-collection mechanism should take care of removing unreferenced objects, but it's good practice to clean up behind yourself as you go, especially when you're dealing with databases and potentially large objects, such as statements and result sets. At the very least, your application will work more efficiently. And it feels good to write "clean" code.

Line 10 is where you actually execute the query. You know that you're not going to get more than one row in the result set, because the book_id is a unique key of the book table.

You might be thinking, "Why should I go through the data manager at all? Couldn't I simply execute the `BookPeer` method from JSP?" Well, you could, but it wouldn't be clean, and dirtiness sooner or later causes problems.

Furthermore, consider the more complex case in which you want to save an order. From the JSP point of view, you only want to call a method of the data manager that takes care of both the customer's data and the shopping cart. Behind the scenes, though, two different tables need to be updated: one for the orders and one for the order details. Therefore, it makes a lot of sense to execute the overall transaction in the data manager (see Listing 4-4) while leaving the updates of individual tables to the peer classes.

Listing 4-4. *The DataManager.insertOrder Method*

```java
public long insertOrder(Customer customer, Hashtable shoppingCart) {
  long returnValue = 0L;
  long orderId = System.currentTimeMillis();
  Connection connection = getConnection();
  if (connection != null) {
    Statement stmt = null;
    try {
      connection.setAutoCommit(false);
      stmt = connection.createStatement();
      try {
        OrderPeer.insertOrder(stmt, orderId, customer);
        OrderDetailsPeer.insertOrderDetails(stmt, orderId, shoppingCart);
        try { stmt.close(); }
        finally { stmt = null; }
        connection.commit();
        returnValue = orderId;
      }
      catch (SQLException e) {
        System.out.println("Could not insert order: " + e.getMessage());
        try { connection.rollback(); }
        catch (SQLException ee) { }
      }
    }
    catch (SQLException e) {
      System.out.println("Could not insert order: " + e.getMessage());
    }
    finally {
      if (stmt != null) {
        try { stmt.close(); }
        catch (SQLException e) { }
      }
      putConnection(connection);
    }
  }
  return returnValue;
}
```

The two lines in bold show you how the data manager asks the peer classes of the tables orders and order_details to do the update. Notice that you pass to them the same statement and order ID. Listing 4-5 shows insertOrder, one of the two methods that do the updates.

Listing 4-5. *The OrderPeer.insertOrder Method*

```
public static void insertOrder(Statement stmt, long orderId,
    Customer customer) throws SQLException {
  String sql = "insert into orders (order_id, delivery_name,"
      + " delivery_address, cc_name, cc_number, cc_expiry) values ('"
      + orderId + "','" + customer.getContactName() + "','"
      + customer.getDeliveryAddress() + "','"
      + customer.getCcName() + "','" + customer.getCcNumber()
      + "','" + customer.getCcExpiryDate() + "')"
      ;
  stmt.executeUpdate(sql);
}
```

Listing 4-6 shows the other method, `insertOrderDetails`.

Listing 4-6. *The OrderDetailsPeer.insertOrderDetails Method*

```
public static void insertOrderDetails(Statement stmt, long orderId,
    Hashtable shoppingCart) throws SQLException {
  String sql;
  Enumeration enumList = shoppingCart.elements();
  while (enumList.hasMoreElements()) {
    CartItem item = (CartItem)enumList.nextElement();
    sql = "insert into order_details (order_id, book_id, quantity,"
        + " price, title, author) values ('" + orderId + "','"
        + item.getBookID() + "','" + item.getQuantity() + "','"
        + item.getPrice() + "','" + item.getTitle() + "','"
        + item.getAuthor() + "')"
        ;
    stmt.executeUpdate(sql);
  }
}
```

The methods throw the SQL exception rather than catch it locally, so that the data manager's method catches it.

What About the XML Syntax?

In Chapter 2, we said that we prefer JSP written with the XML syntax. What impact does that have on what we just said about database access? None! This is a consequence of the MVC model: JSP is the view, while only the model has to do with databases.

However, the switch from traditional to XML syntax has an impact on how you execute the data manager methods. For example, you can write `OrderConfirmation.jsp` to store an order in scripted JSP, as shown in Listing 4-7.

Listing 4-7. *OrderConfirmation.jsp*

```
01: <%@page language="java" contentType="text/html"%>
02: <%@page import="java.util.Hashtable"%>
03: <jsp:useBean id="dataManager" scope="application"
04:    class="eshop.model.DataManager"/>
05: <html>
06: <head>
07:    <meta http-equiv="Content-Type" content="text/html; charset=UTF-8"/>
08:    <title>Order</title>
09:    <link rel="stylesheet" href="/eshop/css/eshop.css" type="text/css"/>
10:    </head>
11: <body>
12: <jsp:include page="TopMenu.jsp" flush="true"/>
13: <jsp:include page="LeftMenu.jsp" flush="true"/>
14: <div class="content">
15:    <h2>Order</h2>
16:    <jsp:useBean id="customer" class="eshop.beans.Customer"/>
17:    <jsp:setProperty property="*" name="customer"/>
18: <%
19:    long orderId = dataManager.insertOrder(
20:                   customer,
21:                   (Hashtable)session.getAttribute("shoppingCart")
22:                   );
23:    if (orderId > 0L) {
24:       session.invalidate();
25:    %>
26:       <p class="info">
27:          Thank you for your purchase.<br/>
28:          Your Order Number is: <%=orderId%>
29:          </p>
30: <%
31:       }
32:    else {
33:       %><p class="error">Unexpected error processing the order!</p><%
34:       }
35:    %>
36:    </div>
37: </body>
38: </html>
```

You can use the XML syntax to write OrderConfirmation.jspx, as shown in Listing 4-8.

Listing 4-8. *OrderConfirmation.jspx*

```
01: <?xml version="1.0" encoding="ISO-8859-1"?>
02: <jsp:root
03:   xmlns:jsp="http://java.sun.com/JSP/Page"
04:   xmlns:c="http://java.sun.com/jsp/jstl/core"
05:   xmlns:fn="http://java.sun.com/jsp/jstl/functions"
06:   xmlns:eshop="urn:jsptld:/WEB-INF/tlds/eshop.tld"
07:   version="2.1"
08:   >
09: <jsp:directive.page
10:   language="java"
11:   contentType="ISO-8859-1"
12:   pageEncoding="ISO-8859-1"
13:   />
14: <jsp:output
15:   doctype-root-element="html"
16:   doctype-public="-//W3C//DTD XHTML 1.0 Strict//EN"
17:   doctype-system="http://www.w3.org/TR/xhtml1/DTD/xhtml1-strict.dtd"
18:   />
19: <html xmlns="http://www.w3.org/1999/xhtml">
20: <head>
21:   <title>Order</title>
22:   <link rel="stylesheet" href="/eshop/css/eshop.css" type="text/css"/>
23:   </head>
24: <body>
25: <jsp:include page="TopMenu.jspx" flush="true"/>
26: <jsp:include page="LeftMenu.jspx" flush="true"/>
27: <div class="content">
28:   <h2>Order</h2>
29:   <jsp:useBean id="customer" class="eshop.beans.Customer"/>
30:   <jsp:setProperty property="*" name="customer"/>
31:   <eshop:insertOrder var="orderID" customer="${customer}"/>
32:   <c:choose>
33:     <c:when test="${orderID > 0}">
34:       <p class="info">
35:         Thank you for your purchase.<br/>
36:         Your Order Number is: <c:out value="${orderID}"/>
37:       </p>
38:     </c:when>
39:     <c:otherwise>
40:       <p class="error">Unexpected error processing the order!</p>
41:     </c:otherwise>
42:   </c:choose>
43:   </div>
44: </body>
45: </html>
46: </jsp:root>
```

Let's concentrate on the highlighted code, where the actual work is done. The saving of the order information in the database, which you do in the JSP file (Listing 4-7) by executing a data manager's method (lines 19-22), you do in the JSPX file (Listing 4-8) by executing a custom action (line 31). The same custom action also invalidates the session (line 24 in `OrderConfirmation.jsp`).

The `if/else` Java construct in lines 23, 31-32, and 34 of the JSP file becomes the JSTL core construct `choose/when/otherwise` in lines 32-33, 38-39, and 41-42 of the JSPX file.

Informing the user of the order acceptance is in HTML and remains basically the same (JSP lines 26-29 become JSPX lines 34-37). In fact, you could have replaced the scripting expression of the JSP page with the EL expression you used in the JSP document, making the code identical.

The introduction of the custom action `insertOrder` is necessary because scriptlets, being Java code, can make assignments and execute methods, while EL expressions cannot. Therefore, when you remove scriptlets because they're not valid XML, you have to move the computation to Java beans or custom actions.

In line 6 of `OrderConfirmation.jspx`, you declare `eshop.tld`, which contains the definition of the `insertMethod` action as shown in Listing 4-9.

Listing 4-9. *The insertMethod Action Defined in eshop.tld*

```
<tag>
  <description>Insert an order into storage</description>
  <display-name>insertOrder</display-name>
  <name>insertOrder</name>
  <tag-class>eshop.tags.InsertOrderTag</tag-class>
  <body-content>empty</body-content>
  <attribute>
    <name>var</name>
    <type>java.lang.String</type>
    <rtexprvalue>true</rtexprvalue>
    </attribute>
  <attribute>
    <name>customer</name>
    <type>eshop.beans.Customer</type>
    <rtexprvalue>true</rtexprvalue>
    </attribute>
  </tag>
```

As you can see, you pass two parameters to the custom action: a string containing the name of the variable where the order ID is to be returned, and an object of type `Customer` containing the customer data (name, address, and credit-card information). You don't absolutely need the second parameter, because the action code could have retrieved the customer data from the page context as follows:

```
(Customer)pageContext.getAttribute("customer")
```

On the other hand, you could have passed to the action a third parameter referencing the shopping cart, but we decided to let the action retrieve it from the session as follows:

```
(Hashtable)pageContext.getSession().getAttribute("shoppingCart")
```

It's not always obvious what constitutes a better design. We felt that the shopping cart, being a session attribute, was obviously shared across JSP documents. Therefore, it was OK for the action to retrieve it directly from the session. The customer data, however, was a page attribute, normally not shared with other modules. Passing it "behind the scenes" to a Java class didn't seem appropriate. Listing 4-10 shows you the action code in its entirety.

Listing 4-10. *InsertOrderTag.java*

```java
package eshop.tags;

import java.util.Hashtable;
import javax.servlet.http.HttpSession;
import javax.servlet.jsp.tagext.TagSupport;
import javax.servlet.ServletContext;
import eshop.beans.Customer;
import eshop.model.DataManager;

public class InsertOrderTag extends TagSupport {
  static final long serialVersionUID = 1L;
  private String var;
  private Customer customer;

  public void setVar(String var) {
    this.var = var;
    }

  public void setCustomer(Customer customer) {
    this.customer = customer;
    }

  public int doEndTag() {
    ServletContext context = pageContext.getServletContext();
    DataManager dataManager =(DataManager)context.getAttribute("dataManager");
    HttpSession session = pageContext.getSession();
    long orderID = dataManager.insertOrder(
        customer,
        (Hashtable)session.getAttribute("shoppingCart")
        );
    if (orderID > 0L) session.invalidate();
    pageContext.setAttribute(var, new Long(orderID).toString());
    return EVAL_PAGE;
    }
}
```

Notice how you obtain the servlet context (corresponding to the JSP implicit object `application`) from `pageContext`, and from it the data manager, so that you can then execute the same `insertOrder` method you invoked directly from JSP when using the traditional scripting syntax.

Possible Alternatives to MySQL

There's no general reason why you shouldn't use MySQL in your applications. Nevertheless, you do have alternatives, and it's worth mentioning them. We have only tested our Eshop application with MySQL, but there's a good chance that it would work exactly the same with other DBMSs.

If you switch DBMSs, there's a good chance that you'll just need to change the values of the init parameters `jdbcDriver` and `dbUrl` in `web.xml` from these values for MySQL:

```
com.mysql.jdbc.Driver
jdbc:mysql://localhost:3306/shop
```

to the values for the other DBMS.

For example, for PostgreSQL (`http://www.postgresql.org/`), the values would look like this:

```
org.postgresql.Driver
jdbc:postgresql://localhost/shop
```

For Firebird (`http://www.firebirdsql.org/`), the values would look like this:

```
org.firebirdsql.jdbc.FBDriver
jdbc:firebirdsql:localhost/3050:D:\\Firebird Datafiles\\shop.fdb
```

At the moment of writing, Sun Microsystems reports that 221 different JDBC drivers exist (see `http://developers.sun.com/product/jdbc/drivers`). Therefore, you should be able to find the driver you need to connect to any database, although it might not be freely available.

If you don't find the right JDBC driver or if it's too expensive, you might be able to use the JDBC-ODBC bridge included in the JVM to connect to any ODBC-compliant database. ODBC refers to an API supported by many database vendors on basically all operating systems. With the JDBC-ODBC bridge, you can also work via JDBC on files in Microsoft Excel format. For example, let's suppose that you have the file shown in Figure 4-2.

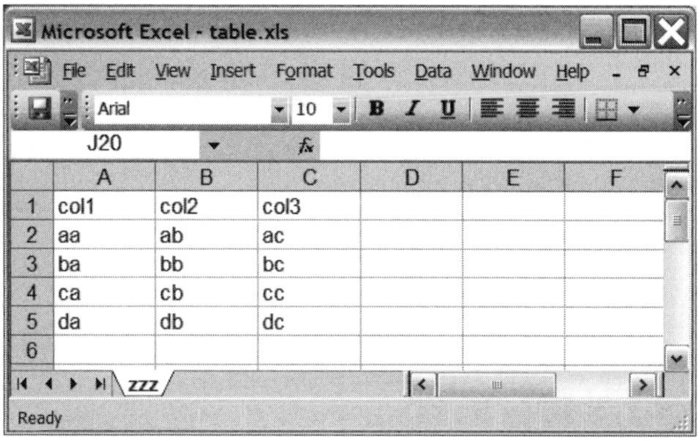

Figure 4-2. *table.xls*

To be able to access this file via the JDBC-ODBC bridge, you first need to associate the file with an ODBC data source. To do so, go to Start ➤ Settings ➤ Control Panel ➤ Administrative Tools ➤ Data Sources (ODBC). There, click on the System DSN tab and then on the Add button, as shown in Figure 4-3.

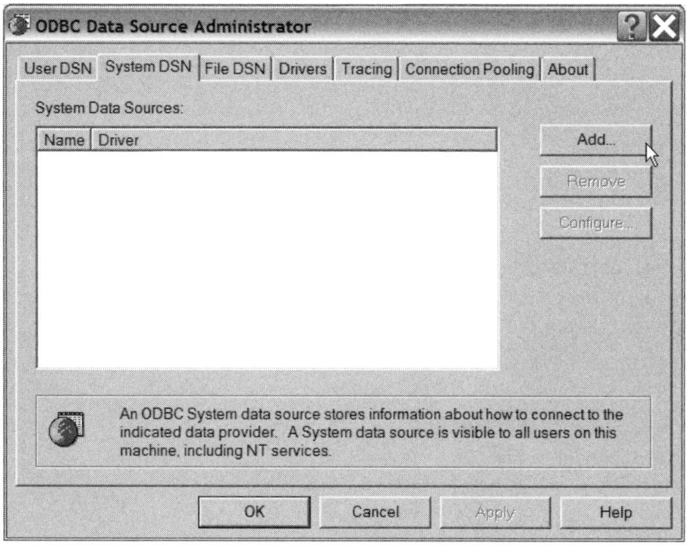

Figure 4-3. *ODBC Data Source control panel*

This opens the Create New Data Source dialog. Scroll the list of possible data sources until you find Microsoft Excel Driver (*.xls). Select it and click on the Finish button. Despite the name of the button, you're not yet done! A new dialog called ODBC Microsoft Excel Setup opens, which lets you select the Excel file and associate it with a data source name. See Figure 4-4.

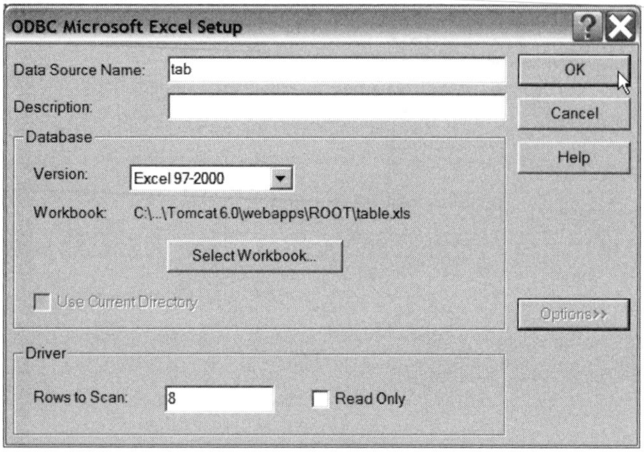

Figure 4-4. *ODBC Microsoft Excel setup*

Click on the Select Workbook... button to select the file. Notice that we've placed the test file (table.xls) in Tomcat's ROOT directory, but it doesn't need to be there. We've chosen tab as a data source name, but you're free to choose any name.

Listing 4-11 shows you a little JSP page to access table.xls as if it were a database.

Listing 4-11. *xls.jsp*

```
<%@page language="java" contentType="text/html"%>
<%@page import="java.sql.*"%>
<html><head><title>XLS - ODBC test</title></head><body>
<%
  Class.forName("sun.jdbc.odbc.JdbcOdbcDriver").newInstance();
  Connection conn = DriverManager.getConnection ("jdbc:odbc:tab");
  Statement stmt = conn.createStatement();
  ResultSet rs = stmt.executeQuery("select * from [zzz$]");
%><table border= "1"><%
  ResultSetMetaData resMetaData = rs.getMetaData();
  int nCols = resMetaData.getColumnCount();
%><tr><%
  for (int kCol = 1; kCol <= nCols; kCol++) {
    out.print("<td><b>" + resMetaData.getColumnName(kCol) + "</b></td>");
    }
%></tr><%
  while (rs.next()) {
    %><tr><%
    for (int kCol = 1; kCol <= nCols; kCol++) {
      out.print("<td>" + rs.getString(kCol) + "</td>");
      }
```

```
  %></tr><%
  }
 %></table><%
 conn.close();
 %>
</body></html>
```

Notice that in the `select` statement, we've used [`zzz$`] as a table name to access the worksheet named `zzz`. Figure 4-5 shows the output of Listing 4-11.

Figure 4-5. *The output of xls.jsp*

One word of warning: you will fail to establish the Java connection if you have the file already open in Excel.

Summary

In this chapter, we introduced you to working with databases and SQL. We explained how to access databases from JSP via the Java SQL API. In particular, we showed you how to establish a connection, insert data, and perform queries. To complete the summary of essential DB operations, we also described how to group elementary updates into transactions. To bring it all together, we described the design of database operations in the Eshop application, and we showed you their implementation both with scriptlets and with the XML syntax. Finally, we mentioned possible alternatives to MySQL and described how you can access a spreadsheet from JSP as if it were a database.

If you think that JSP, HTML, and SQL have not been easy, brace yourself, because in the next chapter, we'll finally talk about JSF!

CHAPTER 5

■ ■ ■

At Face Value (JSF Primer)

In this chapter, we'll discuss JSF and show you how you can use it to create user interfaces for web-based applications. JSF makes the development of web applications easier by:

- Letting you create user interfaces from a set of standard UI components wired to server-side objects

- Making available two JSP custom tag libraries to handle those UI components

- Providing a mechanism for extending the standard UI components

JSF transparently saves state information of the UI components and repopulates forms when they redisplay. This is possible because the states of the components live beyond the life span of HTTP requests. JSF operates by providing a servlet and a component model that includes event handling, server-side validation, data conversion, and component rendering. Not surprisingly, JSF doesn't change the basic page life cycle that you already know from JSP: the client makes an HTTP request, and the server replies with a dynamically generated HTML page.

Be warned that JSF isn't very easy to use, and it requires a non-negligible initial effort to get it going. However, its reward is that once you've familiarized yourself with it, you can develop user interfaces more quickly and efficiently.

FRAMEWORKS

Developers are continuously in search of tools that increase their programming efficiency. Frameworks help in this direction by providing clear processes and predefined components, increasing reusability, and enforcing good programming practices. Let's go through some of the most widely used frameworks and see how they compare with JSF.

Apache Struts was introduced in 2000 and has established itself among developers. Like JSF, Struts is an open source framework that focuses on Java EE web applications. Also like JSF, it enforces the use of an MVC application architecture. However, it does this by providing the controller (the `ActionServlet`), while JSF provides the view (the `FacesServlet`). Visit the Apache Struts home page at `http://struts.apache.org/` for more information.

Struts is better established in the industry than JSF and has (still) better tool support. Contrary to JSF, Struts also supports HTTP GETs, which means that you can bookmark Struts pages. On the other hand, the unification of JSF and JSP ELs makes JSF definitely more attractive. Additionally, with JSP, you're free to name and structure your Java beans as you like, and the configuration is overall simpler. Moreover, open source integrated development environments (IDEs) capable of supporting drag-and-drop JSF components are around the corner.

Apache Tapestry is a framework in which you can develop applications with the MVC architecture. Like JSF, it is based on components. Tapestry focuses on XHTML components and provides binding between those components in the web pages and the corresponding Java objects on the server. In this way, it encourages development in a modular fashion, based on short pieces of code rather than long programs. Check out `http://tapestry.apache.org/` for more information.

Apache Wicket is the most recent addition to the list of Java-based web application frameworks. It is a component-based framework like JSF, but it relies only on HTML and Java, without any additional rendering language such as JSP. Its declared purpose is to make developing web applications "simple and enjoyable again." With this goal in mind, Wicket minimizes the need for configuration and concentrates on making the development of custom components as easy as possible. Go to `http://wicket.apache.org/` for details.

Ruby on Rails is a web application framework that relies on the language Ruby rather than Java. We mention it here because it has received much attention, and you might have heard of it. Its declared aim is to make the development of database-driven web sites faster and easier. To achieve this, it provides code templates called *scaffolding*, which minimize the amount of new code you need to write. Visit `http://www.rubyonrails.org/` for more information.

So, what is best? This is a question you'll have to answer for yourself, based on your own preferences. It's too early to say whether JSF will eventually replace Struts, whether they will both coexist, or whether Struts will remain the more established of the two. We can only say that, while JSF is not the easiest framework to learn, once you understand how it works (and this manual should help you with that!), you won't regret to have made the effort.

The JSF Life Cycle

To be able to use JSF proficiently, you need to have a clear idea of how JSF works. Therefore, before jumping into a practical application, let's take a look at JSF "under the hood."

Figure 5-1 shows the life cycle of a JSF page as it is processed by the JSF servlet. The life cycle applies both to initial and subsequent requests for a page.

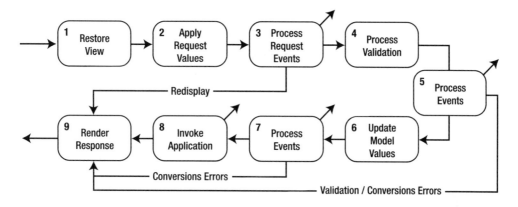

Figure 5-1. *The JSF life cycle*

The up-right arrows you see in the blocks numbered 3, 5, 7, and 8 indicate that the cycle can be interrupted. That happens when the response to be generated doesn't contain any JSF component. In that case, JSF abandons the processing of the request by executing the FacesContext.responseComplete method. Let's go through the life-cycle phases one by one:

1. **Restore View**: The JSF servlet builds the view of the requested page as a component tree that contains the information associated with all components. It also saves the view in a FacesContext instance, thereby making it possible to repopulate the page if necessary—for example, when the user doesn't fill out a form as required. If the same page was displayed before and component states were saved, that information would also be taken into account. In this phase, JSF wires event handlers and validators (if any) to the components.

2. **Apply Request Values**: The JSF servlet goes through the component tree and executes each component's decode method, which extracts values from the request parameters and stores them locally in the component. It also automatically converts the parameters that are associated with object properties of non-string types. Conversion errors cause error messages to be queued to the FacesContext object. In some cases, typically when the user clicks on controls, the servlet also generates request events and queues them to FacesContext.

3. **Process Request Events**: The servlet calls the processEvent method for each component with one or more queued events. Each component decides to handle the events or delegate their handling to event handlers. In any case, the servlet proceeds with the next phase if all executed processEvent methods return false. Otherwise, it jumps directly to the Render Response phase.

4. **Process Validation**: The servlet invokes the validate methods of the validators that had been registered during the Restore View phase. For each validate method that returns false, the servlet queues an error message to the FacesContext.

5. **Process Events**: If validation or conversion errors are generated during the Process Validation phase, control jumps directly to the Render Response phase.

6. **Update Model Values**: Each UI component can be linked to a field in a Java object called the *model object*. During this phase, the values of the linked components are copied to the corresponding fields of the model object by executing the component method `updateModel`, which also does type conversions when necessary. Conversion errors cause error messages to be queued to `FacesContext`.

7. **Process Events**: If it turns out that conversion errors were generated during phase 6, control jumps directly to the Render Response phase.

8. **Invoke Application**: During this phase, the servlet processes the application-level events by executing the corresponding handlers. When the user submits a form or clicks on a link of a JSF application, the JSF servlet generates a corresponding application-level event. One of the tasks you have to do when developing a JSF application is to assign a handler (e.g., a JSP page) to each one of the possible application events.

9. **Render Response**: The servlet creates a response component tree and delegates the rendering of the page to Tomcat. Each component renders itself as Tomcat goes through the corresponding JSF tags. At the end of this phase, the state of the response is saved so that the servlet can access it during the Restore View phase of subsequent requests to the same page.

JSF Custom Tags

The user interface of a JSF application, called a *view*, consists of a tree of UI component objects of types based on the `javax.faces.component.UIComponent` class. Some components are simple, such as a button or a text field. Others are complex, such as a table or a tree control element.

As we've already mentioned, you manipulate the components by means of custom tags, which give you access to their methods. To associate objects of your data model to the corresponding components, you assign to specific attributes of the component tags value expressions that refer to the objects.

The tags associated with rendering HTML components are collected in a custom tag library called (not surprisingly!) html. Here is a list of all possible tags: `column`, `commandButton`, `commandLink`, `dataTable`, `form`, `graphicImage`, `inputHidden`, `inputSecret`, `inputText`, `inputTextarea`, `message`, `messages`, `outputFormat`, `outputLabel`, `outputLink`, `outputText`, `panelGrid`, `panelGroup`, `selectBooleanCheckbox`, `selectManyCheckbox`, `selectManyListbox`, `selectManyMenu`, `selectOneListbox`, `selectOneMenu`, and `selectOneRadio`. The names should already tell you a lot about the purpose of each. For a description of each tag, please refer to Appendix F. In this chapter, we'll only show you how to use some of them through examples.

A second library, called `core`, gives you access to APIs that are independent of a particular render kit:

- **Converters**: They let you convert between the data types of the components and those of your application objects.

- **Listeners**: Based on the JavaBean version 1.0.1 mechanism, a listener to handle events of a certain type is registered with a component.

- **Events**: After the listener is registered with a component, the `FacesServlet` then fires the events by invoking an event notification method of the listener.

- **Validators**: They examine the local value of a component and ensure that it conforms to a set of predefined rules.

The tags defined in the `core` library are `actionListener`, `attribute`, `convertDateTime`, `converter`, `convertNumber`, `facet`, `loadBundle`, `param`, `selectItem`, `selectItems`, `subview`, `validateDoubleRange`, `validateLength`, `validateLongRange`, `validator`, `valueChangeListener`, `verbatim`, and `view`. Please refer to Appendix F for more information on the tags.

Event Handling

Before looking at an application, we want to spend a few words on the JSF mechanism to handle events, because you cannot really understand how JSF works unless you know a thing or two about event handling.

As an example, let's see what role the event handling plays when a user clicks on a submit button. The JSF UI components used to represent button HTML elements are objects of type `javax.faces.component.html.HtmlCommandButton`, which is a class extending the more general `javax.faces.component.UICommand`. As with any other HTML page, by clicking on the `Submit` button of a JSF application, the user triggers the sending to the server of an HTTP request that contains the ID of the button as a parameter name.

As we've already mentioned, during the Apply Request Values phase (phase 2 in the list), the JSF servlet executes the `decode` method of each component of the page. First, the `decode` method scans the parameter names to see whether one matches the ID of the component the method belongs to. In our example, the `decode` method of the `UICommand` object associated with the button clicked by the user finds the component ID among the request parameters, precisely because the user clicked the button. As a result of finding its own ID, the component instantiates an event object of type `javax.faces.event.ActionEvent` and queues it up.

At this point, you have to distinguish between situations in which all the input fields of a form need to be validated and those in which only a partial validation is appropriate. For example, in an online shop such as the Eshop application, the shopper must be able to add further books to the shopping cart even after reaching the checkout page, where she is asked to provide payment information. To make that possible, you must ensure that the validation of the payment data is skipped if the user selects a book category or searches for new titles. If you allowed the validation of empty or partially filled payment fields to proceed, the application would report one or more errors and prevent the shopper from going back to look for new books.

You solve this issue by specifying that the handling of both the book search and the category selection be done during Apply Request Values, while leaving the handling of the payment data to follow the normal life cycle. If it turns out that the user wants to shop for new books rather than complete the checkout, control then jumps directly to the Render Response phase, thereby skipping the intermediate phases where payment data would have been validated and processed.

We'll show you the details of how this is done in the next section.

The JSF Application

If you've installed Java and Tomcat as described in Appendix A, the web applications will reside in the following folder:

```
C:\Program Files\Apache Software Foundation\Tomcat 6.0\webapps
```

To develop a JSF application, you need to follow these steps:

1. Install the JSF JAR files listed in Appendix A.

2. Create an application folder inside webapps with two subfolders named WEB-INF and META-INF. For example, if you name this folder xyz, the URL of the application will be http://localhost:8080/xyz/.

3. Develop the JSP modules and the backing Java beans that constitute the application. The key difference from non-JSF applications is that the JSP modules contain JSF tags.

4. Write the WEB-INF\web.xml file to describe the deployment of your application. Among other things, this is where you tell Tomcat that you want to use the JSF servlet.

5. Write a JSF configuration file named WEB-INF\faces-config.xml. This is where you declare Java beans, so that the JSF servlet can instantiate them, and tell the servlet how to navigate between JSP modules.

Please refer to Appendix A for the details of how to do step 1. Step 2 is trivial. Therefore, we'll start with step 3. As a base for our examples, we'll use the application Eshopx, which is the XML version of the Eshop application we introduced in Chapter 2. In Chapter 8, we'll describe the Eshop* applications in some detail, while in this chapter we'll only show some modules and explain what you need to know in order to understand JSF.

In this section, we'll describe only the tags you need for the JSF version of the online shop application we introduced in Chapter 2. For a brief description of all JSF tags, please refer to Appendix F.

To be able to use the two JSF custom tag libraries, you first need to declare them, as you do with any other tag library. If you're writing JSP pages (i.e., JSP modules with scriptlets), insert the following two lines at the beginning:

```
<%@ taglib uri="http://java.sun.com/jsf/core" prefix="f"%>
<%@ taglib uri="http://java.sun.com/jsf/html" prefix="h"%>
```

If you're writing JSP documents (i.e., JSP modules in XML format), add the following namespace attributes to the root element:

```
xmlns:f="http://java.sun.com/jsf/core"
xmlns:h="http://java.sun.com/jsf/html"
```

In both cases, the result is that JSF core tags have the prefix f, and html tags have the prefix h.

■**Tip** Keep in mind that the purpose of the JSF HTML tag library is to generate HTML code. Therefore, if you're not sure how a tag works, try something out and look at the generated code by displaying the source page on your browser.

---

f:view, h:form, and h:outputText

We've already said that a JSF user interface is called a *view*. Therefore, it shouldn't surprise you that all JSF tags must be enclosed in the <f:view> element. Listing 5-1 shows the welcome page of the Eshopf application (i.e., of a version of Eshop that uses JSF).

Listing 5-1. *index.jspx*

```
<?xml version="1.0" encoding="ISO-8859-1"?>
<jsp:root
  xmlns:jsp="http://java.sun.com/JSP/Page"
  xmlns:f="http://java.sun.com/jsf/core"
  xmlns:h="http://java.sun.com/jsf/html"
  xmlns:c="http://java.sun.com/jsp/jstl/core"
  version="2.1"
  >
<jsp:directive.page
  language="java"
  contentType="ISO-8859-1"
  pageEncoding="ISO-8859-1"
  />
<jsp:output
  doctype-root-element="html"
  doctype-public="-//W3C//DTD XHTML 1.0 Strict//EN"
  doctype-system="http://www.w3.org/TR/xhtml1/DTD/xhtml1-strict.dtd"
  />
<c:url var="cssUrl" value="/css/eshopf.jspx"/>
<html xmlns="http://www.w3.org/1999/xhtml">
<head>
  <title>Welcome</title>
  <link rel="stylesheet" href="${cssUrl}" type="text/css"/>
  </head>
```

```
<body>
  <f:view>
    <h:form>
      <jsp:include page="TopMenu.jspx" flush="true"/>
      <jsp:include page="LeftMenu.jspx" flush="true"/>
      <h:outputText styleClass="content content_h1"
          value="Welcome to e-Shop"/>
    </h:form>
  </f:view>
  </body>
</html>
</jsp:root>
```

As you can see, the page only displays two menus and a welcome sentence. The only differences between this file and the index.jspx of Eshopx are the few lines that we've highlighted. Their purpose is to do the following:

- Declare the namespaces of the JSF tag libraries and assign their prefixes to them.

- Define a view that spans the whole body of the generated HTML page.

- Wrap the menus inside a form.

- Display the message "Welcome to e-Shop."

<h:form> ... </h:form> is expanded to HTML, as shown in the following example:

```
<form id="j_id_jsp_341629961_1" name="j_id_jsp_341629961_1" method="post"
    action="/eshopf/jsp/index.jsf" enctype="application/x-www-form-urlencoded">
...
</form>
```

The id and name attributes are generated automatically and change with every page. The action attribute points to the page itself. The JSF servlet decides whether the same page is then to be reloaded or not.

The h:outputText element is rendered as follows:

```
<span class="content content_h1">Welcome to e-Shop</span>
```

Its attribute styleClass has the same function as the HTML attribute class. Note that this is true for all JSF components. The style content defines the 700-pixel-wide central area of the screen, while content_h1 defines the style of the welcoming message. In the non-JSF version of this application, the second style was defined as .content h1, and the code in index.jspx was as follows:

```
<div class="content"><h1>Welcome to e-Shop</h1></div>
```

Unfortunately, in JSF there is no way of generating the HTML tag <h1>. Therefore, you're forced to create the independent class selector .content_h1 for styling the text.

In general, style sheets and JSF don't work very well together, because CSS relies on the containment of HTML elements inside each other for its "cascading" mechanism. The style .content defined for <div> also applies to whatever is wrapped inside it, including <h1>.

If CSS had provided its own inheritance mechanism, you could have defined for <h1> a style .h1_inheriting_content containing a reference to .content. Then, you could have simply written this element:

```
<h1 class="h1_inheriting_content">Welcome to e-Shop</h1>
```

and used the same style for h:output. As it is, the only way to do it would be to duplicate inside .h1_inheriting_content all the styles that are inside .content. Our solution avoids the duplication. We've discussed this issue of styling because it will present itself over and over again. You can only resolve it by keeping in mind how the different JSF tags are rendered in HTML.

Note In JSF components, you can use the same events associated with HTML elements (onclick, ondblclick, onkeydown, onkeypress, onkeyup, onmousedown, onmousemove, onmouseout, onmouseover, and onmouseup). JSF passes them on to the HTML elements it renders.

---

f:subview, h:panelGroup, h:graphicImage, and h:commandLink

Let's look at the top menu, shown in Listing 5-2.

Listing 5-2. *Partial TopMenu.jspx*

```
01: <f:subview id="viewcart">
02:   <h:panelGroup styleClass="header">
03:     <h:outputText styleClass="logo" value="e-Shopping Center"/>
04:     <h:commandLink styleClass="cart link2" action="showCart" immediate="true">
05:       <h:outputText value="Show Cart "/>
06:       <h:graphicImage url="/images/cart.gif"/>
07:     </h:commandLink>
08:   </h:panelGroup>
09: </f:subview>
```

Listing 5-2 doesn't show the elements xml, jsp:root, and jsp:directive.page because they're present in all JSP documents and just distract from what we need to focus on. The purpose of the element h:subview is equivalent to that of a pair of braces in Java: it limits the scope of its content. For example, the component IDs defined in one subview can be identical to those defined in other subviews of the same page.

With TopMenu.jspx, you don't necessarily need to wrap everything inside a subview, because the content of that document doesn't conflict with what is inside LeftMenu.jspx or with index.jspx. Nevertheless, it's good practice to avoid possible side effects of included modules. Subviews are required to have an ID, which is why we defined id="viewcart", even though we don't actually have any use for it.

In TopMenu.jspx, you encounter three new JSF tags: h:panelGroup, h:graphicImage, and h:commandLink. The h:panelGroup tag is rendered in HTML with a <span> element. Therefore, you use it when a single element is expected but you need to include more than one or to assign the same style to several elements. The UI components inside an h:panelGroup are rendered one after the other as they are encountered. In line 2, you use h:panelGroup to apply the style header.

The h:graphicImage tag is rendered in HTML with <img>, and h:commandLink is how you generate a hyperlink. If you look at how it is rendered in HTML, you'll find a bewildering series of IDs, but in practice, it is equivalent to the following two lines of Eshopx:

```
<a class="link2" href="${myURL}">Show Cart
    <img src="${imageURL}cart.gif" border="0"/></a>
```

JSF transparently passes on to the rendered HTML tag the attributes coords, dir, hreflang, lang, readonly, rel, rev, shape, style, tabindex, target, title, and type.

h:panelGrid, h:inputText, and h:commandButton

LeftMenu.jspx, shown in Listings 5-3, 5-4, and 5-6, shows you some examples of input fields and a way to do tables. We've decided to break up LeftMenu.jspx into three parts for clarity. The *structure*, shown in Listing 5-3, introduces the h:panelGrid component.

Listing 5-3. *LeftMenu.jspx—Structure*

```
<f:subview id="leftMenu">
  <h:panelGrid styleClass="menu">
    Here goes the Search Box - See Listing 5-4
    Here goes the Category Selection Box - See Listing 5-6
    </h:panelGrid>
  </f:subview>
```

The h:panelGrid component is rendered with an HTML <table>, and each component it contains is rendered as an HTML <td> element. With h:panelGrid, you can use the table's attributes dir, lang, style, title, and width. JSF simply passes them on to the rendered <table>.

The optional attribute columns determines the length of the rows. In LeftMenu.jspx, you could have written columns="1", but we omitted it because 1 is the default. Here you need h:panelGrid instead of h:panelGroup, because otherwise the search and category selection boxes would have not been rendered one below the other. The rows are filled in from left to right with the components in the order in which they appeared inside h:panelGrid, from top to bottom. The search box shown in Listing 5-4 consists of some descriptive text, an input text field, and a button to submit the search.

Listing 5-4. *LeftMenu.jspx—Search Box*

```
<h:panelGroup styleClass="box">
  <h:outputText styleClass="box_title" value="Quick Search"/>
  <h:outputText styleClass="box_p" value="Book Title/Author:"/>
  <h:inputText size="15"
      styleClass="box_searchTxt"
      binding="#{shopManager.searchTxt}"
      />
```

```
<h:commandButton
    type="submit" value="Search"
    styleClass="box_searchBtn"
    action="#{shopManager.searchBooks}"
    immediate="true"
    />
</h:panelGroup>
```

The component h:inputText is the JSF equivalent of <input type="text" ... />. JSF transparently passes on to the rendered HTML tag the attributes accesskey, alt, dir, disabled, lang, maxlength, readonly, size, style, tabindex, and title.

The attribute binding="#{shopManager.searchTxt}" shows how you link the input field to a data object on the server. It is also possible to establish a similar link with the value attribute, as the following example taken from the module Checkout.jspx shows:

```
<h:inputText id="name" required="true"
    value="#{shopManager.customer.contactName}"
    requiredMessage="Value is required!"
    />
```

As you can see, value has taken the place of binding. The difference is that with binding, you establish a two-way link, which lets your backing bean modify the value of the field, while with value, the backing bean cannot modify the data entered by the user. The shopManager bean doesn't need to modify the search string entered in LeftMenu.jspx, but you still use binding for reasons that will become clear in a moment.

The component h:commandButton corresponds to <input type="submit" ... />. JSF transparently passes on to the rendered HTML tag the attributes dir, lang, readonly, style, tabindex, title, and type. The attribute action="#{shopManager.searchBooks}" shows how you link the input field to a method on the server.

The attribute immediate="true" tells JSF that the action should be executed during Apply Request Values (phase 2), rather than during Invoke Application (phase 8), which is the default for all actions. In this way, you can be sure that the user is always able to resume shopping from any page, even if it contains invalid input fields (e.g., from the checkout page with empty fields).

This immediate execution of the search action is why you need to use the binding attribute in the h:inputText component. With the value attribute, you could access the search string with the method getValue, but only during Invoke Application (phase 8), after Process Validation (phase 5) and Update Model Value (phase 6) have done their job. This would have been too late, because, as we've just explained, the search action takes place during Apply Request Values (phase 2). By using the binding attribute, you make available to the shop manager *the whole h:inputText component*. As a result, you can invoke the method getSubmittedValue (see line 116 of Listing 5-5) already during Apply Request Value, when the search action is executed.

The attribute required="true" tells JSF that it is invalid for the user to leave the field empty, and requiredMessage defines the corresponding error message. If you omit the requiredMessage attribute, the default error message is something like this:

```
j_id_jsp_548875039_1:address: Validation Error: Value is required.
```

We've already mentioned the ShopManager Java bean. Let's look at it before continuing with the study of LeftMenu.jspx.

The Shop Manager

We've briefly mentioned the JSF configuration file WEB-INF\faces-config.xml. One of the purposes of faces-config.xml is to tell the JSF servlet where to find Java beans. The following code tells JSF to instantiate the class eshop.beans.ShopManager and name the object shopManager, so that you can refer to it in JSF EL expressions:

```
<managed-bean>
  <managed-bean-name>shopManager</managed-bean-name>
  <managed-bean-class>eshop.beans.ShopManager</managed-bean-class>
  <managed-bean-scope>session</managed-bean-scope>
  </managed-bean>
```

This code also specifies that shopManager is to remain available for the duration of the client session. You use shopManager to save the values of the HTTP request parameters locally and to act as an interface between JSF and the Eshop data model, which encapsulates database operations.

In the previous section, we said that the following two attributes realize the linking of user inputs and server entities:

```
binding="#{shopManager.searchTxt}"
action="#{shopManager.searchBooks}"
```

To understand how this works, let's go through the relevant parts of ShopManager.java, as shown in Listing 5-5.

Listing 5-5. *Searching for Books in ShopManager.java*

```
014: private List           books;
...
023: private HtmlInputText searchTxt = new HtmlInputText();
...
099: public HtmlInputText getSearchTxt() {
100:    return searchTxt;
101:    }
...
114: public String searchBooks() {
115:    categoryName=null;
116:    String searchKeyword = (String)searchTxt.getSubmittedValue();
117:    books = dataManager.getSearchResults(searchKeyword);
118:    return "listBooks";
119:    }
...
```

```
137: public void setSearchTxt(HtmlInputText val) {
138:   searchTxt = val;
139:   }
```

The binding attribute listed means that during Update Model Values (phase 6), the JSF servlet saves the search string typed by the user in the attribute searchTxt, which is of type javax.faces.component.html.HtmlInputText. It does so by using the method setSearchTxt. Later in the life cycle, during Render Response (phase 9), it uses the getSearchText method to get the value needed to prefill the input text field in HTML. The HtmlInputTxt class has a series of properties and methods that enable you, among other things, to make it a required input and to validate the value typed in by the user.

The action attribute of the Search button causes the JSF servlet to execute the method searchBooks during Invoke Application (phase 8). As you can see in Listing 5-5, the method simply obtains the value of the search string, executes the dataManager method to obtain the list of books (from the database), saves its result in the object books, and returns the string "listBooks".

If you now look at the following fragment of faces-config.xml, you'll see that by returning "listBooks", the searchBooks method forces JSF to switch from the current page to SearchOutcome.jspx:

```
<navigation-rule>
  <navigation-case>
    <from-outcome>listBooks</from-outcome>
    <to-view-id>/jsp/listBooks.jspx</to-view-id>
    <redirect/>
    </navigation-case>
  </navigation-rule>
```

The presence (or absence) of the redirect element determines how this switch is done. If the redirect is present, as in the example, JSF will send a redirect response to the client that causes the browser to request the new page. Without the redirect element, during Render Response, JSF will directly use the content of the books object to render in HTML the list of books found in the database. But in that case, the list will effectively be a new rendering of the page from which the user launched the search. As a result, the URL shown in the browser will remain unchanged (e.g., http://localhost:8080/eshopf/).

You also could have included this line in the navigation-case element to impose a more restrictive condition on when the page switch should take place:

```
<from-action>#{shopManager.searchBooks}</from-action>
```

However, this would be wrong in this case, because the method dataManager.selectCategory that lists the books in a category also returns "listBooks".

h:dataTable and h:column

Now that you understand how user inputs and actions are bound to data objects and methods, we can complete the study of LeftMenu.jspx. Listing 5-6 shows the part where you select books by category.

Listing 5-6. *LeftMenu.jspx—Category Selection Box*

```
01: <h:panelGroup styleClass="box" id="categBox">
02:    <h:outputText styleClass="box_title" value="Categories"/>
03:    <h:dataTable value="#{shopManager.categories}" var="category">
04:       <h:column>
05:          <h:commandLink
06:             action="#{shopManager.selectCategory}"
07:             value="#{category.name}"
08:             immediate="true"
09:             />
10:       </h:column>
11:    </h:dataTable>
12: </h:panelGroup>
```

JSF renders the h:dataTable component (line 3) with an HTML table element, in which every column is identified by an h:column component (line 4). In addition to the table functionality as you know it from HTML, JSF also provides an iteration mechanism similar to that of c:forEach and linked to the data model. The mechanism is based on two attributes: value, which contains an EL expression that returns a list of items, and var, which contains the name of a variable to which the items of the list are assigned one by one in sequence.

In this case, the EL expression #{shopManager.categories} executes the following method of shopManager:

```
public ListDataModel getCategories() {
  categoriesDataModel.setWrappedData(dataManager.getCategories());
  return categoriesDataModel;
  }
```

with categoriesDataModel defined as follows:

```
private ListDataModel categoriesDataModel = new ListDataModel();
```

The result is that the List of categories obtained from the database via the dataManager.getCategories method is assigned to the value attribute of h:dataTable.

JSF implements an index that goes through all the items of the list, and the attribute var="category" defines the name of the variable that gives access to the current item. In practical terms, this means that when the JSF servlet renders the h:dataTable component during the Render Response phase, it renders the h:commandLink of lines 5-9 for each category found in the database.

f:facet

You've seen that JSF renders h:dataTable/h:column and h:panelGrid with HTML tables. Listing 5-7 shows how you can use the f:facet tag to generate table headers and footers.

Listing 5-7. *Example of f:facet*

```
<h:panelGrid columns="2"
    columnClasses="sc1,sc2" headerClass="sh" rowClasses="sr" styleClass="tc">
  <h:outputText value="11"/>
  <h:outputText value="12"/>
  <f:facet name="footer"><h:outputText value="footer"/></f:facet>
  <f:facet name="header"><h:outputText value="header"/></f:facet>
  <h:outputText value="21"/>
  <h:outputText value="22"/>
</h:panelGrid>
```

Listing 5-8 shows the generated HTML code, which we've indented for clarity.

Listing 5-8. *The Output of the f:facet Example*

```
<table class="tc">
  <thead>
    <tr><th class="sh" colspan="2" scope="colgroup">header</th></tr>
    </thead>
  <tfoot>
    <tr><td colspan="2">footer</td></tr>
    </tfoot>
  <tbody>
    <tr class="sr"><td class="sc1">11</td><td class="sc2">12</td></tr>
    <tr class="sr"><td class="sc1">21</td><td class="sc2">22</td></tr>
    </tbody>
  </table>
```

The example also shows how you can define different styles for the header, the rows, and each column of data. Notice how the sequence of <thead>, <tfoot>, and <tbody> doesn't depend on the order in which you define the corresponding components in JSF.

A facet is a placeholder that has its name as the only attribute and accepts a single component as the content. The name tells the enclosing component what the facet purpose is and where its content is to be rendered.

JSF only defines the two facets we've just described in connection with h:panelGrid, which you can also use with h:dataTable and h:column.

h:message and f:verbatim

The Checkout.jspx module of the Eshopf application asks the user to provide the payment data (name, address, and credit-card information). Listing 5-9 shows the code associated with one of the input items.

Listing 5-9. *Checkout.jspx—Name Entry*

```
<h:panelGrid columns="3" rendered="#{!shopManager.shoppingCartEmpty}"
    style="width:auto">
  ...
  <h:outputText value="Contact Name"/>
  <h:inputText id="name" required="true"
      value="#{shopManager.customer.contactName}"
      requiredMessage="Value is required!"
      />
  <h:message for="name" styleClass="error"/>
  ...
</h:panelGrid>
```

The value of the h:inputText component is associated with the contactName attribute of the object customer, which is an instantiation of the class eshop.beans.Customer. When talking about h:inputText, we explained the meaning of its attributes required and requiredMessage. To complete the picture, we only need to add that h:message lets you decide where and with which style the error message is rendered.

Figure 5-2 shows what Checkout.jspx looks like when you leave one required field empty.

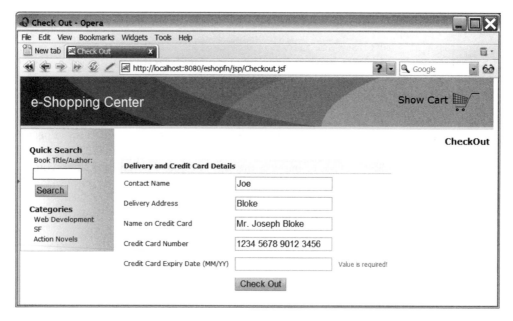

Figure 5-2. *Incomplete input on Checkout.jspx*

A potentially useful tag is `<f:verbatim>`. Its purpose is to let you insert HTML tags where a JSF component is expected. It isn't a practice that we encourage, but sometimes it can make your life much easier. For example, instead of using `h:panelGrid` to arrange components in a single column, you could insert `<f:verbatim><br/></f:verbatim>` between consecutive components.

Using and Creating Converters

As we said when describing the JSF life cycle, the JSF servlet executes the `decode` method of each component during Apply Request Values. The method saves the parameter values locally, but it first needs to convert the input strings to the corresponding types defined in the components, except when the components expect values of type `String`. JSF provides standard converters for the `java.lang` types `Boolean`, `Byte`, `Character`, `Double`, `Enum`, `Float`, `Integer`, `Long`, and `Short`, and for the `java.math` types `BigDecimal` and `BigInteger`.

The standard converters perform a series of checks that you can use to validate, at least in part, the user's input. To do so, you have to enable the reporting of converter messages. For example, in the Eshopf application, the user can update the number of copies of a book that is already in the shopping cart. Clearly, it doesn't make any sense to type a fractional number or a string that is not numeric. Therefore, you can write the input component in the `ShoppingCart.jspx` module as follows:

```
<h:inputText id="quantity" value="#{item.quantity}" size="2"
    required="true"
    requiredMessage="What? Nothing?"
    converterMessage="An integer, please!"
/>
```

Then, you only need to add this line to display the error messages of the standard `Integer` converter:

```
<h:message for="quantity" styleClass="error"/>
```

This is not yet a perfect solution, because the application still accepts negative integers. That is, you can type in `-1`, and the application will happily display negative prices! To see how to solve this problem, you'll have to wait for the section about validators.

Sometimes the standard converters are not sufficient. For example, you might like to save in a database a credit-card number without any dashes or spaces. To make a custom converter, you need to create an implementation of the `javax.faces.Converter` interface that overrides its methods `getAsObject` and `getAsString`. You must implement both directions of the converter. During Apply Request Values (phase 2), the JSF servlet uses the `getAsObject` method to convert the input string to the data model object. During Render Response (phase 9), the JSF servlet uses the `getAsString` method to do the conversion in the opposite direction, so that a string can be included in the HTML response. Once you complete the converter, you have to register it with the application.

To invoke the converter, you need to nest it as a property of `f:converter` or assign it to the `converter` attribute of the input component. Let's go through all the necessary steps one at a time. The converter will just clean up a credit-card number of any non-numeric character.

Notice that it is the task of a validator to check that the credit-card number is valid. This normally takes place during Process Validation (phase 4), while the conversions, as we just said, take place during phases 2 and 9.

Writing the Converter in Java

Listing 5-10 shows the full code of the converter used in Eshopf to convert the credit-card number when checking out.

Listing 5-10. *CCNumberConverter.java*

```java
package eshop.converters;
import javax.faces.convert.Converter;
import javax.faces.context.FacesContext;
import javax.faces.component.UIComponent;
import javax.faces.convert.ConverterException;

public class CCNumberConverter implements Converter {
  //
  // getAsObject extracts from the input string all numeric characters
  public Object getAsObject(FacesContext ctx, UIComponent cmp,
      String val) {
    String convVal = null;
    if ( val != null ) {
      char[] chars = val.trim().toCharArray();
      convVal = "";
      for (int k = 0; k < chars.length; k++) {
        if (chars[k] >= '0' && chars[k] <= '9') {
          convVal += chars[k];
        }
      }
/*
      System.out.println("CCNumberConverter.getAsObject: '"
        + val + "' -> '" + convVal + "'");
*/
    }
    return convVal;
  }
  //
  // getAsString inserts into the object string spaces to make it readable
  // default: nnnn nnnn nnnn nnnn, Amex: nnnn nnnnnn nnnnn
  public String getAsString(FacesContext ctx, UIComponent cmp, Object val)
      throws ConverterException {
    String convVal = null;
    if (val != null) {
      int[] spaces = {3, 7, 11, 99};
      int[] amex = {3, 9, 99};
      String sVal = null;
```

```
        try {
          sVal = (String)val; // The val object should be a String!
          }
        catch (ClassCastException e) {
          throw new ConverterException("CCNumberConverter: Conversion Error");
          }
        int kSpace = 0;
        char[] chars = sVal.toCharArray();
        if (chars.length == 15) spaces = amex;
        convVal = "";
        for (int k = 0; k < chars.length; k++) {
          convVal += chars[k];
          if (spaces[kSpace] == k) {
            convVal += ' ';
            kSpace++;
            }
          }
/*
        System.out.println("CCNumberConverter.getAsString: '"
            + sVal + "' -> '" + convVal + "'");
*/
        }
      return convVal;
      }
  }
```

The getAsObject method simply removes from the input string all the characters that are
not decimal digits. The getAsString method inserts spaces to make the credit-card numbers
more readable.

For example, if you type something such as 12-34. 56Abc78;90123--456 during checkout,
it will be reformatted to 1234 5678 9012 3456 as soon as you press the Check Out button. To
verify that the object is correct, you can use the two println statements that you see commented out in the code. Here are a few examples taken from stdout_*yyyymmdd*.log in Tomcat's
logs folder:

```
CCNumberConverter.getAsObject: 'abc1234 5678 1111x2222' -> '1234567811112222'
CCNumberConverter.getAsString: '1234567811112222' -> '1234 5678 1111 2222'
CCNumberConverter.getAsObject: '  1  23456789  012345' -> '123456789012345'
CCNumberConverter.getAsString: '123456789012345' -> '1234 567890 12345'
```

As you can see, the output of getAsObject, which is also the input of getAsString, is
always stripped of nondigit characters, while the output of getAsString is always formatted
with spaces. Once more, the checking of correctness is a task for a validator, not for the
converter.

Registering the Converter with the Application

You can register the converter with the application by adding the following lines to the `faces-config.xml` file:

```
<converter>
  <converter-id>CCNumberConverter</converter-id>
  <converter-class>eshop.converters.CCNumberConverter</converter-class>
</converter>
```

You can choose any name you like inside the `converter-id` element, while the class in the `converter-class` element must match that of the converter that we described in the previous section.

Using the Converter

Here's how to write the input element for the credit-card number in the `Checkout.jspx` module:

```
<h:inputText id="ccnumber" required="true"
    value="#{shopManager.customer.ccNumber}"
    requiredMessage="Value is required!"
    converter="CCNumberConverter"
    />
```

As you can see, you only need to include the `converter` attribute and assign to it the `converter-id` you've registered in `faces-config.xml`. Alternatively, you also could have nested this element inside the `h:input` component:

```
<f:converter converterId="CCNumberConverter"/>
```

The result would have been the same. This is a permissive converter, because it accepts almost everything without complaining. You could ask yourself whether a 30-character-long string that happens to include 16 digits is a valid credit-card number. We'll leave that up to you.

Using and Creating Validators

How do you ensure that the user of the Eshopf application doesn't succeed in buying a negative number of books? Actually, the application should also reject any attempt of buying zero books. And what about checking the validity of a credit-card number? These are tasks for validators.

JSF features four types of validation mechanisms:

- Built-in validation components

- Application-level validation

- Custom validation components

- Validation methods in backing beans

Let's go through them one by one.

Built-In Validators

JSF provides the following three validation components:

- `f:validateDoubleRange`: It validates that a numeric input is within a given range. It is applicable to values that can be converted to a `double`.

- `f:validateLength`: It validates that the length of the input string is within a given range.

- `f:validateLongRange`: It validates that a numeric input is within a given range. It is applicable to values that can be converted to a `long`.

To use these validation components, you simply nest them inside the `h:input` component you need to validate. For example, to check that only positive quantities can be entered in the Eshopf shopping cart, you modify the `h:inputText` component in `ShoppingCart.jspx` as follows:

```
<h:inputText id="quantity" value="#{item.quantity}" size="2"
    required="true"
    requiredMessage="What? Nothing?"
    converterMessage="An integer, please!"
    validatorMessage="At least one copy!"
    >
  <f:validateLongRange minimum="1"/>
</h:inputText>
```

All three validators also accept the `maximum` attribute to set the upper limit of the range. For example, you can force the user to enter the correct number of credit-card digits by modifying the corresponding `h:inputText` in `Checkout.jspx`:

```
<h:inputText id="ccnumber" required="true"
    value="#{shopManager.customer.ccNumber}"
    converter="CCNumberConverter"
    requiredMessage="Value is required!"
    validatorMessage="Only 15 or 16 digits accepted!"
    >
  <f:validateLength minimum="15" maximum="16"/>
</h:inputText>
```

As the validation takes place after the conversion, the limits of 15 (for American Express) and 16 (for all other credit cards) are applied to the user's input after removing all nondigit characters.

Application-Level Validation

Application-level validation makes sense if you need to validate application logic, as opposed to validating formal correctness of individual fields. For example, before accepting an order, you might like to check that your bank has not blacklisted the credit-card number. Let's see how it works.

In the Eshopf application, when the user clicks on the Check Out button after entering his name and credit-card data, the checkOut method of shopManager is executed, as shown in the following line taken from Checkout.jspx:

```
<h:commandButton value="Check Out" action="#{shopManager.checkOut}"/>
```

The method is as follows:

```
public String checkOut() {
  orderId = dataManager.insertOrder(customer, shoppingCart);
  if (orderId != 0) {
    customer = null;
    shoppingCart.clear();
    }
  return "orderConfirmation";
  }
```

The dataManager.insertOrder method saves the order information in the database. If it fails, the dataManager will log a message to a Tomcat log file (i.e., logs\stdout_*yyyymmdd*.log) and return zero. If the database update succeeds, the value returned will be a unique orderId. In a real-world application, rather than 0, you would return error information to be passed on to the user. The checkOut method returns an outcome that tells JSF what page should be displayed next.

If you want to do some application-level validation, you could insert its logic at the beginning of the checkOut method and make the database update and the method outcome dependent on the validation result. In case of validation failure, you could also send a message to the user, as shown in the following few lines:

```
FacesContext ctxt = FacesContext.getCurrentInstance();
FacesMessage mess = new FacesMessage();
mess.setSeverity(FacesMessage.SEVERITY_ERROR);
mess.setSummary("This is the summary text");
mess.setDetail("This is the detail text");
ctxt.addMessage(null, mess);
```

The message created in this way is a global message, not bound to any particular component, and you can display it with the following JSF component:

```
<h:messages globalOnly="true" styleClass="error"/>
```

If you want to create a message for a particular component, you would need to replace the null argument of ctxt.addMessage with the clientId of the component. The clientId is a string containing all the IDs necessary to identify a particular component. For example, if you have <h:inputText id="it"...> inside <h:form id="fm"...>, the clientId of the input component is fm:it. We recommend that you don't use this option, because it forces you to hard-code the clientId in your Java method.

Custom Validators

In the "Using and Creating Converters" section of this chapter, we explained how to implement a custom converter. To implement a custom validator, you follow an almost identical process:

- Create an implementation of the interface javax.faces.validator.Validator that overrides the validate method.

- Register the validator in faces-config.xml.

- Within your JSF application, refer to the validator in an attribute or a component.

Suppose you want to ensure that the credit-card expiry date provided by the user during checkout is in the form MM/YY and that the card has not expired. Listing 5-11 shows the validator code.

Listing 5-11. *CCExpiryValidator.java*

```
package eshop.validators;
import javax.faces.validator.Validator;
import javax.faces.context.FacesContext;
import javax.faces.component.UIComponent;
import javax.faces.application.FacesMessage;
import javax.faces.validator.ValidatorException;
import java.util.GregorianCalendar;
import java.util.Calendar;

public class CCExpiryValidator implements Validator {
  public CCExpiryValidator() {
    }
  public void validate(FacesContext cntx, UIComponent cmp, Object val) {
    String messS = null;
    String[] fields = ((String)val).split("/", 3);
    if (fields.length != 2) {
      messS = "Expected MM/YY!";
      }
    else {
      int month = 0;
      int year = 0;
      try {
        month = Integer.parseInt(fields[0]);
        year = Integer.parseInt(fields[1]);
        }
      catch (NumberFormatException e) {
        }
```

```
        if (month <= 0  ||  month > 12) {
          messS = "Month " + fields[0] + " not valid!";
          }
        else if (year < 0  ||  year > 99) {
          messS = "Year " + fields[1] + " not valid!";
          }
        else {
          GregorianCalendar cal = new GregorianCalendar();
          int thisMonth = cal.get(Calendar.MONTH) + 1;
          int thisYear = cal.get(Calendar.YEAR) - 2000;
          if (year < thisYear  ||  year == thisYear && month < thisMonth) {
            messS = "Credit card expired!";
            }
          }
        }
    if (messS != null) {
      FacesMessage mess = new FacesMessage(
          FacesMessage.SEVERITY_ERROR, messS, messS);
      throw new ValidatorException(mess);
      }
    }
  }
```

To register the validator with the application, you only need to add the following lines to faces-config.xml—for example, immediately below the registration of the converter:

```
<validator>
  <validator-id>CCExpiryValidator</validator-id>
  <validator-class>eshop.validators.CCExpiryValidator</validator-class>
</validator>
```

If you modify the h:inputText component used in Checkout.jspx for the credit-card expiry date, as follows:

```
<h:inputText id="ccexpiry" required="true"
    value="#{shopManager.customer.ccExpiryDate}"
    requiredMessage="Value is required!"
    >
  <f:validator validatorId="CCExpiryValidator"/>
</h:inputText>
```

you'll be rewarded with error messages like those shown in Figure 5-3.

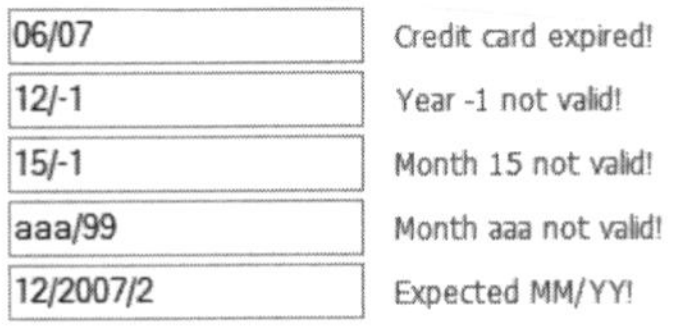

06/07	Credit card expired!
12/-1	Year -1 not valid!
15/-1	Month 15 not valid!
aaa/99	Month aaa not valid!
12/2007/2	Expected MM/YY!

Figure 5-3. *Expiry-date validation in Checkout.jspx*

Validation Methods in Backing Beans

Instead of creating a new class as described in the previous section, you can add a method to a backing bean. In this case, you could do the following:

- Copy the `validate` method to `shopManager.java` inside the class `ShopManager`, as shown in Listing 5-11, and rename it `validateCCExpiry`.

- Copy the imports of `FacesContext`, `UIComponent`, `FacesMessage`, `GregorianCalendar`, and `Calendar` to the beginning of `shopManager.java`.

- Replace the line that throws the `ValidatorException` with `cntx.addMessage(cmp.getClientId(ctxt), mess);`.

That's it! To use this validator instead of the previous one, modify the `h:inputText` in `Checkout.jspx` as follows:

```
<h:inputText id="ccexpiry" required="true"
    value="#{shopManager.customer.ccExpiryDate}"
    validator="#{shopManager.validateCCExpiry}"
    requiredMessage="Value is required!"
    />
```

Creating Custom Components

The functionality of a component is centered on converting a user's inputs (i.e., the HTTP request parameters) to component values (via the `decode` method during Apply Request Values) and converting component values back to HTML (via the `encode` method during Render Response).

When you design a JSF component, you can choose to move encoding and decoding to a separate renderer class. The advantage of that approach is that you can develop more than one renderer for the same component, each with a different representation in HTML. You will then have the same behavior associated with different ways of reading data from the request and writing it to the response.

In general, considering that JSF 1.2 is open source, you might consider modifying an existing component instead of developing a new one, or perhaps, thanks to the separation of components and renderers, modifying an existing renderer.

The root class of all JSF components is the abstract `javax.faces.component.UIComponent`, and the root class of all renderers is `javax.faces.render.Renderer`. To develop a component, though, you're *always* better off if you extend an existing component or, at the very least, the `UIComponentBase` class, which provides default implementations of all abstract methods of `UIComponent`. In this way, you only must develop code for the methods that you need to override. The same goes with the renderer.

To complete the picture of what you need to do in order to have your custom component, you also need to create a custom tag to use it with JSP. The root class of all tag classes is `javax.faces.webapp.UIComponentELTag`. (Up to JSF 1.1, it was `UIComponentTag`, which has now been deprecated.)

In summary, to develop a custom component, you need to go through the following steps, although not necessarily in this order:

- Create a component class that subclasses `UIComponent` by extending an existing component.

- Register the component in `faces-config.xml`.

- Create a renderer class that subclasses `Renderer` and overrides the methods for encoding and decoding.

- Register the renderer in `faces-config.xml`.

- Create a custom tag that subclasses `UIComponentELTag`.

- Create a TLD for the custom tag.

One last word about components and renderers: unless you really think that you'll reuse the same component for different applications, you'll make your life much easier if you keep the renderer inside the component. We'll first show you what to do when they're separate, and then we'll tell you how to keep them together.

We'll show you how to develop a component that combines the functionality of all three standard components needed for accepting a user's input: a label explaining what is expected, the text field to accept the input, and a message to report input errors. In other words, we'll show you how to replace the following JSF code:

```
<h:outputText value="Contact Name"/>
<h:inputText id="name" required="true"
    value="#{shopManager.customer.contactName}"
    requiredMessage="Value is required!"
    />
<h:message for="name" styleClass="error"/>
```

with this custom component:

```
<eshop:inputEntry label="Contact Name" required="true"
    value="#{shopManager.contactName}"
    errorStyleClass="error" requiredMessage="Value is required!"
    />
```

We'll also show you how this new `eshop:inputEntry` component prints an asterisk beside the label if `required="true"`.

Component

The component is actually the easiest part. Let's go through the methods one by one (see Listing 5-12).

Listing 5-12. *InputEntryComponent.java*

```
01: package eshop.components;
02: import javax.faces.component.UIInput;
03: import javax.faces.context.FacesContext;
04:
05: public class InputEntryComponent extends UIInput {
```

```
06:    private String label;
07:    public InputEntryComponent(){
08:      this.setRendererType("eshop.inputEntry");
09:      }
10:    public String getLabel() {
11:      return label;
12:      }
13:    public void setLabel(String label) {
14:      this.label = label;
15:      }
16:
17:    // Overridden methods
18:    public String getFamily() {
19:      return "eshop.inputEntry";
20:      }
21:    public void restoreState(FacesContext ctxt, Object state) {
22:      Object val[] = (Object[])state;
23:      super.restoreState(ctxt, val[0]);
24:      label = (String)val[1];
25:      }
26:    public Object saveState(FacesContext ctxt) {
27:      Object val[] = new Object[2];
28:      val[0] = super.saveState(ctxt);
29:      val[1] = label;
30:      return ((Object)val);
31:      }
32:    }
```

InputEntryComponent is the component initialization. Its only task is to register with the component the string that identifies the renderer. The only property of the component defined in this file is label. This is because you're extending UIInput, which takes care of defining everything that has to do with the input field.

You use the getFamily method to find all the renderers associated with this component. We're planning to create only one renderer, but it's still appropriate to define a family rather than inherit the family of UIInput, because you couldn't use UIInput's renderers with InputEntryComponent.

The state of the component consists of the state of UIInput plus the label property. Therefore, you define its state as an array of two objects. The saveState method forms the array and returns it, so that JSF can save it. The restoreState method receives the state, unpacks it, and stores it locally. Notice how the operations that have to do with UIInput are always delegated to it.

Now that you have the component, you have to register it. You do this by inserting the following lines into faces-config.xml:

```
<component>
  <component-type>eshop.inputEntry</component-type>
  <component-class>eshop.components.InputEntryComponent</component-class>
</component>
```

Renderer

The renderer is a bit trickier than the component. To implement it, you define a class that extends javax.faces.render.Renderer. Start by looking at the three methods that you need to override (see Listing 5-13).

Listing 5-13. *InputEntryRenderer.java—Overridden Methods*

```
56: public void decode(FacesContext ctxt, UIComponent cmp) {
57:    InputEntryComponent ieCmp = (InputEntryComponent)cmp;
58:    Map requestMap = ctxt.getExternalContext().getRequestParameterMap();
59:    String clientId = cmp.getClientId(ctxt);
60:    String val = (String)requestMap.get(clientId);
61:    ((UIInput)ieCmp).setSubmittedValue(val);
62:    }
63: public void encodeBegin(FacesContext ctxt, UIComponent cmp)
64:       throws IOException {
65:    InputEntryComponent ieCmp = (InputEntryComponent)cmp;
66:    ResponseWriter respWr = ctxt.getResponseWriter();
67:    encodeLabel(respWr, ieCmp);
68:    encodeInput(respWr, ieCmp);
69:    encodeMessage(ctxt, respWr, ieCmp);
70:    respWr.flush();
71:    }
72: public Object getConvertedValue(FacesContext ctxt, UIComponent cmp,
73:       Object subVal) throws ConverterException {
74:    Object convVal = null;
75:    ValueExpression valExpr = cmp.getValueExpression("value");
76:    if (valExpr != null) {
77:      Class valType = valExpr.getType(ctxt.getELContext());
78:      if (valType != null) {
79:        convVal = subVal;
80:        if (!valType.equals(Object.class) && !valType.equals(String.class)) {
81:          Converter converter = ((UIInput)cmp).getConverter();
82:          converter =  ctxt.getApplication().createConverter(valType);
83:          if (converter != null ) {
84:            convVal = converter.getAsObject(ctxt, cmp, (String)subVal);
85:            }
86:          }
87:        }
88:      }
89:    return convVal;
90:    }
```

As we said before, the only property that you add to UIInput is label, which the user cannot modify. Therefore, not surprisingly, you only need to decode the input field. In line 57, you typecast the component object to InputEntryComponent, so that you can work with it more comfortably. In line 58, you get the map of the input parameters, and in line 59, you get from the FacesContext the clientId of the component, so that in line 60, you can finally get the input string as typed by the user. After that, you only need to save the input string as a submitted value. Remember that this method is executed during Apply Request Values (phase 2).

The encoding process requires more work than the decoding process, because you have to send to the HTTP response all three components that were combined to form InputEntryComponent. This takes place during Render Response (phase 9). In line 66 of the encodeBegin method, you get the response writer from the FacesContext. After executing the functions that write the three subcomponents, you flush the output, and you're done.

Listing 5-14 shows the method to encode the label. It opens the HTML label element with the startElement method, writes the label with a plain write method, writes an asterisk—but only if the component is required—and closes the label element with the endElement method. The result is something like <label>Contact Name*</label>.

Listing 5-14. *InputEntryRenderer.java—EncodeLabel*

```
private void encodeLabel(ResponseWriter respWr, InputEntryComponent cmp)
    throws IOException {
  respWr.startElement("label", cmp);
  respWr.write(cmp.getLabel());
  if (cmp.isRequired()) {
    respWr.write("*");
    }
  respWr.endElement("label");
  }
```

Listing 5-15 shows the method to encode the input field. It opens the HTML input element, adds the attributes with the writeAttribute method, and closes the element. The three parameters of writeAttribute are the name and value of the HTML attribute and the name of the component property. The result is something like the following element:

```
<input type="text" id="form:nameEntry" name="form:nameEntry" value="" />
```

Listing 5-15. *InputEntryRenderer.java—EncodeInput*

```
private void encodeInput(ResponseWriter respWr, InputEntryComponent cmp)
    throws IOException {
  FacesContext ctxt = FacesContext.getCurrentInstance();
  respWr.startElement("input", cmp);
  respWr.writeAttribute("type", "text", "type");
  respWr.writeAttribute("id", cmp.getClientId(ctxt), "id");
  respWr.writeAttribute("name", cmp.getClientId(ctxt), "name");
  if(cmp.getValue() != null) {
    respWr.writeAttribute("value", cmp.getValue().toString(), "value");
    }
  respWr.endElement("input");
  }
```

Listing 5-16 shows the method to encode the error message. It gets the list of all messages queued for the component but only displays the first one. If you want to display them all, you just need to replace the if keyword with a while. To display the message, the method opens the HTML span element, adds the class attribute to show the message with the correct style, displays the message itself, and closes the element. The result is something like the following element:

```
<span class="error">Value is required!</span>
```

Listing 5-16. *InputEntryRenderer.java—EncodeMessage*

```java
private void encodeMessage(FacesContext ctxt, ResponseWriter respWr,
    InputEntryComponent cmp) throws IOException {
  Iterator it = ctxt.getMessages(cmp.getClientId(ctxt));
  // Notice: an if instead of a while
  if (it.hasNext()){
    FacesMessage mess = (FacesMessage)it.next();
    if (!cmp.isValid()) {
      String errorStyleClass =
          (String)cmp.getAttributes().get("errorStyleClass");
      respWr.startElement("span", cmp);
      respWr.writeAttribute("class", errorStyleClass, "class");
      respWr.write(mess.getDetail());
      respWr.endElement("span");
    }
  }
}
```

To register the renderer, insert the following lines into faces-config.xml:

```xml
<render-kit>
  <renderer>
    <component-family>eshop.inputEntry</component-family>
    <renderer-type>eshop.inputEntry</renderer-type>
    <renderer-class>eshop.renderers.InputEntryRenderer</renderer-class>
  </renderer>
</render-kit>
```

Tag

The custom component is done, but to use it with JSP, you need to define a corresponding custom tag. We already explained how to define custom libraries in Chapter 2. Therefore, we won't spend too many words here on the overall process. Listing 5-17 shows the Java class that implements the tag handler.

Listing 5-17. *InputEntryTag.java*

```java
package eshop.tags;
import javax.el.ValueExpression;
import javax.faces.component.UIComponent;
import javax.faces.webapp.UIComponentELTag;
```

```java
public class InputEntryTag extends UIComponentELTag {
  private ValueExpression  errorStyleClass;
  private ValueExpression  label;
  private ValueExpression  required;
  private ValueExpression  requiredMessage;
  private ValueExpression  value;

  // Setters
  public void setErrorStyleClass(ValueExpression errorStyleClass) {
    this.errorStyleClass = errorStyleClass;
    }
  public void setLabel(ValueExpression label) {
    this.label = label;
    }
  public void setRequired(ValueExpression required) {
    this.required = required;
    }
  public void setRequiredMessage(ValueExpression requiredMessage) {
    this.requiredMessage = requiredMessage;
    }
  public void setValue(ValueExpression value) {
    this.value = value;
    }

  // Overridden methods
  public String getComponentType() {
    return "eshop.inputEntry";
    }
  public String getRendererType() {
    return "eshop.inputEntry";
    }
  protected void setProperties(UIComponent cmp) {
    super.setProperties(cmp);
    if (errorStyleClass != null) {
      cmp.setValueExpression("errorStyleClass", errorStyleClass);
      }
    if (label != null) {
      cmp.setValueExpression("label", label);
      }
    if (required != null) {
      cmp.setValueExpression("required", required);
      }
    if (requiredMessage != null) {
      cmp.setValueExpression("requiredMessage", requiredMessage);
      }
```

```
      if (value != null) {
        cmp.setValueExpression("value", value);
        }
      }
    public void release() {
      super.release();
      errorStyleClass = null;
      label = null;
      requiredMessage = null;
      value = null;
      required = null;
      }
   }
```

As you can see, you define a property for each attribute supported by the tag, but not for the id attribute. The reason is that UIComponentELTag already defines it. Notice that you only have setter methods, without the corresponding getters. This is because you never need the get methods. The setProperties method copies the attribute values from the tag to the component, and the release method cleans up what is no longer needed.

Before you can use the custom tag in JSP, you still need to create a TLD to be placed in WEB-INF\tlds\. See Listing 5-18.

Listing 5-18. *eshop.tld*

```
01: <?xml version="1.0" encoding="ISO-8859-1"?>
02: <taglib xmlns="http://java.sun.com/xml/ns/javaee"
03:     xmlns:xsi="http://www.w3.org/2001/XMLSchema-instance"
04:     xsi:schemaLocation="http://java.sun.com/xml/ns/javaee ➥
http://java.sun.com/xml/ns/j2ee/web-jsptaglibrary_2_1.xsd"
05:     version="2.1">
06:   <description>Eshopf Custom Tags</description>
07:   <tlib-version>1.0</tlib-version>
08:   <short-name>eshop</short-name>
09:   <tag>
10:     <display-name>inputEntry</display-name>
11:     <name>inputEntry</name>
12:     <tag-class>eshop.tags.InputEntryTag</tag-class>
13:     <attribute>
14:       <name>id</name>
15:       <required>false</required>
16:       <rtexprvalue>true</rtexprvalue>
17:     </attribute>
18:     <attribute>
19:       <name>value</name>
20:       <required>false</required>
21:       <deferred-value><type>java.lang.Object</type></deferred-value>
22:     </attribute>
23:     <attribute>
```

```
24:        <name>required</name>
25:        <required>false</required>
26:        <deferred-value><type>boolean</type></deferred-value>
27:      </attribute>
28:      <attribute>
29:        <name>label</name>
30:        <required>false</required>
31:        <deferred-value><type>java.lang.String</type></deferred-value>
32:      </attribute>
33:      <attribute>
34:        <name>errorStyleClass</name>
35:        <required>false</required>
36:        <deferred-value><type>java.lang.String</type></deferred-value>
37:      </attribute>
38:      <attribute>
39:        <name>requiredMessage</name>
40:        <required>false</required>
41:        <deferred-value><type>java.lang.String</type></deferred-value>
42:      </attribute>
43:    </tag>
44:  </taglib>
```

In lines 10 to 12, you define the eshop:inputEntry tag and associate it with the tag handler. The eshop.tags.InputEntryTag string means that you have to place InputEntryTag.class in the folder WEB-INF\classes\eshop\tags\. Below that, you define all attributes and set them to accept the JSF expressions as values, with the exception of id.

With this, you're ready to use the new JSF UI component h:inputEntry. You only need to add the following eshop namespace declaration to the jsp:root element at the beginning of the JSP document:

```
xmlns:eshop="urn:jsptld:/WEB-INF/tlds/eshop.tld"
```

The result will look like the field shown in Figure 5-4.

Contact Name*[   ]Value is required!

Figure 5-4. *Checkout.jspx—eshop:inputEntry*

The disadvantage of the new component compared to separate label, input, and message fields is that it isn't possible to align the input fields vertically. You could add an attribute to the tag to specify the space available for the label, but we'll leave that up to you.

Now that you're done, you might ask, "Why does eshop:inputEntry only support a handful of attributes, while h:inputText supports 40?" That's a good point. We could have added further attributes, such as the size of the input field, which h:inputText passes on to HTML transparently, but our purpose was to be able to replace with a single component the three fields as they are used in Eshopf. More attributes than strictly necessary would have only used up space without adding anything to what you can learn from the example.

Inline Renderer

It's possible to include the rendering functionality inside the component class, so that the component effectively renders itself. As we mentioned before, unless you plan to use more than one renderer with the same component, you might like not to bother with a separate renderer.

To make eshop:inputEntry self-rendering, you need to do the following:

1. Move the methods of InputEntryRenderer.java to InputEntryComponent.java. You'll need to make some cosmetic changes that we'll explain in a moment. You can delete the renderer file.

2. Add the encodeEnd method to InputEntryComponent.java.

3. Return null in the getRendererType method of InputEntryTag.java.

4. Remove the registration of the renderer from faces-config.xml.

The UIInput class, which you extend to make the component, supports the three methods decode, encodeBegin, and getConvertedValue that you used in the separate renderer, but without the UIComponent parameter. It makes a lot of sense, because the component object is directly accessible with the keyword this.

When you remove the cmp parameter from the three methods, you should also remove this line:

```
InputEntryComponent ieCmp = (InputEntryComponent)cmp;
```

from decode and encodeBegin, because it has become useless. Then, make a global replace of cmp and ieCmp with this.

You need the encodeEnd method to override the method in UIComponentBase, which throws a NullPointerException. In fact, you don't need to do anything in encodeEnd; you can just write an empty method:

```
public void encodeEnd(FacesContext context) throws IOException { }
```

Note that you only need this method when a component renders itself, not when it uses a separate renderer class.

In InputEntryTag.java, the getRendererType method returns "eshop.inputEntry". If the method is to use its internal rendering methods, getRendererType has to return null. Finally, remove the seven lines of the render-kit element from faces-config.xml.

web.xml

Listing 5-19 shows the file WEB-INF\web.xml for the application Eshopf.

Listing 5-19. *web.xml*

```
<?xml version="1.0" encoding="ISO-8859-1"?>
<web-app version="2.5" xmlns="http://java.sun.com/xml/ns/j2ee"
  xmlns:xsi="http://www.w3.org/2001/XMLSchema-instance"
```

```
  xsi:schemaLocation="http://java.sun.com/xml/ns/j2ee ➥
http://java.sun.com/xml/ns/j2ee/web-app_2_5.xsd">
  <display-name>eshop</display-name>
  <context-param>
    <param-name>javax.faces.DEFAULT_SUFFIX</param-name>
    <param-value>.jspx</param-value>
  </context-param>
  <servlet>
    <servlet-name>Faces Servlet</servlet-name>
    <servlet-class>javax.faces.webapp.FacesServlet</servlet-class>
    <load-on-startup>1</load-on-startup>
  </servlet>
  <servlet-mapping>
    <servlet-name>Faces Servlet</servlet-name>
    <url-pattern>*.jsf</url-pattern>
  </servlet-mapping>
  <login-config>
    <auth-method>BASIC</auth-method>
  </login-config>
  <resource-ref>
    <res-ref-name>jdbc/mysql</res-ref-name>
    <res-type>javax.sql.DataSource</res-type>
    <res-auth>Container</res-auth>
  </resource-ref>
</web-app>
```

The `context-parameter` element sets the file extension to be `jspx`, which is the extension of JSP documents—that is, JSP modules in XML format, as those of Eshopf. If you had left out this element, the extension would have been `jsp`, which is the extension of JSP pages.

The servlet element points to the class of the standard JSF servlet. By setting the element `servlet-mapping` to `*.jsf`, you specify that the JSP documents are to be accessed with that extension instead of their real extension, which is `jspx`. For example, when you select a book category in Eshopf, the URL displayed in the browser is

```
http://localhost:8080/eshopf/jsp/ListBooks.jsf
```

while the JSP document is actually called `ListBooks.jspx`. This is called *extension mapping*.

The last element, `resource-ref`, states that the resource named `jdbc/mysql` is of type `DataSource`, and that Tomcat does its authentication. Tomcat provides a Java Naming and Directory Interface (JNDI) `InitialContext` for each application. This means that once you've registered a resource in `web.xml`, you can provide in a separate context file all the information necessary to link it to your server environment. For Eshopf, the information is as follows:

```
<Context debug="5" reloadable="true" crossContext="true">
  <Resource name="jdbc/mysql" auth="Container"
    type="javax.sql.DataSource" username="root" password=""
    driverClassName="com.mysql.jdbc.Driver"
    url="jdbc:mysql://localhost:3306/shop" maxActive="8" maxIdle="4"/>
  </Context>
```

As you can see, the resource attributes url, username, and password specify the Eshop*
database and how to access it. The context file must be named context.xml and placed in the
META-INF folder of your application directory.

faces-config.xml

We've already explained all the elements of this file when we talked about the Shop Manager
(<managed-bean> and <navigation-rule>) and when registering a converter (<converter>), a
validator (<validator>), a component (<component>), and a renderer (<render-kit>). We need
to add that it should start with this start tag:

```
<?xml version="1.0" encoding="ISO-8859-1"?>
<faces-config version="1.2" xmlns="http://java.sun.com/xml/ns/javaee"
    xmlns:xi="http://www.w3.org/2001/XInclude"
    xmlns:xsi="http://www.w3.org/2001/XMLSchema-instance"
    xsi:schemaLocation="http://java.sun.com/xml/ns/javaee ➥
http://java.sun.com/xml/ns/javaee/web-facesconfig_1_2.xsd">
```

and end with the corresponding end tag:

```
</faces-config>
```

Table 5-1 lists the navigation cases.

Table 5-1. *Eshopf Navigation Rules*

from-outcome	to-view-id	redirect
checkOut	/jsp/Checkout.jspx	Yes
listBooks	/jsp/ListBooks.jspx	Yes
orderConfirmation	/jsp/OrderConfirmation.jspx	No
showBook	/jsp/BookDetails.jspx	Yes
showCart	/jsp/ShoppingCart.jspx	Yes

Summary

In this chapter, we explained the JSF life cycle and described how JSF works in general. We
then described how we've used JSF to reimplement the user interface of Eshopf, the online
bookshop application that we introduced in Chapter 2. We showed you how to work with the
standard JSF components, and then we explained how to create your own converters, validators, and components. Finally, we briefly described how to tie together the application with
web.xml, faces-config.xml, and context.xml.

You should now be able to write your own application, using this chapter, the code of
Eshopf, and the additional information presented in Appendix F as references.

In the next chapter, we'll talk about XML, how to validate XML documents, and how to
use XML to exchange messages between applications.

CHAPTER 6

■■■

Communicating with XML

HTML is probably the first markup language most of us came into contact with. It's a great language, but it's not without its problems.

For example, HTML mixes content data with the way in which the information is presented, thereby making it difficult to present the same data in different ways and to standardize presentations across multiple sets of data. CSS significantly reduces this problem but doesn't eliminate it 100%, and it also forces you to learn yet another language.

Another problem, partly due to the way in which HTML is defined, is that the browsers are very forgiving about inconsistently written pages. In many cases, they're able to render pages with unquoted attribute values and tags that aren't closed properly. This encourages sloppiness in coding and wastes computer resources.

XML (whose standard is available at `http://www.w3.org/TR/xml`) lets you organize information into a tree-like structure in which each item of information represents a leaf. Its power and flexibility lies in the idea of defining its syntax and a mechanism for defining tags. This makes it possible for you to define your own markup language tailored for the type of information you're dealing with. This also lets you define XHTML, a version of HTML clean of inconsistencies.

We titled this chapter "Communicating with XML" because XML is the perfect vehicle for exchanging structured information. In fact, XML's purpose is precisely to describe information.

We've introduced XML starting from HTML, because you're familiar with HTML and they're both markup languages. However, the usefulness of XML goes well beyond providing a better syntax for HTML. The great advantage of using XML in preference to proprietary formats whenever information needs to be structured is that standardized parsers make the manipulation of XML documents easy. In Chapter 2, we showed you an example of how to parse an XML document in JSP with XML custom tags and XPath.

Many organizations, both private and public, have turned to XML to standardize the representation of information in their respective areas. Some initiatives are ambitious and still in their initial stages, such as the development of a Universal Business Language (UBL) to generate XML-based standards of business documents such as purchase orders and invoices. Other initiatives, such as the Real Estate Transaction Markup Language (RETML) to standardize the encoding of real-estate transactions, have already gone through years of refinements and associated tool development and are being adopted. Still other initiatives, such as the Mind Reading Markup Language (MRML), might just serve the purpose of having fun (see `http://ifaq.wap.org/computers/mrml.html`). The Organization for the Advancement of Structured Information Standards (OASIS), a not-for-profit consortium that promotes the establishment of open standards for the exchange of information, lists more than 600 XML applications and initiatives in `http://xml.coverpages.org/xmlApplications.html`.

The XML Document

To explain XML, we'll start by giving you a simple example that will accompany us throughout this chapter. For this purpose, we'll use a slightly modified portion of the `starfleet.xml` file that we showed you in Listing 2-17 of Chapter 2 (see Listing 6-1).

Listing 6-1. *enterprises.xml*

```
<?xml version="1.0" encoding="ISO-8859-1"?>
<starfleet>
  <title>The two most famous starships in the fleet</title>
  <starship name="USS Enterprise" sn="NCC-1701">
    <class name="Constitution"/>
    <captain>James Tiberius Kirk</captain>
    </starship>
  <starship name="USS Enterprise" sn="NCC-1701-D">
    <class name="Galaxy"/>
    <captain>Jean-Luc Picard</captain>
    </starship>
  </starfleet>
```

The first line defines the standard and the character set used in the document. The tags are always closed, either with an end tag when they have a body (e.g., `<title>...</title>`) or with a slash if they're empty (e.g., `<class .../>`). There can be repeated tags (e.g., starship), and the attribute names are not unique (e.g., name).

As you can see, the tags reflect the logical structure of the data, although there are certainly many ways of structuring the same information. Each tag identifies an *element node* labeled with a name (e.g., starfleet, `title`, and `class`, also called an *element type*), often characterized by *attributes* that consist of a *name* and a *value* (e.g., sn="NCC-1701"), and possibly containing *child nodes* (e.g., captain inside starship, also called *subelements*).

XML documents can also contain processing instructions for the applications that handle them (enclosed between `<?` and `?>`), comments (enclosed between `<!--` and `-->`), and document type declarations (more about that later). Notice that enterprises.xml doesn't provide any information concerning how the data it contains might be presented.

XML relies on the less-than sign to identify the tags. Therefore, if you want to use it for other purposes, you have to escape it by writing the four characters < instead. To escape larger blocks of text, you can use the CDATA section, as in the following example:

```
<![CDATA[<aTag>The tag's body</aTag>]]>
```

Looking at enterprises.xml, you might ask yourself why sn is an attribute of starship, while captain is a child element. Couldn't you make captain an attribute, as in the following example?

```
<starship name="USS Enterprise" sn="NCC-1701" captain="Jean-Luc Picard">
```

Yes, you could. It all depends on what you think you might like to do with the element in the future. With `captain` defined as an element, you can define attributes for it, such as its birth date. This wouldn't be possible if you had defined `captain` as an attribute. And the same applies to the `class` element. You could also replace the `starship` attributes `name` and `sn` with two children elements, but how much sense would it make?

We have to make one last consideration about empty vs. bodied elements. By defining the captain's name as the body of the element, as in:

```
<captain>Jean-Luc Picard</captain>
```

you make it impossible for it to have children elements. Alternatively, you could have defined this:

```
<captain name="Jean-Luc Picard"></captain>
```

perhaps shortened, as in:

```
<captain name="Jean-Luc Picard"/>
```

Defining Your Own XML Documents

The usefulness of being able to use XML tags tailored to your needs is greatly expanded by the possibility of formally specifying them in a separate document. This enables you to verify the validity of the XML documents and also to communicate their structure to others. Without a specification in a standardized format, you would have to describe your document structure in plain language or via examples. It wouldn't be the most efficient way, and it certainly wouldn't be good enough for automatic validation. The two most widely used methods to specify document structures are XML DTDs and XML schemas.

XML DTDs

DTDs are better known than XML schemas, which have been developed more recently. They are also easier to understand. DTDs were originally developed for the XML predecessor, Standard Generalized Markup Language (SGML), and they have a very compact syntax. Listing 6-2 shows how a DTD for `enterprises.xml` would look.

Listing 6-2. *starfleet.dtd*

```
01: <!ELEMENT starfleet (title,starship*)>
02: <!ELEMENT title (#PCDATA)>
03: <!ELEMENT starship (class,captain)>
04: <!ATTLIST
05:     starship name CDATA #REQUIRED
06:     sn CDATA #REQUIRED>
07: <!ELEMENT class EMPTY>
08: <!ATTLIST class name CDATA #REQUIRED>
09: <!ELEMENT captain (#PCDATA)>
```

Line 1 defines the `starfleet` element as consisting of one `title` element and an undefined number of `starship` elements. Replacing the asterisk with a plus sign would require `starship` to occur at least once, and a question mark would mean zero or one starships. If you replaced `starship` with (`starship|shuttle`), it would mean that you could have a mix of `starship` and `shuttle` elements following the `title` (just as an example, because you haven't defined `shuttle`).

Line 2 specifies `title` to be a string of characters (the PC of PCDATA stands for parsed character). Line 7 shows how to specify that an element not be allowed to have a body. To complete the description of how to define elements, we only need to add that if you replaced EMPTY with ANY, it would mean that the element could contain any type of data.

Lines 4–6 specify the attributes for `starship`. The general format of an attribute list declaration is as follows:

```
<!ATTLIST elementName attributeName attributeType defaultValue>
```

where *attributeType* can have a dozen possible values, including CDATA (to indicate character data), an enumeration of all strings allowed (enclosed in parentheses and with bars as separators, as in (`left|right|center`)), ID (to indicate a unique identifier), and IDREF (the ID of another element). The *defaultValue* can be a quoted value (e.g., "0" or "a string"), the keyword #REQUIRED (to indicate that it's mandatory), the keyword #IMPLIED (to indicate that it can be omitted), or the keyword #FIXED followed by a value (to force the attribute to have that value).

XML Schemas

The most significant difference from DTDs is that the schemas are in XML syntax themselves. This makes the schemas more extensible and flexible than DTDs. Furthermore, being in XML format themselves, you can store, handle, and style schemas like any other XML document. W3C describes standardized XML schemas in three documents: http://www.w3.org/TR/xmlschema-0/ (a primer to get you started), http://www.w3.org/TR/xmlschema-1/ (about structures), and http://www.w3.org/TR/xmlschema-2/ (about data types). Unfortunately, schemas are complicated, and the standards aren't trivial to read and understand.

Let's see the XML schema for `enterprises.xml` (see Listing 6-3).

Listing 6-3. *starfleet.xsd*

```
01: <?xml version="1.0" encoding="ISO-8859-1"?>
02: <xsd:schema xmlns:xsd="http://www.w3.org/2001/XMLSchema">
03:   <xsd:annotation>
04:     <xsd:documentation xml:lang="en">
05:       Schema for Starfleet
06:     </xsd:documentation>
07:   </xsd:annotation>
08:   <xsd:element name="starfleet">
09:     <xsd:complexType>
10:       <xsd:sequence>
11:         <xsd:element name="title" type="xsd:string" maxOccurs="1"/>
12:         <xsd:element name="starship" type="ShipType" maxOccurs="unbounded"/>
```

```
13:        </xsd:sequence>
14:      </xsd:complexType>
15:    </xsd:element>
16:   <xsd:complexType name="ShipType">
17:    <xsd:all>
18:      <xsd:element name="class" type="ClassType" minOccurs="1"/>
19:      <xsd:element name="captain" type="xsd:string" minOccurs="1"/>
20:    </xsd:all>
21:    <xsd:attribute name="name" type="xsd:string" use="required"/>
22:    <xsd:attribute name="sn" type="xsd:string" use="required"/>
23:   </xsd:complexType>
24:   <xsd:complexType name="ClassType">
25:    <xsd:attribute name="name" type="xsd:string" use="required"/>
26:   </xsd:complexType>
27:  </xsd:schema>
```

Line 2 establishes that this schema conforms to the standard XML schema. Lines 3-7 are essentially a comment.

Lines 8-15 specify the starfleet element, which is of a complex type, as defined in Line 9. This means that starfleet can have attributes and/or can contain other elements. Line 10 tells you in which way starfleet is complex: it contains a sequence of elements. Elements in xsd:sequence must appear in the order in which they are specified (in this case, title followed by starship).

Line 11 specifies that title can be of type xsd:string, which is a primitive type hard-coded in the standard XML Schema. Line 11 also tells you that there can be maximum one title per starfleet. It is also possible to define minOccurs, and the default for both minOccurs and maxOccurs is 1. This means that by omitting minOccurs, you make title mandatory.

Line 12 declares that the starship element is of type ShipType, which is defined some-where else in starfleet.xsd. This is an alternative to defining the type of an element inside its body, as we did with the starfleet element. Naming a type lets you use it for several element definitions and as a base for more complex types. However, we've only extracted the type specification from the body of starship to make the code more readable. maxOccurs="unbounded" states that there can be as many starships in starfleet as you need.

Lines 16-23 define the type of the starship element. It's a complex type, but it's different from that of starfleet. The xsd:all group means that there can only be up to one element each of all those listed, in any order. This would normally mean that each starship could be empty or contain a class, a captain, or both as children. However, we want to make class and captain mandatory. To achieve this result, we specified the attribute minOccurs="1" for both elements.

Lines 21-22 define the two attributes of starship. The use attribute lets you specify that they are mandatory.

If you now look again at enterprises.xml, you'll notice that the class element has an attribute (name). Because of this attribute, you must define its type as complex, although class has no body. This is done in lines 24-26. As you can see, you specify an empty body by creating a complex type without subelements.

Occurrence Constraints

In `starfleet.xsd`, we used three attributes to limit the number of occurrences: `minOccurs` and `maxOccurs` when declaring elements, and `use` when declaring attributes. While the constraints for elements accept non-negative integers as values (with 1 as the default), `use` can only have one of the following values: `required`, `optional` (the default), and `prohibited`. You can use two additional attributes when declaring either elements or attributes: `default` and `fixed`.

When applied to an attribute, `default` supplies the value of an optional attribute in case it is omitted when you define its element in the XML document (it is an error to provide a default for attributes that are `required`). Note that when you define elements in an XML document, they're always created with all their attributes, whether you explicitly define them in the XML document or not, because their existence is determined by their presence in the schema. When applied to an element, `default` refers to the element content, but it never results in the creation of elements. It only provides content for empty elements.

The `fixed` constraint forces an attribute value or an element content to have a particular value. You can still define a value in the XML document, but it must match the fixed value assigned in the schema.

Primitive and Derived Types

With `xsd:string`, you've already seen an example of primitive types. Table 6-1 summarizes the full list of primitive types.

Table 6-1. *XML Primitive Types*

Type	Example/Description
anyURI	Either an absolute or a relative URI
base64Binary	MIME encoding consisting of A-Z, a-z, 0-9, +, and /, with A = 0 and / = 63
boolean	For example, `true` or `false`
date	Like the date portion of `dateTime`, but with the addition of the time zone
dateTime	For example, `2007-12-05T15:00:00.345-05:00` means 345 milliseconds after 3 PM Eastern Standard Time (EST) of December 5th, 2007; fractional seconds can be omitted
decimal	For example, `123.456`
double	Formatted like `float`, but uses 64 bits
duration	For example, PaYbMcDTdHeMf$S means a years, b months, c days, d hours, e minutes, and f seconds; a minus at the beginning, when present, indicates "in the past"
float	32-bit floating point; for example, `1.2e-4`
gDay	For example, `25`
gMonth	For example, `12`
gMonthDay	For example, `12-25`
gYear	For example, `2007`
gYearMonth	For example, `2007-12`; g stands for Gregorian calendar, which is the calendar we use

Type	Example/Description
hexBinary	Hexadecimal encoding; for example, 1F represents the number 31 and corresponds to a byte containing the bit sequence 01111111
NOTATION	Externally defined formats
QName	Qualified XML name; for example, xsd:string
string	For example, "This is a string"
time	Like the time portion of dateTime

The XML Schema standard also defines additional types called *derived*, among which are those listed in Table 6-2.

Table 6-2. *XML Derived Types*

Type	Example/Description
byte	An integer number between -2^7 (–128) and 2^7–1 (127)
int	An integer number between -2^{31} (–2,147,483,648) and 2^{31}–1 (2,147,483,647)
integer	An integer number
language	A natural language code as specified in the ISO 639 standard (e.g., FR for French and EN-US for American English)
long	An integer number between -2^{63} (–9,223,372,036,854,775,808) and 2^{63}–1 (9,223,372,036,854,775,807)
negativeInteger	An integer number < 0
nonNegativeInteger	An integer number >= 0
nonPositiveInteger	An integer number <= 0
normalizedString	A string that doesn't contain any carriage return, line feed, or tab characters
positiveInteger	An integer number > 0
short	An integer number between -2^{15} (–32,768) and 2^{15}–1 (32,767)
token	A string that doesn't contain any carriage return, line feed, tab characters, leading or trailing spaces, or sequences of two or more consecutive spaces
unsignedByte	An integer number between 0 and 2^8–1 (255)
unsignedInt	An integer number between 0 and 2^{32}–1 (4,294,967,295)
unsignedLong	An integer number between 0 and 2^{64}–1 (18,446,744,073,709,551,615)
unsignedShort	An integer number between 0 and 2^{16}–1 (65,535)

Simple Types

If you need to modify an already defined type without adding attributes or other elements, you can define a so-called *simple type* instead of recurring to a complex one. For example, this code defines a string that can only contain up to 32 characters:

```
<xsd:simpleType name="myString">
  <xsd:restriction base="xsd:string">
    <xsd:maxLength value="32"/>
    </xsd:restriction>
  </xsdLsimpleType>
```

Besides maxLength, you can also apply the length and minLength attributes to list-like types. Additionally, you can also use the whiteSpace and pattern attributes.

The possible values for whiteSpace are preserve (the default), replace, and collapse. With replace, all carriage return, line feed, and tab characters are replaced with simple spaces. With collapse, leading and trailing spaces are removed, and sequences of multiple spaces are collapsed into single spaces.

With pattern, you define a regular expression that must be matched. For example, this code specifies that only strings consisting of at least one letter of the alphabet are valid:

```
<xsd:pattern value="[A-Za-z]+"
```

For nonlist types, you can also use the attributes minExclusive, minInclusive, maxExclusive, maxInclusive, totalDigits, fractionDigits, and enumeration. For example, this code defines a number with three decimal figures >= 10 and < 20:

```
<xsd:simpleType name="xxyyyType">
  <xsd:restriction base="xsd:decimal">
    <xsd:totalDigits value="6"/>
    <xsd:fractionDigits value="3"/>
    <xsd:minInclusive value="10.000"/>
    <xsd:maxExclusive value="20.000"/>
    </xsd:restriction>
  </xsd:simpleType>
```

Here's an example of enumeration:

```
<xsd:simpleType name="directionType">
  <xsd:restriction base="xsd:string">
    <xsd:enumeration value="left"/>
    <xsd:enumeration value="right"/>
    <xsd:enumeration value="straight"/>
    </xsd:restriction>
  </xsd:simpleType>
```

REGULAR EXPRESSIONS

A regular expression is a string that matches a set of strings according to certain rules. Unfortunately, there is no standard syntax for regular expressions. They are used with several applications, including text editors (e.g., vi) and programming languages (e.g., Perl), and in Unix commands and scripting. W3C defines the syntax for regular expressions to be used in XML schemas (http://www.w3.org/TR/xmlschema-2/). Here we give you a summary of that definition in plain English.

The basic component of a regular expression is called an *atom*. It consists of a single character (specified either individually or as a *class* of characters enclosed between square brackets) indicating that any of the characters in the class are a match. For example, both "a" and "[a]" are regular expressions matching the lowercase character 'a,' while "[a-zA-Z]" matches all letters of the English alphabet.

Things can get complicated, because you can also subtract a class from a group or create a *negative group* by sticking a ^ character at the beginning of it. For example, "[(^abc) - [ABC]]" matches any character with the exclusion of the characters 'a,' 'b,' and 'c' in uppercase or lowercase. This is because the group ^abc matches everything with the exclusion of the three letters in lowercase, and the subtraction of [ABC] removes the same three letters in uppercase. Obviously, you could have obtained the same effect with the regular expression "[^aAbBcC]".

The characters \ | .-^?*+{}()[] are special and must be escaped with a backslash. You can also use \n for newlines, \r for returns, and \t for tabs.

An atom followed by a *quantifier* is called a *piece*. Possible quantifiers are ? (the question mark), + (the plus sign), * (the asterisk), and {n,m}, with n <= m indicating non-negative integers. The question mark indicates that the atom can be missing, the plus sign means any concatenation of one or more atoms, the asterisk means any concatenation of atoms (including none at all), and {n,m} means any concatenation of length >= n and <= m (e.g., "[a-z]{2,7}" means all strings containing between two and seven lowercase alphabetic characters). If you omit m but leave the comma in place, you leave the upper limit unbounded. If, on the other hand, you also omit the comma, you define a string of fixed length (e.g., "[0-9]{3}" means a string of exactly three numeric characters). You can concatenate pieces simply by writing them one after the other. For example, to define an identifier consisting of alphanumeric characters and underscores but beginning with a letter, you could write the expression "[a-zA-Z]{1}[a-zA-Z0-9_]*". The general term *branch* is used to indicate a single piece or a concatenation of pieces when the distinction is not relevant.

To specify partial patterns, you can insert at the beginning and/or at the end of each atom a sequence formed with a period and an asterisk. For example, ".*ABC.*" identifies all strings containing in any position the substring ABC. Without dot-asterisk wildcarding, "ABC" only matches a string of exactly three characters of length.

Several branches can be further composed to form the most general regular expression by means of vertical bars. For example, "[a-zA-Z]* | [0-9]*" matches all strings composed entirely of letters or digits but not a mix of the two.

Instead of defining a new simple type by imposing a restriction, you can also specify that it consist of a list of items of an existing simple type. For example, this code defines a type consisting of a series of directions:

```
<xsd:simpleType name="pathType">
  <xsd:list itemType="directionType"/>
  </xsd:simpleType>
```

Finally, besides xsd:restriction and xsd:list, you can define a new simple type by means of xsd:union, which lets you combine two different preexisting types. For example, this code defines a type that can be either a number between 1 and 10 or one of the strings "< 1" and "> 10":

```
<xsd:simpleType name="myNumber">
  <xsd:union>
    <xsd:simpleType>
      <xsd:restriction base="xsd:positiveInteger">
        <xsd:maxInclusive value="10"/>
        </xsd:restriction>
      </xsd:simpleType>
    <xsd:simpleType>
      <xsd:restriction base="xsd:string">
        <xsd:enumeration value="< 1"/>
        <xsd:enumeration value="> 10"/>
        </xsd:restriction>
      </xsd:simpleType>
    </xsd:union>
  </xsd:simpleType>
```

Complex Types

You've already seen some examples of complex types in starfleet.xsd. There are three models that you can use to group the elements contained in a complex type: sequence (in which the elements must appear in the specified sequence), all (in which there can only be up to one element each of all those listed, but they can appear in any order), and choice (in which the contained elements are mutually exclusive). Note that while all can only contain individual elements, sequence and choice can contain other groups. For example, this code:

```
<xsd:sequence>
  <xsd:choice>
    <xsd:element name="no" ... />
    <xsd:all>
      <xsd:element name="yes1" ... />
      <xsd:element name="yes2" ... />
      </xsd:all>
    </xsd:choice>
  <xsd:element name="whatever" ... />
  </xsd:sequence>
```

defines an element that contains one of the following combinations of elements:

- no, whatever

- whatever

- yes1, whatever

- yes2, whatever

- yes1, yes2, whatever

- yes2, yes1, whatever

Complex type definitions provide many additional options, but are not always easy to handle. One might even argue that they've been overengineered. Therefore, to describe them in detail would exceed the scope of this manual. Nevertheless, the information we've provided on primitive and simple types, together with the description of the three model groups of complex types, is already enough to cover most cases.

Validation

An XML document is said to be *valid* if it passes the checks done by a validating parser against the document's DTD or schema. For the parser to be able to operate, the XML document must be *well formed*, which means that all tags are closed, the attributes are quoted, the nesting is done correctly, and so on.

You actually have to validate two documents: the XML file and the DTD or XML schema. In the example, those are enterprises.xml and starfleet.dtd/starfleet.xsd, respectively. The simplest way to do the validation is to use a development environment like Eclipse, which validates the documents as you type.

An alternative is to use online services. For example, the tool available at http://xmlvalidation.com can check XML files, DTD files, and XML schemas. To validate a schema, you can also use the online tool provided by W3C, which provides an authoritative check. Go to http://www.w3.org/2001/03/webdata/xsv and scroll down until you find the section shown in Figure 6-1.

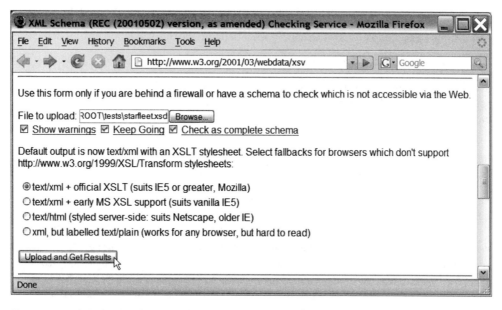

Figure 6-1. *Validating a schema with W3C*

Click on the Browse... button, select starfleet.xsd (or the schema you want to get checked), and then click on Upload and Get Results. You will (should!) see the screen shown in Figure 6-2.

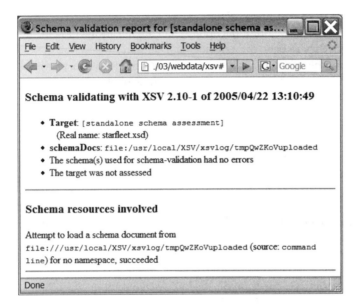

Figure 6-2. *Validation results*

In general, you need to go through three steps to validate an XML document:

1. Associate the document to the DTD/schema against which it is to be validated.

2. Define an exception handler to specify what happens when a validation error is detected.

3. Parse the document with a validating parser.

We'll show you how to control parsers from a JSP page. If you've installed everything as described in Appendix A (and in particular the Xalan package), you'll already have all the software you need.

PARSERS

A parser is a piece of software that breaks down a document into *tokens*, analyzes the syntax of the tokens to form valid expressions, and finally interprets the expressions and performs corresponding actions.

The parsing process therefore implies a validation of the document. The DOM (standardized by W3C) and Simple API for XML (SAX) define, amongst other things, interfaces to perform XML parsing.

DOM parsers build a tree of nodes after loading the whole document in memory. Therefore, they require quite a bit of memory. SAX, on the other hand, parses the documents from streams, and therefore has a smaller memory footprint. The flexibility of the DOM also costs in terms of performance, and DOM implementations tend to be slower than SAX implementations. The two most widely used packages implementing DOM and SAX are Xerces and Java API for XML Processing (JAXP).

Validation Against a DTD

To validate an XML file against a DTD, you have to go through the following steps:

1. Associate the XML document with the DTD by adding a DOCTIME declaration to the XML file. The declaration, which you should insert immediately after the <?xml...?> line, is as follows:

```
<!DOCTYPE starfleet SYSTEM "starfleet.dtd">
```

2. Define an exception handler. This is a Java object of a class that extends org.xml.sax.helpers.DefaultHandler and replaces three of its methods: warning, error, and fatalError. The handler is registered with the parser, which then executes the appropriate method upon encountering a validation problem. The default behavior of DefaultHandler is to do nothing. Therefore, you need to overwrite the methods in order to report the errors. Listing 6-4 shows you the code of a possible handler. It's really up to you to decide what level of reporting you'd like to have, but we have decided to report all validation problems and interrupt the parsing.

Listing 6-4. *ParsingExceptionHandler.java*

```java
package myPkg;
import org.xml.sax.helpers.DefaultHandler;
import org.xml.sax.SAXParseException;
public class ParsingExceptionHandler extends DefaultHandler {
  public SAXParseException parsingException = null;
  public String errorLevel = null;
  public void warning(SAXParseException e) {
    errorLevel = "Warning";
    parsingException = e;
    }
  public void error(SAXParseException e) {
    errorLevel = "Error";
    parsingException = e;
    }
  public void fatalError(SAXParseException e) {
    errorLevel = "Fatal error";
    parsingException = e;
    }
  }
```

As you can see, it's pretty simple. You define two public attributes: one to save the exception generated by the parser, and one to save the error level. You then update the two attributes in each one of the three methods. After each parsing, you can check one of the attributes for null in order to determine whether the parsing succeeded or not. Compile this module from the DOS command line with javac ParsingExceptionHandler.java and copy the resulting .class file into the WEB-INF\classes\myPkg folder of your application directory.

3. Perform the validation. Listing 6-5 shows you a possible implementation for a SAX parser in the form of a JSP page.

Listing 6-5. *starfleet_validate_sax.jsp*

```
01: <%@page language="java" contentType="text/html"%>
02: <%@page import="org.apache.xerces.parsers.SAXParser"%>
03: <%@page import="myPkg.ParsingExceptionHandler"%>
04: <html><head><title>Validate (SAX) starfleet.xml</title></head><body>
05: <%
06:    ParsingExceptionHandler handler = new ParsingExceptionHandler();
07:    SAXParser parser = new SAXParser();
08:    parser.setFeature("http://xml.org/sax/features/validation", true);
09:    parser.setErrorHandler(handler);
10:    try {
11:      parser.parse("webapps/ROOT/tests/enterprises.xml");
12:      }
13:    catch (Exception e) {
14:      // Sax exception already trapped in the handler.
15:      }
16:    if (handler.errorLevel == null) {
17:      out.println("The document is valid.");
18:      }
19:    else {
20:      out.println(
21:          "*** Validation " + handler.errorLevel + ": "
22:          + handler.parsingException
23:          );
24:      }
25:    %>
26: </body></html>
```

We've highlighted the five lines where the critical work is done. You instantiate the exception handler in line 6, you instantiate the SAX parser in line 7, you set the validation feature in the parser in line 8, you register the exception handler with the parser in line 9, and you do the parsing in line 11. The rest is only a piece of code to display the parsing result. For example, if you mistype a closing tag, as in <captain>James Tiberius Kirk</captai>, you get the following message (broken down into two lines):

```
*** Validation Fatal error: org.xml.sax.SAXParseException:
The element type "captain" must be terminated by the matching end-tag "".
```

If you remove the line altogether, you get this message:

```
*** Validation Error: org.xml.sax.SAXParseException: The content of element
type "starship" is incomplete, it must match "(class,captain)".
```

With a typo such as `<class nme="Constitution"/>`, you get this message:

```
*** Validation Error: org.xml.sax.SAXParseException:
Attribute "nme" must be declared for element type "class".
```

and if you rewrite the element, as in `<class name="Constitution" nme="whatever"/>`, you get no error at all, because the DTD simply ignores the additional attribute!

To use a DOM parser instead of SAX, make a copy of `starfleet_validate_sax.jsp` named `starfleet_validate_dom.jsp`, and change SAX to DOM (four occurrences in all). The JSP page then imports and instantiates `org.apache.xerces.parsers.DOMParser` instead of `SAXParser`.

You could also use JAXP instead of SAX, as shown in Listing 6-6.

Listing 6-6. *starfleet_validate_jaxp.jsp*

```
01: <%@page language="java" contentType="text/html"%>
02: <%@page import="javax.xml.parsers.DocumentBuilderFactory"%>
03: <%@page import="javax.xml.parsers.DocumentBuilder"%>
04: <%@page import="org.w3c.dom.Document"%>
05: <%@page import="myPkg.ParsingExceptionHandler"%>
06: <%@page import="java.io.File"%>
07: <html><head><title>Validate starfleet.xml</title></head><body>
08: <%
09:   File docFile = new File("webapps/ROOT/tests/enterprises.xml");
10:   DocumentBuilderFactory dbf = DocumentBuilderFactory.newInstance();
11:   dbf.setValidating(true);
12:   DocumentBuilder db = dbf.newDocumentBuilder();
13:   ParsingExceptionHandler handler = new ParsingExceptionHandler();
14:   db.setErrorHandler(handler);
15:   try {
16:     Document doc = db.parse(docFile);
17:     }
18:   catch (Exception e) {
19:     // Sax exception already trapped in the handler.
20:     }
21:   if (handler.errorLevel == null) {
22:     out.println("The document is valid.");
23:     }
24:   else {
25:     out.println(
26:         "*** Validation " + handler.errorLevel + ": "
27:       + handler.parsingException
28:       );
29:     }
30: %>
```

As you can see, it is somewhat more complicated. In line 9, you create a `File` object for the XML document to be validated (the path is relative to the Tomcat directory). In line 10, you instantiate a document builder factory that you then use in line 12 to manufacture a document builder. But before doing so, in line 11, you switch on the validating feature, as you did with SAX. In lines 13 and 14, you register the exception handler (as you did in lines 6 and 9 of starfleet_validate_sax.jsp), and line 16 is where you load the XML file and do the parsing.

Why use JAXP instead of Xerces? We don't have a satisfying answer to that. We recommend that you pick one method (e.g., SAX with Xerces) and stick to it until there are compelling reasons (e.g., new implementations) that make another choice preferable.

Validation Against a Schema

To validate an XML file against a schema, you have to go through the following steps:

1. Associate the XML document with the schema. Instead of adding a line as you did for DTD validation, you need to add a couple of attributes to the root element:

   ```
   <starfleet
       xmlns:xsi="http://www.w3.org/2001/XMLSchema-instance"
       xsi:noNamespaceSchemaLocation="starfleet.xsd">
   ```

   We've renamed this file from enterprises.xml to enterprises_schema.xml to avoid confusions.

2. Define an exception handler. You can use exactly the same exception handler that you used for DTD validation.

3. Perform the validation. Listing 6-7 shows a modified version of starfleet_validate_sax.jsp to validate enterprises_schema.xml instead of enterprises.xml.

Listing 6-7. *starfleet_validate_sax_schema.jsp*

```
01: <%@page language="java" contentType="text/html"%>
02: <%@page import="org.apache.xerces.parsers.SAXParser"%>
03: <%@page import="myPkg.ParsingExceptionHandler"%>
04: <html><head><title>Validate (SAX) starfleet.xml</title></head><body>
05: <%
06:    ParsingExceptionHandler handler = new ParsingExceptionHandler();
07:    SAXParser parser = new SAXParser();
08:    parser.setFeature("http://xml.org/sax/features/validation", true);
09:    parser.setFeature("http://apache.org/xml/features/validation/schema", true);
10:    parser.setFeature(
11:      "http://apache.org/xml/features/validation/schema-full-checking", true);
12:    parser.setErrorHandler(handler);
13:    try {
14:      parser.parse("webapps/ROOT/tests/enterprises_schema.xml");
15:      }
16:    catch (Exception e) {
17:      // Sax exception already trapped in the handler.
18:      }
```

```
19:    if (handler.errorLevel == null) {
20:      out.println("The document is valid.");
21:      }
22:    else {
23:      out.println(
24:        "*** Validation " + handler.errorLevel + ": "
25:        + handler.parsingException
26:        );
27:      }
28:    %>
29: </body></html>
```

We've highlighted the lines that differ from starfleet_validate_sax.jsp. As you can see, apart from updating the name of the XML file in line 14, you only need to switch on two features of the parser that tell it to use a schema instead of a DTD.

As an alternative to adding the xmlns attributes to the root element of the XML file, you could also specify the schema by setting a property of the parser:

```
parser.setProperty(
"http://apache.org/xml/properties/schema/external-noNamespaceSchemaLocation",
"starfleet.xsd");
```

In any case, the validation errors reported by the parser when using a schema are a bit different from those reported when using a DTD. For example, if you mistype an attribute name, as in <class nme="Constitution"/>, you get:

```
*** Validation Error: org.xml.sax.SAXParseException: cvc-complex-type.4:
Attribute 'name' must appear on element 'class'.
```

and if you rewrite the element, as in <class name="Constitution" nme="whatever"/>, you get:

```
*** Validation Error: org.xml.sax.SAXParseException: cvc-complex-type.3.2.2:
Attribute 'nme' is not allowed to appear in element 'class'.
```

Clearly, the additional work put into writing a schema as compared to a DTD pays in terms of better validation.

What we said about changing SAX to DOM in starfleet_validate_sax.jsp also applies to starfleet_validate_sax_schema.jsp.

To perform JAXP validation with a schema instead of a DTD, you only need to make a couple of minor changes. Obviously, you first have to change enterprises.xml to enterprises_schema.xml in line 9. The only functional change is the insertion after line 11 of the following two configuration settings:

```
dbf.setNamespaceAware(true);
dbf.setAttribute(
  "http://java.sun.com/xml/jaxp/properties/schemaLanguage",
  "http://www.w3.org/2001/XMLSchema");
```

XSL

Extensible Stylesheet Language (XSL) is a language for expressing style sheets that describe how to display XML documents. The specification documents are available from http://www.w3.org/Style/XSL/.

While CSS only needs to define how to represent the predefined HTML tags, XSL has to cope with the fact that there are no predefined tags in XML! How do you know whether a <table> element in an XML file represents a table of data as you know it from HTML or an object around which you can sit for dinner?

That's why XSL is more than a style-sheet language. It actually includes three parts:

- **XSLT**: A language to transform XML documents that can completely change their structure. For example, it can generate an HTML page from XML code.

- **XPath**: A language to navigate in XML documents. See Chapter 2 and Appendix D for more information on XPath.

- **XSL Formatting Objects (XSL-FO)**: A language for formatting XML documents.

The rest of this section will concentrate on the XSLT (i.e., transformation) part of XSL, because we believe that XSL-FO is beyond the scope of this manual. XSL-FO is concerned with *page formatting* (page size, margins, headers, footers, citations, footnotes, and so on), which is very different from the screen formatting and hyperlinking you need for web pages to be viewed rather than printed. In fact, web pages very often print badly.

Just to give you an idea, XSL-FO divides the output into pages, the pages into regions (body, header, footer, and left and right sidebars), the regions into block areas, the block areas into line areas, and the line areas into inline areas. You can define several attributes of these fields and then "flow" your content into them. XSL-FO also provides constructs for lists and tables similar to those you know from HTML.

Example 1: Transformation from One XML Format to Another

In Chapter 2, we showed you starfleet.xml (Listing 2-17), from which we extracted enterprises.xml in this chapter (Listing 6-1), which we later renamed enterprises_schema.xml when we added the schema declaration to it. Besides the fact that enterprises_schema.xml only includes two starships, the differences from the original starfleet.xml are

- The presence of a <title> element

- The removal in the <class> element of the commissioned attribute

- The replacement of the <class> body with an attribute named name

Listing 6-8 shows you an XSL file to extract enterprises_schema.xml from starfleet.xml.

Listing 6-8. *enterprises.xsl*

```
01: <?xml version="1.0" encoding="ISO-8859-1"?>
02: <xsl:stylesheet version="1.0" xmlns:xsl="http://www.w3.org/1999/XSL/Transform">
03: <xsl:output method="xml" version="1.0" encoding="ISO-8859-1" indent="yes"/>
04: <xsl:template match="/">
05:   <starfleet
06:     xmlns:xsi="http://www.w3.org/2001/XMLSchema-instance"
07:     xsi:noNamespaceSchemaLocation="starfleet.xsd">
08:     <title>The two most famous starships in the fleet</title>
09:     <xsl:for-each select="starfleet/starship">
10:       <xsl:if test="@sn='NCC-1701' or @sn='NCC-1701-D'">
11:         <xsl:element name="starship">
12:           <xsl:attribute name="name">
13:             <xsl:value-of select="@name"/>
14:             </xsl:attribute>
15:           <xsl:attribute name="sn">
16:             <xsl:value-of select="@sn"/>
17:             </xsl:attribute>
18:           <xsl:element name="class">
19:             <xsl:attribute name="name">
20:               <xsl:value-of select="class"/>
21:               </xsl:attribute>
22:             </xsl:element>
23:           <xsl:copy-of select="captain"/>
24:           </xsl:element>
25:         </xsl:if>
26:       </xsl:for-each>
27:     </starfleet>
28:   </xsl:template>
29: </xsl:stylesheet>
```

Lines 1 and 2 state that the file is in XML format and specify its namespace. In line 2, you write xsl:stylesheet, but you could also write xsl:transform, because the two keywords are considered synonyms.

Line 3 specifies that the output is also an XML document. This is actually the default, but by writing it explicitly, you can also request that the output be indented. Otherwise, by default, the generated code would be written on a single very long line.

The xsd:template element associates a template to an element, and in line 4, you write match="/" to specify the whole source document. In lines 5-8 and 27, you write the enterprise and title elements to the output.

The loop between lines 9 and 26 is where you scan all the starship elements. Immediately inside the loop, you then select the two starships you're interested in with an xsl:if. In XSL, you also have the choose/when/otherwise construct that you encountered in Chapter 2 when we described JSTL, but in this case, it would not be appropriate, because you do not need an else.

The actual work is done in lines 11-24. The xsl:element and xsl:attribute elements create a new element and a new attribute, respectively, while xsl:value-of copies data from the source XML file to the output. Notice that the XPath expressions in the select attributes are relative to the current element selected by xsl:for-each. Also, notice that the only difference between the source and the output is handled in lines 19-21, where you assign to the name attribute of the class element what was originally in the element's body. The class attribute commissioned is simply ignored, so that it doesn't appear in the output.

The xsl:copy-of element copies the whole element to the output, including attributes and children elements. If you only want to copy the element tag, you can use xsl:copy.

XSL includes more than 30 elements, but the dozen or so that we've described cover the vast majority of what you'll probably need.

Example 2: Transformation from XML to HTML

If you remember, in Chapter 2, we showed you how to use JSP to convert an XML file (starfleet.xml, Listing 2-17) to HTML (starfleet.jsp, Listing 2-18). This time, we want to show you how to do it with XSL. For this purpose, we'll use the enterprises.xml file we showed you at the beginning of this chapter in Listing 6-1. Listing 6-9 shows you the full XSL file.

Listing 6-9. *starfleet.xsl*

```
01: <?xml version="1.0" encoding="ISO-8859-1"?>
02: <xsl:stylesheet version="1.0" xmlns:xsl="http://www.w3.org/1999/XSL/Transform">
03: <xsl:output method="html" version="4.0" encoding="ISO-8859-1" indent="yes"/>
04: <xsl:template match="/">
05: <html><head>
06:   <title>Styling starfleet.xml</title>
07:   <style>th {text-align:left}</style>
08:   </head>
09: <body>
10: <h2><xsl:value-of select="starfleet/title"/></h2>
11: <table border="1">
12:   <tr><th>Name</th><th>S/N</th><th>Class</th><th>Captain</th></tr>
13:   <xsl:for-each select="starfleet/starship">
14:     <xsl:sort select="class/@name"/>
15:     <tr>
16:       <td><xsl:value-of select="@name"/></td>
17:       <td><xsl:value-of select="@sn"/></td>
18:       <td><xsl:value-of select="class/@name"/></td>
19:       <td><xsl:value-of select="captain"/></td>
20:     </tr>
21:   </xsl:for-each>
22:   </table>
23: </body>
24: </html>
25: </xsl:template>
26: </xsl:stylesheet>
```

After the first example (Listing 6-8), it should be clear how this works. There is just one point we'd like to clarify: you can omit line 3 because, although the default output format is XML, XSL automatically recognizes that you're generating HTML if the first tag it encounters is `<html>`. Nevertheless, we recommend that you define the output format explicitly, so that you can set the version, encoding, and indentation options.

Browser Side vs. Server Side

We still haven't told you how to apply an XSL style sheet to an XML file to perform the transformation. This is because we first have to clarify the distinction between browser-side vs. server-side transformation.

The recent versions of all browsers can process XML and XSL. For example, let's say you place `enterprises_schema.xml` in the `webapps\ROOT\test\` folder of the Tomcat directory. By typing `http://localhost:8080/test/enterprises_schema.xml` in Firefox, you immediately see on the left of each element a `-/+` control that lets you collapse it and expand it, as shown in Figure 6-3.

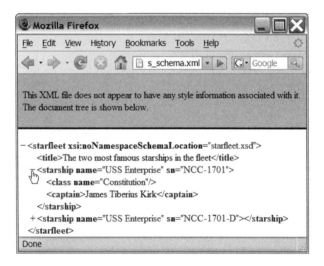

Figure 6-3. *Browsing an XML file without XSL*

This is because the browser "knows" about XML. The message at the top of the page indicates that the browser will display the file as a node tree in a generic way because `enterprises_schema.xml` doesn't refer to any XSL style sheet.

Making the association is simple: insert the following processing instruction immediately below the first line of `enterprises_schema.xml` (i.e., the line with `<?xml...?>`):

```
<?xml-stylesheet type="text/xsl" href="starfleet.xsl"?>
```

Now, if you ask the browser to display `http://localhost:8080/test/` `enterprises_schema.xml`, it will know what style sheet to use. The `href` attribute expects a URL. Therefore, in general, you can also set it to URLs such as `"http://localhost:8080/tests/starfleet.xsl"` or `"/tests/starfleet.xsl"`. We chose to write the relative URL, because we're keeping both files in the same `test` folder, and it makes our lives easier. In any case, Figure 6-4 shows the result.

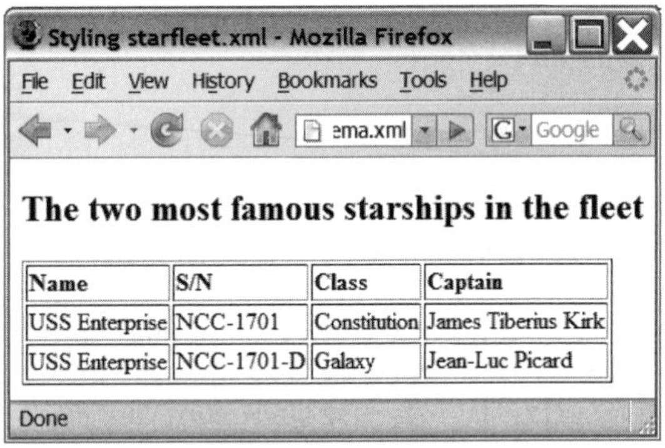

Figure 6-4. *Browsing an XML file with XSL*

Actually, there is one small advantage in keeping XML and XSL files in the same folder: you can view the XML file in a browser without Tomcat by just dragging and dropping it onto the browser window. This doesn't work if you use an absolute URL in the `href`.

If you view the page source (in Firefox, it's the bottom item of the `View` menu), you'll see the XML file, because the browser does the transformation from XML to HTML. The user can also easily obtain your XSL file, because its URL is shown in the XML source. For example, if you're accessing `http://localhost:8080/tests/enterprises_schema.xml`, after viewing its source and discovering the relative URL of the style sheet, you only need to type `http://localhost:8080/tests/starfleet.xsl` to see the XSL file.

The only alternative is to do the transformation on the server and make its output available rather than make the XML and XSL files visible to the browser. Then, you can keep XML and XSL in private folders. Listing 6-10 shows you how to do it with a JSP page.

Listing 6-10. *enterprises_transform.jsp*

```
01: <%@page language="java" contentType="text/html"%>
02: <%@page import="java.io.File"%>
03: <%@page import="java.io.FileOutputStream"%>
04: <%@page import="javax.xml.transform.TransformerFactory"%>
05: <%@page import="javax.xml.transform.Transformer"%>
06: <%@page import="javax.xml.transform.Source"%>
07: <%@page import="javax.xml.transform.SourceLocator"%>
08: <%@page import="javax.xml.transform.TransformerException"%>
09: <%@page import="javax.xml.transform.Result"%>
10: <%@page import="javax.xml.transform.stream.StreamSource"%>
11: <%@page import="javax.xml.transform.stream.StreamResult"%>
12: <%@page import="myPkg.TransformerExceptionHandler"%>
13: <%
```

```
14:    File inFile = new File("webapps/ROOT/tests/enterprises_schema.xml");
15:    File xslFile = new File("webapps/ROOT/tests/starfleet.xsl");
16:    String outFilename = "webapps/ROOT/tests/enterprises_out.html";
17:    TransformerExceptionHandler handler = new TransformerExceptionHandler();
18:    try {
19:      TransformerFactory factory = TransformerFactory.newInstance();
20:      Transformer transformer = factory.newTransformer(new StreamSource(xslFile));
21:      transformer.setErrorListener(handler);
22:      Source source = new StreamSource(inFile);
23:      Result result = new StreamResult(new FileOutputStream(outFilename));
24:      transformer.transform(source, result);
25:      }
26:    catch (TransformerException e) {
27:      }
28:    if (handler.errorLevel == null) {
29:      out.println("Transformation completed.");
30:      }
31:    else {
32:      out.println(
33:          "*** Transformation " + handler.errorLevel + ": "
34:        + handler.transformationException
35:        );
36:      }
37:  %>
```

It looks more complicated than it actually is. Moreover, we've hard-coded the file names for simplicity, but you can stick a simple input form in front of it, and you'll have a small utility you can use to transform all XML files.

enterprises_transform.jsp performs the XML transformation on the server side as follows:

1. It instantiates a generic TransformerFactory and uses it to create a Transformer that implements the transformation defined in the XSL file (lines 19 and 20).

2. It registers with the transformer the exception handler that was instantiated in line 17 (line 21). This is similar to what you did to handle validation exceptions.

3. It opens an input stream to read the XML file and an output stream to write the document that will result from the transformation (lines 22 and 23).

4. It finally does the transformation (line 24).

The exception reporting is almost a carbon copy of the method we described when talking about validation (see Listings 6-5 to 6-7), and the exception handler for transformations (Listing 6-11) is compiled and used exactly like the handler for validations of Listing 6-4.

Listing 6-11. *ParsingExceptionHandler.java*

```java
package myPkg;
import javax.xml.transform.TransformerException;
public class TransformerExceptionHandler
    implements javax.xml.transform.ErrorListener {
  public TransformerException transformationException = null;
  public String errorLevel = null;
  public void warning(TransformerException e) {
    errorLevel = "Warning";
    transformationException = e;
    }
  public void error(TransformerException e) {
    errorLevel = "Error";
    transformationException = e;
    }
  public void fatalError(TransformerException e) {
    errorLevel = "Fatal error";
    transformationException = e;
    }
}
```

The JSP page enterprises_transform.jsp applies the style sheet starfleet.xsl to enterprises_schema.xml to produce enterprises_out.html. If you change the file names in lines 14–16 of enterprises_transform.jsp to starfleet.xml, enterprises.xsl, and enterprises_out.xml, the same page will generate a file functionally identical to enterprises_schema.xml. The only difference is that enterprises_out.xml is not indented like the handmade enterprises_schema.xml.

SOAP

It's important for applications to be able to communicate with each other. This often takes place via Remote Procedure Calls (RPCs), but that mechanism causes compatibility and security problems. Firewalls and proxies have become an integral part of how organizations connect to the Internet, and RPCs don't fit well into the picture.

The purpose of Simple Object Access Protocol (SOAP) is to provide the means of exchanging XML-based information over HTTP regardless of operating systems and programming languages. The latest specs are available from W3C at http://www.w3.org/TR/soap/.

A SOAP message is an XML document that satisfies the following rules:

- It's wrapped inside an Envelope object that identifies it as a SOAP message.

- It uses the namespaces for SOAP envelopes.

- It *doesn't* contain a DTD reference (i.e., a DOCTYPE).

- It *doesn't* contain processing instructions (e.g., <?xml-stylesheet ... ?>).

See Listing 6-12 for a skeleton SOAP message that shows its general structure.

Listing 6-12. *Skeleton SOAP Message*

```
<?xml version="1.0"?>
<soap:Envelope
  xmlns:soap="http://www.w3.org/2001/12/soap-envelope"
  soap:encodingStyle="http://www.w3.org/2001/12/soap-encoding">
<soap:Header>
  ...This is optional...
  </soap:Header>
<soap:Body>
  ...This is mandatory...
  <soap:Fault>
    ...This is optional...
    </soap:Fault>
  </soap:Body>
</soap:Envelope>
```

The Header is how the message originator provides the required application-specific information (e.g., authentication) to the destination. The Body is where the actual message is, and the Fault is where an error notification is placed.

SOAP messages are unidirectional, without any built-in request/response mechanism. It is up to the applications to define messages that acknowledge each other.

For example, the schema shown in Listing 6-13 defines an XML-based protocol to request and obtain a date/time string.

Listing 6-13. *myMess.xsd*

```
<?xml version="1.0" encoding="ISO-8859-1"?>
<xsd:schema xmlns:xsd="http://www.w3.org/2001/XMLSchema">
  <xsd:element name="message">
    <xsd:choice>
      <xsd:element name="reqTime">
        <xsd:complexType></xsd:complexType>
        </xsd:element>
      <xsd:element name="time" type="xsd:string"/>
      <xsd:element name="fault" type="xsd:string"/>
      </xsd:choice>
    </xsd:element>
  </xsd:schema>
```

The message element contains either reqTime (to request a time), time (to return the requested time in its body), or fault (to report a problem).

To handle SOAP messages in Java, you can use the library javax.xml.soap. We've written a JSP page to show you how it is done (see Listing 6-14).

Listing 6-14. *myMess_send.jsp*

```
01: <%@page language="java" contentType="text/html"%>
02: <%@page import="javax.xml.soap.SOAPMessage"%>
03: <%@page import="javax.xml.soap.SOAPEnvelope"%>
04: <%@page import="javax.xml.soap.Name"%>
05: <%@page import="javax.xml.soap.SOAPBody"%>
06: <%@page import="java.io.ByteArrayOutputStream"%>
07: <%@page import="javax.xml.soap.SOAPConnectionFactory"%>
08: <%@page import="javax.xml.soap.SOAPConnection"%>
09: <html><head><title>Send SOAP message</title></head><body>
10: <%
11:    // The following variables are set by myMess_create_mess.jspf
12:    SOAPMessage mess;  SOAPEnvelope env;  SOAPBody body;
13:    %><%@include file="myMess_create_mess.jspf"%><%
14:    Name bodyElemName = env.createName("reqTime", "my", "myMess.xsd");
15:    body.addBodyElement(bodyElemName);
16:    ByteArrayOutputStream baos = new ByteArrayOutputStream(1024);
17:    mess.writeTo(baos);
18:    out.println("<b>---------- Request message ----------</b>");
19:    out.println(baos.toString().replaceAll("<", "<br/>&lt;") + "<br/> ");
20:    SOAPConnectionFactory cf = SOAPConnectionFactory.newInstance();
21:    SOAPConnection conn = cf.createConnection();
22:    SOAPMessage answer = conn.call(mess,
23:        "http://localhost:8080/tests/myMess_reply.jsp");
24:    conn.close();
25:    baos.reset();
26:    answer.writeTo(baos);
27:    out.println("<br/><b>---------- Response message ----------</b>");
28:    out.println(baos.toString().replaceAll("<", "<br/>&lt;") + "<br/> ");
29: </body></html>
```

myMess_send.jsp exchanges SOAP messages with myMess_reply.jsp as follows:

- It generates a new SOAP message by including the JSP segment myMess_create_mess.jspf (line 13).

- It adds a reqTime element to the message body (lines 14 and 15). We included the my prefix because SOAP requires it, and the URI of the schema (myMess.xsd) because it makes our lives easier when we're parsing the message with Java at the receiving end.

- It displays the message to be sent (lines 16-19).

- It creates a SOAP connection (lines 20 and 21).

- It sends the request message and suspends itself until it receives a message response (lines 22 and 23). SOAP itself doesn't include any mechanism to establish connections between systems. Therefore, this connection is only a local Java mechanism to send a message inside an HTTP request and wait for the notification that the corresponding HTTP response has been received. This is also proven by the fact that you don't need to provide the URL of the destination page when instantiating the connection.

- It closes the connection and displays the received message (lines 24-28).

We've highlighted the lines that deal with SOAP. Listing 6-15 shows myMess_create_mess.jspf. To see the output of myMess_send.jsp, check out Listing 6-17 at the end of the chapter.

Listing 6-15. *myMess_create_mess.jspf*

```
01: <%@page import="javax.xml.soap.MessageFactory"%>
02: <%@page import="javax.xml.soap.SOAPConstants"%>
03: <%@page import="javax.xml.soap.SOAPHeader"%>
04: <%@page import="javax.xml.soap.SOAPHeaderElement"%>
05: <%
06:    // It uses the variables mess, env, and body
07:    {
08:      MessageFactory mf =
09:          MessageFactory.newInstance(SOAPConstants.SOAP_1_2_PROTOCOL);
10:      mess = mf.createMessage();
11:      mess.setProperty(SOAPMessage.WRITE_XML_DECLARATION, "true");
12:      mess.setProperty(SOAPMessage.CHARACTER_SET_ENCODING, "ISO-8859-1");
13:      SOAPHeader head = mess.getSOAPHeader();
14:      env = mess.getSOAPPart().getEnvelope();
15:      Name headElemName = env.createName("message", "my", "myMess.xsd");
16:      SOAPHeaderElement headElem = head.addHeaderElement(headElemName);
17:      headElem.setMustUnderstand(true);
18:      body = mess.getSOAPBody();
19:    }
20: %>
```

We've enclosed the segment scriptlet between braces to keep all the instantiated objects local. In general, it's bad practice to write side-effecting code that creates variables outside the scope of the module. In Java, this would also mean that objects hang around longer than necessary, uselessly wasting memory. For the same reason of avoiding side-effecting, we also instantiated mess, env, and body in the including modules rather than where they are set. As a consequence, we needed to move the corresponding declarations to the including module, thereby increasing its size and, as you'll see shortly, duplicating them in more than one module. Nevertheless, coding neatness usually pays!

In line 9, you specify that the latest version of the SOAP protocol be used, as opposed to the default version 1.1. Lines 11 and 12 ensure that the text <?xml version="1.0" encoding="ISO-8859-1" ?> is included at the beginning of the message. In lines 15 and 16, you add a my:message element with the XML namespace attribute to the message header. This is to tell the message recipient how to interpret the element (or elements) you're going to insert in the message body. Line 17 clarifies that the message is only intended for recipients that understand and process the header.

Listing 6-16 shows myMess_reply.jsp, which receives reqTime and returns the current time.

Listing 6-16. *myMess_reply.jsp*

```
01: <%@page language="java" contentType="text/xml"%>
02: <%@page import="javax.xml.soap.SOAPMessage"%>
03: <%@page import="javax.xml.soap.SOAPEnvelope"%>
04: <%@page import="javax.xml.soap.Name"%>
05: <%@page import="javax.xml.soap.SOAPBody"%>
06: <%@page import="java.io.ByteArrayOutputStream"%>
07: <%@taglib uri="http://java.sun.com/jsp/jstl/xml" prefix="x"%>
08: <%@taglib uri="http://java.sun.com/jsp/jstl/core" prefix="c"%>
09: <%
10:    // The following variables are used by myMess_create_mess.jspf
11:    SOAPMessage mess;  SOAPEnvelope env;  SOAPBody body;
12:    %><%@include file="myMess_create_mess.jspf"%><%
13:    int n = request.getContentLength();
14:    byte[] bytes = new byte[n];
15:    request.getInputStream().read(bytes);
16:    String question = new String(bytes);
17:    pageContext.setAttribute("question", question);
18:    %>
19: <x:parse doc="${question}" varDom="dom"/>
20: <x:choose>
21:    <x:when select="count($dom//*[name()='my:reqTime']) = 1">
22:      <%@page import="javax.xml.soap.SOAPBodyElement"%>
23:      <%@page import="java.util.GregorianCalendar"%>
24:      <%
25:        Name bodyElemName = env.createName("time", "my", "myMess.xsd");
26:        SOAPBodyElement be = body.addBodyElement(bodyElemName);
27:        GregorianCalendar cal = new GregorianCalendar();
28:        be.addTextNode(cal.getTime().toString());
29:        %>
30:      </x:when>
31:    <x:otherwise>
32:      <% body.addFault().setFaultString("Unknown request"); %>
33:      </x:otherwise>
34:    </x:choose>
35: <%
36:    ByteArrayOutputStream baos = new ByteArrayOutputStream(1024);
37:    mess.writeTo(baos);
38:    out.print(baos.toString());
39:    %>
```

Notice that `myMess_reply.jsp` includes the same `myMess_create_mess.jspf` you already used in `myMess_send.jsp`.

In lines 13-17, you read the request, which contains the incoming message, and make it available for processing within EL expressions. Line 19 parses the received message into a DOM, so that you can use XPath for easy access.

The selection construct of lines 20-34 is where you analyze the incoming request message and prepare the appropriate response. You only consider `reqTime` (in lines 21-29) and leave any unknown message to be replied to by the `x:otherwise` clause (in line 32). To handle further messages, you would only need to add when blocks, one for each new message.

In line 21, you count how many times the element `my:reqTime` appears in the whole message and check that it is exactly one. This is how you identify the message. If we had wanted to be thorough, we could have checked for the presence of `my:message` in the header before entering the `choose` block and then verified the correct formatting of `reqTime`.

Lines 25-28 are where you prepare the response to `reqTime` by adding the `my:time` element to the body of the message. Notice how lines 25-26 are practically identical to lines 15-16 of `myMess_create_mess.jspf`, where you add `my:message` to the message header. In line 28, you add textual content to `my:time`.

Listing 6-17 shows the output of `myMess_send.jsp`.

Listing 6-17. *The HTML Page Generated by myMess_send.jsp*

```
---------- Request message ----------
<?xml version="1.0" encoding="ISO-8859-1" ?>
<env:Envelope xmlns:env="http://www.w3.org/2003/05/soap-envelope">
<env:Header>
<my:message xmlns:my="myMess.xsd" env:mustUnderstand="true"/>
</env:Header>
<env:Body>
<my:reqTime xmlns:my="myMess.xsd"/>
</env:Body>
</env:Envelope>


---------- Response message ----------
<?xml version="1.0" encoding="ISO-8859-1" ?>
<env:Envelope xmlns:env="http://www.w3.org/2003/05/soap-envelope">
<env:Header>
<my:message xmlns:my="myMess.xsd" env:mustUnderstand="true"/>
</env:Header>
<env:Body>
<my:time xmlns:my="myMess.xsd">Mon Jul 09 10:10:52 CEST 2007
</my:time>
</env:Body>
</env:Envelope>
```

If you edit `myMess_send.jsp` and change `reqTime` to something else in line 14, the `my:time` element in the response will be replaced by the following lines (the tags were originally left-justified, but we indented them for clarity):

```
<env:Fault>
  <env:Code>
    <env:Value>env:Receiver</env:Value>
    </env:Code>
  <env:Reason>
    <env:Text xml:lang="en-US">Unknown request</env:Text>
    </env:Reason>
  </env:Fault>
```

Each env:fault element includes a code and a reason. We only specified a text reason, but several options are available.

Summary

In this chapter, we described the structure and syntax of XML documents, DTDs, and XML schemas, and we showed you how to validate XML documents against DTDs and schemas. We then introduced XSL and presented examples of transformation from XML to XML and from XML to HTML. Finally, we described the SOAP protocol and showed how you can use it to exchange data between JSP pages.

In the next chapter, we'll talk about Tomcat. Among other things, we'll tell you how to create virtual hosts and how to configure the support of encrypted pages.

CHAPTER 7

■■■

Tomcat 6

We've been using Tomcat in all the previous chapters to show you examples of servlets and JSP pages and documents. The moment has finally come to talk about Tomcat itself.

Tomcat is essentially three things:

- A web server

- An application that executes Java servlets

- An application that converts JSP pages and documents into Java servlets

In this chapter, we'll describe the basics of Tomcat's architecture and its directory structure. We'll then show you examples of how to do a couple of useful things.

At the moment of writing, the latest release of Tomcat is 6.0.14, which runs on Java SE 5, implements the Servlet 2.5 and JSP 2.1 specifications, and supports UEL 2.1. Tomcat is the reference implementation (RI) for the Servlet and JSP standards. This means that Tomcat follows the standards closely, and everything running under Tomcat will also run under any other Servlet/JSP container compliant with the standards it implements.

Tomcat is a project of the Apache Software Foundation. Therefore, the authoritative source for obtaining further information on Tomcat is http://tomcat.apache.org/, which provides extensive documentation. As an alternative, you can buy the book *Pro Apache Tomcat 6*,[1] also available as an eBook, which tells you everything you can possibly need to know but is expressed in a more digestible form than that of the original documentation.

Tomcat's Architecture and server.xml

Tomcat's architecture consists of a series of functional components that can be combined according to well-defined rules. The structure of each server installation is defined in the file server.xml, which is located in the conf subdirectory of Tomcat's installation folder.

In the rest of this section, we'll go through the components. Listing 7-1 shows the default server.xml (after removing the comments). We'll refer to it when describing the various components.

---

1. Matthew Moodie and Kunal Mittal (Ed.), *Pro Apache Tomcat 6* (Berkeley, CA: Apress, 2007)

Listing 7-1. *Default server.xml*

```
01: <Server port="8005" shutdown="SHUTDOWN">
02:   <Listener className="org.apache.catalina.core.AprLifecycleListener"➥
 SSLEngine="on" />
03:   <Listener className="org.apache.catalina.core.JasperListener" />
04:   <Listener className=➥
"org.apache.catalina.mbeans.ServerLifecycleListener" />
05:   <Listener className=➥
"org.apache.catalina.mbeans.GlobalResourcesLifecycleListener" />
06:   <GlobalNamingResources>
07:     <Resource name="UserDatabase" auth="Container"
08:               type="org.apache.catalina.UserDatabase"
09:               description="User database that can be updated and saved"
10:               factory="org.apache.catalina.users.MemoryUserDatabaseFactory"
11:               pathname="conf/tomcat-users.xml" />
12:   </GlobalNamingResources>
13:   <Service name="Catalina">
14:     <Connector port="8080" protocol="HTTP/1.1"
15:                connectionTimeout="20000"
16:                redirectPort="8443" />
17:     <Connector port="8009" protocol="AJP/1.3" redirectPort="8443" />
18:     <Engine name="Catalina" defaultHost="localhost">
19:       <Realm className="org.apache.catalina.realm.UserDatabaseRealm"
20:              resourceName="UserDatabase"/>
21:       <Host name="localhost"  appBase="webapps"
22:             unpackWARs="true" autoDeploy="true"
23:             xmlValidation="false" xmlNamespaceAware="false">
24:       </Host>
25:     </Engine>
26:   </Service>
27: </Server>
```

Figure 7-1 shows how the major Tomcat components are organized in hierarchical fashion.

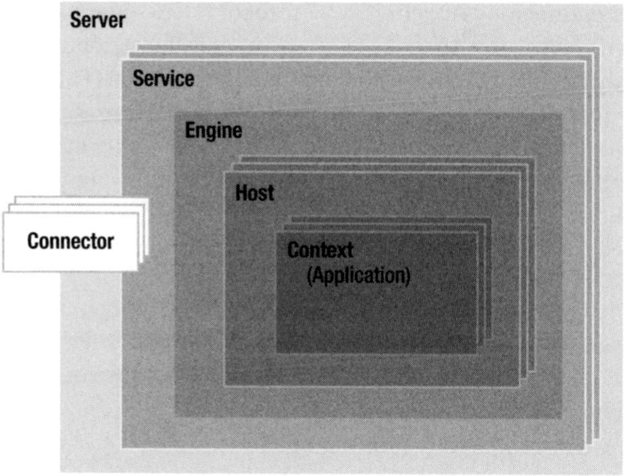

Figure 7-1. *Tomcat's architecture*

Context

The Context is the innermost element of a group of Tomcat components called *containers*, and it represents a single web application.

Tomcat automatically instantiates and configures a standard context upon loading your application. As part of the configuration, Tomcat also processes the properties defined in the WEB-INF\web.xml file of your application folder and makes them available to the application. For example, the web.xml file for Eshopf defines, among other properties, a context parameter and a resource reference (see Listing 5-19).

Connector

The Connector is a component associated with a TCP port that handles the communication between applications and clients (e.g., remote browsers). The default configuration of Tomcat includes a connector to handle HTTP communication. By default, this connector waits for requests coming through port 8080. This is why the URLs of our examples always start with http://localhost:8080/.

Later in this chapter, we'll show you how to change the port number from 8080 to 80, which is the default port for HTTP. Then, you'll be able to access the examples via http://localhost/.

The presence of an HTTP connector is what makes Tomcat a web server. Note that the requests for all applications go through a single instance of this connector. Each new request causes the instantiation of a new thread inside the connector, which remains alive for the duration of the request.

Articles about Tomcat often refer to this connector as "Coyote." Lines 14-16 of Listing 7-1 show how the HTTP connector is defined in server.xml. The connectionTimeout attribute set to 20,000 means that a session is terminated after 5 hours, 33 minutes, and 20 seconds of inactivity, while redirectPort="8443" means that incoming requests that require SSL transport are redirected to port 8443. We'll show you later how you can enable SSL on Tomcat so that it can handle the HTTPS protocol.

By default, Tomcat defines another connector—Apache JServ Protocol (AJP)—which is used to communicate with a web server, such as the Apache HTTP server (see line 17 of Listing 7-1). This connector lets Tomcat only handle dynamic web pages and lets a pure HTML server (e.g., the Apache Web Server) handle the requests for static pages. This maximizes the efficiency with which the requests are handled. Nevertheless, you'll probably be better off keeping it simple and relying on Tomcat to handle all requests, especially if most of your pages are dynamic. Also, consider that the efficiency of Tomcat has been improving with each release.[2] If you don't plan on using a web server together with Tomcat, you can comment out this connector.

Host

The Host container represents a virtual host, which is the association of a name such as www.myDomain.com with the server. A host can contain any number of contexts (i.e., applications).

You can define several hosts on the same server. For example, if you have registered the domain myDomain.com, you can define host names such as w1.myDomain.com and w2.myDomain.com. Later in this chapter, we'll show you how to define a virtual host, but keep in mind that it will only be accessible from the Internet if a domain name server maps its name to the IP address of your computer. For this purpose, you should be able to use the DNS of the company you registered your domain with (i.e., your registrar), but only if you've obtained a fixed IP address from your ISP.

The default configuration of Tomcat includes the host named localhost (see lines 21-24 of Listing 7-1), which you've encountered in many examples. We just said that a host is reachable by name if it is mapped by a DNS to the IP address of the computer. It is obviously not possible to use such a mechanism that relies on external systems to map localhost, which is local by definition. The association between localhost and your computer is done instead by writing an entry in the file C:\Windows\System32\drivers\etc\hosts. We'll come back to this file when we explain how to define a virtual host.

The Host attribute appBase defines the application directory within the Tomcat installation folder. Each application is then identified by its path within that directory. The only exception is the path ROOT, which is mapped to the empty string. The application base directory for localhost is webapps. This means that the application in this directory:

```
C:\Program Files\Apache Software Foundation\Tomcat 6.0\webapps\ROOT\
```

is identified by the empty string. Therefore, its URL is http://localhost:8080/.

The URL of applications in a directory different from ROOT, as in the following example, is http://localhost:8080/*appl-dir*/:

```
C:\Program Files\Apache Software Foundation\Tomcat 6.0\webapps\appl-dir\
```

You can also assign an absolute directory to appBase.

The attribute unpackWARs="true" means that if you drop a WAR file in the appBase directory, Tomcat will automatically expand it into a normal folder. If you set this attribute to false,

---

2. For example, see http://tomcat.apache.org/articles/benchmark_summary.pdf.

the application will run directly from the WAR file. This obviously means a slower execution of the application, because it needs to be unzipped at execution time.

The attribute autoDeploy="true" means that if you drop an application in the appBase directory while Tomcat is running, it will be deployed automatically. Actually, this definition is redundant because the default for autoDeploy is true.

The attributes xmlValidation="false" and xmlNamespaceAware="false" refer to the web.xml files used in this host. If you switch xmlValidation to true but leave xmlNamespaceAware set to false, you'll have a limited validation because the DTDs/schemas will be ignored. We recommend that you leave both attributes set to false. You're better off checking your XMLs with a tool such as Eclipse, which tells you beforehand where the problems are instead of relying on the stack trace that Tomcat displays at execution time.

Engine

The Engine is the highest level of container. It can contain several hosts, but it cannot be contained by any other container component.

An engine must contain one or more hosts, one of which is designated as the default host. The default Tomcat configuration includes the engine Catalina (see line 18 of Listing 7-1), which contains the host localhost (obviously designated to be the default host because it is the only one).

The Catalina engine handles all incoming requests received via the HTTP connector and sends back the corresponding responses. It forwards each request to the correct host and context on the basis of the information contained in the request header.

This Catalina engine is the servlet engine that we mentioned in Chapter 1 (see Figure 1-2).

Service

The purpose of the Service component is to associate one or more connectors to a particular engine.

Tomcat's default configuration includes the service Catalina (see line 13 of Listing 7-1, and yes, it is named like the engine), which associates the HTTP and AJP connectors to the Catalina engine. Accordingly, Connector and Engine are subelements of the Service element.

Server

The Server is the top component, which represents an instance of Tomcat. In can contain one or more services, each with its own engine and connectors.

You might find this hierarchy of components more complicated than necessary, but it provides a flexible structure. In any case, it is unlikely that you'll need more than one instance of Tomcat and more than the default Catalina service and engine.

Listener

The Listener is a Java object that, by implementing the org.apache.catalina.LifecycleListener interface, is able to respond to specific events. The default server.xml, as you can see in lines 2-5 of Listing 7-1, defines four listeners inside the Server component.

The first listener enables the Apache Portable Runtime (APR) library. This library provides functionality that integrates what is made available by the operating system (in our case, Microsoft Windows). Its purpose is to increase portability across OSs. One of the functions of the package is to support OpenSSL if the SSLEngine attribute is set to on (which is the default).

The second listener enables Jasper, which is the JSP engine. For example, this listener is what makes it possible to recompile JSP documents that have been updated.

The third listener enables Java Management Extensions (JMX). This technology, included in Java SE, makes it possible to have remote monitoring and management of system objects, applications, networks, and devices.

The fourth and last listener enables global resources. For example, it makes it possible for us to use JNDI to access a MySQL database in Eshopf (see Listing 5-19).

The bottom line is that these listeners improve or provide some of Tomcat's functionality and should remain untouched.

Global Naming Resources

The GlobalNamingResources element can only be defined inside the Server component. It defines JNDI resources that are accessible throughout the server.

The only resource included in the default server.xml is a user and password memory-based database defined via the file conf/tomcat-users.xml (see lines 7-12 of Listing 7-1). In Appendix D, we've included an example of how you can use this resource to implement user authentication.

Realm

The Realm component can appear inside any container component (Engine, Host, and Context). It represents a database of users, passwords, and user roles. Its purpose is to support container-based authentication. In other words, you can specify an authentication database for each application, host, or engine.

The only realm defined in the default server.xml is in the Catalina engine (see lines 19-20 of Listing 7-1). It refers to the user database defined as a JNDI global resource.

Beside UserDatabaseRealm, the following realm classes are available: JDBCRealm (to connect to a relational database via its JDBC driver), DataSourceRealm (to connect to a JDBC data source named via JNDI), JNDIRealm (to connect to an LDAP directory), and MemoryRealm (to load an XML file in memory).

Cluster

Tomcat supports server clustering by providing the following three functions:

- **Replication of sessions across the clustered servers**: This ensures that a session opened on one server is valid on all other servers.

- **Replication of context attributes**: This makes it possible for you to access the attributes on all servers.

- **Cluster-wide deployment via WAR files**: This ensures that the same application executes on all servers of a cluster.

You can place a `Cluster` element inside an `Engine` or a `Host` container.

Valve

A `Valve` is an element that, when inserted in a `Container` (`Context`, `Host`, or `Engine`), intercepts all the incoming HTTP requests before they reach the application. This gives you the ability to preprocess the requests directed to a particular application, to the applications running in a virtual host, or to all the applications running within an engine.

One of the valves you might like to use is the *access log* valve, which lets you customize request log entries in a file of your choice. Later in this section, we'll show you an example of how to do it.

The *remote address filter* valve lets you selectively block requests on the basis of their source IP address. It supports two attributes—`allow` and `deny`—which accept regular expressions as values (for a brief description of regular expressions, see the "Regular Expressions" sidebar in Chapter 6). For example, this valve allows all requests originated from any of the IP addresses `192.168.*.*` and rejects all the others:

```
<Valve className="org.apache.catalina.valves.RemoteAddrValve"
    allow="192\.168.*"/>
```

On the other hand, with `deny="84.74.97.75"`, it would have allowed all requests with the exception of those coming from the IP address `84.74.97.75`.

The *remote host filter* valve operates like the remote address filter valve but on client host names instead of client IP addresses. For example, this valve only allows requests from hosts belonging to the domain `myweb.com`:

```
<Valve className="org.apache.catalina.valves.RemoteHostValve"
    allow=".*myweb\.com"/>
```

The *request dumper* valve logs details of the incoming requests and therefore is useful for debugging purposes. Here's how you define it:

```
<Valve className="org.apache.catalina.valves.RequestDumperValve"/>
```

The *single sign on* valve, when included in a Host container, has the effect of requiring only one authentication for all the applications of that host. Without this valve, the user would have to enter his ID and password before using each separate application. Here's how you use it:

```
<Valve className="org.apache.catalina.valves.SingleSignOn"/>
```

Loader and Manager

By defining a Loader element inside a Context element, you can replace the standard class-loading mechanism in an application with your own. We see no reason for you to do so, as the default Loader works just fine.

You define a Manager if you want to replace the default session management. As we said concerning the Loader element, it isn't likely that you'll ever need to do so.

Directory Structure

If you've installed Tomcat as we explain in Appendix A, Tomcat will be in the following directory:

```
C:\Program Files\Apache Software Foundation\Tomcat 6.0\
```

From now on, we'll refer to this as the *Tomcat folder*.

The Tomcat folder contains the following subdirectories: bin, conf, lib, logs, temp, webapps, and work, as shown in Figure 7-2. Two of them are pretty obvious: bin is where the Tomcat executable resides, and temp is a working directory for temporary files.

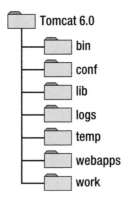

Figure 7-2. *Tomcat's top directories*

conf

The conf directory contains the configuration files that apply to all applications. The server.xml file, which we described in the previous section, is one of them. Besides two property files and one policy file used internally by Tomcat, you'll also see context.xml, tomcat-users.xml, and web.xml, which define defaults for all the applications of the server.

For example, in Chapter 5, we showed you how to use a context.xml file containing a Context element to make the information concerning a MySQL database accessible to Eshopf. On that occasion, context.xml was in the META-INF application subfolder. The same file placed in the conf folder would make the same database data accessible to all applications. For an example of how to use tomcat-users.xml to implement user authentication, please refer to Appendix D.

This conf folder also includes a subfolder for each engine. By default, only a folder named Catalina exists. Inside the engine folder is a folder for each host, containing host-specific context information. By default, only a folder named localhost exists. We'll come back to this later in this chapter, when we tell you how to create virtual hosts.

lib

All the JAR files are kept in the lib directory. Immediately after you complete the installation of Tomcat, this directory will contain the following libraries: annotations-api.jar, catalina.jar, catalina-ant.jar, catalina-ha.jar, catalina-tribes.jar, el-api.jar, jasper.jar, jasper-el.jar, jasper-jdt.jar, jsp-api.jar, servlet-api.jar, tomcat-coyote.jar, tomcat-dbcp.jar, and some libraries for internationalization, such as tomcat-i18n-es.jar and tomcat-i18n-fr.jar.

After installing all the additional packages we recommend, you should also see mysql-connector-java-5.0.6-bin.jar (the JDBC driver for MySQL), jstl.jar and standard.jar (for JSTL), serializer.jar, xalan.jar, xercesImpl.jar, and xml-apis.jar (for XPath and XML manipulation), and jsf-api.jar and jsf-impl.jar (for JSF).

logs

Tomcat keeps its log files in the logs directory. On any given day of operation, you'll see the following files: catalina.*yyyy-mm-dd*.log, jakarta_service_*yyyymmdd*.log, localhost.*yyyy-mm-dd*.log, stderr_*yyyymmdd*.log, and stdout_*yyyymmdd*.log. Additionally, you'll also see admin.*yyyy-mm-dd*.log, host-manager.*yyyy-mm-dd*.log, and manager.*yyyy-mm-dd*.log, but they will systematically be empty.

If you want to write something to the stdout log from JSP, you can simply write to System.out. For example, this code writes a line containing "bla bla bla" in the file stdout_*yyyymmdd*.log:

```
<% System.out.println("bla bla bla"); %>
```

The output of System.err also goes to stdout. Therefore, you won't be able to write to stderr.

Later in this chapter, we'll show you how you can log the requests received by your applications.

webapps

The webapps directory is the application base directory of localhost. The content of any subdirectory of webapps is accessible by browsers. For example, if you create the folder aaa inside webapps and copy into it the file bbb.jsp, you'll be able to execute it by typing this in your browser:

```
http://localhost:8080/aaa/bbb.jsp
```

ROOT

ROOT is the default application folder for localhost. Its name is mapped to the empty string, so you'll be able to execute any file placed into ROOT by appending its name directly to the URL of your host—for example:

```
http://localhost:8080/my_file.jsp
```

work

Tomcat keeps the translation of JSP into Java in the work directory. For example, if you create the file stdout.jsp as follows:

```
<%@page language="java" contentType="text/html"%>
<html><body><% System.out.println("jsp out"); %></body></html>
```

and then place it inside the webapps\ROOT\ folder and execute it by typing this in a browser:

```
http://localhost:8080/stdout.jsp
```

Tomcat will translate it into stdout_jsp.java and compile it into stdout_jsp.class. The two files will be in work\Catalina\localhost_\org\apache\jsp\, where Catalina is the engine name, localhost is the host name, and the underscore indicates that it is the default application of the host.

The Java listing is 68 lines long. Therefore, we won't show it here. However, you should look at least once at how Tomcat converts a JSP page into a servlet. The actual JSP code becomes:

```
out.write("\r\n");
out.write("<html><body>ok");
System.out.println("jsp out");
out.write("</body></html>\r\n");
```

Example: Logging the Requests

To log the incoming requests directed to all applications of a particular host, you only need to include an access log valve in the corresponding Host element of server.xml. For example, this code logs the requests for localhost applications in the localhost-access.*yyyy-mm-dd*.log file:

```
<Valve className="org.apache.catalina.valves.AccessLogValve"
    directory="logs" prefix="localhost-access." suffix=".log"
    pattern="common" resolveHosts="false"/>
```

Listing 7-2 shows some examples of log entries.

Listing 7-2. *localhost-access.2007-08-30.log*

```
01: 127.0.0.1 - - [30/Aug/2007:17:15:22 +0200]➡
 "GET / HTTP/1.1" 200 7354
02: 127.0.0.1 - - [30/Aug/2007:17:15:22 +0200]➡
 "GET /tomcat.gif HTTP/1.1" 200 1934
03: 127.0.0.1 - - [30/Aug/2007:17:15:22 +0200]➡
 "GET /asf-logo-wide.gif HTTP/1.1" 200 5866
04: 127.0.0.1 - - [30/Aug/2007:17:15:22 +0200]➡
 "GET /tomcat-power.gif HTTP/1.1" 200 2324
05: 127.0.0.1 - - [30/Aug/2007:17:15:22 +0200]➡
 "GET /favicon.ico HTTP/1.1" 200 21630
06: 127.0.0.1 - - [30/Aug/2007:17:15:30 +0200]➡
 "GET /RELEASE-NOTES.txt HTTP/1.1" 200 6656
07: 127.0.0.1 - - [30/Aug/2007:17:15:45 +0200]➡
 "GET /tomcat-docs HTTP/1.1" 404 988
08: 127.0.0.1 - - [30/Aug/2007:17:16:00 +0200]➡
 "GET /docs/ HTTP/1.1" 200 13397
09: 127.0.0.1 - - [30/Aug/2007:17:16:00 +0200]➡
 "GET /docs/images/asf-logo.gif HTTP/1.1" 200 7279
10: 127.0.0.1 - - [30/Aug/2007:17:16:00 +0200]➡
 "GET /docs/images/printer.gif HTTP/1.1" 200 438
11: 127.0.0.1 - - [30/Aug/2007:17:16:00 +0200]➡
 "GET /docs/images/tomcat.gif HTTP/1.1" 200 1934
```

Tomcat logged lines 1-5 when we requested the page http://localhost/, line 6 when we requested http://localhost/RELEASE-NOTES.txt, line 7 when we requested http://localhost/tomcat-docs (which doesn't exist), and lines 8-11 when we requested http://localhost/docs/.

Each log entry begins with the IP address of localhost (127.0.0.1), followed by the date and time of the request. The next field is a quoted string (e.g., "GET /docs/ HTTP/1.1"), which contains the type of request (GET), the relative URL of the page (/docs/), and the protocol used (HTTP/1.1). The last two fields are the HTTP status code and the request size in bytes.

The status codes are defined in the standard RFC 2616 (see http://www.w3.org/Protocols/rfc2616/rfc2616-sec10.html). For example, 200 means OK, while 404 means Not Found.

Note how the request for the images contained in the page follows the request of the page itself. Also, after requesting RELEASE-NOTES.txt but before requesting tomcat-docs, we redisplayed Tomcat's home page. Nevertheless, Tomcat made no entry in the log. This is because the browser had cached the page when we requested it the first time and didn't actually send any request to the server. You have to keep this issue of caching in mind if you want to make sense of the access logs, especially since caching can occur not only in the client's browser but also in proxy servers between the client and the server.

If you want to log only the requests directed to a particular application, you can include the valve in a Context element, as in the following example:

```
<Context debug="5" reloadable="true" crossContext="true">
  <Valve className="org.apache.catalina.valves.AccessLogValve"
    directory="logs" prefix="eshop-access." suffix=".log" pattern="common"
    resolveHosts="false"/>
</Context>
```

and place it in the META-INF\context.xml file of the application folder.

The directory attribute specifies where Tomcat creates the log file. In this case, we decided to use the relative path logs, which is where Tomcat keeps all the other logs. The prefix and suffix attributes define the strings to be placed around the log date to form the daily file names. The resolveHosts attribute specifies whether Tomcat should try to resolve the originating IP address into a host name. We strongly recommend that you set it to false, because the name resolution would significantly slow down the logging process.

The pattern attribute defines the format of the log entries. You can form your own pattern by concatenating some of the identifiers listed in Table 7-1 (adapted from the Tomcat 6.0 documentation).

Table 7-1. *Pattern Identifiers*

ID	Function
%a	Remote IP address
%A	Local IP address
%b	Bytes sent, excluding HTTP headers, or - if zero
%B	Bytes sent, excluding HTTP headers
%h	Remote host name (or IP address if resolveHosts is false)
%H	Request protocol
%l	Remote logical username from identd (always returns -)
%m	Request method (GET, POST, and so on)
%p	Local port on which this request was received
%q	Query string (prepended with a ? if it exists)
%r	First line of the request (method and request URI)
%s	HTTP status code of the response
%S	User session ID
%t	Date and time, in Common Log Format
%u	Remote user who was authenticated (if any), else -
%U	Requested URL path
%v	Local server name
%D	Time taken to process the request, in milliseconds
%T	Time taken to process the request, in seconds

pattern="common" tells Tomcat to use the standard log entry format and is equivalent to the pattern %h %l %u %t "%r" %s %b. You can also use the predefined pattern combined, which is like common with the addition of the referer (i.e., the page that made the request) and the user agent (e.g., Firefox).

Example: Tomcat on Port 80

The standard HTTP port is 80, while Tomcat by default waits for incoming requests on port 8080. If you use Tomcat to handle static HTML pages as well dynamic pages, you might like to change the port number to the standard 80, so that no port needs to be specified in the URLs.

All you need to do is update the HTTP connector defined in server.xml. Change the value assigned to the port attribute from 8080 to 80, restart Tomcat, and you're done.

Example: Creating a Virtual Host

Suppose that you register the domain name jsp-jsf.com (not registered at the time of writing) and would like to point it to your server. Normally, you should have a fixed IP address to be able to do it. Unfortunately, unless you ask your ISP to have a fixed address and pay for it, you just get a dynamic IP address from the ISP. In that case, you can still point a domain name to your computer by using the dynamic DNS service offered online by several providers.

In any case, once requests sent to jsp-jsf.com reach your computer, Tomcat must be able to recognize them and send them to the right applications. For that to happen, you have to create a Host element in server.xml and a couple of directories.

Place the following element inside the Catalina Engine element of server.xml:

```
<Host name="www.jsp-jsf.com"  appBase="webapps/www.jsp-jsf.com"
    unpackWARs="true" autoDeploy="true"
    xmlValidation="false" xmlNamespaceAware="false">
  <Alias>jsp-jsf.com</Alias>
  <Valve className="org.apache.catalina.valves.AccessLogValve"
    directory="logs" prefix="www.jsp-jsf.com_access." suffix=".log"
    pattern="common" resolveHosts="false"/>
</Host>
```

Notice that we've defined an Alias, so that the "naked" domain name jsp-jsf.com becomes an alternate name for the host name, which is www.jsp-jsf.com. There is no need to have a www host, but it is what almost everybody expects. Obviously, you could choose any other name. Also, notice that the application base directory has the same name as the host. Any other name would have been perfectly acceptable, but by calling the base directory like the host, you ensure that you'll never get the directories mixed up, regardless of the number of virtual hosts you'll create.

Now create a folder named www.jsp-jsf.com inside conf\Catalina, a second folder also named www.jsp-jsf.com inside webapps, and a third folder named ROOT inside the newly created webapps\www.jsp-jsf.com (all paths relative to the Tomcat folder).

Restart Tomcat, and you're ready to access your host. To test it, you only need to place the following index.html file inside ROOT:

```
<html><head></head><body>Welcome to www.jsp-jsf.com!</body></html>
```

If a DNS entry points to your web address, you'll be able to see your welcome file by typing this line in a browser with or without www:

```
http://www.jsp-jsf.com/
```

To test it without any DNS entry, open the file `C:\Windows\System32\drivers\etc\hosts` and add the following lines to the end:

```
127.0.0.1    www.jsp-jsf.com
127.0.0.1    jsp-jsf.com
```

This maps your domain and host names to the local system. As the communication software checks the file `host` before asking external DNSs to lookup a host name, you'll be able to test your virtual hosts without DNSs. This also allows you to test an application on any computer before deploying it to its final destination.

Example: HTTPS

In this section, we'll explain how to create a secure web site. We'll use the virtual host `www.jsp-jsf.com` that we created in the previous section as a base.

First, create a connector for the HTTPS protocol. The configuration file `server.xml` already includes a connector definition for this purpose, but it is commented out and uses port 8443, which is nonstandard. Simply remove the comments and change 8443 to 443:

```
<Connector port="443" protocol="HTTP/1.1" SSLEnabled="true"
    maxThreads="150" scheme="https" secure="true"
    clientAuth="false" sslProtocol="TLS"/>
```

To keep everything neat, you might also like to remove the `redirectPort="8443"` attribute from the connector for port 80.

A secure protocol requires encryption, so you need to create a security certificate. You can easily do so with the program `keytool` included in the JDK package. Open a DOS window by navigating to `Accessories` ➤ `Command Prompt` and type the following command (we've broken it down into two pieces, but you should enter it on a single line):

```
"C:\Program Files\Java\jdk1.6.0_01\bin\keytool" -genkey -alias tomcat
    -keyalg RSA -keystore ".keystore" -storepass changeit
```

Note that the quotes are necessary. The `keytool` program will ask you a series of questions. Answer with `www.jsp-jsf.com` to the first one and then keep hitting Enter until it asks whether you confirm the previous answers. Confirm and then hit Enter when it asks about the Tomcat key password. This command creates the file named `.keystore` in your `Documents and Settings` directory. If you specified a different user ID when installing Tomcat, you'll have to move the `.keystore` file to the `Documents and Settings` directory of that user.

After restarting Tomcat, open a browser window and type `https://www.jsp-jsf.com/`. The browser will open a dialog like that shown in Figure 7-3.

You see this dialog because the certificate was issued by you instead of by a recognized certificate authority. If you click on the `Examine Certificate...` button, you'll see the dialog shown in Figure 7-4.

Figure 7-3. *Unknown authority*

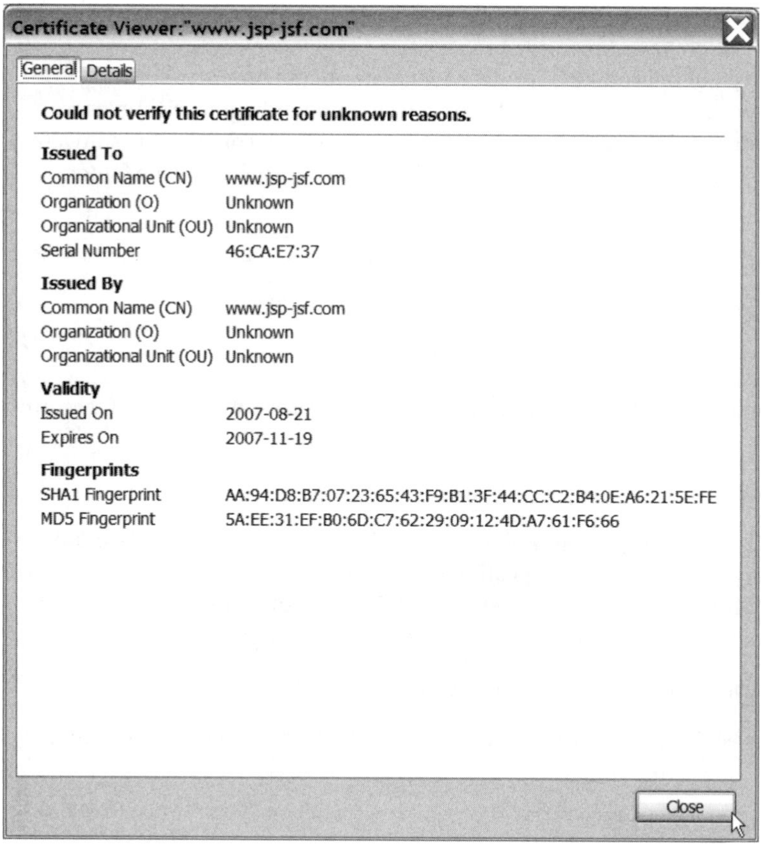

Figure 7-4. *Security certificate*

To keep going, after closing the certificate window, click on Accept this certificate permanently and then on OK.

If the Issued To name on the certificate doesn't match the host name, you'll also get a warning like that shown in Figure 7-5.

Figure 7-5. *Domain name mismatch*

Application Deployment

The simplest way to deploy an application with Tomcat is to create an application folder and place it inside the application base directory of the host.

For example, if you go to the Source Code/Download area of the Apress web site (http://www.apress.com) and download the software package containing the examples we developed for this manual, you'll find that the folder named 05, which contains the software associated with Chapter 5, includes an application folder named eshopf. Copy the folder eshopf to this directory:

```
C:\Program Files\Apache Software Foundation\Tomcat 6.0\webapps\www.jsp-jsf.com
```

and you'll be able to use the application via the following URL:

```
http://www.jsp-jsf.com/eshopf/
```

If you copy the application folder to webapps rather than to webapps\www.jsp-jsf.com, the URL will be:

```
http://localhost/eshopf/
```

Another way of deploying an application is to create a WAR file, as we briefly described at the end of Chapter 1, and place it in the application base directory of the host. Tomcat will then take care of expanding it into the application folder. For example, copy the eshop.war file you find in the folder named G of our software package to this directory:

```
C:\Program Files\Apache Software Foundation\Tomcat 6.0\webapps\www.jsp-jsf.com
```

Wait a few seconds while Tomcat expands it. You'll be able to use the Eshop application via the following URL:

```
http://www.jsp-jsf.com/eshop/shop
```

If you drop the WAR file into `webapps` rather than into `webapps\www.jsp-jsf.com`, the URL will be

```
http://localhost/eshop/shop
```

You can deploy an application without having to restart Tomcat, because the definitions of `localhost` and `www.jsp-jsf.com` contained in `server.xml` include the attributes `unpackWARs="true"` and `autoDeploy="true"`.

You might decide to define hosts that don't support automatic deployment. This would improve security, but would also force you to restart Tomcat in order to deploy or redeploy applications. To resolve this issue, Tomcat's developers have created a manager application that lets you deploy your applications without having to restart Tomcat.

To be able to use the manager application, edit the `server.xml` file and insert the following element into the element that defines the host you want to manage:

```
<Context path="/manager" privileged="true" docBase="manager">
  <Valve className="org.apache.catalina.valves.RemoteAddrValve"
    allow="127.0.0.1"/>
  </Context>
```

The `Valve` element prevents you from using it remotely. Remove the `Valve` element if you want to be able to use it from a system other than that on which you have installed Tomcat. As an added measure of security, the manager application requires you to log in with a user ID that has manager capabilities. You defined such a user ID when you installed Tomcat. If you've forgotten the ID or its associated password, look inside the `tomcat-users.xml` file, which is located in the same `conf` directory as `server.xml`. There you'll find the following element:

```
<user username="userID" password="pass" roles="admin,manager" />
```

Now, if you type the URL `http://localhost/manager/list` in a browser, after logging in with the manager user ID and password, you'll see a page containing the list of all applications of the host:

```
OK - Listed applications for virtual host localhost
/:running:0:ROOT
/manager:running:0:manager
/docs:running:0:docs
/examples:running:0:examples
/host-manager:running:0:host-manager
/eshopf:running:0:eshopf
```

To deploy an application, you need to replace `list` with `deploy`, as in the following example:

```
http://localhost/manager/deploy?path=/yyy&war=file:c:\wars\eshopx.war
```

This command takes the file `c:\wars\eshopx.war`, copies it to `webapps`, which is the application base directory of `locahost`, renames it `yyy.war`, and expands it into the folder `yyy`. It displays a page with the following single line:

```
OK - Deployed application at context path /yyy
```

After that, you can execute the application by typing this URL:

```
http://localhost/yyy/shop
```

Note that you can use both forward and backward slashes for the war parameter, but for the path parameter, you must use forward slashes.

To undeploy the application, type this URL:

```
http://localhost/manager/undeploy?path=/yyy
```

The command removes from webapps both the folder yyy and the file yyy.war that the deploy command had created. It then displays the following message:

```
OK - Undeployed application at context path /yyy
```

Other useful commands are reload, stop, and start, which all accept the path parameter to identify the application.

Summary

In this chapter, we were only able to provide a brief introduction to a complex package. Nevertheless, Tomcat's default configuration already covers the functionality that most people are ever going to need.

We started by describing the components that make up Tomcat. Then, we continued our introduction to Tomcat by explaining how its directories are organized. Finally, we showed some examples of how to modify Tomcat's default configuration. In particular, we explained how to log incoming requests, how to use the standard HTTP ports, and how to create a virtual host, including the handling of encrypted pages.

In the next chapter, we'll complete the description of the Eshop* applications that we've used throughout the book as a source of examples.

CHAPTER 8

■■■

Eshop

In several chapters of this book, we've used examples taken from three different versions of our online bookshop application: Eshop, Eshopx, and Eshopf. In this chapter, we'll complete the description of those applications, so that you can use them as models for your own.

All three versions have the same functionality and generate almost identical HTML pages. Their differences are in the way in which you implement their functionality. The main difference between the two versions we introduced in Chapter 2, Eshop and Eshopx, is that the JSP code in Eshop is in standard JSP syntax, while the code in Eshopx is in XML syntax. The third version of the application, named Eshopf and described in Chapter 5, is quite different from the first two, because we implemented it with JSF. This required us to replace the original servlet with the JSF servlet. Although we used Eshopx as a base for developing Eshopf, we obviously had to rewrite the user interface almost from scratch.

You can download the complete code in the Source Code/Download area of the Apress web site (http://www.apress.com) and install each version of the application by copying the corresponding folder to Tomcat's webapps directory.

The Eshop Application

Toward the beginning of Chapter 2, in the "Objects and Operations" section, we described the objects this application deals with (product categories, books, shopping cart, and order) and the operations the user can perform on those objects. In the "The Eshop Architecture" section, we then described the MVC architecture of Eshop. In particular, we listed the methods of the DataManager class (Table 2-2), described the initialization of the servlet (Listing 2-1 and Table 2-3), summarized how the servlet handles incoming requests, and listed the JSP pages (Table 2-4). We also took you through a typical user session.

In Chapter 4, we showed you the code of Category.java (Listing 4-1) and described the script shop.sql (Listing 4-2), which creates the shop database containing categories, books, and orders. We then devoted the whole "DB Access in Eshop" section to describing how the data manager updates the database via the *peer* methods (Figure 4-1 and Listings 4-3 to 4-6).

In this chapter, we'll start by listing all the subfolders and files in the Eshop application folder (see Listing 8-1, where the folder names are in bold).

Listing 8-1. *The Eshop Files*

css
>   eshop.css

images
>   1.gif, 2.gif, 3.gif, 4.gif, 5.gif, 6.gif
>   bg_header.gif
>   bg_menu.gif
>   cart.gif

jsp
>   BookDetails.jsp
>   Checkout.jsp
>   LeftMenu.jsp
>   OrderConfirmation.jsp
>   SearchOutcome.jsp
>   SelectCatalog.jsp
>   ShoppingCart.jsp
>   TopMenu.jsp

META-INF
>   MANIFEST.MF

WEB-INF
>   web.xml
>   **classes**
>   **eshop**
>   ShopServlet.class
>   ShopServlet.java
>   **beans**
>   Book.class, Book.java
>   CartItem.class, CartItem.java
>   Category.class, Category.java
>   Customer.class, Customer.java
>   **model**
>   BookPeer.class, BookPeer.java
>   CategoryPeer.class, CategoryPeer.java
>   DataManager.class, DataManager.java
>   OrderDetailsPeer.class, OrderDetailsPeer.java
>   OrderPeer.class, OrderPeer.java
>   shop.sql

To complete the description of the ShopServlet class, we need to show you how it selects the appropriate JSP page on the basis of the request, thereby fulfilling its role as a controller. Listing 8-2 shows the code of the doPost method (as we mentioned already in Chapter 1, doGet simply executes doPost).

Listing 8-2. *ShopServlet.java—doPost Method*

```java
protected void doPost(HttpServletRequest request,
    HttpServletResponse response) throws ServletException, IOException {
  String base = "/jsp/";
  String url = base + "index.jsp";
  String action = request.getParameter("action");
  if (action != null) {
    if (action.equals("search"))
      url = base + "SearchOutcome.jsp";
    else if (action.equals("selectCatalog"))
      url = base + "SelectCatalog.jsp";
    else if (action.equals("bookDetails"))
      url = base + "BookDetails.jsp";
    else if (action.matches("(showCart|(add|update|delete)Item)"))
      url = base + "ShoppingCart.jsp";
    else if (action.equals("checkOut"))
      url = base + "Checkout.jsp";
    else if (action.equals("orderConfirmation"))
      url = base + "OrderConfirmation.jsp";
  }
  RequestDispatcher requestDispatcher =
    getServletContext().getRequestDispatcher(url);
  requestDispatcher.forward(request, response);
}
```

As you can see, doPost obtains the request parameter named action and then uses it to form the correct URL of the JSP page. It then uses the request dispatcher obtained from the servlet context to forward control to the page. If no action parameter exists or if it doesn't match any of the expected strings, the servlet will execute the default page (/jsp/index.jsp).

To cover the Eshop functionality in detail, we'll show you what happens in a typical user session, as we already did in Chapter 2. This time, though, instead of showing it from the point of view of the user, we'll look at the behavior of the application on the server. The architecture of Eshop is consistent with the general MVC architecture shown in Figure 1-7.

What Happens When the Application Starts

The user starts the application by typing http://localhost:8080/eshop/shop/ in her browser. The doGet method of ShopServlet is executed, and that simply executes doPost. The doPost method, as we just said, doesn't find a request parameter named action, so it forwards the request to index.jsp.

The index.jsp page, like all other pages of Eshop, displays a header with a link to the shopping cart and a menu on the left-hand side with search and selection controls. It does so by including two separate modules, as follows:

```jsp
<jsp:include page="TopMenu.jsp" flush="true"/>
<jsp:include page="LeftMenu.jsp" flush="true"/>
```

The central area of the page only displays the text welcome to e-Shop.

The TopMenu.jsp module is trivial. Essentially, it consists of the following element:

```
<a class="link2" href="<%=base%>?action=showCart">Show Cart
  <img src="<%=imageURL%>/cart.gif" border="0"/></a>
```

where the two variables are obtained from the application scope:

```
String base = (String)application.getAttribute("base");
String imageURL = (String)application.getAttribute("imageURL");
```

The action parameter set to showCart causes the doPost method of ShopServlet to forward the request to /jsp/ShoppingCart.jsp.

The LeftMenu.jsp module has to do more. It displays a search field and a list of selectable book categories. The code to accept a search request is as follows:

```
<p>Book Title/Author:</p>
  <form style="border: 0px solid; padding: 0; margin: 0;">
    <input type="hidden" name="action" value="search"/>
    <input id="text" type="text" name="keyword" size="15"/>
    <input id="submit" type="submit" value="Search"/>
  </form>
```

Notice the presence of the hidden parameter named action with the value search, which causes ShopServlet to forward the request to /jsp/SearchOutcome.jsp when the user clicks on the Search button to perform a book search.

Here's the code that lists the book categories:

```
<%
    Hashtable categories = dataManager.getCategories();
    Enumeration categoryIds = categories.keys();
    while (categoryIds.hasMoreElements()) {
      Object categoryId = categoryIds.nextElement();
      out.println("<p><a href=" + base + "?action=selectCatalog&id="
        + categoryId.toString() + ">" + categories.get(categoryId) + "</a></p>"
        );
      }
  %>
```

The DataManager method getCategories only executes another method of the data model:

```
public Hashtable getCategories() {
  return CategoryPeer.getAllCategories(this);
  }
```

which interrogates the database to obtain identifiers and names of the available categories (see Listing 8-3).

Listing 8-3. *CategoryPeer.java—getAllCategories Method*

```java
public static Hashtable getAllCategories(DataManager dataManager) {
  Hashtable<String, String> categories = new Hashtable<String, String>();
  Connection connection = dataManager.getConnection();
  if (connection != null) {
    try {
      Statement s = connection.createStatement();
      String sql = "select category_id, category_name from categories";
      try {
        ResultSet rs = s.executeQuery(sql);
        try {
          while (rs.next()) {
            categories.put(rs.getString(1), rs.getString(2));
            }
          }
        finally { rs.close(); }
        }
      finally {s.close(); }
      }
    catch (SQLException e) {
      System.out.println("Could not get categories: " + e.getMessage());
      }
    finally {
      dataManager.putConnection(connection);
      }
    }
  return categories;
  }
```

We've highlighted the lines that do all the work: first, the database query is performed, and then the result is saved in a hash table in which the key is the category ID and the value is the category name.

LeftMenu.jsp uses the content of the hash table to generate one link for each category, as in the following example:

```
<a href=/eshop/shop?action=selectCatalog&id=3>Action Novels</a>
```

Notice that the action parameter is set to selectCatalog. This is done for all categories and causes ShopServlet to forward the request to /jsp/SelectCatalog.jsp when the user clicks on a category name.

As you can see from the code of CategoryPeer.java, we took great care to ensure that the database connection is closed before the method returns. Also notice that we logged a message to the standard output (mapped by Tomcat to the file stdout_*yyyymmdd*.log) if the database couldn't be accessed. In a real-world application, you should throw an exception with an error message to be displayed to the user.

Handling Requests for Book Selection and Book Search

As you saw in the previous section, when the user selects a book category or performs a search, the pages displayed are SelectCatalog.jsp and SearchOutcome.jsp, respectively. Both pages display a list of books and are similar to each other. Actually, they are so alike that we merged them into a single page in the JSF version of the application, Eshopf, as you'll see later in this chapter.

In SelectCatalog.jsp, the requested category is specified by the id parameter. To obtain the category name, you execute the DataManager method getCategoryName:

```
public String getCategoryName(String categoryID) {
  Category category = CategoryPeer.getCategoryById(this, categoryID);
  return (category == null) ? null : category.getName();
  }
```

which loads the category record from the database via the corresponding peer method.

In SearchOutcome.jsp, the search string is in the keyword parameter.

To obtain the list of books, SelectCatalog.jsp executes the following statement in a scriptlet:

```
ArrayList books = dataManager.getBooksInCategory(categoryId);
```

while SearchOutcome.jsp executes this statement:

```
ArrayList books = dataManager.getSearchResults(keyword);
```

For each book in the list, both pages generate a link such as the following one:

```
<a class="link1" href="/eshop/shop?action=bookDetails&bookId=3">Details</a>
```

With the action parameter set to bookDetails, ShopServlet forwards the request to BookDetails.jsp.

Displaying the Book Details

By now, the mechanism should be pretty clear: each JSP page passes its key request parameter to a DataManager method that encapsulates the business logic. This is how the *view* and the *model* of the MVC architecture are kept separate, making it possible for the web page designers and the software developers to work independently. One creates pretty and clear pages, and the other handles the databases. The signatures of the data model methods are the only interface needed between page designers and software developers.

BookDetails.jsp passes the bookId request parameter to the DataManager method getBookDetails:

```
public Book getBookDetails(String bookID) {
  return BookPeer.getBookById(this, bookID);
  }
```

and the BookPeer method getBookById gets the corresponding book record from the database.

To buy the book, the user then clicks on a link that looks like this in HTML:

```
<a class="link1" href="/eshop/shop?action=addItem&bookId=4">Add To Cart</a>
```

With the action parameter set to addItem, ShopServlet forwards the request to ShoppingCart.jsp.

Managing the Shopping Cart

The application displays the shopping cart not only when the user clicks on the Add to Cart link while viewing the book details, but also when the user clicks on the shopping cart link in the header of any page. The difference is that in the first case, the action parameter passed to ShoppingCart.jsp has the value addItem, while in the second case the value is showCart.

The shopping cart itself is an object of type Hashtable stored in a session attribute. The hashtable key is the book ID, while the value is an object of type CartItem. The CartItem class has no methods except the getters and setters for the author, title, price, bookID, and quantity properties.

It's appropriate to save the book price in the shopping cart, because the user should pay the price he sees in the book details when he clicks on Add to Cart, even if the book price stored in the database is then changed before he can complete his order.

For each shopping cart item, ShoppingCart.jsp displays the quantity of books in an input field and adds the Update and Delete buttons enclosed in separate forms. This makes it possible for the user to modify the number of copies he wants to order or remove an item altogether. Here's an example of an update form:

```
<form>
    <input type="hidden" name="action" value="updateItem"/>
    <input type="hidden" name="bookId" value="4"/>
    <input type="text" size="2" name="quantity" value="1"/>
    <input type="submit" value="Update"/>
    </form>
```

and here's an example of a delete form:

```
<form>
  <input type="hidden" name="action" value="deleteItem"/>
  <input type="hidden" name="bookId" value="4"/>
  <input type="submit" value="Delete"/>
  </form>
```

When the user clicks on one of the buttons, ShopServlet forwards the request back to ShoppingCart.jsp.

Before displaying the content of the cart, ShoppingCart.jsp needs to do some work that depends on the value of the action parameter (see Table 8-1).

Table 8-1. *ShoppingCart.jsp—Action Parameter*

Action Value	Additional Parameters	Previous Page
showCart	None	Any
addItem	bookId	BookDetails.jsp
updateItem	bookId, quantity	ShoppingCart.jsp
deleteItem	bookId	ShoppingCart.jsp

To handle addItem, ShoppingCart.jsp obtains the book details from the data manager via the getBookDetails method and creates a new CartItem object, which it then adds to the cart. To handle updateItem, ShoppingCart.jsp uses the setQuantity method to update the quantity in the cart item identified by bookId. To handle deleteItem, ShoppingCart.jsp simply removes the cart item identified by bookId from the cart.

After listing the cart content, ShoppingCart.jsp displays this link:

```
<a class="link1" href="<%=base%>?action=checkOut">Check Out</a>
```

With the action parameter set to checkOut, ShopServlet forwards the request to Checkout.jsp.

Accepting an Order

Checkout.jsp asks the user to provide her personal and financial data. When the user clicks on the Check Out button, the hidden action parameter is set to orderConfirmation, which causes ShopServlet to forward the request to OrderConfirmation.jsp. In real life, you should implement JavaScript/Ajax validation on all the fields.

Providing the Payment Details

In the skeleton implementation, OrderConfirmation.jsp only saves the order in the database. In a real-world situation, it should perform a series of checks, including verifying with a bank that the credit card is valid and not blocked.

All the work to store the order in the database is done in the DataManager method insertOrder, which we've already discussed in Chapter 4.

The Eshopx Application

After completing Eshop, we showed you how to create the Eshopx application by replacing the JSP pages with JSP documents (i.e., modules in XML syntax). This required us to move scriptlet code to JSP custom tags.

Listing 8-4 shows the annotated list of files and folders that constitute Eshopx.

Listing 8-4. *The Eshopx Files*

css
    eshop.jspx (replaces eshop.css)
images (content unchanged)
jsp (all pages rewritten as XML documents)
    BookDetails.jspx
    Checkout.jspx
    LeftMenu.jspx
    OrderConfirmation.jspx
    SearchOutcome.jspx
    SelectCatalog.jspx
    ShoppingCart.jspx
    TopMenu.jspx
META-INF (content unchanged)
WEB-INF
    web.xml (minor update)
    classes
        eshop (ShopServlet unchanged)
            beans (content unchanged)
            model (content unchanged)
            tags (new folder)
                AddBookTag.class, AddBookTag.java
                BookDetailsTag.class, BookDetailsTag.java
                BooksInCartTag.class, BooksInCartTag.java
                BooksInCategoryTag.class, BooksInCategoryTag.java
                CategoryNameTag.class, CategoryNameTag.java
                DeleteBookTag.class, DeleteBookTag.java
                InsertOrderTag.class, InsertOrderTag.java
                RoundToCentTag.class, RoundToCentTag.java
                SearchResultsTag.class, SearchResultsTag.java
                UpdateBookTag.class, UpdateBookTag.java
    tlds (new folder)
        eshop.tld

As you can see, we only changed the *view* part of the application (i.e., the JSP modules), while we didn't need to touch the *controller* and the *model* (i.e., the servlet, the beans, the peer classes, and the data manager).

As we already mentioned, the views of Eshop and Eshopx differ in the implementation but are functionally identical.

Style Sheet

We've replaced the shop.css file used in Eshop with shop.jspx. Listing 8-5 shows the differences between the two files.

Listing 8-5. shop.jspx

```
<?xml version="1.0" encoding="ISO-8859-1"?>
<jsp:root
  xmlns:jsp="http://java.sun.com/JSP/Page"
  xmlns:c="http://java.sun.com/jsp/jstl/core"
  version="2.1"
  >
<jsp:directive.page
  language="java"
  contentType="text/css; charset=ISO-8859-1"
  pageEncoding="ISO-8859-1"
  />
<c:url var="imgUrl" value="/images"/>
<jsp:text>
  ----------  shop.css lines 1 - 42   ----------
  background: url(${imgUrl}/bg_header.gif) no-repeat top left;
  ----------  shop.css lines 44 - 82   ----------
  background: url(${imgUrl}/bg_menu.gif) repeat-y top left;
  ----------  shop.css lines 84 - 105   ----------
  background: url(${imgUrl}/menubar.gif) repeat-x bottom left;
  ----------  shop.css lines 107 - 206  (the last one)  ----------
</jsp:text>
</jsp:root>
```

As you can see, we only wrapped shop.css inside a jsp:text element and changed three lines. If you look at the original lines, it should become clear why we did it:

```
background: url(/eshop/images/bg_header.gif) no-repeat top left;
background: url(/eshop/images/bg_menu.gif) repeat-y top left;
background: url(/eshop/images/menubar.gif) repeat-x bottom left;
```

The string "/eshop/images" of shop.css has become "${imgUrl}" in shop.jspx, and if you look at the beginning of shop.jspx, you'll notice that the variable imgUrl is set as follows:

```
<c:url var="imgUrl" value="/images"/>
```

The advantage of doing it with the EL expression is that c:url takes care of adding the application folder (i.e., /eshop) before the relative URL /images. This makes it possible to deploy the application in any folder. You should try to avoid hard-coding paths.

Obviously, you need to change the way in which the style sheet is loaded in the JSP modules. In Eshop, with shop.css, you needed to include the following line in the <head> element:

```
<link rel="stylesheet" href="/eshop/css/eshop.css" type="text/css"/>
```

In Eshopx, with shop.jspx, you need to write this line:

```
<c:url var="cssUrl" value="/css/eshop.jspx"/>
```

and then include the following line in the <head>:

```
<link rel="stylesheet" href="${cssUrl}" type="text/css"/>
```

By doing so, you remove the hard coded /eshop path from all JSP modules, which is good.

web.xml

When moving from Eshop to Eshopx, we only changed the definitions of two parameters in web.xml: base and imageURL. The definition of base changed from /eshop/shop to /shop, because in Eshop, we used base as follows:

```
<a class="link1" href="<%=base%>?action=checkOut">Check Out</a>
```

while in Eshopx, we first define the page attribute myURL:

```
<c:url value="${base}" var="myURL">
  <c:param name="action" value="checkOut"/>
  </c:url>
```

and then use the attribute to make the link, as follows:

```
<a class="link1" href="${myURL}">Check Out</a>
```

As we said when talking about the style sheet, c:url accepts in the value attribute URLs relative to the application folder, and then completes them to make them relative to the server root. Within Eshop, you must include the application folder in base, because you don't form the URL with c:url.

The definition of imageURL changed from /eshop/images/ to /images/ because we used imageURL in Eshop as follows:

```
<img src="<%=imageURL%>cart.gif" border="0"/>
```

while in Eshopx, we first define the page attribute imgURL:

```
<c:url value="${imageURL}" var="imgURL"/>
```

and then use the attribute in the img element:

```
<img src="${imgURL}cart.gif" border="0"/>
```

Thanks to these two changes, you could remove all hard-coded references to the application directory in Eshopx.

JSP Documents

To explain how we converted the JSP pages of Eshop (with extension jsp) to the corresponding JSP documents of Eshopx (with extension jspx), we'll go through one example in detail.

Listing 8-6 shows OrderConfirmation.jsp. We chose it because it is one of the simplest modules.

Listing 8-6. *OrderConfirmation.jsp*

```
01: <%@page language="java" contentType="text/html"%>
02: <%@page import="java.util.Hashtable"%>
03: <jsp:useBean id="dataManager" scope="application"
04:   class="eshop.model.DataManager"/>
05: <html>
06: <head>
07:   <meta http-equiv="Content-Type" content="text/html; charset=UTF-8"/>
08:   <title>Order</title>
09:   <link rel="stylesheet" href="/eshop/css/eshop.css" type="text/css"/>
10: </head>
11: <body>
12: <jsp:include page="TopMenu.jsp" flush="true"/>
13: <jsp:include page="LeftMenu.jsp" flush="true"/>
14: <div class="content">
15:   <h2>Order</h2>
16:   <jsp:useBean id="customer" class="eshop.beans.Customer"/>
17:   <jsp:setProperty property="*" name="customer"/>
18: <%
19:     long orderId = dataManager.insertOrder(
20:                     customer,
21:                     (Hashtable)session.getAttribute("shoppingCart")
22:                     );
23:     if (orderId > 0L) {
24:       session.invalidate();
25:   %>
26:       <p class="info">
27:         Thank you for your purchase.<br/>
28:         Your Order Number is: <%=orderId%>
29:       </p>
30: <%
31:     }
32:     else {
33:       %><p class="error">Unexpected error processing the order!</p><%
34:     }
35:   %>
36:   </div>
37: </body>
38: </html>
```

When converting to the XML syntax, you first need to replace the first 10 lines of the JSP page with those shown in Listing 8-7.

Listing 8-7. *Top Portion of OrderConfirmation.jspx*

```
01: <?xml version="1.0" encoding="ISO-8859-1"?>
02: <jsp:root
03:   xmlns:jsp="http://java.sun.com/JSP/Page"
04:   xmlns:c="http://java.sun.com/jsp/jstl/core"
05:   xmlns:eshop="urn:jsptld:/WEB-INF/tlds/eshop.tld"
06:   version="2.1"
07:   >
08: <jsp:directive.page
09:   language="java"
10:   contentType="ISO-8859-1"
11:   pageEncoding="ISO-8859-1"
12:   />
13: <jsp:output
14:   doctype-root-element="html"
15:   doctype-public="-//W3C//DTD XHTML 1.0 Strict//EN"
16:   doctype-system="http://www.w3.org/TR/xhtml1/DTD/xhtml1-strict.dtd"
17:   />
18: <c:url var="cssUrl" value="/css/eshop.jspx"/>
19: <html xmlns="http://www.w3.org/1999/xhtml">
20: <head>
21:   <title>Order</title>
22:   <link rel="stylesheet" href="${cssUrl}" type="text/css"/>
23:   </head>
```

In XML format, you no longer need to declare the Java classes, but you need to declare the namespaces of JSP, the JSTL core, and the custom library. The page directive becomes a `jsp:directive.page` element. Also, notice that the style sheet is loaded differently, as we explained in a previous section.

Lines 11-17 of `OrderConfirmation.jsp` remain practically the same, the only difference being that now the two modules have the extension `jspx`. The last three lines (36-38) also remain the same. You only have to append the end tag of `jsp:root`.

The major changes take place in lines 18-35. They are replaced by the code shown in Listing 8-8.

Listing 8-8. *Central Portion of OrderConfirmation.jspx*

```
31: <eshop:insertOrder var="orderID" customer="${customer}"/>
32: <c:choose>
33:   <c:when test="${orderID > 0}">
34:     <p class="info">
35:       Thank you for your purchase.<br/>
36:       Your Order Number is: <c:out value="${orderID}"/>
```

```
37:        </p>
38:      </c:when>
39:    <c:otherwise>
40:      <p class="error">Unexpected error processing the order!</p>
41:    </c:otherwise>
42:  </c:choose>
```

Line 31 of OrderConfirmation.jspx is the XML equivalent of lines 19-24 plus line 31 of OrderConfirmation.jsp. Notice that in Eshop, the order ID is returned by the insertOrder method and stored in the scripting variable orderID, while in Eshopx, the order ID is stored into the EL variable orderID directly by the custom tag eshop:insertOrder.

The if/else of lines 23 and 32 in the JSP code is replaced in the JSPX code by the elements c:choose/c:when/c:otherwise of lines 32-33 and 39. As we said on other occasions, you cannot use c:if because a c:else doesn't exist.

To complete the picture, let's look at Listing 8-9, which shows the doEndTag method of InsertOrderTag.java.

Listing 8-9. *InsertOrderTag.java—doEndTag Method*

```
public int doEndTag() {
  ServletContext context = pageContext.getServletContext();
  DataManager dataManager =(DataManager)context.getAttribute("dataManager");
  HttpSession session = pageContext.getSession();
  long orderID = dataManager.insertOrder(
      customer,
      (Hashtable)session.getAttribute("shoppingCart")
      );
  if (orderID > 0L) session.invalidate();
  pageContext.setAttribute(var, new Long(orderID).toString());
  return EVAL_PAGE;
  }
```

Not surprisingly, here you find (highlighted in bold) the code originally in lines 19-24 of OrderConfirmation.jsp that execute the dataManager method insertOrder and terminate the user session if the insertion succeeds.

On the basis of this example, you should now be able to figure out how to convert the other modules. In the next section, you'll find additional information concerning the eshop custom tag library.

Custom Tags and TLD

EL expressions can include bean properties. This means that they can invoke "getter" methods. What they cannot do is invoke methods that require parameters. You can work around that difficulty by setting an attribute with c:set and picking it up in a bean method.

For example, in `SelectCatalog.jspx`, the request parameter `id` specifies a book category, and you need to know the category name. This operation requires a database search, which you can implement with the following custom tag:

```
<eshop:categoryName var="cat" catID="${param.id}"/>
```

This accepts the ID as an input and sets the variable `cat` to the category name. The `doEndTag` method of `CategoryNameTag.java` is simple:

```
public int doEndTag() {
  ServletContext context = pageContext.getServletContext();
  DataManager dataManager =(DataManager)context.getAttribute("dataManager");
  pageContext.setAttribute(var, dataManager.getCategoryName(catID));
  return EVAL_PAGE;
  }
```

The `getCategoryName` method of the data manager (invoked exclusively by the `doEndTag` method of `CategoryNameTag.java`) is even simpler:

```
public String getCategoryName(String categoryID) {
  Category category = CategoryPeer.getCategoryById(this, categoryID);
  return (category == null) ? null : category.getName();
  }
```

Instead of defining the custom tag, you could add the `categoryID` property to the data manager:

```
private String categoryID = "0";
public void setCategoryID(String categoryID) {
  this.categoryID = categoryID;
  }
```

and remove its input parameter from the `getCategoryName` method.

Then, in `SelectCatalog.jspx`, you could replace the `eshop:categoryName` element with `jsp:setProperty` to set the `categoryID` and `c:setVar` to invoke the `getCategoryName` method:

```
<jsp:setProperty name="dataManager" property="categoryID"
    value="${param.id}"/>
<c:set var="cat" value="${dataManager.categoryName}"/>
```

The result would be the same. We didn't do this because it makes the code less "transparent," but it is ultimately a matter of taste. We just want to make the point that you can replace the input parameters of bean methods by setting bean properties with `jsp:setProperty`. Then, you only need to name the methods like getters (e.g., getWhatever), and you'll be able to execute them with an expression such as `${myBean.whatever}`.

In any case, we decided to implement nontrivial functionality in a custom tag library. In total, we introduced ten tags, as shown in Table 8-2.

Table 8-2. *eshop Custom Tag Library*

Name	Attributes	Where Used
bookDetails	var, bookID	BookDetails.jspx
insertOrder	var, customer	OrderConfirmation.jspx
searchResults	var, keyword	SearchOutcome.jspx
categoryName	var, catID	SelectCatalog.jspx
booksInCategory	var, catID	SelectCatalog.jspx
addBook	bookID	ShoppingCart.jspx
updateBook	bookID, quantity	ShoppingCart.jspx
deleteBook	bookID	ShoppingCart.jspx
booksInCart	items	ShoppingCart.jspx
roundToCent	var, value	ShoppingCart.jspx

Listing 8-10 shows an example of a TLD tag entry.

Listing 8-10. *A TLD Tag Definition*

```
<tag>
  <description>Insert an order into storage</description>
  <display-name>insertOrder</display-name>
  <name>insertOrder</name>
  <tag-class>eshop.tags.InsertOrderTag</tag-class>
  <body-content>empty</body-content>
  <attribute>
    <name>var</name>
    <type>java.lang.String</type>
    <rtexprvalue>true</rtexprvalue>
  </attribute>
  <attribute>
    <name>customer</name>
    <type>eshop.beans.Customer</type>
    <rtexprvalue>true</rtexprvalue>
  </attribute>
</tag>
```

The Eshopf Application

Although we used Eshopx as a basis for the JSF version of our application example, its architecture is quite different from that of the previous two versions. This is partly due to the fact that we had to replace ShopServlet with the standard FacesServlet class. In the process, we also removed the custom tags we had introduced in Eshopx. In this section, we'll refer to the Eshopf application as described in Chapter 5 after the addition of a custom converter, a custom validator, and a custom component with a separate renderer.

Listing 8-11 shows the annotated list of files and folders that constitute Eshopf. When we mark a folder as "unchanged," we mean that the folder content is identical to that of Eshopx, not of the original Eshop. We mark with "rewritten" the modules of Eshopf that are completely different from the corresponding modules of Eshopx, while "updated" means that the differences are not substantial.

Listing 8-11. *The Eshopf Files*

```
css
    eshopf.jspx  (updated version of eshop.jspx)
images  (content unchanged)
jsp
    BookDetails.jspx  (updated)
    Checkout.jspx  (updated)
    LeftMenu.jspx  (updated)
    ListBooks.jspx  (update of SelectCatalog.jspx + SearchOutcome.jspx)
    OrderConfirmation.jspx  (updated)
    ShoppingCart.jspx  (updated)
    TopMenu.jspx  (updated)
META-INF
    MANIFEST.MF  (unchanged)
    context.xml  (new file)
WEB-INF
    faces-config.xml  (new file)
    web.xml  (rewritten)
    classes
        eshop  (ShopServlet removed)
            beans
                Book.class, Book.java  (unchanged)
                CartItem.class, CartItem.java  (updated)
                Category.class, Category.java  (unchanged)
                Customer.class, Customer.java  (unchanged)
                ShopManager.class, ShopManager.java  (new file)
            components  (new folder)
                InputEntryComponent.class, InputEntryComponent.java
            converters  (new folder)
                CCNumberConverter.class, CCNumberConverter.java
            model
                BookPeer.class, BookPeer.java  (unchanged)
                CategoryPeer.class, CategoryPeer.java  (minor update)
                DataManager.class, DataManager.java  (updated)
                OrderDetailsPeer.class, OrderDetailsPeer.java  (unchanged)
                OrderPeer.class, OrderPeer.java  (unchanged)
                shop.sql  (unchanged)
            renderers  (new folder)
                InputEntryRenderer.class, InputEntryRenderer.java
```

```
tags   (removed all the custom tags of eshopx)
     InputEntryTag.class, InputEntryTag.java   (new file)
validators   (new folder)
     CCExpiryValidator.class, CCExpiryValidator.java
tlds
  eshop.tld   (rewritten)
```

In fact, we described almost everything in Chapter 5. In this chapter, we'll systematically go through the changes we made to Eshopx to transform it into Eshopf.

web.xml and context.xml

In Eshopx, we defined our own servlet (ShopServlet.java) to implement the controller part of the MVC architecture. In Eshopf, we replaced our servlet with the standard FacesServlet. As a result, we almost entirely rewrote the web.xml file from scratch. In particular, we replaced this servlet element used in the web.xml version of Eshopx:

```
<display-name>ShopServlet</display-name>
<servlet-name>ShopServlet</servlet-name>
<servlet-class>eshop.ShopServlet</servlet-class>
```

with this:

```
<servlet-name>Faces Servlet</servlet-name>
<servlet-class>javax.faces.webapp.FacesServlet</servlet-class>
<load-on-startup>1</load-on-startup>
```

We also changed the servlet-mapping element from this:

```
<servlet-name>ShopServlet</servlet-name>
<url-pattern>/shop/*</url-pattern>
```

to this:

```
<servlet-name>Faces Servlet</servlet-name>
<url-pattern>*.jsf</url-pattern>
```

To access the database containing books, book categories, and orders, we defined the initialization parameters jdbcDriver, dbURL, dbUserName, and dbPassword in Eshopx. They were used in ShopServlet to set up an object of type DataManager, which implemented the model part of the MVC architecture and interfaced to the database. The replacement of ShopServlet with FacesServlet forced us to implement a different mechanism in Eshopf for passing the database parameters to the data manager.

We defined the database as a resource external to the application by creating the context.xml file in the META-INF folder with the following content:

```
<Context debug="5" reloadable="true" crossContext="true">
  <Resource name="jdbc/mysql" auth="Container"
    type="javax.sql.DataSource" username="root" password=""
    driverClassName="com.mysql.jdbc.Driver"
    url="jdbc:mysql://localhost:3306/shop" maxActive="8" maxIdle="4"/>
  </Context>
```

We then registered the resource in the `web.xml` file as follows:

```
<resource-ref>
  <res-ref-name>jdbc/mysql</res-ref-name>
  <res-type>javax.sql.DataSource</res-type>
  <res-auth>Container</res-auth>
  </resource-ref>
```

To complete the transition from Eshopx to Eshopf, we also removed the definition of the initialization parameters base and imageURL from `web.xml`, because they were no longer needed, and we added the element to direct Tomcat to perform the basic authentication needed to access the resource. Listing 5-19 shows the full `web.xml` file of Eshopf.

Style Sheet

CSS lets you define new styles by adding attributes to already defined styles. This "cascading" mechanism is a form of inheritance, and therefore it requires an underlying hierarchical structure. CSS uses the structure provided by HTML documents instead of creating its own. This is fine as long as you write the HTML code yourself or generate it with JSP. When you use JSF, though, the control you have on the generated HTML is reduced. As a result, you have to pay greater attention when designing the style sheets.

When converting Eshopx to Eshopf, we encountered this issue in several places and had to modify the style-sheet file accordingly. We mentioned a specific example in the "f:view, h:form, and h:outputText" section of Chapter 5.

In general, if you compare the files `eshop.jspx` of Eshopx and `eshopf.jspx` of Eshopf, you'll see that there are a dozen differences. In fact, this issue concerning style sheets is a disadvantage of using JSF, but it becomes less and less important as you become familiar with the HTML code that JSF generates. Furthermore, you'll normally start developing directly with JSF. When converting Eshopx into Eshopf, we were dealing with an existing user interface that we wanted to alter as little as possible.

JSP Documents

We had to modify all JSP documents. This shouldn't surprise you when you consider that the JSP documents generate the HTML pages that the user sees in her web browser. In Chapter 5, we described all the JSF components you need for Eshopf. Therefore, it wouldn't make much sense to do it again here. In this section, we'll only tell you how JSF allows you to merge two separate JSP documents of Eshopx (`SelectCatalog.jspx` and `SearchOutcome.jspx`) into a single document of Eshopf (`ListBooks.jspx`).

The two modules were already very similar in Eshopx. Without considering page titles, text headers, and error messages, the differences boiled down to less than a handful of lines. In `SearchOutcome.jspx`, we were using the custom tag eshop:searchResults, while in `SelectCatalog.jspx`, we were first obtaining the category name with eshop:categoryName and then the list of books with eshop:booksInCategory.

After converting the two modules to use JSF, the list of books in both cases was obtained from a property of shopManager. When the user performed a search via the search field of `LeftMenu.jspx`, the method used to fill in the list of books in shopManager was searchBooks, while when the user selected a category, the method used was selectCategory.

The only difference left between the two modules was in a couple of messages. To make the merging possible, we added the categoryName property to shopManager and reset it to null within the searchBooks method. In this way, we could use the name of the category as a flag, because it would be null after a search and non-null after a category selection.

Perhaps we could have also merged the JSP documents in Eshopx, but it would have required some "awkward" coding, while it works out quite naturally with JSF.

Java Modules

One major change we made was to replace the custom tags defined in Eshopx with the eshop.beans.ShopManager class. We did this to take into account the functionality of JSF.

For example, to update the number of copies of a book in Eshopx, you can use the custom tag UpdateBook. Listing 8-12 shows the code to implement the tag.

Listing 8-12. *Eshopx—UpdateBookTag.java*

```java
package eshop.tags;

import java.util.Hashtable;
import javax.servlet.jsp.tagext.TagSupport;
import javax.servlet.http.HttpSession;
import eshop.beans.CartItem;

public class UpdateBookTag extends TagSupport {
  static final long serialVersionUID = 1L;
  private String bookID;
  private String quantity;

  public void setBookID(String bookID) {
    this.bookID = bookID;
    }

  public void setQuantity(String quantity) {
    this.quantity = quantity;
    }

  public int doEndTag() {
    HttpSession session = pageContext.getSession();
    Hashtable shoppingCart = (Hashtable)session.getAttribute("shoppingCart");
    CartItem item = (CartItem)shoppingCart.get(bookID);
    if (item != null) {
      item.setQuantity(quantity);
      }
    return EVAL_PAGE;
    }
}
```

In Eshopf, the following JSF component takes care of updating the number of copies:

```
<h:inputText id="quantity" value="#{item.quantity}" size="2" required="true"
    requiredMessage="What? Nothing?" converterMessage="An integer, please!"
    validatorMessage="At least one copy!">
  <f:validateLongRange minimum="1"/>
  </h:inputText>
```

As a result, when you trigger an update by pressing the corresponding button, as shown here:

```
<h:commandButton action="#{shopManager.updateItem}" value="Update"/>
```

there's nothing left for the updateItem function to do, as you can see here:

```
public String updateItem() { return null; }
```

Another example is the RoundToCent tag, which rounds amounts in dollars to two decimal places in Eshopx. This is necessary, because sometimes the result of multiplying the price of a book by the ordered quantity results in a sequence of 9s after the decimal point. Here is an example of its usage taken from ShoppingCart.jspx:

```
<eshop:roundToCent var="itemPrice" value="${item.quantity * item.price}"/>
```

In Eshopf, we introduced the subtotal attribute to eshop.beans.CartItem.java and added the functionality to recalculate it and round it to two decimals after every shopping cart update. This is the only update we made to the four eshop.beans modules.

Of the eshop.model modules, we only needed to modify CategoryPeer.java and DataManager.java. In CategoryPeer.java, we changed the getAllCategories method to return a list of categories instead of an object of type java.util.Hashtable. We then changed the getCategories methods in DataManager.java and ShopManager.java accordingly. This allowed us to display the list of categories in LeftMenu.jspx with the following JSF element without having to do any type conversion:

```
<h:dataTable value="#{shopManager.categories}" var="category">
```

In DataManager, besides the change to the getCategories method that we've already discussed and the removal of the getCatIDs method that was no longer needed, we only updated the algorithm used in the getConnection method to open a database connection. This was necessary because we had replaced the database initialization parameters of Eshopx with a JNDI resource.

In Eshopx, DataManager opened a database connection by invoking the static getConnection method of the java.sql.DriverManager class:

```
conn = DriverManager.getConnection(getDbURL(), getDbUserName(), ➥
getDbPassword());
```

The dbURL, dbUserName, and dbPassword attributes were set by ShopServlet using the servlet initialization parameters. In Eshopf, DataManager opens a database connection with this code:

```
Context ctx = new InitialContext();
if (ctx != null){
  Context envContext  = (Context)ctx.lookup("java:/comp/env");
  if (envContext != null) {
    DataSource ds = (DataSource)envContext.lookup("jdbc/mysql");
    if (ds != null) {
      conn = ds.getConnection();
      }
    }
  }
```

In Eshopf, we also added Java modules to implement a custom JSF component, a converter, a renderer, and a validator. Please refer to the corresponding sections of Chapter 5 for their description.

Summary

In this chapter, we completed the description of the various versions of the online bookshop example and explained what we had to do in order to convert standard JSP syntax to XML syntax and to use JSF.

With this chapter, we complete the main body of the book. We shocked you with a demanding first chapter, talked about Java and JSP in Chapter 2, described HTTP and HTML in Chapter 3, introduced SQL and the handling of databases in Chapter 4, showed examples of JSF in Chapter 5, covered XML in Chapter 6, and described Tomcat's architecture in Chapter 7.

Next, eight appendixes will give you detailed information on what we've described through the examples in the main eight chapters. Appendix A will explain how to install all the packages we've referred to, Appendixes B through F will provide a reference for what we covered in Chapters 1 to 5, Appendix G will provide some information on the Eclipse integrated development environment (IDE), and Appendix H will list all the acronyms we've used in this book.

What more is there to say?

We hope that you'll find this book useful. In a few cases, we could have gone a bit deeper or provided additional examples, but we had to set limits somewhere!

We wish you all the best. Good programming!

■ ■ ■

Installing Everything

To be able to develop and run web applications, you need to download and install several packages from the Internet. They will occupy at least 300MB of disk space for Java and Tomcat alone, and twice as much if you want to install the Eclipse IDE. We successfully tested our code on at least four different systems, including a Windows XP with 512MB of memory and a 1.8GHz Pentium 4, and a Windows Vista with 1GB of memory and a 2.6GHz AMD Athlon 64 X2. We also tested on a virtual Windows XP system installed on a VMware Server 1.0.2 with only 256MB of memory.

All the instructions contained in this appendix are for Windows XP, because at the moment of writing (mid 2007), XP is still more widely used than Vista. In any case, the differences between the two systems concerning installation are minimal.

By the time you're reading this book, there probably will be newer releases of everything we describe. Nevertheless, you should be able to adapt our instructions to the latest versions without any problem. In fact, in most cases, we expect that our instructions will apply to the latest releases without any change (apart from the version numbers!). To avoid clogging up the instructions with obsessive warnings, we won't mention this issue again in the rest of this appendix.

We recommend that you install the various packages in the order in which we list them in the following sections.

This appendix is exclusively about standard packages. Therefore, you won't find here anything concerning the examples that we've developed for this manual. You can download our examples from the Source Code/Download area of the Apress web site (http://www.apress.com). Together with the code, you'll also find a readme file with the necessary installation instructions.

Java

Nothing runs without Java, and you need two different packages: the runtime environment, which lets you execute Java, and the JDK, which lets you compile Java sources into executable classes.

You can download these packages together from Sun Microsystems' web site. Here's what you need to do:

1. Go to http://java.sun.com/javase/downloads/index.jsp.

2. Click on the Download button beside JDK 6 Update 1.

3. Select Accept License Agreement and wait for the page to reload itself.

4. Click on the Windows Offline Installation, Multi-language link, which downloads the file jdk-6u1-windows-i586-p.exe (56MB).

5. Execute the file.

6. Accept the license agreement when requested.

7. The installation wizard opens a dialog named Custom Setup. Click on the Next > button without changing the default settings. It will probably take a few minutes to install the JDK.

8. Another Custom Setup dialog appears, this time for the runtime environment. Again, click on the Next > button without changing the default settings.

At this point, you should have the folder C:\Program Files\Java\ with two subfolders: jdk1.6.0_01 and jre1.6.0_01.

In order to be able to compile Java from the command line, you need to add the JDK path to the PATH environment variable. From the Windows Start menu, select Settings, Control Panel, and System. When the System Properties dialog opens, click on the Advanced tab. Figure A-1 shows what you'll see.

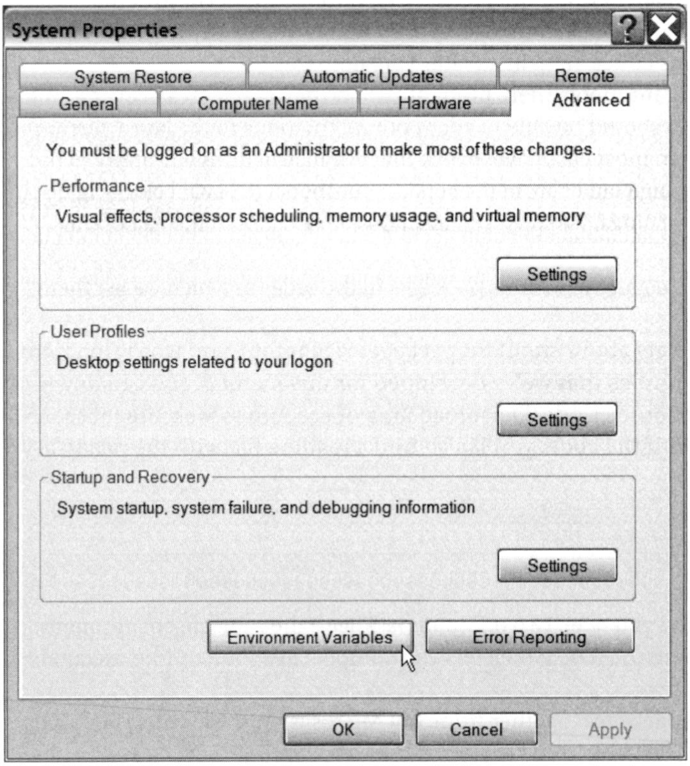

Figure A-1. *The System Properties dialog*

Click on the `Environment Variables` button to open the dialog shown in Figure A-2.

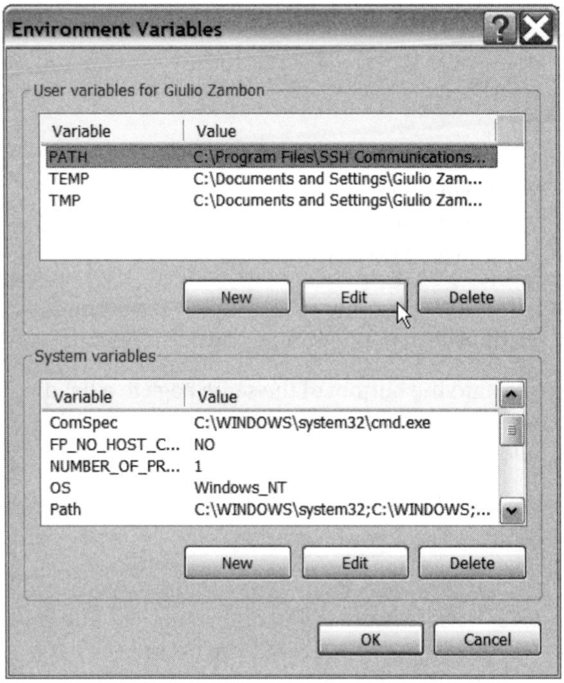

Figure A-2. *The Environment Variables dialog*

As you can see, there are two "path" variables: one in the user's list and one in the system's list. You have to add the JDK path to one of them. If you're the only user who needs to compile Java classes, you should update the `PATH` variable in the upper list. In any case, the procedure to update a variable is the same for both lists: by double-clicking the entry you need to update, you'll open the edit dialog shown in Figure A-3.

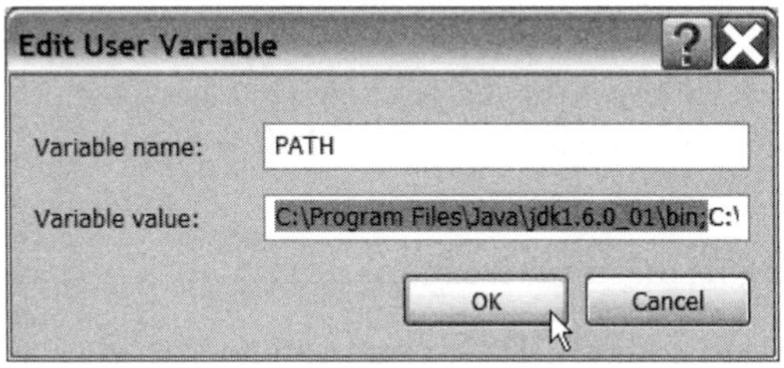

Figure A-3. *The Edit User Variable dialog*

Figure A-3 shows the text that we added at the very beginning:

```
C:\Program Files\Java\jdk1.6.0_01\bin;
```

The semicolon at the end is essential, because it separates the new path from the existing ones. Do not insert additional spaces before or after.

Click on the OK button to save the changes. Do it another couple of times until the System dialog closes.

Tomcat

Tomcat is the Java web server—that is, the servlet container that lets you run JSP pages and documents. If you've already installed an older version of Tomcat, you should remove it before installing a new version. Here's how you install Tomcat 6 correctly:

1. Go to http://tomcat.apache.org/download-60.cgi. Immediately below the second heading (Quick Navigation), you'll see three links: KEYS, 6.0.13, and Archives.

2. By clicking on 6.0.13, you'll be taken toward the bottom of the same page to a heading with the same version number. Below the version heading, you'll see the subheading Core and, below that, three links as follows: Windows Service Installer (pgp, md5).

3. Click on Windows Service Installer to download the file apache-tomcat-6.0.13.exe (approximately 5MB).

4. Before launching the installer file, you have to check its integrity. To do so, you need a small utility to calculate its checksum. One freeware utility that works just fine is MD5, of mst software GmbH. Download the file mstMD520e.exe from http://www.mstsoftware.com/cFreeware.aspx, execute it, accept the license agreement, and select the normal installation (instead of the custom one). Then launch the program C:\Program Files\mst software\mst MD5\mstMD5.exe and drag the Tomcat installer file on the little window that appears. You'll see a checksum string of 32 hex digits, such as d5322de3e2adada0dc569bb4cc7c1153.

5. Go back to the page with the links Windows Service Installer (pgp, md5) and click on md5. This opens a page containing a single line of text that should begin with the checksum calculated by the mstMD5.exe utility.

6. Now that you've verified the correctness of the Tomcat installer, launch it.

7. After you agree to the terms of the license, you'll see the dialog shown in Figure A-4. Click on the plus sign before the Tomcat item and select Service and Native before clicking on the Next > button.

8. Click on Next > once more without changing the install location.

9. You'll be asked to specify the connector port and user ID plus password for the administrator login. Leave the port set to 8080, because all the examples in this manual refer to port 8080. If you want, you can always change it later to the HTTP standard port (which is 80). For the user ID and password, you might as well use your Windows username and password. It is not critical.

10. At this point, you'll be asked to provide the path of a JRE. This is the path you saw when installing Java (in the previous section). With the version of Java we have, the correct path is C:\Program Files\Java\jre1.6.0_01.

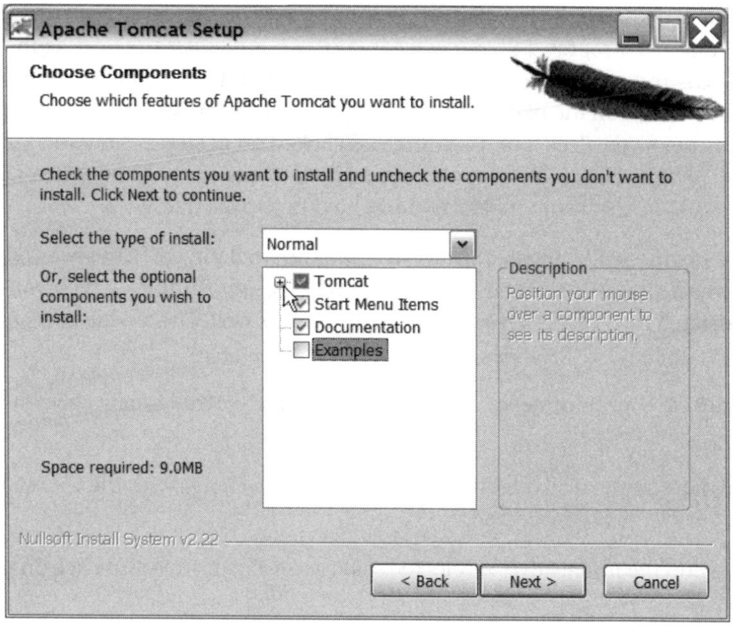

Figure A-4. *The Choose Components dialog*

MySQL

To support a web application, you need a DBMS. MySQL is the most widely used DBMS, and you can install it as follows:

1. Go to `http://dev.mysql.com/downloads/mysql/5.0.html`.

2. Scroll down until you arrive to the two headings, `Windows Downloads` and `Windows x64 Downloads`. Here you should choose the version to download depending on whether you have a 32-bit or a 64-bit CPU. A 32-bit MySQL version running on a 64-bit CPU works less efficiently. Therefore, we would normally advise you to download the 64-bit package if you have a 64-bit CPU. To find out what CPU you have, you only need to click on the `Start` menu and select `Settings`, then `Control Panel`, and finally `System`. Unless you see a 64 mentioned somewhere, you can conclude that you have a 32-bit CPU. However, MySQL only provides the 64-bit version of the full package *without* the installation wizard. You probably don't want to be bothered with a manual installation, so we suggest that you download the 32-bit version labeled `Windows (x86) ZIP/ Setup.EXE (5.0.41, 47.0MB)`. Right-click on the `Pick a mirror` link and open it in a new tab or window.

3. Before you can download the file `mysql-5.0.41-win32.zip`, you can register with MySQL, although this isn't strictly necessary. In any case, if you scroll down the page, you'll see a series of mirror sites from which you can download the software. Click on one of the links marked `HTTP` or `FTP` to download.

4. Before you proceed with the installation, you should verify that its checksum is correct. To do so, launch `C:\Program Files\mst software\mst MD5\mstMD5.exe`, drag the `mysql-5.0.41-win32.zip` file to its window, and check that the calculated checksum matches that shown on the page `http://dev.mysql.com/downloads/mysql/5.0.html` immediately below the `Pick a mirror` link you clicked on in step 2. Now you know why we told you to right-click `Pick a mirror`: we wanted you to have the Message-Digest algorithm 5 (MD5) checksum handy, without having to page back.

5. You have to unzip the file. If you don't have a program to do it, you can always download it for free from the Internet. For example, the `ZipCentral` utility, which you can download from `http://zipcentral.iscool.net/`, works well. The zip file contains `Setup.exe`. Launch it.

6. Click on the `Next >` button, select `Complete`, click on `Next >`, and finally click on `Install`.

7. Click through a couple of advertising slides and then on `Finish` with the `Configure the MySQL Server now` box selected.

8. After clicking on the initial `Next >`, select `Standard Configuration` and click on `Next >` once more.

9. You'll see two option boxes. Be sure that they are both selected before clicking on `Next >`. The first option is to run MySQL as a service from startup. The second one lets you use MySQL from the command line. You want to be able to do so in order to execute SQL scripts.

10. The next dialog lets you select a couple of options concerning security. In particular, it lets you choose a root password, enable access to the MySQL server from remote systems, and create an anonymous account. The defaults are that there is no root password, no remote access, and no anonymous user. If you're installing MySQL exclusively to support web applications, you might as well uncheck the `Modify Security Settings` box and click on `Next >`. Tomcat will be the only user of MySQL, and it will be local, regardless of whether you will access your web application from the same system or remotely. Obviously, the safest thing to do would be to define a password, but we leave that up to you.

11. Press the `Execute` button and, when the control comes back, `Finish`. Welcome to MySQL!

JDBC

Before being able to access MySQL from Java, you need a JDBC driver. You can download it from MySQL and install it as follows:

1. Go to `http://dev.mysql.com/downloads/connector/j/5.0.html`.

2. You'll see the `Source and Binaries (zip)` version 5.0.6 (8.3MB) entry. Notice the MD5 code that you'll need to check the correct downloading of the package. Right-click on the corresponding `Pick a mirror` link and open it in a new tab or window.

3. Register with MySQL or simply click on the `No thanks, just take me to the downloads!` link.

4. Click on an `HTTP` or `FTP` link to download the `mysql-connector-java-5.0.6.zip` file, and then extract everything to your desktop. You'll see a new folder named `mysql-connector-java-5.0.6`.

5. Open the folder and copy the `mysql-connector-java-5.0.6-bin.jar` file to the `C:\Program Files\Apache Software Foundation\Tomcat 6.0\lib\` Folder. Alternatively, you can copy it to the `WEB-INF\lib\` folder of each web application that needs to access a database.

6. Restart Tomcat.

That's it. The package also contains documentation on using JDBC with examples.

MySQL Tools

From the MySQL site, you can download free tools to browse and work with databases in a comfortable way. The package includes `MySQL Administrator 1.2`, `MySQL Query Browser 1.2`, and `MySQL Migration Toolkit 1.1`. To download and install them, follow these steps:

1. Go to `http://dev.mysql.com/downloads/gui-tools/5.0.html`.

2. Scroll down until you find `Windows (x86)` version 5.0-r12 (17.4MB). Notice the MD5 code that you'll need to check the correct downloading of the package. Right-click on the corresponding `Pick a mirror` link and open it in a new tab or window.

3. Register with MySQL or simply click on the `No thanks, just take me to the downloads!` link.

4. Click on an `HTTP` or `FTP` link to download the `mysql-gui-tools-5.0-r12-win32.msi` file, and then execute it.

5. Click `Next >` once, accept the license agreement, and then keep clicking on `Next >`, `Install`, and `Finish` until the dialog disappears, without changing anything.

Tomcat and MySQL Checks

First of all, you should check that the Tomcat and MySQL services are running. To do so, click on the Windows `Start` menu and select `Settings`, `Control Panel`, `Administrative Tools`, and `Services`. You'll see a list with dozens of entries. Scrolling down the list, among the many entries, you should see the two listed in Table A-1.

Table A-1. *Running Services*

Name	Description	Status	Startup Type	Log On As
Apache Tomcat	Apache Tomcat 6.0.13 Server– (http://tomcat.apache.org/)	Started	Automatic	Local System
MySQL		Started	Automatic	Local System

You can stop and start Tomcat by right-clicking on the icon in the notification area of the Windows toolbar, but to restart MySQL, you have to right-click its entry in the Services panel (not that it's likely you'll ever need to restart it!).

The next basic test you should do is to open a web browser and type localhost:8080. Figure A-5 shows what you should see.

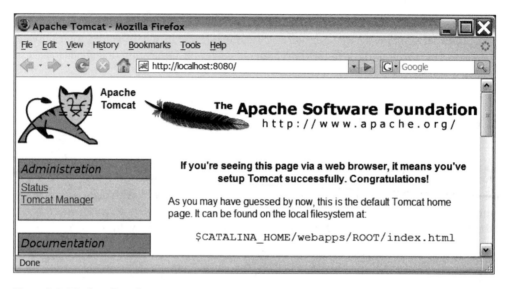

Figure A-5. *The localhost home page*

To check MySQL, you can click on the Windows Start menu and select Programs, MySQL, MySQL Server 5.0, and MySQL Command Line Client. This opens a DOS window with a request to provide a password. If you have followed our advice in step 10 of the MySQL installation procedure, just hit Return, and you'll get a mysql> prompt.

Open the shop.sql file (shown in Listing 4-2) included in the software package for this manual with any text editor, such as Notepad. Copy all lines with the exception of the first one (i.e., drop database shop;) and paste them after the mysql> prompt. It should accept the code without complaining. Type exit.

To see the database content, go to Start, Programs, MySQL, and MySQL Query Browser. This opens a dialog that you have to fill in, as shown in Table A-2, in order to connect to your MySQL server.

Table A-2. *Logging in to the MySQL Query Browser*

Field Name	Type This
Stored Connection:	Leave it empty.
Server Host:	localhost
Port:	Leave it set to 3306.
Username:	root
Password:	Leave it empty, unless you defined a password in step 10 of the MySQL installation procedure.
Default Schema:	shop

Click on the OK button. You should see a window with several frames. Type `select * from books` in the top frame and click on the Execute green button marked with a lightning bolt. You should see what's shown in Figure A-6 (although we have adjusted the column widths to show you all the columns).

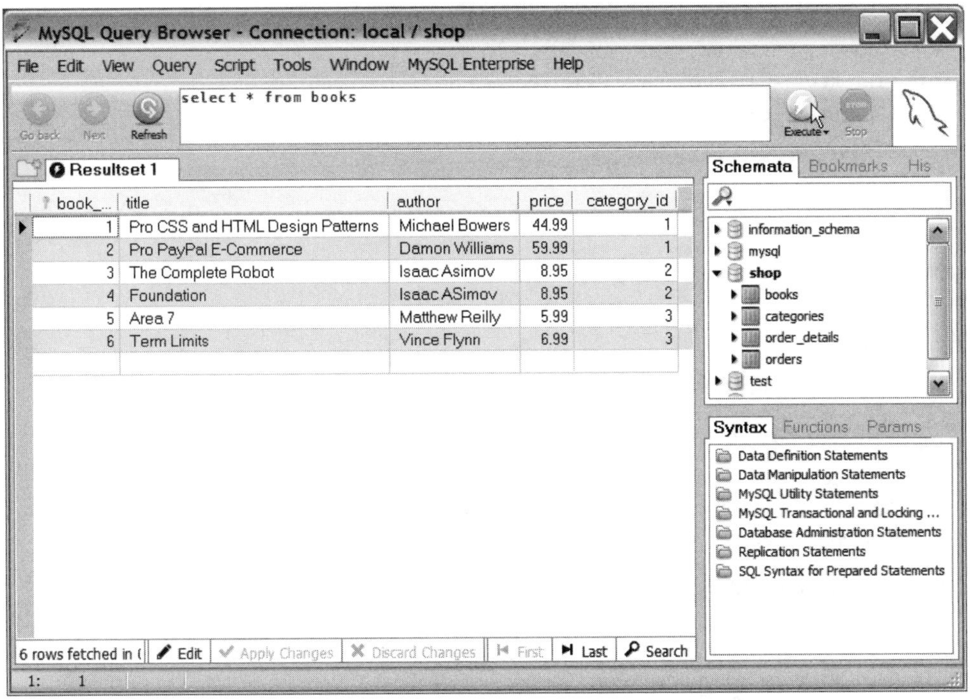

Figure A-6. *Browsing MySQL*

To complete the test of Tomcat and MySQL, you need to check that you can access the database from Java. To do so, execute the JSP page shown in Listing A-1.

Listing A-1. *jdbc.jsp*

```
<%@page language="java" contentType="text/html"%>
<%@page import="java.sql.*"%>
<html><head><title>JDBC test</title></head><body>
<%
  Class.forName("com.mysql.jdbc.Driver");
  Connection conn = DriverManager.getConnection(
      "jdbc:mysql://localhost:3306/shop", "root", "");
  Statement stmt = conn.createStatement();
  ResultSet rs = stmt.executeQuery("select * from books");
%><table border= "1"><%
  ResultSetMetaData resMetaData = rs.getMetaData();
  int nCols = resMetaData.getColumnCount();
```

```
  %><tr><%
  for (int kCol = 1; kCol <= nCols; kCol++) {
    out.print("<td><b>" + resMetaData.getColumnName(kCol) + "</b></td>");
    }
  %></tr><%
  while (rs.next()) {
    %><tr><%
    for (int kCol = 1; kCol <= nCols; kCol++) {
      out.print("<td>" + rs.getString(kCol) + "</td>");
      }
    %></tr><%
    }
  %></table><%
  conn.close();
  %>
</body></html>
```

Create the following folder:

```
C:\Program Files\Apache Software Foundation\Tomcat 6.0\webapps\ROOT\tests
```

and place in it the `jdbc.jsp` file. Then start a web browser and type this URL:

```
http://localhost:8080/tests/jdbc.jsp
```

You should see a table with the books in the Eshop database, as shown in Figure A-7.

book_id	title	author	price	category_id
1	Pro CSS and HTML Design Patterns	Michael Bowers	44.99	1
2	Pro PayPal E-Commerce	Damon Williams	59.99	1
3	The Complete Robot	Isaac Asimov	8.95	2
4	Foundation	Isaac ASimov	8.95	2
5	Area 7	Matthew Reilly	5.99	3
6	Term Limits	Vince Flynn	6.99	3

Figure A-7. *The output of jdbc.jsp*

You still need to install some libraries, but you're basically in business!

JSTL

Follow these simple steps to install JSTL:

1. Go to `http://jakarta.apache.org/taglibs/doc/standard-doc/intro.html`.

2. Scroll down the page until you find `Standard-1.1 Taglib News` and follow the `Apache Jakarta Project Mirrors` link of the most recent `Standard Taglib` version (version 1.1.2 since October 2004).

3. Follow the `taglibs` link at the end of the `Downloads` section.

4. Follow the `Standard 1.1 Taglib` link of the `Taglibs Downloads` section.

5. Finally, download the `jakarta-taglibs-standard-1.1.2.zip` file (< 1MB) by clicking on the `1.1.2.zip` link close to the bottom of the page.

6. Unzip the file, go to the `lib` directory, and copy the two `jstl.jar` and `standard.jar` files to `C:\Program Files\Apache Software Foundation\Tomcat 6.0\lib\`. Alternatively, you can copy them to the `WEB-INF\lib\` folder of each web application that uses JSTL.

7. Restart Tomcat. You might also have to clear the cache of your browser.

For your information, `jstl.jar` contains the class library `javax.servlet.jsp.jstl.*`, while `standard.jar` contains `org.apache.taglibs.standard.*`. The actual tag handlers are in `org.apache.taglibs.standard.tag.rt.*`, while the functions are in `org.apache.taglibs.standard.functions.Function.class`.

Listing A-2 shows you a JSP document that uses the `core` and `sql` JSTLs to access the `Books` table of the Eshop database. It produces the same output produced by `jdbc.jsp`, as shown in Figure A-7.

Listing A-2. *jdbc.jspx*

```
<?xml version="1.0" encoding="ISO-8859-1"?>
<jsp:root
  xmlns:jsp="http://java.sun.com/JSP/Page"
  xmlns:c="http://java.sun.com/jsp/jstl/core"
  xmlns:sql="http://java.sun.com/jsp/jstl/sql"
  version="2.1"
  >
<jsp:directive.page
  language="java"
  contentType="ISO-8859-1"
  pageEncoding="ISO-8859-1"
  />
<jsp:output
  doctype-root-element="html"
  doctype-public="-//W3C//DTD XHTML 1.0 Strict//EN"
  doctype-system="http://www.w3.org/TR/xhtml1/DTD/xhtml1-strict.dtd"
  />
<html xmlns="http://www.w3.org/1999/xhtml">
<head><title>JDBC/JSTL test</title></head><body>
<sql:setDataSource driver="com.mysql.jdbc.Driver"
  url="jdbc:mysql://localhost:3306/shop"
  user="root" password="" var="dataSource"
  />
<sql:query var="books" dataSource="${dataSource}">
  select * from books
  </sql:query>
```

```
<table border= "1">
  <tr>
    <c:forEach var="colName" items="${books.columnNames}">
      <td><b><c:out value="${colName}"/></b></td>
      </c:forEach>
    </tr>
  <c:forEach var="row" items="${books.rowsByIndex}">
    <tr>
      <c:forEach var="col" items="${row}">
        <td><c:out value="${col}"/></td>
        </c:forEach>
      </tr>
    </c:forEach>
  </table>
</body></html>
</jsp:root>
```

XPath

To be able to use XPath together with the JSTL XML library, you have to install a couple of JAR files. Here's how you do it:

1. Go to `http://www.apache.org/dyn/closer.cgi/xml/xalan-j/`.

2. Click on the first link you'll see below the `Apache Download Mirrors` header. What link it actually is depends on where you are, as the web site chooses the mirror site that is more likely to work best for you.

3. Scroll down the page until you see a `.zip` link marked as `Latest binary release`. For us, it was `xalan-j_2_7_0-bin.zip` (16MB). Click it to download the file.

4. Unzip the file, and copy the four `xalan.jar`, `xercesImpl.jar`, `serializer.jar`, and `xml-apis.jar` files to `C:\Program Files\Apache Software Foundation\Tomcat 6.0\lib\`. Alternatively, you can copy them to the `WEB-INF\lib\` folder of each web application that uses XPath.

5. If you really want to be picky and get the latest version of Xerces from its official distribution directory, go through the following steps:

    a. Go to `http://www.apache.org/dyn/closer.cgi/xml/xerces-j/`.

    b. Click on the first link below the `Apache Download Mirrors` header.

    c. Scroll down until you find the zip file marked `Latest binary release`. For us, it was `Xerces-J-bin.2.9.0.zip` (6.6MB). Click the link to download the file.

    d. Unzip the file and copy the `xercesImpl.jar`, `serializer.jar`, and `xml-apis.jar` libraries to Tomcat's `lib` directory `C:\Program Files\Apache Software Foundation\Tomcat 6.0\lib\`, thereby overwriting the versions you had installed in step 4.

The version of Xerces we downloaded with `xalan.jar` was 2.7.1 (dated 2005-08-06), while the version downloaded separately was 2.9.0 (dated 2006-11-22).

6. Restart Tomcat. You might also have to clear the cache of your browser.

Xalan implements the XSLT XML transformation language and XPath, while Xerces lets you parse and manipulate XML.

To test it, you can use the Starfleet example of Chapter 2: `starfleet.xml` (Listing 2-17) and `starfleet.jsp` (Listing 2-18). Actually, we might as well use this opportunity to convert the JSP page `starfleet.jsp` to the JSP document `starfleet.jspx` (see Listing A-3).

Listing A-3. *starfleet.jspx*

```
<?xml version="1.0" encoding="ISO-8859-1"?>
<jsp:root
  xmlns:jsp="http://java.sun.com/JSP/Page"
  xmlns:c="http://java.sun.com/jsp/jstl/core"
  xmlns:x="http://java.sun.com/jsp/jstl/xml"
  version="2.1"
  >
<jsp:directive.page
  language="java"
  contentType="ISO-8859-1"
  pageEncoding="ISO-8859-1"
  />
<jsp:output
  doctype-root-element="html"
  doctype-public="-//W3C//DTD XHTML 1.0 Strict//EN"
  doctype-system="http://www.w3.org/TR/xhtml1/DTD/xhtml1-strict.dtd"
  />
<c:import url="starfleet.xml" var="sf"/>
<x:parse doc="${sf}" varDom="dom"/>
<html xmlns="http://www.w3.org/1999/xhtml">
<head>
  <title>Parsing starfleet.xml</title>
  <style>th {text-align:left}</style>
  </head>
<body>
<table border="1">
  <tr><th>Name</th><th>S/N</th><th>Class</th><th>Year</th><th>Captain</th></tr>
  <x:forEach var="tag" select="$dom//starship">
    <tr>
      <td><x:out select="$tag/@name"/></td>
      <td><x:out select="$tag/@sn"/></td>
      <td><x:out select="$tag/class"/></td>
      <td><x:out select="$tag/class/@commissioned"/></td>
      <td><x:out select="$tag/captain"/></td>
      </tr>
```

```
        </x:forEach>
      </table>
  </body>
  </html>
  </jsp:root>
```

The result should be identical to that shown in Figure 2-9.

JavaServer Faces

To use JSF, you need to download yet another couple of JAR files:

1. Go to `https://javaserverfaces.dev.java.net/servlets/ProjectDocumentList`.

2. You'll see a folder list. Click on the plus sign preceding the `release` (0) link or directly on the link. This makes a list of subfolders visible, each one containing a different JSF release.

3. Click on the link of the last subfolder, marked `1.2_04 P02` (4), to display a table of downloadable files on the right-hand side of the page.

4. Click on the top link, marked `jsf-1_2_04-p02.zip`. This starts the download of the most recent stable version of JSF, released by rlubke on Wednesday, May 23, 2007 at 6:20:27 PM (5.38MB).

5. Unzip the package and copy the two JAR files `jsf-api.jar` and `jsf-impl.jar` that you find in its `lib` folder to the `lib` folder of Tomcat.

To test the installation, execute the `eshopf` application.

APPENDIX B

■■■

HTML Characters

A sequence of 1s and 0s is universally used to represent bits of information stored in computers, and a byte is a sequence of 8 bits. But the meaning of those bits depends on the context in which they are utilized. For example, the sequence 01000001 may be used to represent a capital A but, if interpreted as a number in binary form, may correspond to the decimal number 65. To understand this, consider that a binary representation of a decimal number consists of a series of 1s and 0s, each used to *switch on* or *off* a power of 2. A number is usually written with the least significant digit in the right-most position, preceded on its left by digits with increasing significance. Therefore, the right-most bit of a number in binary form holds the place for $2^0 = 1$ (exactly as the 5 of the decimal number 65 refers to $10^0 = 1$), the second right-most refers to $2^1 = 2$ (as the 6 of 65 refers to $10^1 = 10$), and so on to the left-most bit of the byte, which represents $2^7 = 128$. In 01000001, the only two powers of 2 *switched on* are 0 and 6, so the sequence represents $2^0 + 2^6 = 1 + 64 = 65$.

Traditionally, modern computers have encoded characters in ASCII, which uses 7 bits. While this was sufficient to represent the English alphabet, it quickly became evident that it was completely inadequate to satisfy the needs of the majority of the world population, with all its languages and alphabets. ASCII was then expanded into the ISO 8859-1 (ISO Latin1) standard, which uses all 8 bits of a byte to define additional characters, such as the diacritical German letters. According to Global Reach, in 2004, almost two-thirds of people with access to the Internet were of a non-English-speaking background (see `http://global-reach.biz/globstats/index.php3`). More and more names of people and domains will require accented characters in addition to the plain-English alphabet. Sooner or later, you'll need them too.

Nowadays, the ISO 8859-1 standard is the most widely used to represent the characters found in the majority of Western European languages and might be the only character set you'll ever need to know. However, you must be aware of the fact that there are several other character sets to represent Eastern European languages such as Russian or Greek and non-European languages such as Arabic or Mandarin. In this appendix, you'll only find the description of ISO 8859-1. You can find the list of character sets you may use when developing a web application on the IANA's web site (`http://www.iana.org/assignments/character-sets`).

As we mentioned in Chapter 3, you have to pay attention to special characters when naming paths, JSP/HTML modules, and parameters, and replace them with their hex equivalent. Similar problems occur when coding in HTML; the only real difference is that you don't need to remember hex values and can use mnemonics instead. These special sequences of characters are called *HTML entities*. Table B-1 lists all 256 characters of ISO Latin1 together with their decimal and hex values and the corresponding HTML entity name.

For example, an ampersand (as you've already seen in Chapter 3) corresponds to 26 hex and should be replaced with & inside HTML.

Table B-1. *ISO 8859-1 and HTML*

ISO	Decimal Value	Hex Value	HTML
NUL	0	0	
SOH	1	1	
STX	2	2	
ETX	3	3	
EOT	4	4	
ENQ	5	5	
ACK	6	6	
BEL	7	7	
BS	8	8	
HT	9	9	
NL	10	a	
VT	11	b	
NP	12	c	
CR	13	d	
SO	14	e	
SI	15	f	
DLE	16	10	
DC1	17	11	
DC2	18	12	
DC3	19	13	
DC4	20	14	
NAK	21	15	
SYN	22	16	
ETB	23	17	
CAN	24	18	
EM	25	19	
SUB	26	1a	
ESC	27	1b	
FS	28	1c	
GS	29	1d	
RS	30	1e	
US	31	1f	
SP	32	20	
!	33	21	
"	34	22	"
#	35	23	
$	36	24	

ISO	Decimal Value	Hex Value	HTML
%	37	25	
&	38	26	&amp;
'	39	27	
(	40	28	
)	41	29	
*	42	2a	
+	43	2b	
,	44	2c	
–	45	2d	
.	46	2e	
/	47	2f	
0	48	30	
1	49	31	
2	50	32	
3	51	33	
4	52	34	
5	53	35	
6	54	36	
7	55	37	
8	56	38	
9	57	39	
:	58	3a	
;	59	3b	
<	60	3c	&lt;
=	61	3d	
>	62	3e	&gt;
?	63	3f	
@	64	40	
A	65	41	
B	66	42	
C	67	43	
D	68	44	
E	69	45	
F	70	46	
G	71	47	
H	72	48	
I	73	49	

Continued

Table B-1. *Continued*

ISO	Decimal Value	Hex Value	HTML
J	74	4a	
K	75	4b	
L	76	4c	
M	77	4d	
N	78	4e	
O	79	4f	
P	80	50	
Q	81	51	
R	82	52	
S	83	53	
T	84	54	
U	85	55	
V	86	56	
W	87	57	
X	88	58	
Y	89	59	
Z	90	5a	
[	91	5b	
\	92	5c	
]	93	5d	
^	94	5e	
_	95	5f	
`	96	60	
a	97	61	
b	98	62	
c	99	63	
d	100	64	
e	101	65	
f	102	66	
g	103	67	
h	104	68	
i	105	69	
j	106	6a	
k	107	6b	
l	108	6c	
m	109	6d	
n	110	6e	

ISO	Decimal Value	Hex Value	HTML
o	111	6f	
p	112	70	
q	113	71	
r	114	72	
s	115	73	
t	116	74	
u	117	75	
v	118	76	
w	119	77	
x	120	78	
y	121	79	
z	122	7a	
{	123	7b	
|	124	7c	
}	125	7d	
~	126	7e	
DEL	127	7f	
	128	80	
	129	81	
	130	82	
	131	83	
	132	84	
	133	85	
	134	86	
	135	87	
	136	88	
	137	89	
	138	8a	
	139	8b	
	140	8c	
	141	8d	
	142	8e	
	143	8f	
	144	90	
	145	91	
	146	92	
	147	93	

Continued

Table B-1. *Continued*

ISO	Decimal Value	Hex Value	HTML
	148	94	
	149	95	
	150	96	
	151	97	
	152	98	
	153	99	
	154	9a	
	155	9b	
	156	9c	
	157	9d	
	158	9e	
	159	9f	
	160	a0	
¡	161	a1	&iexcl;
¢	162	a2	&cent;
£	163	a3	&pound;
¤	164	a4	&curren;
¥	165	a5	&yen;
¦	166	a6	&brvbar;
§	167	a7	&sect;
¨	168	a8	&uml;
©	169	a9	&copy;
ª	170	aa	&ordf;
«	171	ab	&laquo;
¬	172	ac	&not;
	173	ad	­ [soft hyphen, non-printing]
®	174	ae	&reg;
¯	175	af	&macr;
°	176	b0	&deg;
±	177	b1	&plusmn;
²	178	b2	&sup2;
³	179	b3	&sup3;
´	180	b4	&acute;
µ	181	b5	&micro;
¶	182	b6	&para;
•	183	b7	&middot;

ISO	Decimal Value	Hex Value	HTML
¸	184	b8	&cedil;
¹	185	b9	&sup1;
º	186	ba	&ordm;
»	187	bb	&raquo;
¼	188	bc	&frac14;
½	189	bd	&frac12;
¾	190	be	&frac34;
¿	191	bf	&iquest;
À	192	c0	&Agrave;
Á	193	c1	&Aacute;
Â	194	c2	&Acirc;
Ã	195	c3	&Atilde;
Ä	196	c4	&Auml;
Å	197	c5	&Aring;
Æ	198	c6	&AElig;
Ç	199	c7	&Ccedil;
È	200	c8	&Egrave;
É	201	c9	&Eacute;
Ê	202	ca	&Ecirc;
Ë	203	cb	&Euml;
Ì	204	cc	&Igrave;
Í	205	cd	&Iacute;
Î	206	ce	&Icirc;
Ï	207	cf	&Iuml;
Ð	208	d0	&ETH;
Ñ	209	d1	&Ntilde;
Ò	210	d2	&Ograve;
Ó	211	d3	&Oacute;
Ô	212	d4	&Ocirc;
Õ	213	d5	&Otilde;
Ö	214	d6	&Ouml;
×	215	d7	&times;
Ø	216	d8	&Oslash;
Ù	217	d9	&Ugrave;
Ú	218	da	&Uacute;
Û	219	db	&Ucirc;
Ü	220	dc	&Uuml;

Continued

Table B-1. *Continued*

ISO	Decimal Value	Hex Value	HTML
Ý	221	dd	Ý
Þ	222	de	Þ
ß	223	df	ß
à	224	e0	à
á	225	e1	á
â	226	e2	â
ã	227	e3	ã
ä	228	e4	ä
å	229	e5	å
æ	230	e6	æ
ç	231	e7	ç
è	232	e8	è
é	233	e9	é
ê	234	ea	ê
ë	235	eb	ë
ì	236	ec	ì
í	237	ed	í
î	238	ee	î
ï	239	ef	ï
∂	240	f0	ð
ñ	241	f1	ñ
ò	242	f2	ò
ó	243	f3	ó
ô	244	f4	ô
õ	245	f5	õ
ö	246	f6	ö
÷	247	f7	÷
ø	248	f8	ø
ù	249	f9	ù
ú	250	fa	ú
û	251	fb	û
ü	252	fc	ü
ý	253	fd	ý
þ	254	fe	þ
ÿ	255	ff	ÿ

■ ■ ■

HTML Reference

In Chapter 3, we explained how to write a web page with HTML. In this appendix, you'll find a brief description of all HTML elements. You won't find the following elements, because they've been deprecated in HTML 4.01/XHTML 1.0: `<applet>`, `<basefont>`, `<center>`, `<dir>`, `<font>`, `<isindex>`, `<menu>`, `<s>`, `<strike>`, `<u>`, and `<xmp>`. We'll also restrict ourselves to strict compliance to XHTML (rather than transitional), with the exception that we'll describe the tags associated with frames (for which no strict validation is possible). The tags within each section are in alphabetical order.

Standard Attributes

Most elements support a standard set of attributes. We'll describe them in this section rather than repeat them when discussing individual elements.

Core Attributes

Core attributes are not valid in `<base>`, `<head>`, `<html>`, `<meta>`, `<param>`, `<script>`, `<style>`, and `<title>`.

class

The `class` attribute accepts as a value the name of a class to which the element belongs. Use it as a style-sheet selector. For example, if you define the class `warning_text`, as in:

```
<style> p.warning_text {color:red} </style>
```

you can then use the class name in the appropriate element as follows:

```
<p class="warning_text" id="warn1">This text is displayed in red</p>
```

id

The `id` attribute associates an element with a unique identifier within the document. Use it whenever you need to identify a particular element. For example, if you write `<a id="point1"/>` somewhere within a long web page stored in `mypage.html`, you'll be able to jump directly to that position by clicking on a hyperlink created with this code:

```
<a href="http://mysite.com/mypage.html#point1">go to my page point 1</a>
```

To jump there from within the same page, you don't need to include the full URI, but only the locator part, as in

```
<a href="#point1">go to point 1</a>
```

style

The `style` attribute identifies an inline style definition. It's good to be able to define simple one-off styles within the HTML page, but if you use the same styles in several elements, you should define them by placing a `<style>` element inside the `<head>` element. If you define styles to be used in more than one document, you should write a separate style sheet and load it by placing a `<link>` element inside the `<head>` element.

The following is a simple example of a style definition using the `style` attribute:

```
<table style="font-weight:bold; background-color:#C0C0C0">
```

title

The `title` attribute displays tooltip text when the cursor is held over the element.

Language Attributes

Language attributes are not valid in `<base>`, `<br>`, `<frame>`, `<frameset>`, `<hr>`, `<iframe>`, `<param>`, and `<script>`.

dir

You use the `dir` attribute to set the text direction. It can have the values `ltr` (left-to-right) and `rtl` (right-to-left).

lang

The `lang` attribute sets the language of the element and accepts a language code as a value. The valid language codes are listed in RFC 1766 (`http://rfc.net/rfc1176.txt`). Each language code consists of a primary code of one or two letters and possibly a dash followed by a sub-code. Examples of valid language codes are `en` for English, `he` for Hebrew, `en-US` for American English, and `x-klingon` for Star Trek's Klingon language.

The setting of a language can assist search engines, speech synthesizers, and spell and grammar checkers, to name a few. It can also help render language-specific features such as hyphenation.

Keyboard Attributes

You're probably never going to use keyboard attributes, but we'll list them just to be thorough.

accesskey

The `accesskey` attribute assigns a keyboard key to an element. By pressing that key when the page is displayed in a browser, the user shifts the focus to that element. This was meant as a way of helping people with some disabilities, but it doesn't work well, and not all keys are possible with all browsers. We haven't got it to work with Mozilla Firefox 2.0.0.2. Also, you're supposed to press the Alt key while pressing the `accesskey`, so you run into trouble with Microsoft Internet Explorer because Alt is used to give all sorts of commands. Good luck!

tabindex

The `tabindex` attribute lets you specify the sequence of fields in a form when you tab through them. Again, we couldn't get it to work as expected in either Firefox or Internet Explorer.

Document Structure and Information

The following elements define the document structure and its meta information and general formatting.

<!— ... —>

The `<!-- ... -->` pair defines a comment, such as `<!-- This is a comment -->`. The browser ignores everything enclosed between the brackets.

<base>

When placed in the `<head>` element, the `<base>` element defines a base URL for all the links in a page. For example, if you write `<base href="http://my-site.com/images/"/>` and then `<img src="apict.gif"/>`, the browser will load the image from `http://my-site.com/images/apict.gif`.

You can also use the `target` attribute to define where the browser opens the links that appear in your page when the viewer clicks on them. For example,

- `<base target="_blank"/>` opens in a new window

- `<base target="_parent"/>` opens in the parent frameset

- `<base target="_self"/>` opens in the same frame

- `<base target="_top"/>` opens in the full body of the window

<body>

Place the `<body>` element directly inside `<html>`. It defines the body of the page. This is where everything happens.

The `<br/>` element inserts a single line break.

<h1> to <h6>

The `<h1>` through `<h6>` elements define headers 1 through 6.

<head>

Place the `<head>` element directly inside `<html>`. It defines information about the document. Between `<head>` and `</head>`, you can include elements that refer to the whole document—in particular, `<base>`, `<link>`, `<meta>`, `<script>`, `<style>`, and `<title>`.

<hr/>

The `<hr/>` element defines a horizontal rule.

<html>

The `<html>` element defines an HTML document. The whole document is enclosed between `<html>` and `</html>`.

<meta/>

Place the `<meta/>` element inside `<head>`. It defines information about your page for search engines and other applications. We could write a whole chapter on meta attributes and their use. Because this is a reference, we'll limit ourselves to the basics.

You can use several instances of this element within your document's `<head>`. For example, you could include all of the following:

```
<meta name="description" content="This is my marvelous page on..."/>
<meta name="keywords" content="HTML, XHTML, CSS, XML"/>
<meta name="revised" content="1.0.7" />
```

It should be clear how it works: the `content` attribute specifies the meta information as a line of text, while the `name` attribute specifies how to interpret the value of the `content` attribute. The `name` attribute can assume several values beside `"description"`, `"keywords"`, and `"revised"`. For example, if you write `<meta name="robot" content="noindex"/>`, your page won't be listed in search engines. Another possible attribute is `http-equiv`. As with the `name` attribute, the value of `http-equiv` specifies how to interpret the value of `content`:

```
<meta http-equiv="refresh" content="10"/>
<meta http-equiv="expires" content="Thu, 31 Dec 2009 23:59:59 GMT"/>
```

The first line tells the browser that the page should be reloaded after 10 seconds. The second line forces a reloading of the document even if the page is cached. Additional possible values are `content-type` and `set-cookie`.

The third and last possible attribute is `scheme`, which defines how to interpret what follows. This provides full flexibility to use `<meta>` for special and proprietary applications. For example, in `<META scheme="USA" name="date" content="01-04-1999"/>`, the value `USA` is used to indicate that the date is the 4th of January. You could use `Australia` to indicate that the date is the 1st of April.

<p> and <p/>

The `<p>` element defines a paragraph. Browsers should render `<p/>` with an empty line.

\<title\>

Place \<title\> inside \<head\>. It defines the document title. Always define a title for your documents.

Character Formatting

This section lists the elements you need to define special character formatting. See Figure C-1.

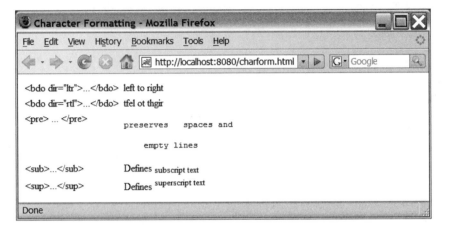

Figure C-1. *Character formatting*

\<bdo\>

The \<bdo\> element defines the direction of text display—for example:

```
<bdo dir="rtl">this will be written right to left</bdo>
<bdo dir="ltr">this will be written left to right</bdo>
```

\<pre\>

The \<pre\> element defines preformatted text. The text enclosed between \<pre\> and \</pre\> is displayed in a monospaced font and with all line breaks and empty lines as typed. For example, \<pre width="72"\> limits the number of characters per line to 72.

\<sub\>, \<sup\>

The \<sub\> and \<sup\> elements define subscripted and superscripted text, respectively.

Character Styling

The character styling elements define how the characters are presented. The \<basefont\>, \<font\>, \<s\>, \<strike\>, and \<u\> elements have been deprecated. Even though the rest have not been deprecated, you can achieve better control and better results using styles. See Figure C-2.

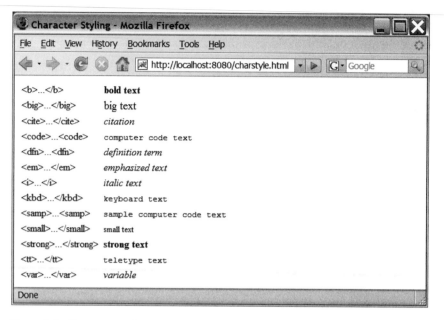

Figure C-2. *Character styling*

<b>, <strong>

The <b> and <strong> elements define bold and strong text, respectively. As you can see from Figure C-2, Firefox renders them identically in **bold**.

<big>

The <big> element defines big text.

<cite>, <dfn>, <em>, <i>, <var>

The <cite>, <dfn>, <em>, <i>, and <var> elements define a citation, a definition term, emphasized text, italic text, and a variable, respectively. As you can see from Figure C-2, Firefox renders them identically in *italic*.

<code>, <kbd>, <samp>, <tt>

The <code>, <kbd>, <samp>, and <tt> elements define computer code, keyboard, sample computer code, and teletype text, respectively. As you can see from Figure C-2, Firefox renders them identically in a monospaced font.

<small>

The <small> element defines small text.

Blocks

Block elements define how special blocks of characters are rendered. You probably won't use them often.

<abbr>

The <abbr> element defines an abbreviation. When you pass your cursor over the abbreviation text, the browser shows the full text (see Figure C-3). It isn't guaranteed to work, but Firefox renders it correctly. Internet Explorer 7 shows the full text but doesn't dot-underline the abbreviation.

Figure C-3. *Abbreviations in Firefox*

<acronym>

The <acronym> element defines an acronym. Its purpose is to give information to browsers, spell checkers, translation systems, and search engines. It looks and behaves like <abbr>.

<address>

The <address> element defines post addresses, signatures, and similar information. It is usually rendered in italic.

<blockquote>

The <blockquote> element defines a long quotation, which is rendered with spacing all around, as shown in Figure C-4.

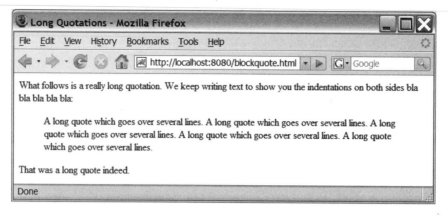

Figure C-4. *Long quotations with* `<blockquote>`

It supports the `cite` attribute, which takes the URL of the document you're quoting from. Use it for your own reference or for tools that analyze the page.

<del> and <ins>

The `<del>` element defines text that was deleted from the document, while the `<ins>` element defines text that was inserted into the document. The text enclosed between `<del>` and `</del>` is rendered with strikethrough characters, while the text enclosed between `<ins>` and `</ins>` is rendered with underlined characters. Both elements support the `cite="URL"` and `datetime="YYYYMMDD"` attributes, which you can use for reference purposes.

<q>

The `<q>` element defines a short quotation. The browser should replace the `<q>` and `</q>` tags with double quotes when rendering the page. Firefox does this correctly, but Internet Explorer, up to and including release 7, simply ignores it. Like the `blockquote` element, this element supports the `cite` attribute.

Links

You use link elements to link the document to other documents.

<a>

The `<a>` element defines an anchor and may only appear in the `<body>`. It supports several attributes, but the most important is `href`, which is used to show clickable hyperlinks. When used with the `href` attribute, the `<a>` element is at the core of what HTML is all about and effectively justifies the HT of HTML.

The following examples show how to create hyperlinks:

```
<a href="http://aSite.com/anotherPage.html">hyperlink to another page</a>
<a href="aPage.html"><img src="image.gif"/></a>
<a href="#point1">go to point 1</a>
<a href="mailto:first.last@domain.com" title="Send feedback">First Last</a>
```

The first example shows how to create a normal link to a URL. In the second example, the text of the link is replaced with a clickable image. The third example shows how to use this element to link to an anchor within the same page. The fourth and last example shows how to link to an email address.

Creating a Clickable Map

You can use the `<a>` element together with `<object>` and `<map>` to create a clickable map (see Figure C-5) by associating different URIs to sections of an image.

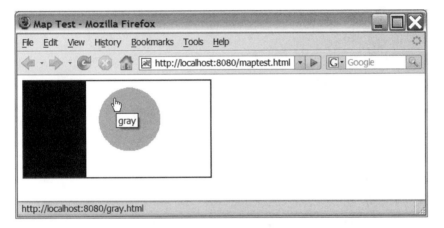

Figure C-5. *Status bar and screen tip pointing to gray in a map test*

Notice how the status bar shows a link to gray.html, and the screen tip also states gray. Now look at Figure C-6 and notice how with the cursor just outside the gray circle, both the link target and the screen tip have changed.

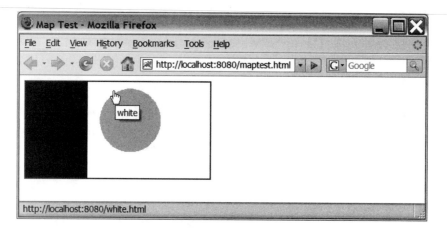

Figure C-6. *Status bar and screen tip pointing to white in a map test*

Listing C-1 shows how you can implement a clickable map.

Listing C-1. *maptest.html*

```
<!DOCTYPE html PUBLIC "-//W3C//DTD XHTML 1.0 Strict//EN"
  "http//www.w3.org/TR/xhtml1/DTD/xhtml1-strict.dtd">
<html xmlns="http//www.w3.org/1999/xhtml" xmllang="en" lang="en">
<head><title>Map Test</title></head>
<body>
<object data="maptest.gif" usemap="#map" type="image/gif"
  width="300" height="150">
  <map name="map" id="map">
    <ul>
      <li><a href="black.html" shape="rect" coords="0,0,100,150"
            title="black"/></li>
      <li><a href="gray.html" shape="circ" coords="170,60,50"
            title="gray"/></li>
      <li><a href="white.html" shape="rect" coords="100,0,300,150"
            title="white"/></li>
    </ul>
  </map>
</object>
</body>
</html>
```

The `<object>` element of `type="image/gif"` specifies the name of a `<map>` element to be associated with the GIF image. The `<map>` element contains a list of hyperlinks assigned to different regions of the image.

We'll describe `<object>` and `<map>` in more detail in their own sections. However, concerning the `<a>` element, notice how the `shape` and `coords` attributes are set to identify the three clickable areas. The `shape` attribute can have the following values: `rect`, `rectangle`, `circ`, `circle`, `poly`, and `polygon`. The coordinates are defined in `coords` as a comma-separated list of numeric values. Table C-1 shows the meaning of the numeric values associated with each shape.

Table C-1. *Meaning of the coords Attribute*

shape	coords
rect/rectangle	x and y of the top-left corner, x and y of the bottom-right corner. For example, the white rectangle in Figure C-6 has coords set to "100,0,300,150".
circ/circle	x and y of the center, radius. For example, the gray circle in Figure C-6 has coords set to "170,60,50"; 170 and 60 are the coordinates of the center, and 50 is the length of the radius.
poly/polygon	x and y of each vertex. For example, coords="0,0,50,0,0,30" defines a rectangular triangle with a side of length 50 parallel to the x axis, a side of length 30 parallel to the y axis, and the right angle in the top-left corner of the map.

The x coordinate is measured horizontally from left to right, and the y coordinate is measured vertically from top to bottom. The top-left corner of the map always represents the origin of the coordinates, with x=0, y=0. In the example, the bottom-right corner of the map has the coordinates x=300, y=150.

Target Attributes

You've already seen that you use href to specify the target URL. Other attributes associated with the target are hreflang and charset, which specify the language of the target and its character set, respectively. We've already talked about languages in this appendix when describing the standard lang attribute. We also mentioned possible character sets when we introduced HTML in Chapter 3. The charset attribute expects as a value strings such as "iso-8859-1" (the normal Western alphabet) and "x-euc" (Extended Unix Code Japanese).

You use the type attribute only for information. Future browsers could do something with it, but for the time being, you can do without it. You'll find the official reference of MIME types in http://www.iana.org/assignments/media-types/, but it isn't easy reading.

Two attributes, rel and rev, define the relationship between the document and the URL target in the href attribute. In particular, rel defines how the target relates to the document containing the link, while rev defines how the document relates to the target (*rev* stands for reverse relationship). Valid values for both rel and rev are one or more of the following keywords separated by commas: alternate, appendix, bookmark, chapter, contents, copyright, designates, glossary, help, index, next, prev, section, start, stylesheet, and subsection. The reason for having a reverse relationship is that the target might not be a web page. In that case, it wouldn't be possible to define the reverse relationship in the target itself.

You can use rel and rev for information, but some applications could also use them to handle pages in a particular way. For example, a client could decide to preload the page linked with rel="next" to save loading time in case the user actually follows a chain of links in sequence.

<link/>

The <link/> element defines a resource reference. It is basically identical to <a> and supports exactly the same attributes, but <a> can only appear in the <body> of a page, while <link> can only appear within the `<head>` (more than once). You can use `<link>` with the `rel` and `rev` attributes to establish relationships with other documents, and in particular to tell the browser to render the document elements according to an external style sheet, as in the following example, where "/myStyles/aStyleSheet.css" is the URL of the file containing the style sheet:

```
<link rel="stylesheet" href="/myStyles/aStyleSheet.css" type="text/css"/>
```

You can also combine styles contained in several files by defining the `title` attribute with the same value, as in the following example:

```
<link rel="stylesheet" href="/myStyles/generic.css" title="allStyles"
    type="text/css"/>
<link rel="stylesheet" href="/myStyles/forms.css" title="allStyles"
    type="text/css"/>
```

Frames

In Chapter 3, we stated that you have to use the `frameset` DOCTYPE to validate your XHTML page if you want to use frames. We also implicitly expressed our disliking of frames. However, if you really want to use them, here they are. The general concept is that you define a frameset with a certain number of rows and columns and then design a page to occupy each cell/frame of the set.

For example, let's say you want to define a frameset, as in Listing C-2.

Listing C-2. *frameset.html*

```
<!DOCTYPE html PUBLIC "-//W3C//DTD XHTML 1.0 Frameset//EN"
  "http//www.w3.org/TR/xhtml1/DTD/xhtml1-frameset.dtd">
<html xmlns="http//www.w3.org/1999/xhtml" xmllang="en" lang="en">
<head><title>Example of frames: Frameset</title></head>
<frameset rows="30%, *" cols="*, 60%">
  <frame src="framea.html"/>
  <frame src="frameb.html"/>
  <frame src="framec.html"/>
  <frame src="framed.html"/>
</frameset>
</html>
```

You'll see four frames, as they appear in Figure C-7.

Figure C-7. *A simple frameset*

Listing C-3 shows the source of frame A.

Listing C-3. *framea.html*

```
<!DOCTYPE html PUBLIC "-//W3C//DTD XHTML 1.0 Frameset//EN"
  "http//www.w3.org/TR/xhtml1/DTD/xhtml1-frameset.dtd">
<head>
  <title>Example of frames: Frame A</title>
  <style type="text/css">body {background-color: white}</style>
  </head>
<body>
this is frame A
</body>
</html>
```

The code for frames B, C, and D is substantially identical to `framea.html`, but with the A replaced by the appropriate letter in a couple of places and the background color set to #hc0c0c0, #808080, and #404040, respectively.

<frame>

The `<frame>` element defines a subwindow (a frame) when used inside the `<frameset>` element. The following sections describe all the attributes for the `<frame>` element, but be aware that we've tested them only with Firefox 2.0.0.2. They might (and probably will!) behave differently with Internet Explorer.

frameborder

When set to "0" or "no" in all the frames of a frameset, the `frameborder` attribute disables the display of the 3D border between frames. In any case, the spacing of six pixels between frames remains, and the frame size can still be adjusted. If you want to remove the border completely, add `frameborder="no"` to `<frameset>`, not to all `<frame>` elements.

longdesc

The longdesc attribute accepts as a value a URL containing the description of the frame contents. It is only used for browsers that don't handle frames.

marginheight

Set the marginheight attribute to the number of pixels you want to leave as a margin at the top and bottom of the frame.

marginwidth

Set the marginwidth attribute to the number of pixels you want to leave to the left and right of the frame.

name

The name attribute defines a unique frame name to be used within scripts.

noresize

When the noresize attribute is present (with or without any value), it prevents the viewer from resizing a frame by clicking and dragging its border. Obviously, it also limits the resizing of all other frames in the same column or row. In the simple example shown in Figure C-7, if you block the resizing of one frame, you also automatically block the resizing of all others at the same time.

scrolling

You can set the scrolling attribute to yes, no, or auto. With auto, which is the default, the browser displays the vertical and/or horizontal scrollbars as needed. With yes, both scrollbars are always displayed, whether you need them or not. With no, no scrollbar is ever displayed.

src

The src attribute accepts as a value the URL of the page to be displayed inside the frame.

<frameset>

The <frameset> element defines a set of frames and supports the attributes listed in the following sections.

border

The border attribute sets the size of the border in pixels (the default is six). If you set it to zero, it has the same effect as frameborder="no".

cols

The cols attribute defines how much space to assign to each column of frames within the browser window. The value consists of as many comma-separated width definitions as columns, and each width definition can be either a percentage or an asterisk. The columns for which you define an asterisk share the space left after subtracting the percentages. For example, by defining cols="10%, *, 50%, *", you set the width of the first column to 10% of the browser window and the width of the third column to 50%. The second and fourth columns then get half each of the remaining 40%.

If you define a total of more than 100%, the percentages are adjusted in proportion. For example, if you assign 50% and 150% to two columns, the first one actually gets 25% and the second one 75%. In that case, the columns with asterisks get no space at all, exactly as if you had specified a width of 0%. This might not be as useless as it sounds, because the viewer can always make the columns visible by dragging their border with the mouse (unless you've blocked them with noresize).

You can also define the width in pixels rather than in percentage.

frameborder

When set to "0" or "no", the frameborder attribute completely disables the display of the 3D border between frames.

rows

The rows attribute defines how much space to assign to each row of the frames within the browser window. For a description of possible values, please see what we wrote for the frameset attribute cols.

\<noframes\>

The \<noframes\> element defines a no-frame section within a frameset. If the browser *does not* support frames, it will display what is between \<noframes\> and \</noframes\>. To see what this means in practice for the frameset.html example, check out Listing C-4. We've highlighted the lines we had to add to cater for frameless browsers.

Listing C-4. *frameset.html Modified for Frameless Browsers*

```
<!DOCTYPE html PUBLIC "-//W3C//DTD XHTML 1.0 Frameset//EN"
   "http//www.w3.org/TR/xhtml1/DTD/xhtml1-frameset.dtd">
<html xmlns="http//www.w3.org/1999/xhtml" xmllang="en" lang="en">
<head>
  <title>Example of frames: Frameset</title>
  <style type="text/css"> <!--
    .cell_a {background-color: white;}
    .cell_b {background-color: #c0c0c0;}
    .cell_c {background-color: #808080;}
    .cell_d {background-color: #404040;}
    --> </style>
</head>
```

```
<frameset rows="30%, *" cols="*, 60%">
  <frame src="framea.html"/>
  <frame src="frameb.html"/>
  <frame src="framec.html"/>
  <frame src="framed.html"/>
  <noframes>
    <body>
      <table cellpadding="5" border="1">
        <tr>
          <td class="cell_a">this is frame A</td>
          <td class="cell_b">this is frame B</td>
        </tr>
        <tr>
          <td class="cell_c">this is frame C</td>
          <td class="cell_d">this is frame D</td>
        </tr>
      </table>
    </body>
  </noframes>
</frameset>
</html>
```

As you can see, we basically had to repeat the contents of all the frames inside
`frameset.html`. It's a nightmare to maintain, even if the result, which you can see in Figure C-8,
doesn't really match the original with frames.

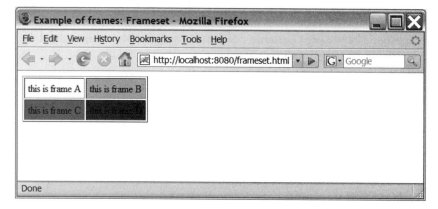

Figure C-8. *A simple frameset with a frameless browser*

■**Tip** To disable the handling of frames in Firefox for testing purposes, view the `about:config` page and
double-click on the line that starts with `browser.frames.enable`. The status will change to `user set`, and
the value will change to `false`. It takes effect after restarting the browser. Switch it back to the default in
the same way.

\<iframe\>

The \<iframe\> element, which stands for *inline frame*, lets you define a frame within any HTML page without having to use a frameset. For example, let's say you want to load the four pages framea.html, frameb.html, framec.html, and framed.html into four iframes, as shown in Figure C-9.

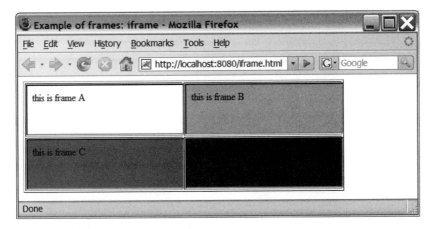

Figure C-9. *Example of iframe*

You'd have to use the code shown in Listing C-5.

Listing C-5. *iframe.html*

```
<!DOCTYPE html PUBLIC "-//W3C//DTD XHTML 1.0 Frameset//EN"
  "http//www.w3.org/TR/xhtml1/DTD/xhtml1-frameset.dtd">
<html xmlns="http//www.w3.org/1999/xhtml" xmllang="en" lang="en">
<head><title>Example of frames: iframe</title></head>
<body>
  <table border="1">
    <tr>
      <td width="250" height="75">
        <iframe src="framea.html" width="100%" height="100%">
          <a href="framea.html" target="_blank">frame A</a>
          </iframe>
        </td>
      <td width="250" height="75">
        <iframe src="frameb.html" width="100%" height="100%">
          <a href="frameb.html" target="_blank">frame B</a>
          </iframe>
        </td>
      </tr>
```

```
    <tr>
      <td width="250" height="75">
        <iframe src="framec.html" width="100%" height="100%">
          <a href="framec.html" target="_blank">frame C</a>
        </iframe>
      </td>
      <td width="250" height="75">
        <iframe src="framed.html" width="100%" height="100%">
          <a href="framed.html" target="_blank">frame D</a>
        </iframe>
      </td>
    </tr>
  </table>
 </body>
</html>
```

In fact, you could have written each table cell much more simply, as follows:

```
<td><iframe src="framea.html"></iframe></td>
```

but the size of each frame would have defaulted to 300 pixels of width and 150 of height, and we didn't want to have them so big in this example. Alternatively, you could have simply defined width="250" and height="75" as attributes of the <iframe> elements rather than of the table cells, but we preferred to set the size of the cells in case the browser doesn't support frames. In that case, as you can see in Figure C-10, the browser should render what is between <iframe> and </iframe>. If you had set the size inside the <iframe> rather than the <td> elements, the browser would have ignored them, causing the page to appear quite different. We said "the browser should render" because it didn't work with Firefox when we disabled the frames. It also didn't work with Opera running under Windows XP, but it did work with Opera under Windows Vista.

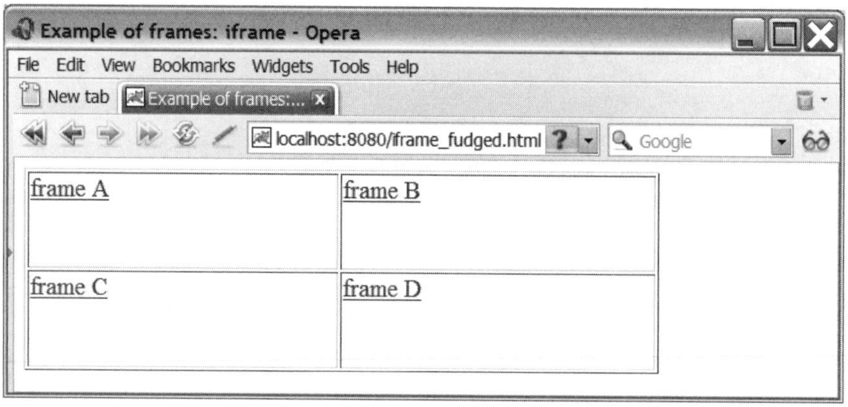

Figure C-10. *Example of iframe with a frameless browser*

■**Tip** To disable the handling of frames in Opera for testing purposes, go to `Tools` ➤ `Preferences`, click on the `Advanced` tab, select `Content`, and then click on the `Style Options` button.

Let's go through the list of attributes in a more systematic way.

frameborder, longdesc, name, scrolling, src

See the descriptions under the `<frame>` element.

align

The `align` attribute specifies how to align the iframe with respect to the surrounding text. It accepts the following values: `left`, `right`, `top`, `middle`, and `bottom`.

height, width

The `height` and `width` attributes define the dimensions of the frame within which the linked page is loaded. You can express these attributes in pixels or in percentages of the surrounding container.

marginheight, marginwidth

The `marginheight` and `marginwidth` attributes define the top/bottom and left/right size, respectively, of the frame border in pixels.

Input

This section describes how to use forms to make the browser accept the viewer's input and send it to the server.

The <form> element

You use the `<form>` element to direct the browser to accept user input and send it to a specified URL. A form can contain several types of controls.

Only the `action` attribute is required. It accepts the target URL as a value. The `target` attribute is only accepted with transitional and frameset validation, but it's still widely used. Go to the description of the `<base>` tag at the beginning of this appendix to read a description of `target`. The following sections list the other possible attributes.

accept

The `accept` attribute is a comma-separated list of MIME content types that the server is allowed to accept when processing the form. Here's an example of a correct usage of this attribute:

```
accept="text/html, image/gif, video/mpeg"
```

As we said earlier in this appendix, you can find a list of valid media types at `http://www.iana.org/assignments/media-types/`. This attribute lets you tell the server what the user is allowed to input into the form. In practice, it is unlikely that you'll need it.

accept-charset

The `accept-charset` attribute is a comma-separated list of character sets allowed within the form. We talked about character sets in Chapter 3. A valid example for this attribute is as follows:

```
accept-charset="iso-8859-1, x-euc"
```

The default is the language of the document containing the form.

enctype

The `enctype` attribute defines the MIME type to be used by the browser when encoding the content of the form. The default `"application/x-www-form-urlencoded"` will serve you well in most cases. You should set it to `"multipart/form-data"` in forms used to upload files.

method

The `method` attribute accepts two values: `get` and `post`. As we explained in Chapter 3, you should use `post` when sending more than a few dozen bytes or characters of data to the server. Keep in mind, though, that you can only bookmark pages obtained with a GET request. Furthermore, when you refresh a page obtained with a POST request, the browser will ask for your authorization to resend data to the server.

name

The `name` attribute defines a unique frame name to be used within scripts.

Text Input

To accept text from the user, you can use one of two elements: `<input>` or `<textarea>`. With `<input>`, you can also decide whether the text is displayed on the screen while the user types it in (with the attribute `type="text"`) or not (with `type="password"`). Note that `"text"` is the default type for `<input>`, but we advise you to define it explicitly, because it makes the code clearer and also ensures that all browsers will behave as expected.

See Figure C-11 for examples of `<input>` and `<textarea>`.

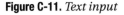

Figure C-11. *Text input*

See Listing C-6 for the source code.

Listing C-6. *form_text.html*

```
<!DOCTYPE html PUBLIC "-//W3C//DTD XHTML 1.0 Strict//EN"
  "http//www.w3.org/TR/xhtml1/DTD/xhtml1-strict.dtd">
<html xmlns="http//www.w3.org/1999/xhtml" xmllang="en" lang="en">
<head><title>Examples of text input</title></head>
<body>
<form action="">
  <table  cellpadding="5" border="1">
    <tr>
      <td>&lt;input type="text" size="10" name="t"/></td>
      <td><input type="text" size="10" name="t"/></td>
      </tr>
    <tr>
      <td>&lt;input type="password" maxlength="10" name="p"/></td>
      <td><input type="password" maxlength="10" name="p"/></td>
      </tr>
    <tr>
      <td>&lt;textarea name="ta"><br/>
The quick brown fox jumps over the lazy dog.&lt;/textarea></td>
      <td><textarea name="ta">
The quick brown fox jumps over the lazy dog.</textarea></td>
      </tr>
    </table>
  <input type="submit"/>
  </form>
</body>
</html>
```

Note how we used < to prevent the browser from interpreting the code fragments we wanted to display in clear. Also note that each element has the name attribute set to a unique value. The server uses the name to identify the parameter. For example, if you type "blabla" inside the first text field and submit it, it will be as if you had appended ?t=blabla to the URL.

The <input> element, with either the type="text" or the type="password" attribute, can have the additional attributes maxlength and size. Both have numeric values, but while maxlength sets a limit to the number of characters that can be typed into the field, size only uses the given number of characters to determine the dimension of the field as it appears in the browser. However, don't try to figure it out; trial and error will do.

The <textarea> element accepts two attributes: cols and rows, with the obvious meaning. The default for cols is 20, and the default for rows is 3.

Additionally, all text input elements accept the disable and readonly attributes.

Buttons and Images

You can define a button in several ways, as shown in Figure C-12. All allow the disable attribute.

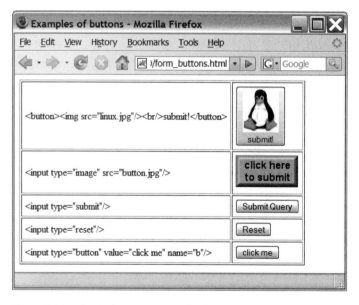

Figure C-12. *HTML elements to render buttons*

Perhaps the most obvious way of defining a button is with the <button> element. As you can see from Figure C-12, you can then use images and text to make your button interesting. You can also define the attribute type="submit" (the default), type="reset", or type="button". A "reset" button returns all input fields of the form to the values they had before any user input. You can use a button of type "button" to execute a JavaScript on the client side, and you can assign to it a default value with the value attribute. You can also use the name attribute.

<input type="submit"/>, <input type="reset"/>, and <input type="button"/> let you define standard buttons. You can specify the text to be displayed inside the button with the

value attribute. Note that the name attribute is allowed with type="button", but not with type="submit" and type="reset".

`<input type="image" src="image-file"/>` is yet another way to create submit buttons. However, the behavior is slightly different: when you use an image to create a submit button and you click on it to submit, the browser sends to the server two additional parameters named x and y and representing the position of the cursor within the image, with 0,0 indicating the top-left corner of the image, x increasing from left to right, and y increasing from the top down. Furthermore, if you add to the element the attribute name="whatever", the browser will name the parameters whatever.x and whatever.y instead of simply x and y.

If you define the name attribute and also define the value="val" attribute, the browser will send the whatever=val parameter in addition to the coordinates. Finally, with image buttons, you can define the alt attribute to specify text associated with the image. A nice feature of Firefox is that it displays the *hand cursor* on image buttons (while it keeps the *arrow cursor* on the other types of buttons).

With an appropriate server-side script, you can use the coordinate parameters to create an image map, but then the script would have to do all the analysis to determine what region was clicked and then forward the request to the appropriate page. It would require quite a bit of coding. Look at the description of the elements `<a>` and `<img>` for easier ways of making clickable maps.

Choices

You have two controls that let you make choices: check boxes and radio buttons. Check boxes let you choose more than one value, while radio buttons are used for exclusive alternatives. See Figure C-13 for some examples.

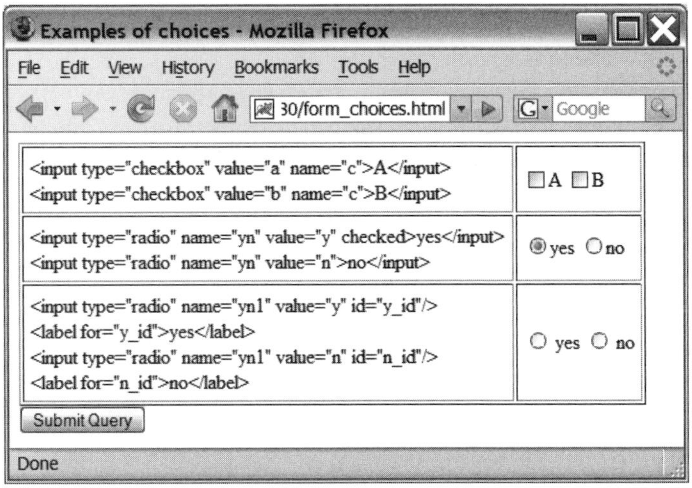

Figure C-13. *HTML elements to render check boxes and radio buttons*

Both check boxes and radio buttons accept the checked attribute to set a default. You identify groups of radio buttons by giving the same name to all elements of each group. This also applies to check boxes, but it's less important for them, because they're not exclusive within each group. Notice in Figure C-13 that we've shown two different ways of displaying radio buttons—one without labels and one with labels. The only difference is that the labels are clickable. Therefore, you can click the yes and no labels of the second pair of radio buttons to make a selection, while with the first pair, you must click directly on the buttons.

Selections

If you need to be able to choose one or more of several possibilities, check boxes and radio buttons become awkward. The solution is to use a <select> element containing as many <option> subelements as you need. See Figure C-14 for an example.

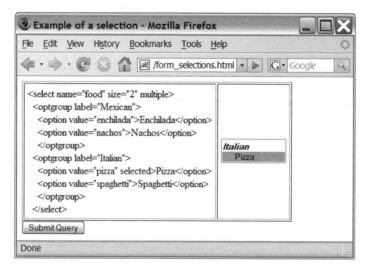

Figure C-14. *HTML elements to render menu selections*

size="2" defines the number of lines to be displayed. You can use the <optgroup> subelements recursively to group the items in a hierarchical fashion. The multiple attribute lets you select several individual items by pressing the Control key while clicking, or several adjacent items by pressing the Shift key instead.

Sets of Fields

You can group fields that belong logically together. See Figure C-15 for an example.

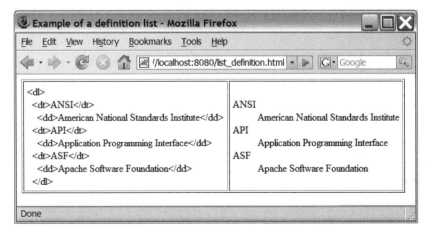

Figure C-15. *Grouping sets of fields*

This is pretty self-explanatory. Note that you can use `<fieldset>` recursively to create sets within sets.

Files

Use `<input type="file" name="f"/>` to upload a file. The browser takes care of displaying the `Browse` button and the field to type in file name and path. Be sure that you define the `method="post"` and `enctype="multipart/form-data"` attributes in the `<form>` element.

Lists

We have to distinguish between definition lists, ordered list, and unordered lists. Figure C-16 shows a definition list.

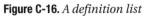

Figure C-16. *A definition list*

You can see what an ordered list looks like in Figure C-17.

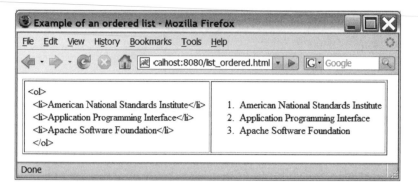

Figure C-17. *An ordered list*

Figure C-18 shows how an unordered list appears.

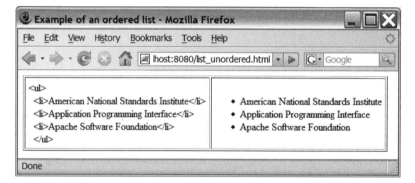

Figure C-18. *An unordered list*

You used to be able to use some attributes to personalize the lists, but they have been deprecated. Use styles instead.

Images

When you display an image, you can decide to make it clickable by wrapping its definition inside an <a> element. Further, you can associate a map to it, so that clicking it on different areas will result in different pages being loaded.

The <img> element

The <img> element defines an image, as in <img src="mugshot.jpg" alt="John Doe"/>. The src attribute defines the URL of the image, and alt defines a short description of the image that appears when the mouse is passed over it. Both attributes are required when strict validation of either HTML 4 or XHTML 1 is applied.

Other attributes are height, width, longdesc, ismap, and usemap.

height and width

The height and width attributes force the image into a rectangle of defined dimensions. You can specify the dimensions both in pixels and in a percentage of the original size. It's best to use images that you don't need to resize via HTML.

longdesc

The longdesc attribute accepts as a value a URL containing the description of the image.

ismap

The ismap attribute tells the browser that the image is used with a server-side map. For example, when you click on the image of this link:

```
<a href="/imagemaps/example.map">
  <img src="/images/example.gif" alt="server-side image map" ismap/>
</a>
```

the browser sends to example.map the coordinates of the cursor, whereby 0,0 indicates the top-left corner of the image, x increases from left to right, and y increases from the top down. The server must then have an application that processes the coordinates and selects the appropriate page to be returned to the browser (most web servers have it). The example.map file is actually a map definition file for that application. We advise you to forget server-side maps and use client-side maps. With a server-side map, you would have to learn how to write the map configuration file, which is not trivial. Also, why should you load your server with map processing when the client can do everything?

usemap

The usemap attribute accepts the URL of a map, which tells the browser what pages to load when you click on different areas of the image. This mechanism is said to define a client-side image map, because it is the browser that decides which page to load. We showed you an example of such a map when we described the element <a>. We used the element <object type="image/gif"> to define the image, but you can also use <img>, as shown in Listing C-7.

Listing C-7. *maptest_img.html*

```
<!DOCTYPE html PUBLIC "-//W3C//DTD XHTML 1.0 Strict//EN"
  "http//www.w3.org/TR/xhtml1/DTD/xhtml1-strict.dtd">
<html xmlns="http//www.w3.org/1999/xhtml" xmllang="en" lang="en">
<head><title>Map Test with img</title></head>
<body>
<img src="maptest.gif" usemap="#map" width="300" height="150"/>
<map name="map" id="map"><table><tr>
  <td><a href="black.html" shape="rect" coords="0,0,100,150"
    title="black"/></td>
  <td><a href="gray.html" shape="circ" coords="170,60,50"
    title="gray"/></td>
```

```
  <td><a href="white.html" shape="rect" coords="100,0,300,150"
    title="white"/></td>
  </tr></table></map>
</body>
</html>
```

The page will look exactly as shown in Figures C-5 and C-6. Notice that, compared with Listing C-1 of `maptest.html`, we've replaced in `maptest_img.html` the unordered list with a table. The `<map>` element requires itemized content, and both lists and tables will do. However, in `maptest.html`, the element `<map>` was defined within `<object>`, while in `maptest_img.html`, it is not. Therefore, a bullet of the unordered list became visible. With `<table>`, nothing is visible.

More on Image Maps

We've already shown how to build image maps when describing `<a>` and `<img>`. However, there is still something we should add to complete this subject. Instead of using lists or tables to define a map, you can use the `<area>` element, as shown in Listing C-8.

Listing C-8. *maptest_area.html*

```
<!DOCTYPE html PUBLIC "-//W3C//DTD XHTML 1.0 Strict//EN"
  "http//www.w3.org/TR/xhtml1/DTD/xhtml1-strict.dtd">
<html xmlns="http//www.w3.org/1999/xhtml" xmllang="en" lang="en">
<head><title>Map Test with areas</title></head>
<body>
<img src="maptest_area.gif" usemap="#map" width="300" height="150"/>
<map name="map" id="map">
  <area nohref shape="rect" coords="280,130,300,150" title="nothing"/>
  <area href="black.html" shape="rect" coords="0,0,100,150" title="black"/>
  <area href="gray.html" shape="circ" coords="170,60,50" title="gray"/>
  <area href="white.html" shape="rect" coords="100,0,300,150" title="white"/>
  </map>
</body>
</html>
```

As you can see, the differences between `maptest_area.html` and `maptest_img.html` or `maptest.html` appear to be only cosmetic. However, look at the line of code in bold:

```
<area nohref shape="rect" coords="280,130,300,150" title="nothing"/>
```

It defines an area without any link. This can be useful, especially because `<map>` examines the areas in a well-defined order, from the last to the first. That's why the circle takes precedence over the white rectangle. This also means that the `nohref` area in the example takes precedence over all others. Therefore, you can *cut out holes* in your map, regardless of what lies *behind*. You can also create a nonresponsive background when using irregularly shaped maps. Notice how in Figure C-19 the cursor maintains its arrow shape when you place it on the dead corner.

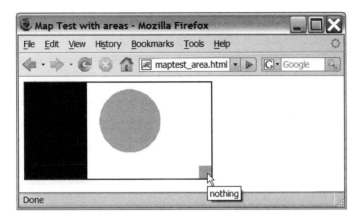

Figure C-19. *An image map with a dead corner*

Tables

A table consists of rows and columns, with cells containing text, images, and other components. In almost every chapter of this book, you'll find examples of tables. Tables are an easy
way to present components in an organized fashion. You need several elements to build
tables, and these elements share a few standard attributes that we want to describe first to
avoid duplications.

Standard Attributes

We'll describe the attributes that apply to more than one element.

align, char, and charoff

The `align` attribute defines the horizontal alignment of the content in a table cell. It can have
the following values: `left`, `right`, `center`, `justify`, and `char`.

In particular, `align="char"` means that the text is aligned with respect to one particular
character. The default for this character is the period, so that numbers with decimal digits are
displayed with the periods aligned vertically. To change the character, use the attribute `char`,
as in `char=";"`, to use a semicolon in place of the default period. You also have the possibility
of introducing an offset in the alignment with the attribute `charoff`. For example,
`charoff="10%"` shifts the alignment to the right by 1/10 of the cell size, while `charoff="-10"`
shifts it to the left by 10 pixels. It sounds cool, doesn't it? Well, forget it, because neither Firefox
nor Internet Explorer nor Opera render `align="justify"` and `align="char"`. There goes our
beloved conformance to standards! We're keeping this description in this book because the
problem might be fixed in the near future and also because we don't want to waste the time
we invested in testing it.

valign

The valign attribute defines the vertical alignment of the content in a table cell. It can have the following values: top, middle, bottom, and baseline. Baseline means that the characters are aligned on the same line of text regardless of their size. Figure C-20 clearly shows the differences.

Figure C-20. *The four possible values of the valign attribute*

width

The width attribute defines the width of a table cell. You can express it either in pixels or as a percentage of the whole table width. Please note that the browsers tend to have a lot of initiative when it comes to rendering tables. You cannot really rely on this attribute. Trial and error and using different browsers is advisable.

Table Structure

You use the element <table> to define a table. Inside <table>, immediately after the start tag, you can place a single <caption> element to identify a string that the browsers display immediately above the table.

Use the <tr> element to define rows within the table, and use <td> to define cells (i.e., columns) within the rows. If you want, you can use <th> for the table header instead of <tr>. The browsers will highlight it in bold.

To facilitate scrolling and printing of long tables, you can flag some rows at the top and/or at the bottom of the table as having particular significance. To do so, place the header rows inside the <thead> element, the footer rows inside the element <tfoot>, and the rest of the rows inside the <tbody> element.

You can also define attributes of columns before defining the rows that contain the actual table cells. You do this with the <col> element, which is not as useless as it might appear at first, because tables are defined one cell at a time. Therefore, without <col>, you have to define the cell attributes for each individual cell. With <col>, you can define those attributes only once for all the cells belonging to one column. It potentially avoids a lot of repetitions and makes the code more readable. Unfortunately, before you get excited about <col>, be aware that it only works with Internet Explorer. Firefox and Opera simply ignore it.

<table> Attributes

With strict validation, <table> doesn't support any of the standard table attributes we've already described, with the exception of width. Its value, when expressed as a percentage, refers to the browser window, so that <table width="100%"> defines a table as wide as the whole window.

border, frame, and rules

You use the border attribute to define the thickness in pixels of the border enclosing the table. The default is border="0", but we encourage you to specify it in any case. With any border greater than zero, each individual cell is highlighted by a thin border.

Once you've defined a border of nonzero thickness, you can use the frame attribute to define which sides of the border surrounding the whole table will be visible. Table C-2 shows the possible values. The default (i.e., without the frame attribute) is "border".

Table C-2. *Values of the frame Attribute*

Value	Meaning
void	No border at all
above	Top side
below	Bottom side
hsides	Horizontal side (top and bottom)
lhs	Left-hand side
rhs	Right-hand side
vsides	Vertical sides (left-hand side and right-hand side)
box	All four sides
border	All four sides (same as box)

The rules attribute defines the horizontal and vertical divider lines between rows and columns. It can have the following values: none, groups, rows, cols, and all. The rules are single lines, not the thin cell borders that are shown when the rules attribute is missing. With rules="groups", the lines are only drawn between the groups of columns defined with <colgroup>. Figure C-21 shows some examples of tables with different combinations of frames and rules.

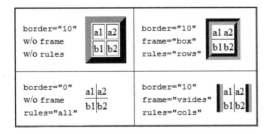

Figure C-21. *Rendering of table frames and rules*

Notice that the appearance of the outer table border is different between the two examples in the first row. It turns out that this is due to the presence of the rules attribute.

Rows

You can define a table row using the `<tr>` element (table row). It accepts the standard table attributes `align`, `char`, `charoff`, and `valign`.

Cells

You can use two elements to define cells: `<th>` (table header) for header cells and `<td>` (table data) for all other cells. The only difference between the two elements is that the browsers normally render the text in header cells in bold. Therefore, everything we'll say about `<td>` will also apply to `<th>`.

Note that cell elements are contained inside row elements. That's why we talk about cells rather than columns. In other words, it's your responsibility to ensure that each row element includes the correct number of cell elements.

Besides supporting all the standard table attributes, `<td>` accepts the following attributes: `abbr`, `axis`, `colspan`, `headers`, `rowspan`, and `scope`.

abbr

The `abbr` attribute specifies an abbreviated version of the cell content.

axis

The `axis` attribute provides a way of categorizing cells. Its value is a string identifying the category. Nonvisual browsers use this attribute.

colspan and rowspan

`colspan` and `rowspan` let you expand a cell over several columns and rows. They require a bit of care. For example, let's say you want to generate the table you see in Figure C-22.

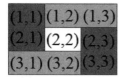

Figure C-22. *Grouping of table columns and rows with colspan and rowspan*

To create this table, use the code in Listing C-9.

Listing C-9. *cr_span.html*

```
<!DOCTYPE html PUBLIC "-//W3C//DTD XHTML 1.0 Strict//EN"
  "http//www.w3.org/TR/xhtml1/DTD/xhtml1-strict.dtd">
<html xmlns="http//www.w3.org/1999/xhtml" xmllang="en" lang="en">
<head>
  <title>Example of colspan and rowspan</title>
  <style type="text/css">body {font-size:16pt}</style>
```

```
    <style type="text/css">.g1 {background-color: #c0c0c0}</style>
    <style type="text/css">.g2 {background-color: #808080}</style>
    </head>
<body>
<table cellpadding="2" border="1" rules="all">
  <tr>
    <td rowspan="2" class="g2">(1,1)<br/>(2,1)</td>
    <td colspan="2" class="g1">(1,2) (1,3)</td>
    </tr>
  <tr>
    <!-- (2,1) was defined one row up -->
    <td>(2,2)</td>
    <td rowspan="2" class="g2")>(2,3)<br/>(3,3)</td>
    </tr>
  <tr>
    <td colspan="2" class="g1">(3,1) (3,2)</td>
    <!-- (3,3) was defined one row up -->
    </tr>
  </table>
</body>
</html>
```

headers

The headers attribute is a space-separated list of cell IDs that supply header information for the cell. Its purpose is to allow text-only browsers to render the header information for the cells. Listing C-10 shows you how it is used.

Listing C-10. *td_headers.html*

```
<!DOCTYPE html PUBLIC "-//W3C//Dtd XHTML 1.0 Strict//EN"
  "http//www.w3.org/TR/xhtml1/Dtd/xhtml1-strict.dtd">
<html xmlns="http//www.w3.org/1999/xhtml" xmllang="en" lang="en">
<head><title>Test of td headers attribute</title></head>
<body>
<table border="1">
  <caption>Average Height</caption>
  <tr>
    <th id="c">Country</th>
    <th id="m">Males</th><th id="f">Females</th>
    </tr>
  <tr>
    <td id="au" headers="c">Australia</td>
    <td headers="m au">5 ft 10.2</td><td headers="f au">5 ft 4.5</td>
    </tr>
```

```
    <tr>
      <td id="us" headers="c">U.S.A.</td>
      <td headers="m us">5 ft 9.4</td><td headers="f us">5 ft 4</td>
      </tr>
    </table>
</body>
</html>
```

Note that headers has no effect on how the table is rendered on normal browsers.

scope

The scope attribute specifies that the cell provides header information for the row that contains it (scope="row"), the column (scope="col"), the row group (scope="rowgroup"—i.e., the rows identified by one of the elements <thead>, <tbody>, or <tfoot>), or the column group (scope="colgroup"—we'll describe the colgroup attribute shortly).

Columns

As we said in the "Table Structure" section, you should be able to define attributes for all the cells in a column by means of the <col> element. Unfortunately, at least for the time being, it only works with Internet Explorer. Actually, it works in part also with Firefox, as you can see from Figure C-23, where the second column should have a gray background (and it does) and the third column should be right-aligned (and it isn't).

first	second	third
column	column	column
only defaults	in gray	right aligned

Figure C-23. *Example of* <col> *with Firefox*

Listing C-11 shows the page source code for Figure C-23.

Listing C-11. *table_col.html*

```
<!DOCTYPE html PUBLIC "-//W3C//Dtd XHTML 1.0 Strict//EN"
  "http//www.w3.org/TR/xhtml1/Dtd/xhtml1-strict.dtd">
<html xmlns="http//www.w3.org/1999/xhtml" xmllang="en" lang="en">
<head><title>Test of table col element</title></head>
<body>
<table border="1">
  <col/>
  <col style="background-color:#C0C0C0"/>
  <col align="right"/>
  <tr><th>first</th><th>second</th><th>third</th></tr>
  <tr><td>column</td><td>column</td><td>column</td></tr>
```

```
<tr><td>only defaults</td><td>in gray</td><td>right aligned</td></tr>
  </table>
</body>
</html>
```

As you can see from Listing C-11, there are three `<col>` elements that apply to the three columns of the table, from left to right. It isn't necessary to have all the `<col>` elements before the `<tr>` elements or to have as many `<col>` elements as the number of columns actually present in the table. You can freely mix `<col>` and `<tr>`. What counts is only the order in which you write the `<col>` elements.

Column Groups

You can identify groups of contiguous columns with the table element `<colgroup>`. In addition to all standard table attributes, it also accepts the span attribute, which defines how many columns from left to right are to be grouped. In connection with the table attribute rules, you can use column groups to decide when to show column separators. For example, see Listing C-12.

Listing C-12. *table_colgroup.html*

```
<!DOCTYPE html PUBLIC "-//W3C//Dtd XHTML 1.0 Strict//EN"
  "http//www.w3.org/TR/xhtml1/Dtd/xhtml1-strict.dtd">
<html xmlns="http//www.w3.org/1999/xhtml" xmllang="en" lang="en">
<head>
  <title>Test of table colgroup element</title>
  <style type="text/css">body {font-size:16pt}</style>
  </head>
<body>
<table border="1" cellpadding="2" rules="groups">
  <colgroup span="1"/>
  <colgroup span="2"/>
  <tr><td>(1,1)</td><td>(1,2)</td><td>(1,3)</td><td>(1,4)</td></tr>
  <tr><td>(2,1)</td><td>(2,2)</td><td>(2,3)</td><td>(2,4)</td></tr>
  <tr><td>(3,1)</td><td>(3,2)</td><td>(3,3)</td><td>(3,4)</td></tr>
  </table>
</body>
</html>
```

The code in Listing C-12 results in the table shown in Figure C-24.

(1,1)	(1,2) (1,3)	(1,4)
(2,1)	(2,2) (2,3)	(2,4)
(3,1)	(3,2) (3,3)	(3,4)

Figure C-24. *Example of* `<colgroup>`

Theoretically, you could use the style attribute of `<colgroup>` to define styles shared by all the columns of the groups, but unfortunately this mechanism only works with Internet Explorer. You could also include `<col>` elements inside `<colgroup>`, but again, this only works with Internet Explorer.

Table Header, Body, and Footer

With the table elements `<thead>`, `<tbody>`, and `<tfoot>`, you can split all the rows of a table in three groups: header, body, and footer. This allows browsers to perform a more intelligent scrolling of long tables. In practice, you can use them to separate cells horizontally, as shown in Figure C-25.

(1,1)	**(1,2)**	**(1,3)**
(2,1)	(2,2)	(2,3)
(3,1)	(3,2)	(3,3)
(4,1)	(4,2)	(4,3)
(5,1)	**(5,2)**	**(5,3)**
(6,1)	**(6,2)**	**(6,3)**

Figure C-25. *Example of* `<thead>`, `<tbody>`, *and* `<tfoot>`

Listing C-13 shows you how to create the table shown in Figure C-25.

Listing C-13. *table_rowgroup.html*

```
<!DOCTYPE html PUBLIC "-//W3C//Dtd XHTML 1.0 Strict//EN"
  "http//www.w3.org/TR/xhtml1/Dtd/xhtml1-strict.dtd">
<html xmlns="http://www.w3.org/1999/xhtml" xmllang="en" lang="en">
<head>
  <title>Test of table row grouping</title>
  <style type="text/css">body {font-size:16pt}</style>
  </head>
<body>
<table border="1" cellpadding="2" rules="groups">
  <colgroup span="1"/>
  <thead style="font-weight:bold; background-color:#C0C0C0">
    <tr><td>(1,1)</td><td>(1,2)</td><td>(1,3)</td></tr>
    </thead>
  <tr><td>(2,1)</td><td>(2,2)</td><td>(2,3)</td></tr>
  <tr><td>(3,1)</td><td>(3,2)</td><td>(3,3)</td></tr>
  <tr><td>(4,1)</td><td>(4,2)</td><td>(4,3)</td></tr>
```

```
    <tfoot style="font-weight:bold">
      <tr><td>(5,1)</td><td>(5,2)</td><td>(5,3)</td></tr>
      <tr><td>(6,1)</td><td>(6,2)</td><td>(6,3)</td></tr>
      </tfoot>
    </table>
</body>
</html>
```

As you can see, contrary to what happens with column groups, the styling works. Notice that we've only defined a header and a footer. It would be better programming to define the body as well.

Styles

You've already seen several examples of style sheets, and we outlined the CSS standard in Chapter 3. In this section, we'll only provide a brief description of the generic HTML elements that let you use styles in an HTML page.

\<div\> and \<span\>

You can use both \<div\> and \<span\> to apply styles to sections of a document, as in the following example:

```
<div style="color:red">
  <p>a red paragraph</p>
  <p>a red paragraph <span style="color:green">with green</span> in it</p>
  </div>
```

As you can see, \<div\> can contain paragraphs, while \<span\> cannot. This is because \<div\> identifies a block and can therefore contain other block-level elements (such as \<p\> and \<table\>), while \<span\> can only contain inline-level elements (such as \<a\> and \<img\>). So far, so good. However, the standards don't clearly distinguish between block-level and inline-level elements. Moreover, some elements are sometimes considered to be block-level and sometimes inline-level. Usually, the browsers display a new line before rendering a block-level element, but this also is not always true. The elements that are certainly block-level are \<address\>, \<blockquote\>, \<dl\>, \<fieldset\>, \<form\>, \<h1\>, \<h2\>, \<h3\>, \<h4\>, \<h5\>, \<h6\>, \<hr\>, \<noframes\>, \<noscript\>, \<ol\>, \<p\>, \<pre\>, \<table\>, and \<ul\>. The elements that are certainly inline-level are \<a\>, \<abbr\>, \<acronym\>, \<b\>, \<bdo\>, \<big\>, \<br\>, \<cite\>, \<code\>, \<dfn\>, \<em\>, \<i\>, \<img\>, \<input\>, \<kbd\>, \<label\>, \<q\>, \<samp\>, \<select\>, \<small\>, \<strong\>, \<sub\>, \<sup\>, \<textarea\>, \<tt\>, and \<var\>. For all the others, we cannot give you a clear indication.

We recommend using \<div\> only to apply styles to whole sections of a document. To apply styles to a single element (e.g., a \<table\>), you should define the style attribute directly in the start tag of the element itself. In fact, if you use several styles, it would make your code more maintainable if you defined the corresponding classes in a separate style-sheet file. Use \<span\> even more sparingly, just for one-off styling of strings.

\<style>

Place the \<style> element inside the \<head> element to define a style that will apply to the whole document. If you use the same styles in different documents, you should place them in a separate style-sheet file and load it with the \<link> element, as shown toward the beginning of this appendix.

The \<style> element requires the type attribute, as illustrated in the following example:

```
<style type="text/css"> h1 {color: red} h2 {color: green} </style>
```

See Listings C-3, C-4, C-7, C-9, and C-11 for further examples. Use the optional attribute media to specify the destination of the style information. See Table C-3 for a list of valid media values.

Table C-3. *Values Valid for the* media *Attribute*

Value	Purpose
all	For all devices (default)
aural	For speech synthesizers
braille	For braille tactile-feedback devices
handheld	For handheld devices with small screens and limited bandwidth
screen	For nonpaged computer screens
print	For paged media and for documents viewed on screen in print-preview mode
projection	For projectors
tty	For media using a fixed-pitch character grid, such as teletypes
tv	For TV-type devices with low resolution and limited scroll ability

Programming

If you expect to find \<applet> in this section, please be aware that it has been deprecated. Use \<object> instead.

\<object> and \<param>

Listing C-1 shows how to use the elements \<object type="image/gif"> and \<a> to make a clickable map (see Figures C-5 and C-6) with a GIF image. However, you can use \<object> to embed objects of any MIME type (listed in http://www.iana.org/assignments/media-types/), including applets. This is important, because the \<applet> element has been deprecated.

You can also use \<object> to download a video clip, as in the following example:

```
<object data=myClip.mpeg type="video/mpeg" height="120" width="180">
  <p>Click <a href=MyMovie.mpeg>here</a> to download</p>
  </object>
```

Now, to embed an applet using the `<object>` element is anything but easy. Assuming that your `Applet` class is `MyA.class` and that it is archived together with all other necessary classes in a JAR file named `MyA.jar`, with the now deprecated `<applet>` element you might have included in your HTML document something like the following line:

```
<applet code="MyA" archive="MyA.jar" height="200" width="300"></applet>
```

With strict XHTML, you have to include the following to be sure that both Internet Explorer and Firefox can render the page correctly:

```
<!--[if !IE]>-->
  <object classid="java:MyA.class"
    codetype="application/x-java-applet"
    archive="MyA.jar"
    height="200" width="300">
    <!--<![endif]-->
<object classid="clsid:8AD9C840-044E-11D1-B3E9-00805F499D93"
  height="200" width="300">
  <param name="code" value="MyA"/>
  <param name="archive" value="MyA.jar"/>
  </object>
<!--[if !IE]>-->
  </object>
  <!--<![endif]-->
```

Just to make it safer, you should also tell the browser where the Java plug-in can be found on the Sun server. To do it, include the following attribute inside the innermost `<object>` start tag:

```
codebase="http://java.sun.com/update/1.5.0/jinstall-1_5_0-windows-i586.cab"
```

This refers to Java 5, which was the latest version at the time of writing this chapter. Obviously, you don't need it if the plug-in has already been installed. If, by any chance, you're using the Konqueror browser, insert the following line between the first `<object>` start tag and the line containing the first `endif`:

```
<param name="archive" value="MyA.jar"/>
```

With `<param>`, you can define the applet parameters, as in the following example:

```
<param name="theParName" value="the ParValue"/>
```

Unfortunately, because of the `<object>` duplication necessary to cater for all browsers, the parameters have to be duplicated as well. So this code:

```
<applet code="MyA" archive="MyA.jar" height="200" width="300">
  <param name="aName" value="whatever"/>
  <param name="anotherName" value="blabla"/>
  </applet>
```

now becomes:

```
<!--[if !IE]>-->
  <object classid="java:MyA.class"
    codetype="application/x-java-applet"
    archive="MyA.jar"
    height="200" width="300">
    <param name="aName" value="whatever"/>
    <param name="anotherName" value="blabla"/>
    <!--<![endif]-->
<object classid="clsid:8AD9C840-044E-11D1-B3E9-00805F499D93"
  height="200" width="300">
  <param name="code" value="MyA"/>
  <param name="archive" value="MyA.jar"/>
  <param name="aName" value="whatever"/>
  <param name="anotherName" value="blabla"/>
  </object>
<!--[if !IE]>-->
  </object>
  <!--<![endif]-->
```

To top it off, while using `<applet>` to define the URL holding the JAR file, you only needed to define the `codebase` attribute, as in `codebase="myApplets"`. Now, however, you have to pass it to the object as a `<param>`, as in `<param name="codebase" value="myApplets"/>`. And obviously, you need to do it twice, once for each one of the two objects.

Perhaps you're thinking of switching back from strict to transitional validation, so that you can keep using `<applet>`. You have our sympathy, but resist the temptation, because in the future, you might no longer be able to do it, and it is healthy to be rigorous.

Beside `name` and `value`, `<param>` can also have the optional attribute `type`, which defines the MIME type of the parameter, and `valuetype`, which accepts the values `data` (the default), `ref`, and `object`. With `data`, the value is evaluated and passed to the object as a string. With `ref`, the value is a URI pointing to runtime values. With `object`, the value coincides with the value of the `id` attribute of an `<object>` in the same document.

Anyhow, let's now look at the remaining possible attributes you can define for `<object>`. In the applet example, you've already seen `archive`, `classid` (a class ID value as set in the Windows registry or a URL), `codebase`, `codetype`, `height`, and `width`. You also have `data` (the URL of the object data, an alternative to `classid`), `declare` (to delay the instantiation of the object to when it is needed), `standby` (text to be displayed while the object is being loaded), `type` (the MIME type of the data, an alternative to `codetype`), and `usemap`, which you saw when we described clickable maps.

<script> and <noscript>

Use `<script>` to define a client-side script, as in the following example:

```
<script type="text/javascript">
<!--
document.write("Now: " + new Date());
//-->
</script>
```

The script displays the current date and time like this:

```
Now: Mon Mar 26 2007 19:12:17 GMT-0800
```

The strings `<!--` and `-->` wrap the script inside an HTML comment, so that browsers that cannot handle the `<script>` element are told to ignore its content. You need the double slash to comment out `-->` for browsers that do understand JavaScript; otherwise, they would get confused. This is a piece of trivia that we couldn't resist telling you, but nowadays all browsers can handle JavaScript. Therefore, you no longer need to do this. Only old *code warriors* insist on doing it!

If the script is long or if you use it in several documents, you should store it in a separate file and load it by defining the `src` attribute, which accepts as a value the URL of the file—for example, `<script type="text/javascript" src="myScript.js"></script>`. Please note that you need both the start and end tags. The form `<script ... />` is not valid.

`<noscript>` defines text displayed by browsers that can process the `<script>` element but do not understand the scripting language you specify. By including something like this line in your page:

```
<noscript>Please enable JavaScript to view this page correctly!</noscript>
```

you'll notify the users who have disabled JavaScript in their browser.

JSP Reference

In Chapter 2, we explained JSP through a series of examples. Here, we'll provide several additional examples and a more systematic description of JSP 2.1. This appendix is consistent with the documents `jsp-2_1-fr-spec.pdf` and `jsp-2_1-el-spec.pdf`, which together constitute version 2.1 of the JSR 245 standard (consisting of two documents, JavaServer Pages Specification Version 2.1 and Expression Language Specification Version 2.1). You can download both documents from the JCP web site (`http://jcp.org/`).

There are three types of elements in JSP pages: *directive*, *action*, and *scripting*. Directive elements are messages to the JSP container. Their purpose is to provide information on the page itself necessary for its translation. As they have no association with each individual request, directive elements output no data to the HTML response.

Action elements specify activities that need to be performed when the page is requested. They can use, modify, and/or create objects, and they may affect the way in which data is sent to the output. In addition to the standard action elements, it is possible to specify extensions in the form of custom tag libraries. JSTL is one such extension, which we mention here because it has been standardized by Sun Microsystems and is universally available.

Scripting elements can be declarations, scriptlets, and expressions, but they all are Java fragments capable of manipulating Java objects, invoking their methods, and catching Java exceptions. Like actions, they execute when the page is requested, and they can send data to the output.

EL was introduced in JSP 2.0 as an alternative to the scripting elements. You can use EL expressions in action attributes specified to be capable of accepting runtime expressions. You can also use EL in JSP templates (JSP files that include parameterized content).

Object Scopes

Whether objects are created explicitly within JSP pages when processing a request or implicitly by Tomcat, you cannot use them properly unless you know in which scope they are available. There are four possible scopes. In order of increasing generality, they are *page*, *request*, *session*, and *application*.

Implicit Objects

The JSP container (i.e., Tomcat) defines several objects that you can use within the scripting elements. They are `application`, `config`, `exception`, `pageContext`, `out`, `request`, `response`, and session. For a detailed description of the implicit object methods, refer to jsp-2_1-fr-spec.pdf or to the Java EE 5 API (http://java.sun.com/javaee/5/docs/api/).

The application Object

The application object is an instance of the class org.apache.catalina.core. ApplicationContextFacade, which Tomcat defines to implement the interface javax.servlet.ServletContext. It provides access to the resources shared within the web application. For example, by adding an attribute (which can be an object of any type) to application, you can ensure that all JSP files that make up your web application have access to it.

Example: Using an Attribute to Enable and Disable Conditional Code

One of the advantages of using JSP is that the web server doesn't need to reinterpret the source file of a page every time a client requests that page. The JSP container translates each JSP page into a Java file and compiles it into a class, but this only happens when you update the JSP source. You might like to be able to switch on or off some particular functionality for debugging or other purposes, without having to recompile the whole application when you flip the switch. To achieve this result, you only need to wrap the functionality in question inside a conditional statement, as follows:

```
if (application.getAttribute("do_it") != null) {
  /* ...place your "switchable" functionality here... */
  }
```

You also need to include two small JSP pages in your application. The first one sets the attribute (see Listing D-1).

Listing D-1. *do_it.jsp*

```
<%@page language="java" contentType="text/html"%>
<html><head><title>Conditional code ON</title></head>
<body>Conditional code
<%
  application.setAttribute("do_it", "");
  if (application.getAttribute("do_it") == null) out.print("not");
  %>
enabled</body></html>
```

The second one removes the attribute (see Listing D-2).

Listing D-2. *do_it_not.jsp*

```
<%@page language="java" contentType="text/html"%>
<html><head><title>Conditional code OFF</title></head>
<body>Conditional code
<%
```

```
application.removeAttribute("do_it");
if (application.getAttribute("do_it") == null) out.print("not");
%>
enabled</body></html>
```

When you want to enable the conditional code, you just type the URL of do_it.jsp in your browser, and when you want to disable it, you type do_it_not.jsp. Until you disable it or restart Tomcat, the conditional code will remain enabled in all pages of your application. Notice that you've just set the attribute do_it to an empty string, but you can also define different values to have a finer selection of code to be activated.

Example: Using an Attribute to Control Logging

You might find it useful to be able to control the logging of some events to a particular file dynamically. To do so, you need to include two JSP files in your application. Listing D-3 shows the first one, log_on.jsp.

Listing D-3. *log_on.jsp*

```
<%@page language="java" contentType="text/html"%>
<%@ page import="MyClasses.*"%>
<html><head><title>Switch the log ON</title></head><body>
<%
  MyLog log = (MyLog)application.getAttribute("logFile");
  if (log == null) {
    try {
      log = new MyLog("logs/mylog.log");
      application.setAttribute("logFile", log);
      log.println("Logging enabled");
      out.println("Logging enabled");
      }
    catch (Exception e) {
      out.println(e.getMessage());
      }
    }
  else {
    log.println("Attempt to enable logging");
    out.println("Logging was already enabled");
    }
  %>
</body></html>
```

Listing D-4 shows the second JSP file, log_off.jsp.

Listing D-4. *log_off.jsp*

```
<%@page language="java" contentType="text/html"%>
<%@ page import="MyClasses.*"%>
<html><head><title>Switch the log OFF</title></head><body>
<%
  MyLog log = (MyLog)application.getAttribute("logFile");
  if (log != null) {
    log.println("Logging disabled");
    log.close();
    application.removeAttribute("logFile");
    }
  %>
Done.
</body></html>
```

After checking that there is no application attribute named logFile, log_on.jsp instantiates the MyLog class and saves the object as an application attribute named logFile. After that, you can easily make an entry in the log file from any JSP of the same application. You only need to do the following:

```
<%@ page import="MyClasses.*"%>
<%
  MyLog log = (MyLog)application.getAttribute("logFile");
  if (log != null) log.println("This is my entry in the log");
  %>
```

In log_off.jsp, after checking that the logFile attribute exists, you close the log file and remove the attribute. The logging is then disabled in all JSPs of the application, because any attempt to get the logFile attribute returns a null.

The only piece of the puzzle that you still need is how to make the MyLog class. This is also simple: inside the WEB-INF\classes\ directory of your application, create a subdirectory named MyClasses, where you move the class file you obtain by compiling the Java source shown in Listing D-5 with javac.

Listing D-5. *MyLog.java*

```
/* MyLog.java - Implements a log class */
package MyClasses;
import java.util.*;
import java.text.*;
import java.io.*;
public class MyLog {
  private static final SimpleDateFormat TIME_FMT =
                       new SimpleDateFormat("yyyy-MM-dd HH:mm:ss:SSS");
  private static PrintWriter log = null;
  public MyLog(String logpath) throws IOException {
    log = new PrintWriter(new FileWriter(logpath, true));
    }
```

```
public static synchronized void println(String s) {
  log.println(TIME_FMT.format(new java.util.Date()) + " - " + s);
  log.flush();
  }
public static synchronized void close() {
  log.close();
  }
}
```

MyLog.java opens your log file in append mode and adds the date to your entry before writing it into the file. Notice that the methods are synchronized, so that several pages can log entries at the same time without getting mixed up. An alternative would have been to make MyLog a subclass of PrintWriter. Then you could have had all the methods of PrintWriter available, and you wouldn't have needed to define a close method within MyLog. However, we wanted to have the methods synchronized, although it might have been a bit overkill.

In any case, the logs look like this:

```
2007-04-26 17:39:05:843 - Logging enabled
2007-04-26 17:39:10:531 - This is a log
2007-04-26 17:39:29:640 - Logging disabled
```

Example: Using an init Parameter to Increase Application Portability

Sooner or later, you'll need to port your application to a different environment. Perhaps you'll need to change a database name, user ID, and/or password. The initialization parameters exist precisely for this purpose.

First, you need to include the parameter definitions in the web.xml file that's inside the WEB-INF folder of your application root directory. You need to insert the lines shown in Listing D-6 between the <web-app> and </web-app> tags.

Listing D-6. *XML Fragment to Define Initialization Parameters*

```
<context-param>
  <param-name>dbName</param-name>
  <param-value>my-database-name</param-value>
  </context-param>
<context-param>
  <param-name>dbUser</param-name>
  <param-value>my-userID</param-value>
  </context-param>
<context-param>
  <param-name>dbPass</param-name>
  <param-value>my-password</param-value>
  </context-param>
```

To access the parameters from within any JSP page, you just need to type something like the following:

```
String dbName = application.getInitParameter("dbName");
String dbUser = application.getInitParameter("dbUser");
String dbPass = application.getInitParameter("dbPass");
```

The config Object

The config object is an instance of the org.apache.catalina.core.StandardWrapperFacade class, which Tomcat defines to implement the interface javax.servlet.ServletConfig. Tomcat uses this object to pass information to the servlets.

The following config method is the only one you might ever use, and its usage is trivial:

```
config.getServletName()
```

This returns the servlet name, which is the string contained in the <servlet-name> element defined in the WEB-INF\web.xml file. <servlet-name> is inside <servlet>, which is in turn inside <web-app>. In the Ebookshop example from Chapter 1, the servlet name was EBookshopServlet. The default name is jsp.

The exception Object

The exception object is an instance of a subclass of Throwable (e.g., java.lang. NullPointerException) and is only available in error pages.

Listing D-7 shows you two methods to send the stack trace to the output. The first one, using getStackTrace, gives you access to each trace element as an object of type java.lang.StackTraceElement, which you can then analyze with methods such as getClassName, getFileName, getLineNumber, and getMethodName.

Listing D-7. *stack_trace.jsp*

```
<%@page language="java" contentType="text/html"%>
<%@page import="java.util.*, java.io.*"%>
<%@page isErrorPage="true"%>
<html><head><title>Print stack trace</title></head><body>
From exception.getStackTrace():<br/>
<pre><%
  StackTraceElement[] trace = exception.getStackTrace();
  for (int k = 0; k < trace.length; k++) {
    out.println(trace[k]);
  }
%></pre>
Printed with exception.printStackTrace(new PrintWriter(out)):
<pre><%
  exception.printStackTrace(new PrintWriter(out));
%></pre>
</body></html>
```

Notice the directive `<%@page isErrorPage="true"%>`, without which the implicit variable `exception` is not defined. Listing D-8 shows a simple example of how you can use an error page.

Listing D-8. *cause_exception.jsp*

```
<%@page language="java" contentType="text/html"%>
<%@ page errorPage="stack_trace.jsp"%>
<html><head><title>Cause null pointer exception</title></head><body>
<%
  String a = request.getParameter("notThere");
  int len = a.length(); // causes a null pointer exception
  %>
</body></html>
```

Notice the `<%@ page errorPage="stack_trace.jsp"%>` directive, which links the error page of Listing D-7 to the occurrence of exceptions. To cause a `NullPointerException`, we tried to get a request parameter that doesn't exist and then accessed it. Also, we didn't use `try`/`catch` to trap the exception; if we had, the error page would have not been executed.

The out Object

Most manuals state that `out` is an instance of the `javax.servlet.jsp.JspWriter` class, which you can use to write into the response. This is not entirely correct, because `JspWriter` is an abstract class, and as such, it cannot be instantiated. In reality, `out` is an instance of the non-abstract class `org.apache.jasper.runtime.JspWriterImpl`, which extends `JspWriter`. Tomcat defines `JspWriterImpl` precisely to implement the `JspWriter` methods. For all practical purposes, this is inconsequential to you, but some of you sharp-eyed readers might have thought that we were talking about instantiating an abstract class. It usually pays to be precise.

The `JspWriter` class includes the definition of a handful of fields. You won't need them, but mentioning them gives us the opportunity to give you some useful information.

The `autoFlush` field tells you whether the `JspWriter` is flushed automatically when its buffer fills up or whether an `IOException` is thrown upon overflow. The default for `out` is `true`, which means that Tomcat will send a partial response to the client if the buffer fills up. You can set it to `false` with the directive `<%@page autoFlush="false"%>`, and you should do so if you expect the client to be an application. However, sending the response in "chunks" is perfectly OK when the client is a browser. In case you use `autoflush="false"`, though, you should also use `<%@page buffer="size-in-kb"%>` to ensure that the output buffer is large enough to store your largest response. This field is protected, but you can obtain its value with the `isAutoFlush` method.

The `bufferSize` field is the size in bytes of the output buffer. The default for `out` is 8,192 bytes. It's a protected field, but you can obtain its value with the `getBufferSize` method.

There are also three constant integer fields (`DEFAULT_BUFFER`, `NO_BUFFER`, and `UNBOUNDED_BUFFER`, of type `public static final int`), but you can safely ignore them. Just for the record, they're used to test whether the `JspWriter` is buffered and uses the default buffer size, is not buffered, or is buffered with an unbounded buffer, respectively. Besides the fact that you have no variable or attribute to check against these values, you're well served by the `getBufferSize` method (which returns 0 if the output is not buffered), in any case.

You've already seen in several examples that you can use print and println to write to the output buffer. As an argument, you can use any of the eight primitive data types of Java (boolean, char, byte, short, int, long, float, and double), an array of characters (char[]), an object (java.lang.Object), or a string (java.lang.String). In practice, you'll usually use a String argument, as in the following example:

```
out.print("fun(" + arg + ") = " + fun(arg));
```

Here, fun(arg) is executed, and both arg and the value returned by fun(arg) are automatically converted to strings to be concatenated with the rest.

The write method, inherited from java.io.Writer, sends a portion of an array of characters or of a string to the output. For example, if cbuf is a variable of type char[], out.write(cbuf, off, len) will write a portion of cbuf, with off being the offset of the first character and len being the number of characters to be copied. You could achieve the same result by extracting a part of the array with the following code and then printing it with print:

```
char[] portion = java.util.Arrays.copyOfRange(cbuf, off, off+len-1)
```

However, it would be less efficient, because first you would be copying a portion of the original array—an operation you don't need when using write.

You're not likely to use any of the other methods. In any case, you should avoid using close, which closes the output stream. Tomcat closes the stream when it is needed, and you don't want to fiddle with it.

The pageContext Object

Most manuals state that pageContext is an instance of the javax.servlet.jsp.PageContext class to access all objects and attributes of a JSP page. Similar to what we said concerning JspWriter, this is only partly true, because this class, like JspWriter, is also abstract. In reality, pageContext is an instance of the nonabstract class org.apache.jasper.runtime.PageContextImpl, which extends PageContext.

The PageContext class defines several fields, including PAGE_SCOPE, REQUEST_SCOPE, SESSION_SCOPE, and APPLICATION_SCOPE, which identify the four scopes. It also supports more than 40 methods, about half of which are inherited from the javax.servlet.jsp.JspContext class.

You have to pay particular attention when using the removeAttribute method, which accepts either one or two arguments. For example, pageContext.removeAttribute ("attrName") removes the attribute from *all* scopes, while the following code only removes it from the page scope:

```
pageContext.removeAttribute("attrName", PAGE_SCOPE)
```

The request Object

The request variable gives you access within your JSP page to the HTTP request sent to it by the client. It's an instance of the org.apache.catalina.connector.RequestFacade class, which Tomcat defines to implement the javax.servlet.http.HttpServletRequest and javax.servlet.ServletRequest interfaces.

■**Caution** You cannot mix methods that handle parameters with methods that handle the request content. For example, if you execute request.getParameter, getReader and getInputStream will then fail. Also, keep in mind that in a JSP page, you can use either getReader or getInputStream, not both.

Example: Listing the Headers

Listing D-9 shows code that displays the request headers.

Listing D-9. *req_headers.jsp*

```
<%@page language="java" contentType="text/html"%>
<%@page import="java.util.*"%>
<html><head><title>Request Headers</title></head><body>
<%
  Enumeration headers = request.getHeaderNames();
  int kh = 0;
  while (headers.hasMoreElements()) {
    String hName = (String)headers.nextElement();
    out.println("------- " + hName);
    Enumeration hValues = request.getHeaders(hName);
    while (hValues.hasMoreElements()) {
      out.println("<br/>   " + hValues.nextElement());
      }
    out.println("<br/>");
    }
  %>
</body></html>
```

Figure D-1 shows the request headers generated by Firefox.

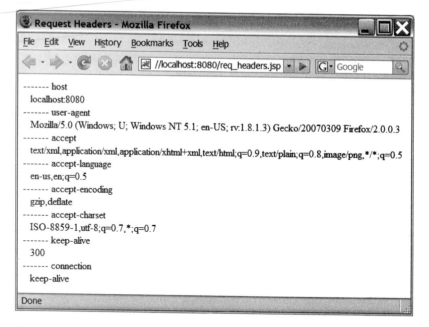

Figure D-1. *Request headers generated by Firefox*

Figure D-2 shows the request headers generated by Opera.

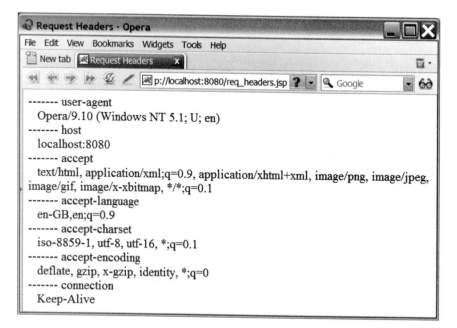

Figure D-2. *Request headers generated by Opera*

Figure D-3 shows the request headers generated by Internet Explorer.

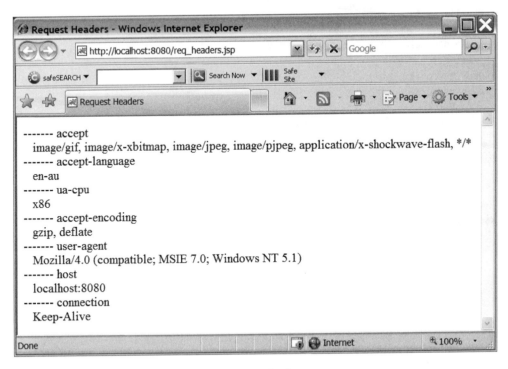

Figure D-3. *Request headers generated by Internet Explorer*

Example: User Authentication

The browsers can display a user/password dialog to provide a basic authentication mechanism. First, you have to define roles and users in the tomcat-users.xml file that you find in Tomcat's conf folder. Listing D-10 shows you what you should insert into tomcat-users.xml to define the canDoThis and canDoThat roles together with a couple of new users.

Listing D-10. *tomcat-users.xml Fragment*

```
<tomcat-users>
  <role rolename="canDoThis"/>
  <role rolename="canDoThat"/>
  <user username="aBloke" password="whatever" roles="canDoThis"/>
  <user username="bigCheese" password="yes!" roles="canDoThis,canDoThat"/>
</tomcat-users>
```

The tomcat-users.xml file is shared by all applications, but this doesn't prevent you from using the roles only for specific applications. Suppose that you want to use a password to protect all the pages inside a particular folder of an application. To do so, you have to edit the WEB-INF\web.xml file in the application's root directory. Listing D-11 shows you the code you should insert inside the <web-app> element. We've highlighted the three main tags.

Listing D-11. *web.xml Fragment*

```xml
<security-role>
  <role-name>canDoThis</role-name>
  <role-name>canDoThat</role-name>
  </security-role>
<security-constraint>
  <web-resource-collection>
    <web-resource-name>This</web-resource-name>
    <url-pattern>/this/*</url-pattern>
    </web-resource-collection>
  <auth-constraint>
    <role-name>canDoThis</role-name>
    </auth-constraint>
  </security-constraint>
<security-constraint>
  <web-resource-collection>
    <web-resource-name>That</web-resource-name>
    <url-pattern>/that/*</url-pattern>
    <http-method>GET</http-method>
    </web-resource-collection>
  <auth-constraint>
    <role-name>canDoThat</role-name>
    </auth-constraint>
  </security-constraint>
<login-config>
  <auth-method>BASIC</auth-method>
  </login-config>
```

As you can see, you first declare the security roles defined in `tomcat-users.xml`. Then you define two security constraints. Each security constraint can actually include several resources and authority constraints. The `<url-pattern>` subelements state which folders or pages require protection. Finally, you state that the `BASIC` authentication method should be applied.

That's it! When you first attempt to access a page in a protected folder, the browser asks you to provide user identification and a password, as shown in Figure D-4.

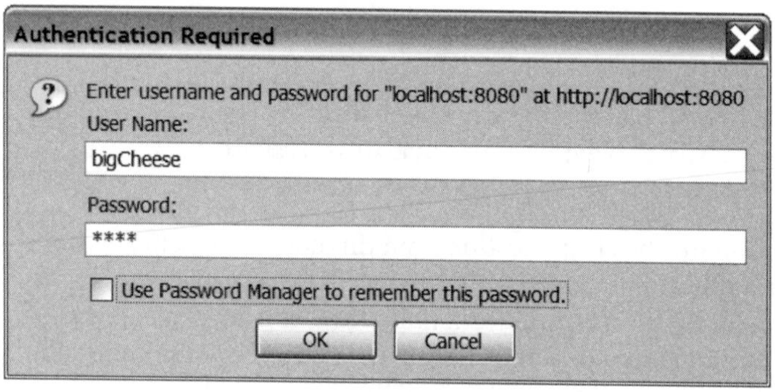

Figure D-4. *Basic authentication*

The only way of logging out is to close the browser and reopen it. Now, after logging in, you're able to verify that the getAuthType method returns "BASIC" instead of null, getRemoteUsers returns "bigCheese" instead of null, isUserInRole("canDoThat") returns true, and getUserPrincipal() also returns a Principal object with name "bigCheese".

Example: Reading the Request Body

You can read the request content with either getInputStream or getReader (but not both for the same request). Listing D-12 shows you an example with getInputStream.

Listing D-12. *req_getInputStream.jsp*

```jsp
<%@page language="java" contentType="text/html"%>
<%@page import="java.util.*, java.io.*"%>
<%
  int     len = request.getContentLength();
  byte[] buf = null;
  int     n = 0;
  if (len > 0) {
    buf = new byte[len];
    n = request.getInputStream().read(buf);
    }
%>
<html><head><title>Test request.getInputStream</title></head><body>
  <form action="" method="post" enctype="multipart/form-data">
    <input type="hidden" name="oneTwoThree" value="123"/>
    <input type="file" name="fil"/>
    <input type="submit"/>
    </form>
  <table border="1">
    <tr><td>getContentType()</td><td><%=request.getContentType()%></td></tr>
    <tr><td>getContentLength()</td><td><%=len%></td></tr>
<%
    out.print("<tr><td>getInputStream(): " + n + "</td><td><pre>");
    for (int k = 0; k < n; k++) out.print((char)buf[k]);
    out.println("</pre></td></tr>");
  %>
    </table>
</body></html>
```

Listing D-13 shows you an example with getReader. There are several methods to read the content, but the important thing to keep in mind is that getInputStrem returns data in binary form and unbuffered, while getReader returns buffered characters.

Listing D-13. *req_getReader.jsp*

```
<%@page language="java" contentType="text/html"%>
<%@page import="java.util.*, java.io.*"%>
<%
  int    len = request.getContentLength();
  String s = "";
  if (len > 0) {
    char[] cbuf = new char[len];
    int    n = request.getReader().read(cbuf, 0, len);
    s = new String(cbuf);
  }
%>
<html><head><title>Test request.getReader</title></head><body>
  <form action="" method="post">
    <input type="hidden" name="oneTwoThree" value="123"/>
    <input type="hidden" name="fourFiveSix" value="456"/>
    <input type="submit"/>
    </form>
  <table border="1">
    <tr><td>getContentType()</td><td><%=request.getContentType()%></td></tr>
    <tr><td>getContentLength()</td><td><%=len%></td></tr>
    <tr><td>getReader(): <%=s.length()%></td><td><pre><%=s%></pre></td></tr>
    </table>
</body></html>
```

Figure D-5 shows the output of req_getInputStream.jsp.

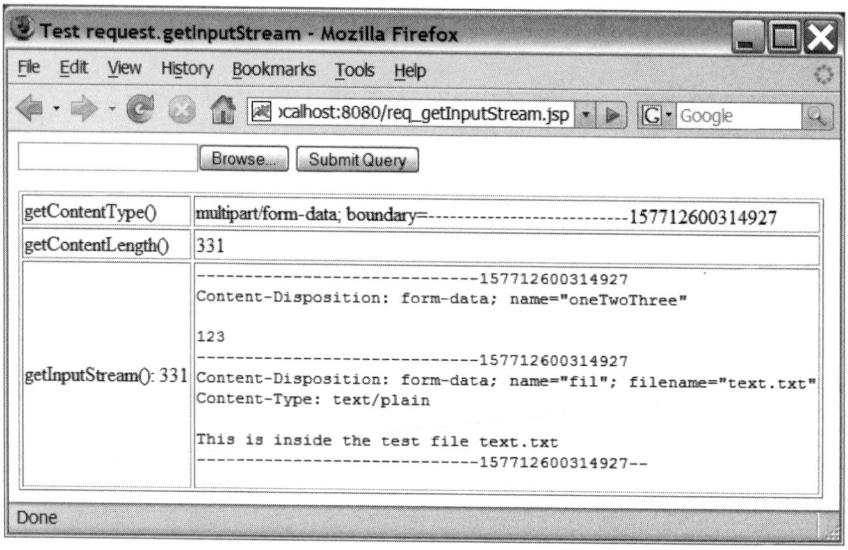

Figure D-5. *Output of req_getInputStream.jsp*

We've uploaded the file named `text.txt`, which only contains the text `This is inside the test file text.txt`. In the real world, the file would perhaps contain a formatted document, an image, or a video clip. With this example, you can also get an idea of the multipart format. As you can see, the content type actually contains a definition of the boundary, which is then used inside the request body to separate its parts. Each part consists of a header followed by an empty line and its content. Figure D-6 shows the output of `req_getReader.jsp`.

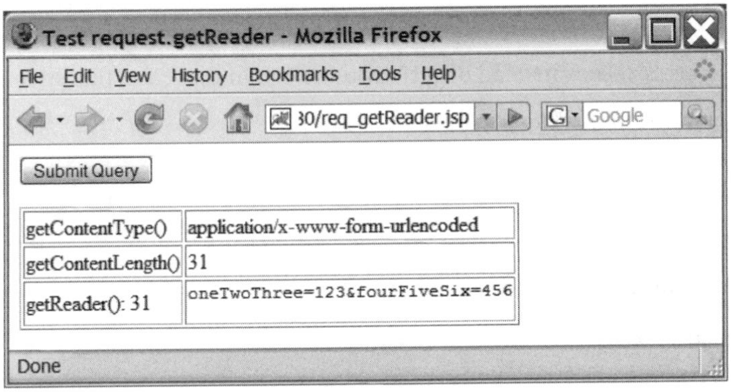

Figure D-6. *Output of req_getReader.jsp*

Example: Getting the Parameters

You can easily obtain a parameter value by executing `request.getParameter("parName")`, but a parameter might have more than one value, in which case you would only get the first value and not even be aware that more exist. Or, you might not know in advance what parameters are available. Listing D-14 shows you how to retrieve the map of parameters and all their values.

Listing D-14. *req_params.jsp*

```
<%@page language="java" contentType="text/html"%>
<%@page import="java.util.*, java.io.*"%>
<%
  Map      map = request.getParameterMap();
  Object[] keys = map.keySet().toArray();
  %>
<html><head><title>Request Parameters</title></head><body>
  Map size = <%=map.size()%>
  <table border="1">
    <tr><td>Map element</td><td>Par name</td><td>Par value[s]</td></tr>
<%
    for (int k = 0; k < keys.length; k++) {
      String[] pars = request.getParameterValues((String)keys[k]);
      out.print("<tr><td>" + k + "</td><td>'" + keys[k] + "'</td><td>");
      for (int j = 0; j < pars.length; j++) {
```

```
            if (j > 0) out.print(", ");
            out.print("'" + pars[j] + "'");
            }
         out.println("</td></tr>");
         }
   %>
      </table>
</body></html>
```

You could have used getParameterNames instead of getParameterMap. In that case, this code:

```
Enumeration enumPar = request.getParameterNames();
```

would have replaced this code:

```
Object[] keys = map.keySet().toArray();
```

The loop to get through all parameters would have changed from:

```
for (int k = 0; k < keys.length; k++)  {
```

to:

```
while (enumPar.hasMoreElements()) {
```

and to get the parameter names one by one, you would have used enumPar.nextElement() instead of (String)keys[k]. It wouldn't have really made any difference in the example, but with a map, you would get the parameter names in alphabetical order, while with the other method, you wouldn't. Furthermore, a Map object comes with some useful methods. For example, containsValue lets you check whether the map contains a given value.

If you copy req_params.jsp to Tomcat's webapps\ROOT directory and type the following URL in your browser:

```
http://localhost:8080/req_params.jsp?a=b&c=d&a=zzz&empty=&empty=&1=22
```

you get what is shown in Figure D-7.

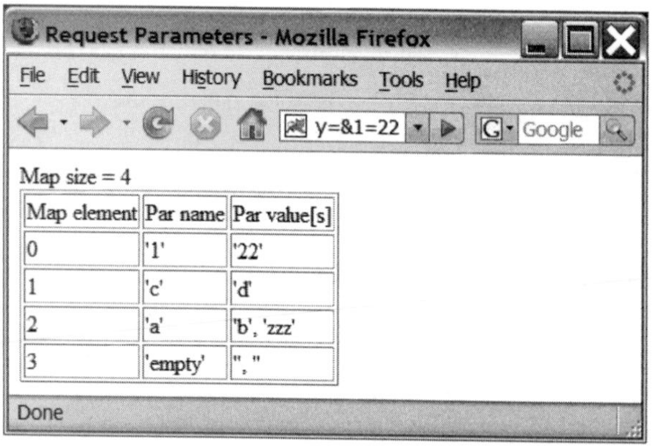

Figure D-7. *Output of req_params.jsp*

Notice that the parameter aptly named empty appears twice in the query string, which results in two empty strings in the parameter map. Also, looking at the parameter a, you'll notice that the values are returned in the same order in which they appear in the query string.

The response Object

The response variable gives you access within your JSP page to the HTTP response to be sent back to the client. It is an instance of the org.apache.catalina.connector.ResponseFacade class, which Tomcat defines to implement the interfaces javax.servlet.http. HttpServletResponse and javax.servlet.ServletResponse.

The HttpServletResponse interface includes the definition of 41 status codes (of type public static final int) to be returned to the client as part of the response. The HTTP status codes are all between 100 and 599. The range 100-199 is reserved to provide information, 200-299 to report successful completion of the requested operation, 300-399 to report warnings, 400-499 to report client errors, and 500-599 to report server errors.

The normal status code is SC_OK (200), and the most common error is SC_NOT_FOUND (404), which occurs when the client requests a page that doesn't exist. Working with Tomcat, the most common server error is SC_INTERNAL_SERVER_ERROR (500). You get it when there is an error in a JSP. You can use these constants as arguments of the sendError and setStatus methods.

The session Object

The variable session gives you access within your JSP page to the current client session. It is an instance of the org.apache.catalina.session.StandardSessionFacade class, which Tomcat defines to implement the javax.servlet.http.HttpSession interface.

To start a new session, you need to close and restart your browser. The session object supports a dozen methods, including setMaxInactiveInterval, but be aware that setMaxInactiveInterval doesn't work with Tomcat and JSP. However, you can set the timeout for your application (e.g., 40 minutes) by inserting a <session-config> element in the WEB-INF\web.xml file in your application folder within the webapps Tomcat folder. You need to place the following code inside the <web-app> element:

```
<session-config>
  <session-timeout>40</session-timeout>
  </session-config>
```

Alternatively, you can change Tomcat's default (which is 30 minutes) by inserting the same <session-config> element in the \conf\web.xml file you find inside the Tomcat home directory.

The session is the perfect place to save user information after a login. You only need to store it into an attribute, as in the following example:

```
session.setAttribute("upref", preferences);
```

Here you store an object of type UserPrefs named preferences in a session attribute named upref.

In all the pages of your application, you can then retrieve that information with something like this:

```
UserPrefs preferences = (UserPrefs)session.getAttribute("upref");
```

By doing so, you don't need to access a user database in each JSP page until the user closes his browser or the session expires after a long period of inactivity.

Standard Directive Elements

The standard directives are executed when the JSP page is translated into Java. Their syntax is as follows:

```
<%@ directive-name attr1="value1" [attr2="value2"...] %>
```

where `directive-name` can be `page`, `include`, or `taglib`.

The page Directive

The page directive defines several page-dependent properties expressed through attributes. These properties should appear only once in a JSP page (unless the multiple instances all have the same value).

You can write more than one page directive in a JSP page, and they will all apply. Their order or position of appearance within the page is generally irrelevant.

A typical page starts with the following directive:

```
<%@page language="java" contentType="text/html"%>
```

This is often followed by another page directive that specifies which Java libraries are needed—for example:

```
<%@page import="java.io.*, java.util.*"%>
```

However, it is preferable to import individual classes rather than whole libraries.

The page directive supports the following attributes: `autoFlush`, `buffer`, `contentType`, `errorPage`, `extends`, `import`, `info`, `isELIgnored`, `isErrorPage`, `language`, `pageEncoding`, `session`, and `trimDirectiveWhitespaces`.

Listing D-15 shows you a simple program to test concurrency.

Listing D-15. *concurrency.jsp*

```
<%@page language="java" contentType="text/html"%>
<%@page isThreadSafe="false"%>
<%! int k = 0;%>
<html><head><title>Concurrency</title></head><body>
<%
  out.print(k);
  int j = k + 1;
  Thread.sleep(5000);
```

```
  k = j;
  out.println(" -> " + k);
  %>
</body></html>
```

The program declares the instance variable k, copies it to the variable j, increments j, waits for five seconds, and copies the incremented j back to k. It also displays k at the beginning and at the end.

If you reload the page several times, you'll see that k is increased every time the page refreshes. Now view the page in another browser (not just another browser window, because caching plays funny tricks); for example, view it in Opera if you normally use Firefox. If you keep reloading the page in the two browsers, you'll see the k keeps increasing regardless of which browser you're looking at. This is because k is an instance variable.

Now reload the page in the first browser and then in the second browser. Do you notice how the second browser takes longer to refresh? This is because you've set isThreadSafe="false", and Tomcat doesn't execute the servlet code for the two requests at the same time. However, k keeps increasing across the browsers with each page refresh.

Now remove the page directive that sets isThreadSafe to false and repeat the test. When you reload the page on both browsers almost simultaneously, they refresh the page at the same time but with the same value of k! This is because the second execution of the servlet starts while the first one is "holding" for five seconds.

We introduced the five-second delay to be sure that you would see the problem. In the real world, the time interval between incrementing j and saving it back to k would be vanishingly small. Therefore, you might keep trying for years and never see the problem. Nevertheless, to rely on "it will never happen" when developing code is a bad practice. Other factors might influence the timing, and then you might see a problem once a day or worse. It could have a damaging effect on how users consider your web site.

Anyhow, there's a better alternative to relying on Tomcat to make the threads safe. Look at Listing D-16.

Listing D-16. *concurrency2.jsp*

```
<%@page language="java" contentType="text/html"%>
<%!
  int k = 0;
  Object syncK = new Object();
  %>
<html><head><title>Concurrency</title></head><body>
<%
  synchronized(syncK) {
    out.print(k);
    int j = k + 1;
    Thread.sleep(5000);
    k = j;
    out.println(" -> " + k);
    }
  %>
</body></html>
```

You protect the critical part of the code by enclosing it in a synchronized block. The syncK variable, being defined in a declaration element, is an instance variable shared like k among all the requests. We haven't used k because synchronized requires an object. In this simple case, instead of creating a new object specifically to protect the code, we could have used this, representing the servlet itself. But in general, if there were more than one block of code to protect, it wouldn't be a good idea. The best strategy to optimize efficiency, besides staying locked as little as possible, is to use specific locks.

The include Directive

The include directive merges the content of another file into a JSP page. Tomcat does it before translating the page to produce Java code and a servlet class. For example, this code includes the file named whatever with the ext extension in the same directory as the including file:

```
<%@include file="whatever.ext"%>
```

Any text file with any extension will do.

As the merging is done before the page is translated, all the HTML tags and JSP variables are available to the code stored in the included file. That said, you have to be careful not to go overboard with these inclusions, because with code spread over several fragments, your pages could quickly become unmaintainable.

The taglib Directive

You can extend the number of available JSP tags by directing Tomcat to use tag libraries. The taglib directory identifies a tag library and specifies what prefix is used to distinguish the new tags. For example, this code:

```
<%@taglib uri="http://mysite.com/mytags" prefix="my" %>
```

makes it possible for you to write the following line as part of your JSP page:

```
<my:oneOfMyTags> ... </my:oneOfMyTags>
```

See the "JSP's Tag Extension Mechanism" section in Chapter 2 to find out how to make your own tag libraries.

As another example, this code includes the core JSTL:

```
<%@taglib uri="http://java.sun.com/jsp/jstl/core" prefix="c" %>
```

Standard Action Elements

The standard actions are executed when Tomcat receives an HTTP request from a client. Their syntax is as follows:

```
<jsp:action-name attr1="value1" [attr2="value2"...]> ... </jsp:action-name>
```

action-name can be element, forward, getProperty, include, plugin, setProperty, text, and useBean. Additional action elements can only be used inside other actions. They are attribute, body, fallback, param, and params.

There are two additional action elements—invoke and doBody—but you can only use them within tag files.

jsp:element, jsp:attribute, and jsp:body

With the jsp:element action element, you can define XML elements dynamically. To see what this means in practice, have a look at Listing D-17. You need to define XML elements dynamically if the output of your JSP is an XML file that you're using to exchange data with other modules and applications rather than an HTML page to be displayed in a browser. The word *dynamically* is important, because it means that the XML elements can be generated at request time rather than statically at compile time.

Listing D-17. *actel_element_attribute.jsp*

```
<%@page language="java" contentType="text/html"%>
<html
  xmlns="http://www.w3c.org/1999/xhtml"
  xmlns:jsp="http://java.sun.com/JSP/Page"
  >
<head><title>Action elements: element, attribute</title></head>
<body>
<jsp:element name="myElem">
  <jsp:attribute name="myElemAttr">myElemAttr's value</jsp:attribute>
  <jsp:body>myElem's body</jsp:body>
  </jsp:element>
<br/>
<jsp:include page="text.txt"/>
<br/>
<jsp:include>
  <jsp:attribute name="page">text.txt</jsp:attribute>
  </jsp:include>
</body>
</html>
```

The JSP page shown in Listing D-17 generates the HTML output shown in Listing D-18.

Listing D-18. *The Output of actel_element_attribute.jsp*

```
<html
  xmlns="http://www.w3c.org/1999/xhtml"
  xmlns:jsp="http://java.sun.com/JSP/Page"
  >
<head><title>Action elements: element, attribute</title></head>
```

```
<body>
<myElem myElemAttr="myElemAttr's value">myElem's body</myElem>
<br/>
This is inside the test file text.txt
<br/>
This is inside the test file text.txt
</body>
</html>
```

We've highlighted two parts of the listings. The first highlight shows how to use jsp:element, jsp:attribute, and jsp:body to generate an XML element. Be aware of the fact that if you don't define a jsp:body element, the XML element generated by jsp:element will be empty, as in the following example:

```
<myElem myElemAttr="myElemAttr's value"/>
```

The second highlight shows how you can use jsp:attribute to move the page attribute of the jsp:include action to inside its body. At the beginning of the section, we said that jsp:element lets you define XML elements dynamically, because you can use EL expressions to set its attributes, as in the following example:

```
<jsp:element name="${expression1}">
  <jsp:attribute name="${expression2}">${expression3}</jsp:attribute>
  <jsp:body>${expression4}</jsp:body>
  </jsp:element>
```

jsp:forward and jsp:param

With jsp:forward, you can terminate processing of the current JSP page and pass control to another resource of the same application. With jsp:param, you can add additional parameters to the request. For example, this code shows you how to forward the request to a dynamically determined page after adding to it a new parameter:

```
<% String dest = "/myJspPages/" + someVar; %>
<jsp:forward page="<%=dest%>">
  <jsp:param name="newParName" value="newParValue"/>
  </jsp:forward>
```

This action is equivalent to the following scriptlet:

```
<%
  String dest = "/myJspPages/" + someVar;
  RequestDispatcher rd = application.getRequestDispatcher(dest
      + "?newParName=newParValue");
  rd.forward(request, response);
  %>
```

Note that the output buffer is cleared before forwarding the request. This means that what you have already written to it will be lost. If some output has already been sent to the client, this will cause the throwing of the IllegalState Exception.

If you don't need to add parameters, you can write jsp:forward as an empty element:

```
<jsp:forward page="relative-URI"/>
```

jsp:include

You can use jsp:include to insert into the current page the output generated by another resource of the same application. The included resource (e.g., another JSP page) has access to the request parameters, and you can add additional parameters with jsp:param (see jsp:forward for an example of how jsp:param is used). With the optional flush="true" attribute, you can direct Tomcat to flush the output buffer before executing the jsp:include. By default, the buffer is not flushed. Note that the included resource is not allowed to change the response headers or status code.

In its simplest form, a jsp:include looks like the following example:

```
<jsp:include page="/misc/copyleft.html"/>
```

You might think that <jsp:include page="..."/> is the same as <%@include file="..."%>, but this is definitely not the case. The most important difference is that while the include directive includes the content of a file without any processing, the jsp:include action includes the *output* of the included resource. If the resource is a JSP page, this makes a big difference. In practical terms, this also means that JSP pages to be included with jsp:include must be well formed and complete pages rather than simply JSP fragments.

To illustrate a subtle consequence of the different mechanisms of inclusion, we've prepared a small test page (see Listing D-19).

Listing D-19. *includes.jsp*

```
<%@page language="java" contentType="text/html"%>
<html><head><title>A</title></head><body>
<table border="1">
  <tr><th>Includes</th><th>B</th><th>C is with</th></tr>
  <tr><td>act</td><td>act</td><td><jsp:include page="d/b_act.jsp"/></td></tr>
  <tr><td>act</td><td>dir</td><td><jsp:include page="d/b_dir.jsp"/></td></tr>
  <tr><td>dir</td><td>act</td><td><%@include file="d/b_act.jsp"%></td></tr>
  <tr><td>dir</td><td>dir</td><td><%@include file="d/b_dir.jsp"%></td></tr>
  </table>
</body></html>
```

As you can see, we first included the d/b_act.jsp and d/b_dir.jsp files with an include action and then with an include directive. The two files contain these lines, respectively:

```
<%@page language="java" contentType="text/html"%><jsp:include page="c.txt"/>
<%@page language="java" contentType="text/html"%><%@include file="c.txt"%>
```

We placed a c.txt file (only containing the letter A) in the directory of includes.jsp and a second c.txt file (only containing the letter B) in the d directory. Table D-1 shows the result.

Table D-1. *The Output of includes.jsp*

Mechanism to Include b*.jsp	Mechanism to Include c*.txt	Letter Displayed
jsp:include	jsp:include	B
jsp:include	@include	B
@include	jsp:include	A
@include	@include	B

As you can see, includes.jsp displays the letter B in all cases except when you implement the outer inclusion with the include directive and the inner inclusion with the jsp:include action. This means that only with that particular combination of file inclusions, includes.jsp accesses the c.txt file that is in the same directory. In the other three cases, includes.jsp accesses the c.txt file that is in the d directory together with b_act.jsp and b_dir.jsp. To understand these results, you have to know that when Tomcat translates a JSP page into a Java class, it replaces <jsp:include page="fname"/> with an execution of the method org.apache.jasper.runtime.JspRuntimeLibrary.include(request, response, "fname", out, false), while <%@include file="fname"%> results in the copying of the *content* of the fname file. Therefore, in the third case of the example, the <jsp:include page="c.txt"/> inside b_act.jsp is replaced with an include(request, response, "c.txt", out, false), and then the whole b_act.jsp is copied into includes.jsp. That's why the servlet picks up the file in the directory of includes.jsp. The fact that b_act.jsp was in a different directory was lost when its include directive was replaced by the file content.

We decided to spend so much effort on this issue because the inclusion mechanism is often misunderstood and causes many people to knock their heads against the wall when files seem to disappear.

jsp:plugin, jsp:params, and jsp:fallback

To tell a browser how to run an applet by means of the Java plug-in, you need to utilize an <object> or <embed> HTML construct (which one depends on the browser). This ensures that the browser downloads the plug-in if necessary or notifies the user if that is not possible. The plugin action lets you generate the appropriate browser-dependent construct. Unfortunately, at the moment of writing, this works with Internet Explorer and Opera but not with Firefox. See Listing D-20 for an example.

Listing D-20. *applet.jsp*

```
<%@page language="java" contentType="text/html"%>
<html><head><title>Applet</title></head><body>
<jsp:plugin type="applet" code="MyApplet.class"
  codebase="/tests" height="100" width="100">
  <jsp:params>
    <jsp:param name="line" value="Well said!"/>
    </jsp:params>
  <jsp:fallback>Unable to start plugin</jsp:fallback>
  </jsp:plugin>
</body></html>
```

The example also shows you how to use jsp:params, which lets you define parameters needed by your applet, and jsp:fallback, which lets you define a message to be displayed if the embedding of the applet fails.

If you want to try it yourself, Listing D-21 shows you the code for a simple applet.

Listing D-21. *MyApplet.java*

```java
import java.awt.*;
import java.applet.*;
public class MyApplet extends Applet {
  String line;
  public void init() {
    line = getParameter("line");
    }
  public void paint(Graphics page) {
    page.setColor(Color.red);
    page.fillRect(0, 0, 50, 50);
    page.setColor(Color.green);
    page.fillRect(50, 0, 50, 50);
    page.setColor(Color.blue);
    page.fillRect(0, 50, 50, 50);
    page.setColor(Color.yellow);
    page.fillRect(50, 50, 50, 50);
    page.setColor(Color.black);
    page.drawString(line, 10, 40);
    }
}
```

Figure D-8 shows the result of Listing D-21.

Figure D-8. *The output of applet.jsp*

jsp:plugin accepts several attributes. Some are specific for the action element (type, jreversion, nspluginurl, and iepluginurl), while many more are as defined by HTML. They are code, codebase, align, archive, height, hspace, name, vspace, title, width, and mayscript, whereby height and width accept runtime expression values. You can find more information on the HTML attributes in Appendix C under the "Programming" heading. Of the action-specific attributes, you've seen how we used type in the example; jreversion lets you specify the version number of the JRE specification you require (the default is 1.2), and nspluginurl and iepluginurl let you specify where the JRE plug-in can be downloaded for Netscape Navigator and Internet Explorer, respectively.

jsp:text

You can use the jsp:text action to write template text in JSP pages and documents. Its syntax is straightforward:

```
<jsp:text>Template data</jsp:text>
```

Its body cannot contain other elements; it can only contain text and EL expressions. Note that in XML files, you cannot use expressions such as ${whatever > 0}, because the greater-than signs are illegal. Instead, use the gt form, such as ${whatever gt 0}.

jsp:useBean, jsp:getProperty, and jsp:setProperty

The jsp:useBean action declares a scripting variable and associates a Java object to it. It accepts the attributes beanName, class, id, scope, and type, of which only id is mandatory.

If you type <jsp:useBean id="objName"/>, Tomcat will check whether an object named objName exists in pageContext. If it exists, Tomcat will create a variable named objName with the same type as the object, so that you can access the object in subsequent JSP scripting elements. If the object doesn't exist, Tomcat will throw a java.lang.InstantiationException.

If you type <jsp:useBean id="objName" scope="aScope"/> with aScope set to one of the words page, request, session, or application, Tomcat will behave like we described in the previous paragraph, but it will look for the objName object in the given scope rather than in pageContext.

You use jsp:useBean not only to access an already created object but also to create it. You determine whether a bean is created and what type of variable is made available for JSP scripting via the three remaining attributes: class, type, and beanName.

If you specify class and set it to a fully qualified class name (i.e., with its package, as in java.lang.String) but specify neither type nor beanName, Tomcat will instantiate in the given scope (in the page context, by default) an object of the given class and create a scripting variable of the same data type named like the value of the id attribute. If you also specify type together with class, Tomcat will set the data type of the new object to the value of the type attribute. You can set the type attribute to the same class as the class attribute (which is equivalent to omitting type), to a superclass of class, or to an interface implemented by class.

If you specify the beanName attribute instead of class, Tomcat will behave as if you had specified class, but only after attempting to find a serialized bean of that class. Serializing a bean means that the object's data is converted to a byte stream and saved in a file with the extension ser. Tomcat expects to find serialized objects together with the application classes. For example, a serialized bean of the xxx.yyy.Zzz class is expected to be in the WEB-INF\classes\xxx\yyy\Zzz.ser file. This mechanism lets you save an object in a file and then load it into your JSP page. You can actually have several serialized beans of the same class (e.g.,

Zzz.ser, Zzz_test.ser, Zzz25.ser, and abc.ser). Fortunately, the designers of JSP have thought this issue through and allowed you to set the value of beanName at request time (the other attributes must be hard-coded), so that you can parameterize your page for what concerns loading serialized objects.

If you specify type and set it to a fully qualified class name but specify neither class nor beanName, Tomcat won't instantiate any object and will instead look for it in the given scope. If it finds it, Tomcat will make it available as an object of the given type rather than of the class from which it was instantiated.

A word of caution concerning scopes: don't confuse the scope of the bean as specified with the jsp:useBean attribute scope with the scope of the scripting variable that Tomcat associates to the bean. For example, this code instantiates a String object that remains available as long as the session remains valid:

```
<jsp:useBean class="myPkg.MyClass" id="myObj" scope="session"/>
```

You'll be able to access it via a scripting variable named myObj in any page within the same session with the following statement:

```
<jsp:useBean id="myObj" type="myPkg.MyClass" scope="session"/>
```

However, the scope of the scripting variable is determined by where within your page you execute jsp:useBean, as with the declaration of any other scripting variable.

Incidentally, jsp:useBean with class, id, and scope="session" is exactly the same as doing the following:

```
MyClass myName = new MyClass();
session.setAttribute("myObj", myObj);
```

and jsp:useBean with id, type, and scope="session" is the same as this:

```
MyClass myObj = (MyClass)session.getAttribute("myObj");
```

With jsp:setProperty, you can set object attributes, and with jsp:getProperty, you can send attribute values to the output buffer. For example, see the class defined in Listing D-22.

Listing D-22. *MyClass.java*

```
package myPkg;
import java.io.Serializable;
public class MyClass implements java.io.Serializable {
  private int i;
  public MyClass() {i = 0;}
  public void setI(int i) {this.i = i;}
  public int getI() {return i;}
  }
```

It is the code of the myPkg.MyClass class with one integer attribute. To be able to use this class as a Java bean, we've made it implement the Serializable interface, and we've defined two methods to set and get the attribute. Without the two methods setI and getI, the attribute i would not be recognized as a bean property. The names of the methods *must* consist of the words *get* and *set*, followed by the name of the attribute with the first letter capitalized.

Take a look at Listing D-23, which shows how to use jsp:setProperty and jsp:getProperty.

Listing D-23. *myObj.jsp*

```
<%@page language="java" contentType="text/html"%>
<%@page import="java.util.*, myPkg.MyClass"%>
<html><head><title>myObj</title></head><body>
<jsp:useBean id="obj" class="myPkg.MyClass" scope="session">
  <jsp:setProperty name="obj" property="i" value="11"/>
  </jsp:useBean>
<jsp:getProperty name="obj" property="i"/>
<jsp:setProperty name="obj" property="i" value="22"/>
<jsp:getProperty name="obj" property="i"/>
</body></html>
```

The highlighted part is where you create the bean object. There you also see that jsp:useBean can have a body, which you can use to initialize the object's attributes. The code inside the body is not executed if the bean fails to be instantiated. The first jsp:getProperty sends the value of i to the output immediately after initialization, while the second one does the same after a jsp:setProperty has modified it. After removing additional empty lines and spaces, the HTML response to the client is as follows:

```
<html><head><title>myObj</title></head><body>
11
22
</body></html>
```

In jsp:setProperty, you can replace the value attribute with param. In that case, the property is set to the value of the request parameter you specify. But it gets better: if you omit both value and param and use an asterisk as a value for the property attribute, all the properties will be set to the values of the corresponding request parameters (if they are there). For example, suppose that you have the class MyClass from Listing D-22 but with an additional attribute named k. The following two lines will set the two attributes i and k to the values of the corresponding request parameters:

```
<jsp:useBean id="obj" class="myPkg.MyClass" scope="session"/>
<jsp:setProperty property="*" name="obj"/>
```

The alternative way of achieving the same result without jsp:useBeans and jsp:setProperty would be to do the following:

```
MyClass obj = new MyClass();
obj.setI(Integer.parseInt(request.getParameter(i)));
obj.setK(Integer.parseInt(request.getParameter(k)));
```

And just think, this system works for as many attributes and parameters as you have!

XPath

XPath is a language that lets you identify nodes in XML documents. You need XPath expressions to set the select attribute of JSTL XML actions.

XPath distinguishes between seven types of nodes: document/root, comment, element, attribute, text, processing instruction, and namespace. For example, take a look at the following XML document:

```
<?xml version="1.0" encoding="ISO-8859-1"?>
<starfleet xmlns:zzz="http://myWeb.com/whatever">
  <!-- bla bla -->  <?myAppl "xyz"?>
  <starship name="USS Enterprise" sn="NCC-1701">
    <captain>James (Jim) T. Kirk</captain>
    </starship>
  </starfleet>
```

<starfleet> is the document (or root) node, <!-- bla bla --> is a comment node, <captain>...</captain> is an element node, sn="NCC-1701" is an attribute node, the string James (Jim) T. Kirk is a text node, <?myAppl "xyz"?> is a processing-instruction node, and xmlns:zzz="http://myWeb.com/whatever" is a namespace node.

■Note Processing instructions in an XML document provide information for the application that uses the document.

A *node set* is a group of nodes considered collectively. A node set resulting from the execution of an XPath expression doesn't necessarily contain several nodes. It can consist of a single node or even none. Keep in mind that the nodes belonging to a node set can be organized in a tree, but not necessarily. For example, the expression $myDoc//C identifies all C elements in a document that was parsed into the variable myDoc. It is unlikely that they form a tree.

Syntax

To identify one or more nodes, you need to navigate through the tree structure of an XML document from your current position within the tree (the *context node*) to the target[s]. The path description consists of a series of steps separated by slashes, whereby each step includes the navigation direction (the *axis specifier*), an expression identifying the node[s] (the *node test*), and a condition to be satisfied (the *predicate*) enclosed between square brackets.

A slash at the beginning indicates that the path begins at the root node, while paths relative to the context node begin without a slash. Two consecutive colons separate the axis specifier and the node test. For example, this code identifies the second attribute of all B elements immediately below the root element A:

```
/child::A/child::B/attribute::*[position()=2]
```

You can express the same path with an abbreviated syntax, as follows:

```
/A/B/@*[2]
```

where `child`, `::`, and `position()=` are simply omitted, and `attribute` is represented by `@`.

Table D-2 shows the possible axis specifiers and their abbreviated syntax.

Table D-2. *Axis Specifiers*

Specifier	Abbreviated Syntax
ancestor	Not available (n/a)
ancestor-or-self	n/a
attribute	@
child	Default; do not specify it
descendant	//
descendant-or-self	n/a
following	n/a
following-sibling	n/a
namespace	n/a
parent	.. (i.e., two dots)
preceding	n/a
preceding-sibling	n/a
self	. (i.e., a single dot)

As node tests, you can use node names with or without a namespace prefix, or you can use an asterisk to indicate all names. With abbreviated syntax, an asterisk on its own indicates all element nodes, and @* indicates all attributes.

You can also use `node()` as a node test to indicate all possible nodes of any type. Similarly, `comment()` indicates all comment nodes, `text()` indicates all text nodes, and `processing-instruction()` indicates all processing instruction nodes.

For example, this code selects all elements B descendant of A that have the attribute xx set to 'z':

```
A//B[@xx='z']
```

while this code selects all elements C anywhere in the tree that have the attribute yy:

```
//C[@yy]
```

To form expressions besides the operators we've already shown (i.e., slash, double slash, and square brackets), you have available all standard arithmetic and comparison operators (i.e., +, -, *, div, mod, =, !=, <, <=, >, and >=). Additionally, you have and and or for boolean operations, and the union operator | (i.e., the vertical bar) to merge two node sets.

References to variables are indicated by sticking a dollar sign before them, as shown in the following example:

```
<x:parse doc="${sf}" varDom="dom"/>
<x:forEach var="tag" select="$dom//starship">
```

Here we've parsed an XML document into the variable dom and then used $dom when we referred to it in an XPath expression.

Functions

The XPath standard (http://www.w3.org/TR/xpath) specifies a set of core functions that all implementations of XPath must support. They are divided into node set, string, boolean, and number functions.

Scripting Elements

With scripting elements, you can place code inside a JSP page. However, they are difficult to maintain. Therefore, you should use action elements and custom tags when possible.

There are three types of scripting elements: *scriptlets*, *expressions*, and *declarations*.

Scriptlets

A scriptlet is a block of code enclosed between <% and %>. For example, this code includes two scriptlets that let you switch HTML code on or off depending on a condition:

```
<% if (condition) { %>
<p>This is only shown if the condition is satisfied</p>
<%   } %>
```

Expressions

The value obtained calculating an expression enclosed between <%= and %> is inserted into the page. For example, in this code, the value resulting from creating a new date is displayed:

```
<%@page import="java.util.Date"%>
Server date and time: <%=new Date()%>
```

Any expression will do, provided it results in a value. For example, <%=(condition) ? "yes" : "no"%> is valid, because it calculates to a string, and it's equivalent to <%if (condition) out.print("yes") else out.print("no");%>.

Declarations

A variable declaration enclosed between <%! and %> is an instance variable shared by all requests for the same page. See the "Example: Testing Concurrency" section for an example on how you can use it.

APPENDIX E

■ ■ ■

SQL Quick Reference

Structured Query Language (SQL) is the most widely used language to interact with DBMSs. The purpose of this appendix is not to provide a comprehensive manual of SQL, but rather to list and explain the most common concepts, terms, and statements. Most DBMSs don't support the whole SQL standard. Moreover, vendors sometimes add nonstandard elements that, in practice, prevent full portability across DBMSs. In this appendix, we'll limit ourselves to standard elements. To help you identify nonstandard keywords, we've included Table E-12 at the end of this appendix, which shows the keywords defined as reserved by ISO/IEC 9075-2:2003, which is part of the latest SQL standard.

SQL Terminology

Data is organized in *tables* consisting of *rows* and *columns*. This is a natural way of organizing data, and you're probably familiar with it through the use of spreadsheets. Nevertheless, although there are some similarities, a database table is *not* an Excel worksheet. For example, in a spreadsheet, you can assign data types to individual cells, while in a database, all the cells of a column have the same data type. The column definitions, each with their name and the type of data permitted, represent the data structure of the table.

For example, a table of employees would probably include columns named `FirstName`, `LastName`, and `SocialSecurityNumber` containing strings of text; columns named `EmployeeNumber` and `YearSalary` containing numbers; and columns named `DateOfBirth` and `EmployedSince` containing dates. The data associated with each employee would then all be stored into a row.

A *field* is an individual data item within a table, corresponding to the intersection of a row and a column. This would be a cell in a spreadsheet.

One or more columns can be identified as unique keys, used to identify each individual employee. For this purpose, you could use one of the columns mentioned previously (e.g., `EmployeeNumber`), or you could use the combination of first and last name. The unique key used in preference over the others is called the *primary key*.

An additional type of key is the *foreign key*. In this case, the column is defined as a reference (i.e., a pointer) to a unique key of another table. Besides avoiding duplication of data, this type of constraint increases the consistency of the database. For example, a table containing customer contracts could include a column pointing to the employee number defined in the employee table. This would ensure that each contract would be associated with an existing salesperson.

The DBMS can build an *index* for each key, so that the data can be retrieved more quickly. This will obviously slow down insertion and deletion of rows, because the DBMS will have to spend time updating the indexes, but most databases are more frequently interrogated than modified. Therefore, it usually pays to define indexes, at least those that can speed up the most common queries. Here you have a hint of another difference from Excel: in a database table, the data items are not moved around once they're inserted.

Sometimes it's useful to present only some columns and rows, as if they were a table in their own right. Such virtual tables are called *views*. Under certain circumstances (we'll discuss this further when we describe individual statements later in this chapter), you can also use views to collect columns from different tables and handle them as if they belong to a single table. With a view, you consider the result of a database query as if it were a separate table.

Transactions

Transactions deserve a little more attention, because they represent a key concept in database operations. A *transaction* indicates a series of database operations that have to be performed without interruption—that is, without any other operation "sneaking in" between them. To make sense of this, you have to think in terms of concurrent access to the same tables.

For example, imagine the following scenario in which two money transfers involve three bank accounts:

1. Transfer $100 from account A to account B

2. Transfer $200 from account B to account C

Conceptually, each transfer consists of the following operations:

- Read the balance of the source account.

- Reduce it.

- Write it back.

- Read the balance of the destination account.

- Increase it.

- Write it back.

Now, imagine that the second transfer starts while the first one is not yet completely done, as Table E-1 illustrates.

Table E-1. *Sequence of Elementary Operations*

Step	Transaction	Elementary Operation
1	1	Read the balance of account A.
2	1	Reduce the balance of account A by $100.
3	1	Write back the balance of account A.
4	1	Read the balance of account B.
5	1	Increase the balance of account B by $100.
6	**2**	**Read the balance of account B.**
7	2	Reduce the balance of account B by $200.
8	2	Write back the balance of account B.
9	2	Read the balance of account C.
10	2	Increase the balance of account C by $200.
11	**1**	**Write back the balance of account B.**
12	2	Write back the balance of account C.

The owner of account B is going to be very happy, because she will end up with $200 more than what she actually owns. The problem is that the two operations numbered 6 and 11 should not have been executed in that order. Let's say that account B had $500 initially. At the end, it should hold $500 + $100 – $200 = $400, but this is not what happened. Just before the end of the first transfer, when the balance of $600 was about to be written back, the second transfer started. The balance of account B stored in the database was changed as a result of the second transfer, but when the first transfer resumed and completed, the balance of $600 was written back to account B. The effect of the second transfer was "forgotten." As far as account B was concerned, it was as if the second transfer hadn't happened!

You can solve this problem by handling each transfer as a transaction. The second transfer won't start until the first one is completed, and by then, the balance of account B will have been updated to reflect the first transfer.

A transaction is characterized by four properties—atomicity, consistency, isolation, and durability (ACID):

- **Atomicity**: It guarantees that either all the individual steps of an operation are performed or none at all. It must not be possible to perform partial transactions.

- **Consistency**: It refers to the fact that a transaction is not supposed to violate the integrity of the database. For example, it shouldn't be able to store a negative value in a numeric field that is supposed to be positive.

- **Isolation**: It means that concurrent operations cannot see intermediate values of a transaction. This is clearly what didn't happen in step 6 of the example, when the balance of account B could be read even though the transaction that was modifying it was not yet complete. Unfortunately, the serialization of the transactions (i.e., performing them one after the other) has an impact on performance precisely when there is a high workload. Lack of isolation is a problem in the example, but this is not always the case. For example, it might not matter that searches on a list of products take place while products are being added or removed. Given the potential impact on performance, you might decide in some cases to ignore the existence of concurrent transactions.

- **Durability**: It refers to the capacity of a DBMS to guarantee that a transaction, once completed, is never going to be "forgotten," even after a system failure.

Conventions

We'll use the following conventions to describe SQL statements:

- SQL keywords that you must enter exactly as shown are in uppercase (e.g., CREATE).

- Variable values are in lowercase (e.g., db_name).

- Elements that you can omit are enclosed in square brackets (e.g., [DEFAULT]).

- References to further definitions are enclosed in angle brackets (e.g., <create_spec>).

- The ellipsis immediately preceding a closing square bracket means that you can repeat the element enclosed between the brackets (e.g., [<create_spec> ...]).

- Mutually exclusive alternatives are enclosed in curly brackets and separated by vertical bars (e.g., {DATABASE | SCHEMA}). You must enter one (and only one) of them.

- We close every statement with a semicolon, although, strictly speaking, it is not part of the official syntax. We do so because it makes for easier reading and to remind you that you must type the semicolon when including the statement in scripts.

For example, Listing E-1 shows that the SQL statement used to create a database begins with the CREATE keyword followed by either DATABASE or SCHEMA and a database name. It is then possible (but not mandatory) to add one or more <create_spec> elements, the meaning of which is defined separately.

Listing E-1. *Example of an SQL Statement*

```
CREATE {DATABASE | SCHEMA} db_name [<create_spec> ...];
<create_spec> = {
    [DEFAULT] CHARACTER SET charset_name
    [DEFAULT] COLLATION collation_name
    }
```

Statements

In general, regardless of whether we're talking about database organization, table structure, or actual data, you'll need to perform four basic operations: create, retrieve, update, and delete (CRUD). The corresponding SQL statements begin with a keyword that identifies the operation (e.g., INSERT, SELECT, UPDATE, or DELETE), followed when necessary by a keyword specifying on what type of entity the operation is to be performed (e.g., DATABASE, TABLE, or INDEX) and by additional elements. You use the SELECT statement for retrieving information.

You can create databases, tables, and indexes with the CREATE statement, update them with ALTER, and delete them with DROP. Similarly, you can create and delete views with CREATE and DROP, but you cannot update them once you've created them. You use INSERT to create new rows within a table, and you use DELETE to delete them. The UPDATE statement lets you modify entire rows or one or more individual fields within them.

That said, you won't find anything about ALTER DATABASE and ALTER INDEX in this appendix, because there is very little you can update in a database or an index definition once you've created them, and there is no agreement among DBMS vendors. Table E-2 shows a summary of the possible combinations of keywords.

Table E-2. *SQL Keywords to Create, Update, and Delete*

Entity	Create	Update	Delete
DATABASE	CREATE	n/a	DROP
TABLE	CREATE	ALTER	DROP
INDEX	CREATE	n/a	DROP
VIEW	CREATE	—	DROP
Row	INSERT	UPDATE	DELETE

In many applications, the structure of databases, tables, indexes, and views, once initially defined, remains unchanged. Therefore, you'll often need within your applications only the statements operating on rows and fields. In any case, you'll certainly need SELECT, which you use to interrogate databases both in terms of their structure and the data they contain. Finally, to complete the list of statements you're likely to need when developing applications, we'll also describe START TRANSACTION, COMMIT, and ROLLBACK.

SQL interprets all text enclosed between /* and */ as comments and ignores it.

Note In all statements, you can always use the column position within the table instead of the column name. Column numbering in SQL starts with 1. In some particular cases, this can be useful, but use it sparingly, because it leads to errors and code that's difficult to maintain.

The WHERE Condition

When you want to retrieve, update, or delete rows, you obviously have to identify them within the corresponding SQL statement. You do this with the WHERE keyword followed by a <where_condition>. Listing E-2 shows you the format of this condition. We explain WHERE before discussing individual statements, because you'll need it for several of them.

Listing E-2. *The WHERE Condition*

```
<where_condition> = {
    col_name {= | < | > | <= | >= | !< | !> | <> | !=} <val>
    | col_name [NOT] BETWEEN <val> AND <val>
    | col_name [NOT] LIKE <val> [ESCAPE <val>]
    | col_name [NOT] IN (<val> [, <val> ...])
    | col_name IS [NOT] NULL
    | col_name [NOT] CONTAINING <val>
    | col_name [NOT] STARTING [WITH] <val>
    | NOT <search_condition>
    | <where_condition> OR <where_condition>
    | <where_condition> AND <where_condition>
    | (<where_condition>)
    }
<val> = A valid SQL expression that results in a single value
```

Note that the WHERE condition is more powerful (and complex) than what we explain here. You could actually include complete query statements within a condition and use the result of a first search to delimit the scope of the successive one. However, to explain such techniques involving subqueries would go beyond the scope of this manual.

We'll describe the listed possibilities by simply showing and explaining valid examples of WHERE selections on a hypothetical employee table:

- lastname = 'Smith' selects all employees with the family name Smith.

- startdate < '2000-01-01' selects all employees who joined the company before the beginning of the century.

- startdate BETWEEN '2006-01-01' AND '2006-12-31' selects all employees who joined the company in 2006, while startdate NOT BETWEEN '2006-01-01' AND '2006-12-31' selects those who didn't.

- lastname LIKE 'S%' selects all employees whose family name starts with S. You can use more than one percent sign in a condition. For example, lastname LIKE 'S%z%a' selects all names that start with S, end with a, and have a z somewhere in between. While the percent sign stands for any number of characters (including none), the underscore stands for exactly one character. For example, lastname NOT LIKE '_' selects all names that contain at least two characters. The ESCAPE keyword lets you search for strings containing one of the escape characters. For example, lastname LIKE '%!%%' ESCAPE '!' selects all names that contain a percent sign in any position.

- firstname IN ('John', 'Jack') selects all employees who have either John or Jack as their first name.

- middlename IS NULL selects all employees who have no middle name.

- lastname CONTAINING 'qu' selects all employees who have the string *qu* in their family name. This is identical to lastname LIKE '%qu%'.

- `lastname STARTING WITH 'Sm'` selects all employees whose family name starts with *Sm*. This is identical to `lastname LIKE 'Sm%'`.

- You can use the logical operators `NOT`, `AND`, and `OR` to build complex conditions. For example, `startdate >= '2006-01-01' AND startdate <= '2006-12-31'` is equivalent to `startdate BETWEEN '2006-01-01' AND '2006-12-31'`. To avoid ambiguities, use the parentheses to set the order of execution. For example, `lastname CONTAINING 's' OR (lastname CONTAINING 'q' AND lastname NOT CONTAINING 'qu')` selects all employees whose family names contain an *s* or a *q*, but only if the *q* is not followed by a *u*. The statement `(lastname CONTAINING 's' OR lastname CONTAINING 'q') AND lastname NOT CONTAINING 'qu'` would not select names containing both *s* and *qu*. A name such as *quasi* would be selected by the first condition but not by the second one.

As a final remark, you should be aware of the fact that wherever we've talked about column names, you can also use column numbers. For example, if `lastname` is the third column of the employee table, `lastname = 'Smith'` is equivalent to `3 = 'Smith'`. However, we encourage you to use column names rather than column positions, which can always change.

Data Types

When designing your database, you have to decide what type of data you need to store in the columns of your tables. SQL supports different data types to store numbers, text, date/time, and unspecified data (called LOB, for large object), as summarized in Listing E-3.

Listing E-3. *The SQL Data Types*

```
<data_type> = {<num_dt> | <datime_dt> | <text_dt> | <lob_dt>}
```

Numbers

The space reserved in memory for the numeric data types determines their precision—that is, the number of digits they can have. Java and JSP specify the space allocated for each data type, so that they are the same regardless of operating systems and virtual machines. Unfortunately, the same cannot be said of SQL, where the precision of the data types is vendor-dependent. Therefore, you always have to refer to the manual of your DBMS if you want to be sure that your applications will work correctly. Listing E-4 shows how you specify a numeric data type.

Listing E-4. *The SQL Data Types for Numbers*

```
<num_dt> = {
     {DECIMAL | DEC | NUMERIC} [(precision [, scale])]
   | {SMALLINT | INTEGER | INT | BIGINT | REAL | FLOAT | DOUBLE PRECISION}
   }
```

The types `DECIMAL` (which can be abbreviated to `DEC`) and `NUMERIC` require you to specify the total number of digits and the number of decimal places. For example, you specify numbers of the type `xxxx` as `(4)`, numbers of the type `xxx.y` as `(4,1)`, and numbers of the type `0.yyy` as `(3,3)`. The scale must never exceed the precision. As different DBMS vendors set different defaults, you should always at least specify the precision. When doing so, keep in mind that 18 decimal digits require 64 bits. Therefore, larger precisions might not be accepted by all DBMSs.

The difference between DECIMAL and NUMERIC is that with DECIMAL, the DBMS is free to allocate more space than the minimum required in order to optimize access speed, while with NUMERIC, the number of digits allocated is exactly what you specify as precision.

The other types are easier to use but require some attention, because, once more, different DBMS vendors allocate different numbers of bytes for the different data types. If you don't pay attention, you'll risk writing code that won't be portable.

The first three types refer to integer types of different sizes (INT is just an abbreviation for INTEGER), while the other three refer to numbers with a decimal point. Table E-3 shows the ranges possible with different numbers of bits, and their corresponding data type in Java.

Table E-3. *Space Occupied by Numeric Data*

Bits	Minimum	Maximum	Java Type
16	−32,768	32,767	short
32	−2,147,483,648	2,147,483,647	int
64	−9,223,372,036,854,775,808	9,223,372,036,854,775,807	long
32	1.175×10^{-38}	3.402×10^{38}	~float
64	2.225×10^{-308}	1.797×10^{308}	~double

Table E-4 lists the number of bits allocated by some vendors to the different SQL data types.

Table E-4. *Vendor-Specific Numeric Data Types*

Vendor	SMALLINT	INTEGER	BIGINT	REAL	FLOAT	DOUBLE PRECISION
MySQL	16	32	64	32	32	64
PostgreSQL	16	32	64	32		64
FirebirdSQL	16	32			32	64
Microsoft SQL Server	16	32	64	32	64	
Oracle		38			126	

FirebirdSQL supports 64-bit integers, but it doesn't recognize the type BIGINT. You have to use INT64. Microsoft SQL Server and Oracle aren't open source DBMSs, but given their large customer bases, we thought that you might be interested to know.

Date and Time

Listing E-5 shows how dates and times are defined in SQL, but its simplicity is somewhat misleading, because the DBMSs of different vendors behave differently.

Listing E-5. *The SQL Data Types for Date and Time*

```
<datime_dt> = {DATE | TIME | TIMESTAMP}
```

One area where the vendors don't agree is the range of dates. MySQL accepts dates between the year 1000 AD and the year 9999 AD, PostgreSQL between 4713 BC and 5874897 AD, and FirebirdSQL between 100 AD and February 32767 AD. The bottom line is that any date within our lifetimes should be accepted by every DBMS!

You can use DATE when you're not interested in the time of the day. It occupies 4 bytes. TIME stores the time of the day in milliseconds and occupies 8 bytes. TIMESTAMP manages to fit both the date and the time of the day in milliseconds into 8 bytes.

You can set date and time values in different formats, but we recommend that you conform to the ISO 8601 standard and set dates as 'YYYY-MM-DD', times as 'HH:MM', 'HH:MM:SS', or 'HH:MM:SS.mmm', and timestamps as a standard date followed by a space and a standard time, as in 'YYYY-MM-DD HH:MM:SS.mmm'. In particular, pay attention to years specified with only two digits, because the different DBMSs interpret the dates differently. MySQL has defined the DATETIME type, but as it accepts the standard TIMESTAMP, we see no reason for you to adopt it. We mention it here only because you'll probably encounter it sooner or later.

Text

Listing E-6 shows how you specify strings of characters.

Listing E-6. *The SQL Data Types for Text*

```
<text_dt> = {CHAR | CHARACTER | VARCHAR | CHARACTER VARYING} [(int)]
```

There are only two data types for text: CHARACTER and VARCHAR. CHAR is a synonym of CHARACTER, and CHARACTER VARYING is a synonym of VARCHAR. Use CHARACTER to store strings of fixed length, and VARCHAR for strings of variable length.

For example, a field of type CHARACTER (16) always occupies 16 bytes. If you use it to store a string of only 6 characters, it will be left-justified and right-padded with 10 spaces. If you attempt to store a string of 19 characters, you'll only succeed if the last 3 characters are spaces, in which case the DBMS will remove them. Different DBMSs set different limits to the maximum number of characters you can store into a CHARACTER data type, but they will all accept 255 characters. If you need more than that, check the user manual of the DBMS you're using.

The practical difference between VARCHAR and CHARACTER is that with VARCHAR, the DBMS stores the strings as they are, without padding. Also, with VARCHAR, you should be able to store up to 32,767 characters with all DBMSs.

Large Objects

LOBs let you store a large amount of data, including binary data, in tables. This is an alternative to saving data in files and then storing their URIs into the database. In some cases, you might find it useful to access the data as normal files outside the DBMS.

■**Note** A URI is a generalization of a URL. Strictly speaking, the name location of a code fragment (i.e., the #whatever that you sometimes see in your browser's address field) is part of the URI but not of the URL, which only refers to the whole resource. Unfortunately, the definition of URI came when the term URL had already become universally known. That's why most people, including many specialists, keep referring to URLs when they should really be talking about URIs.

We have to distinguish between binary large objects (BLOBs) and character large objects (CLOBs). Unfortunately, once more, the major DBMS vendors haven't agreed. See Listing E-7 for the correct definition of LOBs.

Listing E-7. *The SQL Data Types for Large Objects*

```
<lob_dt> = {<blob_dt> | <clob_dt>}
<blob_dt> = {
      BLOB(maxlen)      /* MySQL */
    | BYTEA             /* PostgreSQL */
    | BLOB(maxlen, 0)   /* FirebirdSQL */
    }
<clob_dt> = {
      TEXT              /* MySQL */
    | TEXT              /* PostgreSQL */
    | BLOB(maxlen, 1)   /* FirebirdSQL */
    }
```

LOBs can store up to 64KB of data, but this limit is likely to change in the future. SQL Server can already store GBs, and we're used to images that take up MBs of disk space. With the current limit, the LOBs are of limited use.

SELECT

SELECT retrieves data from one or more tables and views. See Listing E-8 for a description of its format.

Listing E-8. *The SQL Statement SELECT*

```
SELECT [ALL | DISTINCT ]
   {* | <select_list> [[<select_list>] {COUNT (*) | <function>}]
   [FROM <table_references> [WHERE <where_condition>]
     [GROUP BY col_name [ASC | DESC], ... [WITH ROLLUP]
       [HAVING <where_condition>]
       ]
     ]
   [ORDER BY <order_list>]
   [LIMIT {[offset,] row_count | row_count OFFSET offset}]
   ;
```

```
<select_list> = col_name [, <select_list>]
<table_references> = one or more table and/or view names separated by commas
<order_list> = col_name [ASC | DESC] [, <order_list> ...]
<function> = {AVG | MAX | MIN | SUM | COUNT} ([{ALL | DISTINCT}] <val>)
```

In part, the complication of SELECT is due to the fact that you can use it in two ways: to retrieve actual data or to obtain the result of applying a function to the data. To make it worse, some of the elements only apply to one of the two ways of using SELECT. To explain how SELECT works, we'll split the two modes of operation.

SELECT to Obtain Data

Listing E-9 shows how you use SELECT to obtain data.

Listing E-9. *SELECT to Obtain Data*

```
SELECT [ALL | DISTINCT ] {* | <select_list>}
    [FROM <table_references> [WHERE <where_condition>]]
    [ORDER BY <order_list>]
    [LIMIT {[offset,] row_count | row_count OFFSET offset}]
    ;
<select_list> = col_name [, <select_list>]
<table_references> = one or more table and/or view names separated by commas
<order_list> = col_name [ASC | DESC] [, <order_list> ...]
```

Conceptually, it is simple: SELECT one, some, or all columns FROM one or more tables or views WHERE certain conditions are satisfied, then present the rows ORDERed as specified. Some examples will clarify the details:

- SELECT * is the simplest possible SELECT, but you'll probably never use it. It returns everything you have in your database.

- SELECT * FROM table is the simplest practical form of SELECT. It returns all the data in the table you specify. The DBMS returns the rows in the order it finds most convenient, which is basically meaningless to us. Instead of a single table, you can specify a mix of tables and views separated by commas.

- SELECT a_col_name, another_col_name FROM table still returns all the rows of a table, but for each row, it returns only the values in the columns you specify. Use the keyword DISTINCT to tell the DBMS that it should *not* return any duplicate set of fields.

- SELECT * FROM table WHERE condition only returns the rows for which the condition you specify is satisfied. Most SELECTs include a WHERE condition. Often only a single row is selected—for example, when the condition requires a unique key to have a particular value.

- `SELECT * FROM table ORDER BY col_name` returns all the rows of a table ordered on the basis of a column you specify. Note that you can provide more than one ordering. For example, `SELECT * FROM employee_tbl ORDER BY last_name, first_name` returns a list of all employees in alphabetical order. Append to the statement the keyword `DES` to specify descending orderings.

- `SELECT * FROM table LIMIT first, count` returns `count` rows starting from `first`. You can obtain the same result with `SELECT * FROM table LIMIT count OFFSET first`. Be warned that not all DBMSs support both formats. We discourage you to use this element, because it doesn't deliver entirely predictable results. We only include it here because you could find it useful to debug some database problem.

SELECT to Apply a Function

Sometimes you need to obtain some global information on your data and are not interested in the details. This is where the second format of `SELECT` comes to the rescue. Listing E-10 shows how you use `SELECT` to apply a function.

Listing E-10. *SELECT to Apply a Function*

```
SELECT [ALL | DISTINCT ] [<select_list>] {COUNT (*) | <function>}
    [FROM <table_references>
        [GROUP BY col_name [ASC | DESC], ... [WITH ROLLUP]
          [HAVING <where_condition>]
          ]
        ]
    ;
<select_list> = col_name [, <select_list>]
<table_references> = one or more table and/or view names separated by commas
<function> = {AVG | MAX | MIN | SUM | COUNT} ([{ALL | DISTINCT}] <val>)
```

Here are some examples of how you apply a function with `SELECT`:

- `SELECT COUNT (*) FROM employee_tbl` counts the number of rows in the employee table.

- `SELECT department, citizenship, gender COUNT(employee_id) FROM employee_tbl GROUP BY department, citizenship, gender` provides counts of employees for each possible department, citizenship, and gender combination. If you append `WITH ROLLUP` to the statement, you'll also obtain partial totals, as shown in Table E-5.

- `SELECT last_name COUNT(first_name) FROM employee_tbl GROUP BY first_name HAVING COUNT(first_name) > 1` counts the number of first names for each family name but only reports the family names that appear with more than one first name. `HAVING` has the same function for the aggregated values produced by `GROUP BY` that `WHERE` had for data selection.

Table E-5. *Employees per Department, Citizenship, and Gender*

Department	Citizenship	Gender	Count
Dev	India	Male	1
Dev	India	NULL	1
Dev	USA	Female	2
Dev	USA	Male	3
Dev	USA	NULL	5
Dev	NULL	NULL	6
Ops	Canada	Male	2
Ops	Canada	NULL	2
Ops	USA	Female	4
Ops	USA	Male	3
Ops	USA	NULL	7
Ops	NULL	NULL	9
Sales	USA	Female	7
Sales	USA	Male	5
Sales	USA	NULL	12
Sales	NULL	NULL	12
NULL	NULL	NULL	27

JOINs

When describing SQL terminology, we said that a foreign key is a reference to a unique key of another table. This means that information associated with each unique value of that key can be in either table or in both. For example, in a database representing a bookstore, you could imagine having one table with book authors and one with books. The name of the author would be a unique key in the authors' table and would appear as a foreign key in the books' table. For example, Table E-6 shows the authors' table.

Table E-6. *Authors' Table*

Name	City
Isaac Asimov	New York (NY)
David Baldacci	Alexandria (VA)
Matthew Reilly	Sydney (Australia)

Table E-7 shows the books' table.

Table E-7. *Books' Table*

Title	Author
I, Robot	Isaac Asimov
Foundation	Isaac Asimov
Contest	Matthew Reilly
Scarecrow	Matthew Reilly
BlaBlaBla	NULL

If you perform the query `SELECT * FROM books, authors;`, the DBMS will return 15 combined rows, the first 7 of which are shown in Table E-8.

Table E-8. *Disjoined Query on Books and Authors*

Title	Author	Name	City
I, Robot	Isaac Asimov	Isaac Asimov	New York (NY)
Foundation	Isaac Asimov	Isaac Asimov	New York (NY)
Contest	Matthew Reilly	Isaac Asimov	New York (NY)
Scarecrow	Matthew Reilly	Isaac Asimov	New York (NY)
BlaBlaBla	NULL	Isaac Asimov	New York (NY)
I, Robot	Isaac Asimov	David Baldacci	Alexandria (VA)
Foundation	Isaac Asimov	David Baldacci	Alexandria (VA)

In other words, all books would be paired with all authors. This doesn't look very useful. You can get a more useful result when you perform the following query:

```
SELECT * FROM books, authors WHERE author = name;
```

Table E-9 shows the result.

Table E-9. *Traditional Joined Query on Books and Authors*

Title	Author	Name	City
I, Robot	Isaac Asimov	Isaac Asimov	New York (NY)
Foundation	Isaac Asimov	Isaac Asimov	New York (NY)
Contest	Matthew Reilly	Matthew Reilly	Sydney (Australia)
Scarecrow	Matthew Reilly	Matthew Reilly	Sydney (Australia)

You can achieve the same result with the `JOIN` keyword:

```
SELECT * FROM books [INNER] JOIN authors ON (author = name);
```

The result is the same, but conceptually, the `JOIN` syntax is clearer, because it states explicitly that you want to join two tables matching the values in two columns.

There is another type of `JOIN`, called `OUTER JOIN`, which also selects rows that appear in one of the two tables. For example, this line of code returns the result shown in Table E-10:

```
SELECT * FROM books LEFT [OUTER] JOIN authors ON (author = name);
```

while this line of code returns the result shown in Table E-11:

```
SELECT * FROM books RIGHT [OUTER] JOIN authors ON (author = name);
```

Table E-10. *LEFT JOIN Query*

Title	Author	Name	City
I, Robot	Isaac Asimov	Isaac Asimov	New York (NY)
Foundation	Isaac Asimov	Isaac Asimov	New York (NY)
Contest	Matthew Reilly	Matthew Reilly	Sydney (Australia)
Scarecrow	Matthew Reilly	Matthew Reilly	Sydney (Australia)
BlaBlaBla	NULL	NULL	NULL

Table E-11 shows the result of a `RIGHT JOIN` query on author names.

Table E-11. *RIGHT JOIN Query*

Title	Author	Name	City
I, Robot	Isaac Asimov	Isaac Asimov	New York (NY)
Foundation	Isaac Asimov	Isaac Asimov	New York (NY)
Contest	Matthew Reilly	Matthew Reilly	Sydney (Australia)
Scarecrow	Matthew Reilly	Matthew Reilly	Sydney (Australia)
NULL	NULL	David Baldacci	Alexandria (VA)

To decide of which table you want to include all rows, choose `LEFT` or `RIGHT` depending on whether the table name precedes or follows the `JOIN` keyword in the `SELECT` statement.

You'd probably like to obtain a list with the names of all authors, regardless of whether they appear only in the first table, only in the second table, or in both tables. Can you have a `JOIN` that is both `LEFT` and `RIGHT` at the same time? The answer is that the SQL standard defines a `FULL JOIN`, which does exactly what you want, but MySQL doesn't support it.

CREATE DATABASE

`CREATE DATABASE` creates a new, empty database. See Listing E-11 for a description of its format.

Listing E-11. *The SQL Statement CREATE DATABASE*

```
CREATE {DATABASE | SCHEMA} db_name [<create_spec> ...];
<create_spec> = {
    [DEFAULT] CHARACTER SET charset_name
    [DEFAULT] COLLATION collation_name
    }
```

The DATABASE and SCHEMA keywords are equivalent, and the DEFAULT keyword is only descriptive. The default character set determines how strings are stored in the database, while the collation defines the rules used to compare strings (i.e., precedence among characters).

When using SQL with Java and JSP, you need to specify the Unicode character set in which each character is stored in a variable number of bytes. With a minimal database creation statement such as CREATE DATABASE 'db_name', you risk getting the US-ASCII character set, which is incompatible with Java. Therefore, always specify Unicode, as in the following statement: CREATE DATABASE 'db_name' CHARACTER SET utf8.

In fact, there are several Unicode character sets, but utf8 is the most widely used and also the most similar to ASCII. As such, it is the best choice for English speakers. You don't need to bother with specifying any collation. The default will be fine.

CREATE TABLE

CREATE TABLE creates a new table, together with its columns and integrity constraints, in an existing database. See Listing E-12 for a description of its format.

Listing E-12. *The SQL Statement CREATE TABLE*

```
CREATE TABLE tbl_name (<col_def> [, <col_def> | <tbl_constr> ...]);
<col_def> = col_name <data_type> [DEFAULT {value | NULL}] [NOT NULL] [<col_constr>]
<col_constr> = [CONSTRAINT constr_name] {
        UNIQUE
    |   PRIMARY KEY
    |   REFERENCES another_tbl [(col_name [, col_name ...])]
          [ON {DELETE | UPDATE} { NO ACTION | SET NULL | SET DEFAULT | CASCADE }]
    |   CHECK (<where_condition>)
    }
<tbl_constr> = [CONSTRAINT constr_name] {
        {PRIMARY KEY | UNIQUE} (col_name [, col_name ...])
    |   FOREIGN KEY (col_name [, col_name ...]) REFERENCES another_tbl
          [ON {DELETE | UPDATE} {NO ACTION | SET NULL | SET DEFAULT | CASCADE}]
    |   CHECK (<where_condition>)
    }
```

To understand how CREATE TABLE works, concentrate on the first line of Listing E-12. It says that a table definition consists of a table name followed by the definition of one or more columns and possibly some table constraints. In turn, each column definition consists of a column name followed by the definition of a data type, a dimension, a default, and possibly some column constraints.

The following examples and comments should make it clear:

- `CREATE TABLE employee_tbl (employee_id INTEGER)` creates a table with a single column of type `INTEGER` and without any constraint. If you want to ensure that the employee ID cannot have duplicates, append the `UNIQUE` constraint to the column definition as follows: `CREATE TABLE employee_tbl (employee_id INTEGER UNIQUE)`.

- With `DEFAULT`, you can set the value to be stored in a field when you insert a new row. For example, the column definition `employee_dept VARCHAR(64) DEFAULT ''` sets the department to an empty string (without the `DEFAULT` element, the field is set to `NULL`). Note that this is different from `NULL`. This distinction is important when working with Java and JSP, because you can rest assured that a variable containing an unforeseen `NULL` will sooner or later cause a runtime exception. To avoid setting a field to `NULL` by mistake, append `NOT NULL` to a column definition. This will ensure that you get an error when your code is causing the problem and not later when you hit the unexpected `NULL`. It will make debugging your code easier.

- The column constraints `UNIQUE` and `PRIMARY KEY` ensure that the values stored in that column are unique within the table. You can specify the `PRIMARY KEY` constraint only for one column of each table, while you can specify `UNIQUE` even for all columns of a table, if that is what you need.

- Use the column constraint `REFERENCES` to force consistency checks between tables. For example, if you store the list of departments in the table `department_tbl`, which includes the column `dept_name`, you could use `REFERENCES` to ensure that all new employee records will refer to existing departments. To achieve this result, when you create the employee table, define the department column as follows: `employee_dept VARCHAR(64) REFERENCES department_tbl (dept_name)`. This will make it impossible for the creator of the employee record to enter the name of a nonexisting department. Note that you must have defined the referenced columns with the `UNIQUE` or `PRIMARY KEY` constraints. It wouldn't make sense to reference a column that allows duplicate values, because then you wouldn't know which row you would actually be referring to.

- The `ON DELETE` and `ON UPDATE` elements, which you can append to the `REFERENCES` column constraint, tell the DBMS what you want to happen when the referenced column (or columns) are deleted or updated. For example, if the department named `'new_product'` is merged into `'development'` or renamed to `'design'`, what should happen with the records of employees working in that department? You have four possibilities to choose from. With `NO ACTION`, you direct the DBMS to leave the employee record as it is. With `SET NULL` and `SET DEFAULT`, you choose to replace the name of the updated or deleted department with `NULL` or the default value, respectively. With `CASCADE`, you tell the DBMS to repeat for the referencing record what has happened with the referenced one. That is, if the `employee_dept` column of the employee table has the `ON UPDATE CASCADE` constraint, you can change the department name in the department table and automatically get the same change in the employee table. Great stuff! If you have the constraint `ON DELETE CASCADE` and remove a department from the department table, all the employee records of the employee table referencing that department will disappear. This is not necessarily what you might like to happen. Therefore, you should be careful when applying these constraints.

- The CHECK column constraint only lets you create columns that satisfy the specified check condition. For example, to ensure that a bank account can only be opened with a minimum balance of $100, you could define a column named initial_balance with the following constraint: CHECK (initial_balance >= '100.00').

- The table constraints are similar to the column constraints, both in meaning and syntax. However, there is one case in which you must use the table constraints: when you want to apply the UNIQUE or PRIMARY KEY constraints to a combination of columns rather than to a single one. For example, you might need to require that the combination of first and last name be unique within an employee table. You could achieve this result with the following table constraint: UNIQUE (last_name, first_name).

- The purpose of CONSTRAINT constraint_name is only to associate a unique name to a constraint. This then allows you to remove the constraint by updating the table with the DROP constraint_name element. As you never know whether you'll need to remove a constraint in the future, you should play it safe and name it. If you don't, you might one day have to re-create a table without a constraint and transfer the data from the original constrained version.

Note Constraints are good to help maintain database integrity, but they reduce flexibility. What you initially considered unacceptable values might turn out to be just unlikely but perfectly valid. Therefore, only create the constraints that you're really sure about. With increasing experience, you'll develop a feel for what's best.

CREATE INDEX

CREATE INDEX creates an index for one or more columns in a table. You can use it to improve the speed of data access, in particular when the indexed columns appear in WHERE conditions. See Listing E-13 for a description of its format.

Listing E-13. *The SQL Statement CREATE INDEX*

```
CREATE [UNIQUE] [{ASC[ENDING] | DESC[ENDING]}] INDEX index_name
    ON tbl_name (col_name [, col_name ...])
    ;
```

For example, CREATE UNIQUE INDEX empl_x ON employee_tbl (last_name, first_name) creates an index in which each entry refers to a combination of two field values. Attempts to create employee records with an existing combination of first and last name will fail.

CREATE VIEW

CREATE VIEW lets you access data belonging to different tables as if each were part of a single table. Only a description of the view is stored in the database, so that no data is physically duplicated or moved. See Listing E-14 for a description of its format.

Listing E-14. *The SQL Statement CREATE VIEW*

```
CREATE VIEW view_name [(view_col_name [, view_col_name ...])]
    AS <select> [WITH CHECK OPTION];
    ;
<select> = A SELECT statement without ORDER BY elements
```

Here are some examples of CREATE VIEW:

- CREATE VIEW female_employees AS SELECT * FROM employee_tbl WHERE gender = 'female' creates a view with all female employees.

- CREATE VIEW female_names (last, first) AS SELECT last_name, first_name FROM employee_tbl WHERE gender = 'female' creates a similar view but only contains the name columns of the employee table rather than the full rows. Notice that the column names of the view are matched one by one with the column names of the table.

- CREATE VIEW phone_list AS SELECT last_name, first_name, dept_telephone, phone_extension FROM employee_tbl, department_tbl WHERE department = dept_no creates a view with columns from both the employee and the department tables. The columns of the view are named like the original columns, but it would have been possible to rename them by specifying a list of columns enclosed in parentheses after the view name. The WHERE condition is used to match the department numbers in the two tables, so that the department telephone number can be included in the view. Note that views that join tables are read-only.

- When a view only refers to a single table, you can update the table by operating on the view rather than on the actual table. The WITH CHECK OPTION element prevents you from modifying the table in such a way that you could then no longer retrieve the modified rows. For example, if you create a view WITH CHECK OPTION containing all female employees, it won't allow you to use the view to enter a male employee or to change the gender of an employee. Obviously, you would still be able to do those operations by updating the employee table directly.

INSERT

INSERT stores one or more rows in an existing table or view. See Listing E-15 for a description of its format.

Listing E-15. *The SQL Statement INSERT*

```
INSERT INTO {tbl_name | view_name} [(col_name [, col_name ...])]
    {VALUES (<val> [, <val> ...]) | <select>};
    ;
<select> = A SELECT returning the values to be inserted into the new rows
```

You can use INSERT to create one row in a table (or view) from scratch or to create one or more rows by copying data from other tables, as shown in the following examples:

- INSERT INTO employee_tbl (employee_id, first_name, last_name) VALUES ('999', 'Joe', 'Bloke') creates a new row for the employee Joe Bloke. All the columns not listed after the table name are filled with their respective default values. You could omit the list of column names, but the values would be stored beginning from the first column in the order in which the columns were created. Be sure that you get the correct order.

- INSERT INTO foreigners SELECT * from employee_tbl WHERE citizenship != 'USA' copies the full records of all employees who are not U.S. citizens to the foreigners table. Note that this is different from creating a view of foreign employees, because the records are actually duplicated and stored in a different table. With a view, you would only specify a different way of accessing the same data. Be extremely cautious when INTO and SELECT refer to the same table. You could create an endless insertion loop. It's best if you simply refrain from inserting rows by copying the data from rows that are in the same table.

DROP

DROP is the statement you use when you want to remove a database, a table, an index, or a view. See Listing E-16 for a description of their format.

Listing E-16. *The SQL DROP Statements*

```
DROP DATABASE;
DROP TABLE tbl_name;
DROP INDEX index_name;
DROP VIEW view_name;
```

DROP DATABASE removes the database you're connected to. The rest are pretty self-explanatory. Just one point: with DROP INDEX, you cannot eliminate the indexes that the DBMS creates automatically when you specify the UNIQUE, PRIMARY KEY, or FOREIGN KEY attribute for a column.

DELETE

DELETE removes one or more rows from an existing table or a view that is not read-only. See Listing E-17 for a description of its format.

Listing E-17. *The SQL Statement DELETE*

```
DELETE FROM {tbl_name | view_name} [WHERE <where_condition>];
```

ALTER TABLE

ALTER TABLE modifies the structure of an existing table. See Listing E-18 for a description of its format.

Listing E-18. *The SQL Statement ALTER TABLE*

```
ALTER TABLE tbl_name <alter_tbl_op> [, <alter_tbl_op> ...];
<alter_tbl_op> = {
        ADD <col_def>
    |   ADD <tbl_constr>
    |   DROP col_name
    |   DROP CONSTRAINT constr_name
    |   <alter_col_def>
    }
<alter_col_def> = {
        ALTER [COLUMN] col_name SET DEFAULT <val>       /* MySQL, postgreSQL */
    |   ALTER [COLUMN] col_name DROP DEFAULT            /* MySQL, postgreSQL */
    |   CHANGE [COLUMN] col_name <col_def>              /* MySQL */
    |   MODIFY [COLUMN] <col_def>                       /* MySQL */
    |   ALTER [COLUMN] col_name { SET | DROP } NOT NULL /* PostgreSQL */
    |   RENAME [COLUMN] col_name TO new_col_name        /* PostgreSQL */
    |   ALTER [COLUMN] col_name TO new_col_name         /* FirebirdSQL */
    |   ALTER [COLUMN] TYPE new_col_type                /* FirebirdSQL */
    }
```

As you can see from Listing E-18, the DBMS vendors once more haven't managed to agree on how you can modify columns.

The addition or removal of columns and table constraints is pretty straightforward. Refer to CREATE TABLE for a description of <col_def> and <tbl_constr>.

What you can do in terms of changing the definition of an existing column depends on which DBMS you've chosen. Only MySQL gives you full flexibility in redefining the column with ALTER TABLE tbl_name CHANGE col_name <col_def>. Note that <col_def> must be complete, including a column name. If you don't want to change the name of a column, you can use its current name within <col_def>. In fact, besides being compatible with Oracle, the only reason for having MODIFY is that you don't need to type the same column name twice.

UPDATE

UPDATE modifies the content of one or more existing rows in a table (or view). See Listing E-19 for a description of its format.

Listing E-19. *The SQL Statement UPDATE*

```
UPDATE {tbl_name | view_name} SET col_name = <val> [, col_name = <val> ...]
    [WHERE <where_condition>]
    ;
```

For example, use the statement UPDATE employee_tbl SET first_name = 'John' WHERE first_name = 'Jihn' to correct a typing error. Nothing could be simpler.

SET TRANSACTION and START TRANSACTION

The purpose of a transaction is to ensure that nobody else can "sneak in" and modify rows after you've read them but before you've updated them in the database. The DBMS can achieve this by locking the rows you read within a transaction until you commit your updates. As with other statements, different DBMSs behave differently. Listing E-20 shows what you need to do with MySQL and PostgreSQL.

Listing E-20. *Start a Transaction with MySQL and PostgreSQL*

```
SET TRANSACTION ISOLATION LEVEL READ COMMITTED;
START TRANSACTION;
```

Listing E-21 shows what you need to do with FirebirdSQL.

Listing E-21. *Start a Transaction with FirebirdSQL*

```
SET TRANSACTION ISOLATION LEVEL READ COMMITTED;
```

As you can see, to start a transaction with MySQL and PostgreSQL, you have to execute a SET TRANSACTION and a START, while you only need to execute SET TRANSACTION without START when starting a transaction with FirebirdSQL. Note that all three DBMSs provide additional options, but we'll only show a mode of operation that is common to them all.

You need to specify the ISOLATION LEVEL if you want to write portable code, because the three DBMSs have different defaults.

COMMIT and ROLLBACK

COMMIT confirms the updates you've performed since starting the current transaction and terminates it. ROLLBACK discards the updates and returns the database to its condition prior to the current transaction. Their syntax couldn't be simpler: COMMIT; and ROLLBACK;.

Reserved SQL Keywords

Table E-12 shows all the reserved SQL keywords.

Table E-12. *Reserved SQL Keywords*

ABC...	Keyword
A	ADD, ALL, ALLOCATE, ALTER, AND, ANY, ARE, ARRAY, AS, ASENSITIVE, ASYMMETRIC, AT, ATOMIC, and AUTHORIZATION
B	BEGIN, BETWEEN, BIGINT, BINARY, BLOB, BOOLEAN, BOTH, and BY
C	CALL, CALLED, CASCADED, CASE, CAST, CHAR, CHARACTER, CHECK, CLOB, CLOSE, COLLATE, COLUMN, COMMIT, CONNECT, CONSTRAINT, CONTINUE, CORRESPONDING, CREATE, CROSS, CUBE, CURRENT, CURRENT_DATE, CURRENT_DEFAULT_TRANSFORM_GROUP, CURRENT_PATH, CURRENT_ROLE, CURRENT_TIME, CURRENT_TIMESTAMP, CURRENT_TRANSFORM_GROUP_FOR_TYPE, CURRENT_USER, CURSOR, and CYCLE
D	DATE, DAY, DEALLOCATE, DEC, DECIMAL, DECLARE, DEFAULT, DELETE, DEREF, DESCRIBE, DETERMINISTIC, DISCONNECT, DISTINCT, DOUBLE, DROP, and DYNAMIC

ABC...	Keyword
E	EACH, ELEMENT, ELSE, END, END-EXEC, ESCAPE, EXCEPT, EXEC, EXECUTE, EXISTS, and EXTERNAL
F	FALSE, FETCH, FILTER, FLOAT, FOR, FOREIGN, FREE, FROM, FULL, and FUNCTION
G	GET, GLOBAL, GRANT, GROUP, and GROUPING
H	HAVING, HOLD, and HOUR
I	IDENTITY, IMMEDIATE, IN, INDICATOR, INNER, INOUT, INPUT, INSENSITIVE, INSERT, INT, INTEGER, INTERSECT, INTERVAL, INTO, IS, and ISOLATION
J	JOIN
L	LANGUAGE, LARGE, LATERAL, LEADING, LEFT, LIKE, LOCAL, LOCALTIME, and LOCALTIMESTAMP
M	MATCH, MEMBER, MERGE, METHOD, MINUTE, MODIFIES, MODULE, MONTH, and MULTISET
N	NATIONAL, NATURAL, NCHAR, NCLOB, NEW, NO, NONE, NOT, NULL, and NUMERIC
O	OF, OLD, ON, ONLY, OPEN, OR, ORDER, OUT, OUTER, OUTPUT, OVER, and OVERLAPS
P	PARAMETER, PARTITION, PRECISION, PREPARE, PRIMARY, and PROCEDURE
R	RANGE, READS, REAL, RECURSIVE, REF, REFERENCES, REFERENCING, RELEASE, RETURN, RETURNS, REVOKE, RIGHT, ROLLBACK, ROLLUP, ROW, and ROWS
S	SAVEPOINT, SCROLL, SEARCH, SECOND, SELECT, SENSITIVE, SESSION_USER, SET, SIMILAR, SMALLINT, SOME, SPECIFIC, SPECIFICTYPE, SQL, SQLEXCEPTION, SQLSTATE, SQLWARNING, START, STATIC, SUBMULTISET, SYMMETRIC, SYSTEM, and SYSTEM_USER
T	TABLE, THEN, TIME, TIMESTAMP, TIMEZONE_HOUR, TIMEZONE_MINUTE, TO, TRAILING, TRANSLATION, TREAT, TRIGGER, and TRUE
U	UNION, UNIQUE, UNKNOWN, UNNEST, UPDATE, USER, and USING
V	VALUE, VALUES, VARCHAR, and VARYING
W	WHEN, WHENEVER, WHERE, WINDOW, WITH, WITHIN, and WITHOUT
Y	YEAR

■ ■ ■

JSF Quick Reference

In this appendix, we'll describe all the JSF tags in the core and html tag libraries. When we mention JSF life-cycle phases, we're referring to the diagram shown at the beginning of Chapter 5 (Figure 5-1). The tag description is consistent with JSF version jsf-1.2_04-b16-p02. The main source of information for this chapter is the original Sun Microsystems' TLD documentation available online at http://java.sun.com/javaee/javaserverfaces/1.2/docs/tlddocs/index.html.

JSF core Tag Library

The JSF core tag library contains actions that are independent of rendering aspects. In the tables listing the attributes of each tag, ValExpr means the class javax.el.ValueExpression. Note that you can omit all attributes unless we explicitly indicate that they are required.

To be able to use the library, insert the following line at the beginning of your JSP pages in standard format:

```
<%@ taglib uri="http://java.sun.com/jsf/core" prefix="f"%>
```

Add the following namespace attribute to the root element of your JSP documents:

```
xmlns:f="http://java.sun.com/jsf/core"
```

f:actionListener

The f:actionListener element registers for a UIComponent an instantiation of a class that implements the ActionListener interface. Action listeners process action events during the Apply Request Values or Invoke Application phases of the JSF life cycle. This is done only when developing application frameworks, not when developing applications in the Tomcat environment. Normally, to act on an event, you'd do what we do in the Eshopf application: implement a method of a backing bean to handle the event and then refer to that method via a method expression assigned to the appropriate attribute of the component's tag. Table F-1 lists the element's attributes.

Table F-1. *f:actionListener Attributes*

Name	Type	Description
type	ValExpr evaluating to String	Java class name of an ActionListener
binding	ValExpr evaluating to javax. faces.event.ActionListener	An object that implements the ActionListener interface

f:attribute

The f:attribute element adds an attribute to a UIComponent. Table F-2 lists the element's attributes.

Table F-2. *f:attribute Attributes*

Name	Type	Description
name	ValExpr evaluating to String	The name of the attribute to be added
value	ValExpr evaluating to Object	The value of the attribute to be added

f:converter

The f:converter element creates for a UIComponent an instance of the javax.faces.convert.Converter class registered under a converter ID. Table F-3 lists the element's attributes.

Table F-3. *f:converter Attributes*

Name	Type	Description
converterId	ValExpr evaluating to String	Identifier of the Converter class
binding	ValExpr evaluating to javax. faces.convert.Converter	An object that implements the Converter interface

f:convertDateTime

The f:convertDateTime element creates a DateTimeConverter instance for a UIComponent. Table F-4 lists the element's attributes.

Table F-4. *f:convertDateTime Attributes*

Name	Type	Description
binding	ValExpr evaluating to javax. faces.convert. DateTimeConverter	An instance of the DateTimeConverter class.
dateStyle	ValExpr evaluating to String	Valid values are default, short, medium, long, and full. The default value is default, which is only applied if the attribute type is date or both.

Name	Type	Description
locale	ValExpr evaluating to Object	Locale whose predefined styles for dates and times are used during formatting or parsing. The default value is the Locale returned by FacesContext.getViewRoot().getLocale(). The value must be either a Visual Basic (VB) expression that evaluates to a java.util.Locale instance, or a String that is valid to pass as the first argument to the java.util.Locale(String language, String country) constructor. The empty string is passed as the second argument.
pattern	ValExpr evaluating to String	Custom formatting pattern that determines how the date/time string is to be formatted and parsed.
timeStyle	ValExpr evaluating to String	Valid values are default, short, medium, long, and full. The default value is default, which is only applied if the attribute type is time or both.
timeZone	ValExpr evaluating to Object	The value must be either a VB expression that evaluates to a java.util.TimeZone instance, or a String that is a time zone ID as described in the javadocs for java.util.TimeZone.getTimeZone().
type	ValExpr evaluating to String	Valid values are date, time, and both. The default value is date.

f:convertNumber

The f:convertNumber element creates a NumberConverter instance for a UIComponent. Table F-5 lists the element's attributes.

Table F-5. *f:convertNumber Attributes*

Name	Type	Description
currencyCode	ValExpr evaluating to String	ISO 4217 currency code, applied only when formatting currencies.
currencySymbol	ValExpr evaluating to String	Currency symbol, applied only when formatting currencies.
groupingUsed	ValExpr evaluating to Boolean	Flag specifying whether the formatted output is to contain grouping separators. The default value is true.
integerOnly	ValExpr evaluating to Boolean	Flag specifying whether only the integer part of the value is to be formatted and parsed. The default value is false.
locale	ValExpr evaluating to java.util.Locale	Locale whose styles for numbers are to be used during formatting and parsing. If not specified, the Locale returned by FacesContext.getViewRoot().getLocale() is used.

Continued

Table F-5. *Continued*

Name	Type	Description
maxFractionDigits	ValExpr evaluating to Integer	Maximum number of digits to be formatted in the fractional portion of the output.
maxIntegerDigits	ValExpr evaluating to Integer	Maximum number of digits to be formatted in the integer portion of the output.
minFractionDigits	ValExpr evaluating to Integer	Minimum number of digits to be formatted in the fractional portion of the output.
minIntegerDigits	ValExpr evaluating to Integer	Minimum number of digits to be formatted in the integer portion of the output.
pattern	ValExpr evaluating to String	Custom formatting pattern determining how the string representing a number is to be formatted and parsed.
type	ValExpr evaluating to String	Specifies how the string representing a number is to be formatted and parsed. Valid values are number, currency, and percent. The default value is number.
binding	ValExpr evaluating to javax.faces.convert.NumberConverter	An instance of the NumberConverter class.

f:facet

The f:facet element creates a named facet for a UIComponent. Table F-6 lists the element's attributes.

Table F-6. *f:facet Attributes*

Name	Type	Description
name (required)	String	Name of the facet

f:loadBundle

The f:loadBundle element loads a resource bundle localized for the current view and makes it accessible as a request attribute of type java.util.Map named as specified in the var tag attribute. The Map object must not throw a MissingResourceException. Instead, a get() call made for a key that doesn't exist in the Map object must return the literal string "???KEY???", where KEY is the key being looked up unsuccessfully. If the ResourceBundle doesn't exist, a JspException must be thrown. Table F-7 lists the element's attributes.

Table F-7. *f:loadBundle Attributes*

Name	Type	Description
basename	ValExpr evaluating to String	Base name of the resource bundle to be loaded.
var (required)	String	Name of a request scope attribute under which the resource bundle is to be made available as a Map object.

f:parameter

The f:parameter element adds a UIParameter child component to a UIComponent. For example, if you have a backing bean registered as myBean with this property:

```
String myMess = "{0}, I {1} agree with you!";
```

then the following JSF component will print Jane, I agree with you! or Jane, I do not agree with you!, depending on the string stored in aResult:

```
<h:outputFormat value="#{myBean.myMess}">
  <f:param value="Jane"/>
  <f:param value="#{myBean.aResult}"/>
  </h:outputFormat>
```

Table F-8 lists the element's attributes.

Table F-8. *f:parameter Attributes*

Name	Type	Description
binding	ValExpr evaluating to javax.faces.component.UIComponent	Backing bean property bound to the component instance for which the parameter is created
id	String	Identifier of the UIParameter component
name	ValExpr evaluating to String	Name of the parameter to be created
value	ValExpr evaluating to Object	Value of the parameter to be set

f:phaseListener

The f:phaseListener element registers an instantiation of a class that implements the PhaseListener interface. JSF then executes the registered PhaseListener every time the processing for each standard phase of the life cycle begins or ends. Table F-9 lists the element's attributes.

Table F-9. *f:phaseListener Attributes*

Name	Type	Description
type	ValExpr evaluating to String	Fully qualified Java class name of the PhaseListener to be registered
binding	ValExpr evaluating to javax.faces.event.PhaseListener	An object implementing the PhaseListener interface

f:selectItem

The f:selectItem element adds an option to a UIComponent. Table F-10 lists the element's attributes.

Table F-10. *f:selectItem Attributes*

Name	Type	Description
binding	ValExpr evaluating to javax.faces.component.UIComponent	Value binding the expression to a backing bean property.
id	String	Component identifier of the option component to be created.
itemDescription	ValExpr evaluating to String	Description of this option, for use in development tools.
itemDisabled	ValExpr evaluating to Boolean	Flag to disable the option. The default value is false.
itemLabel	ValExpr evaluating to String	Label to be displayed to the user for this option.
escape	ValExpr evaluating to String	Flag to escape sensitive characters in the value of the itemLabel attribute. The default value is true.
itemValue	ValExpr evaluating to Object	Value returned if the user selects this option.
value	ValExpr evaluating to javax.faces.model.SelectItem	Value binding the expression pointing at a SelectItem instance containing the information for this option.

f:selectItems

The f:selectItems element adds a set of options to a UIComponent. Table F-11 lists the element's attributes.

Table F-11. *f:selectItems Attributes*

Name	Type	Description
binding	ValExpr evaluating to javax.faces.component.UIComponent	Value binding the expression to a backing bean property.
id	String	Component identifier of the options component to be created.
value	ValExpr evaluating to javax.faces.model.SelectItem	Value binding the expression pointing at a SelectItem instance containing the information for this set of options.

f:setPropertyActionListener

The f:setPropertyActionListener element creates an ActionListener instance and registers it for a UIComponent. This ActionListener causes the value of the value attribute to be set into the ValueExpression given by the target attribute. Table F-12 lists the element's attributes.

Table F-12. *f:setPropertyActionListener Attributes*

Name	Type	Description
value (required)	ValExpr evaluating to Object	To be stored as the value of the target attribute
target (required)	ValExpr evaluating to Object	Destination of the value attribute

f:subview

The f:subview element is a container action for all JSF actions included via jsp:include, the JSTL action c:import, or any other custom action with an equivalent behavior. Table F-13 lists the element's attributes.

Table F-13. *f:subview Attributes*

Name	Type	Description
binding	ValExpr evaluating to javax.faces.component.UIComponent	Value binding the expression to a backing bean property.
id (required)	String	Component identifier.
rendered	ValExpr evaluating to Boolean	Flag indicating whether this component (and its children) should be rendered. The default is true.

f:validateDoubleRange

The f:validateDoubleRange element registers a DoubleRangeValidator instance for a UIComponent. Table F-14 lists the element's attributes.

Table F-14. *f:validateDoubleRange Attributes*

Name	Type	Description
maximum	ValExpr evaluating to Double	Maximum value allowed for this component
minimum	ValExpr evaluating to Double	Minimum value allowed for this component
binding	ValExpr evaluating to javax.faces.validator.DoubleRangeValidator	An instance of the DoubleRangeValidator class

f:validateLength

The f:validateLength element registers a LengthValidator instance for a UIComponent. Table F-15 lists the element's attributes.

Table F-15. *f:validateLength Attributes*

Name	Type	Description
maximum	ValExpr evaluating to Integer	Maximum length allowed for this component
minimum	ValExpr evaluating to Integer	Minimum length allowed for this component
binding	ValExpr evaluating to javax. faces.validator. LengthValidator	An instance of the LengthValidator class

f:validateLongRange

The f:validateLongRange element registers a LongRangeValidator instance for a UIComponent. Table F-16 lists the element's attributes.

Table F-16. *f:validateLongRange Attributes*

Name	Type	Description
maximum	ValExpr evaluating to Long	Maximum value allowed for this component
minimum	ValExpr evaluating to Long	Minimum value allowed for this component
binding	ValExpr evaluating to javax. faces.validator. LongRangeValidator	An instance of the LongRangeValidator class

f:validator

The f:validator element registers for a UIComponent an instantiation of a class that implements the Validator interface. Table F-17 lists the element's attributes.

Table F-17. *f:validator Attributes*

Name	Type	Description
validatorId	ValExpr evaluating to String	Validator identifier
binding	ValExpr evaluating to javax. faces.validator.Validator	An object that implements the Validator interface

f:valueChangeListener

The f:valueChangeListener element registers for a UIComponent an instantiation of a class that implements the ValueChangeListener interface. What we said concerning f:actionListener also applies to this tag. Table F-18 lists the element's attributes.

Table F-18. *f:valueChangeListener Attributes*

Name	Type	Description
type	ValExpr evaluating to String	Java class name of a ValueChangeListener
binding	ValExpr evaluating to javax. faces.event. ValueChangeListener	An object that implements the ValueChangeListener interface

f:verbatim

The f:verbatim element creates for a UIComponent a child component that renders its body. In practice, it makes it easy for you to embed HTML code in a JSF module. Table F-19 lists the element's attributes.

Table F-19. *f:verbatim Attributes*

Name	Type	Description
escape	ValExpr evaluating to Boolean	Flag indicating that the generated output must be escaped. The default value is false.
rendered	ValExpr evaluating to Boolean	Flag indicating whether this component should be rendered. The default value is true.

f:view

The f:view element is a container for all JSF actions . Table F-20 lists the element's attributes.

Table F-20. *f:view Attributes*

Name	Type	Description
locale	ValExpr evaluating to java. util.Locale or to a String that is converted to a Locale	Locale to use for localizing this page.
renderKitId	ValExpr evaluating to String	Identifier for the RenderKit object to use for rendering this page.
beforePhase	javax.el.MethodExpression	Points to a method with signature void beforePhase(javax.faces.event.PhaseEvent). This method is then executed before each phase except for Restore View.
afterPhase	javax.el.MethodExpression	Points to a method with signature void after-Phase(javax.faces.event.PhaseEvent). This method is then executed after each phase except for Restore View.

JSF html Tag Library

The JSF html tag library contains tags for all UIComponent and HTML RenderKit renderer combinations defined in the JSF Specification. As for the core tag library, we abbreviate javax.el.ValueExpression with ValExpr.

To be able to use the library, insert the following line at the beginning of your JSP pages in standard format:

```
<%@ taglib uri="http://java.sun.com/jsf/html" prefix="h"%>
```

Add the following namespace attribute to the root element of JSP documents:

```
xmlns:h="http://java.sun.com/jsf/html"
```

The current release of the html tag library includes 25 components and 99 attributes, 36 of which are used by at least 10 different components. To avoid 611 repeated descriptions of attributes, we'll describe the shared attributes only once in a separate section. When describing each component, we'll list the shared attributes but only describe the attributes that are used exclusively by that component or that have different behavior with different components.

h:column

The h:column element renders a single column of data within a parent h:dataTable component. The included UI components are rendered from the top down, in the order in which they appear.

Possible subelements are

- `<f:facet name="header">..</facet>` (zero or one)

- `<f:facet name="footer">..</facet>` (zero or one)

- JSF UI components (one or more)

This element supports the following shared attributes: binding, footerClass, headerClass, id, and rendered.

There are no specific attributes.

h:commandButton

The h:commandButton element renders a button to submit an input form.

It generates the following HTML element: `<input type="submit"../>` (default only).

There are no possible subelements.

This element supports the following shared attributes: accesskey, action, actionListener, alt, binding, dir, disabled, id, immediate, label, lang, onblur, onchange, onclick, ondblclick, onfocus, onkeydown, onkeypress, onkeyup, onmousedown, onmousemove, onmouseout, onmouseover, onmouseup, onselect, readonly, rendered, style, styleClass, tabindex, title, and value.

It supports the following specific attributes: image and type (see Table F-21).

Table F-21. *Specific Attributes of h:commandButton*

Name	Type	Description
image	ValExpr evaluating to String	Absolute or relative URL of the image to be displayed for this button. If this attribute is specified, the input element will be of type image.
type	ValExpr evaluating to String	Type of button to create. Valid values are submit and reset. If not specified or not a valid value, the default value will be submit.

h:commandLink

The h:commandLink element renders a hyperlink to another page or to another location of the same page that acts like a form's Submit button when clicked.

It generates the following HTML element: <a..>..</a>

Possible subelements are

- <h:outputText../> (zero or more)

- <h:graphicImage../> (zero or more)

It supports the following shared attributes: accesskey, action, actionListener, binding, charset, coords, dir, disabled, hreflang, id, immediate, lang, onblur, onclick, ondblclick, onfocus, onkeydown, onkeypress, onkeyup, onmousedown, onmousemove, onmouseout, onmouseover, onmouseup, rel, rendered, rev, shape, style, styleClass, tabindex, target, title, and value.

It has the following specific attribute: type (see Table F-22).

Table F-22. *Specific Attributes of h:commandLink*

Name	Type	Description
type	ValExpr evaluating to String	The content type of the resource designated by this hyperlink.

h:dataTable

The h:dataTable element renders an HTML table compliant with the HTML 4.01 specification.

It generates the following HTML element:

<table..><thead>..</thead><tbody>..</tbody><tfoot>..</tfoot></table>

Possible subelements are

- <f:facet name="header">..</facet> (zero or one)

- <f:facet name="footer">..</facet> (zero or one)

- <h:column> (one or more)

This element supports the following shared attributes: bgcolor, binding, border, captionClass, captionStyle, cellpadding, cellspacing, columnClasses, dir, footerClass, frame, headerClass, id, lang, onclick, ondblclick, onkeydown, onkeypress, onkeyup, onmousedown, onmousemove, onmouseout, onmouseover, onmouseup, rendered, rowClasses, rules, style, styleClass, summary, title, and value.

It supports the following specific attributes: first, rows, var, and width (see Table F-23).

Table F-23. *Specific Attributes of h:dataTable*

Name	Type	Description
first	ValExpr evaluating to int	Row number of the first row to be displayed, whereby 0 indicates the first row.
rows	ValExpr evaluating to int	The number of rows to be displayed, starting with the row identified by the attribute first. If rows is set to 0, all available rows are displayed.
var	String	Name of a request-scoped attribute under which the model data for the current row is to be made accessible.
width	ValExpr evaluating to String	Width of the entire table.

h:form

The h:form element renders an input form.

It generates the following HTML element: <form..>..</form>

Possible subelements are JSF UI components (zero or more).

This element supports the following shared attributes: binding, dir, id, lang, onclick, ondblclick, onkeydown, onkeypress, onkeyup, onmousedown, onmousemove, onmouseout, onmouseover, onmouseup, rendered, style, styleClass, target, and title.

It supports the following specific attributes: accept, acceptcharset, enctype, onreset, onsubmit, and prependId (see Table F-24).

Table F-24. *Specific Attributes of h:form*

Name	Type	Description
accept	ValExpr evaluating to String	List of content types that a server processing this form is to handle correctly.
acceptcharset	ValExpr evaluating to String	List of character encodings for input data that are to be accepted by the server processing this form.
enctype	ValExpr evaluating to String	Content type used to submit the form to the server. If not specified, the default value is application/x-www-form-urlencoded.
onreset	ValExpr evaluating to String	JavaScript code to be executed when this form is reset.
onsubmit	ValExpr evaluating to String	JavaScript code to be executed when this form is submitted.
prependId	ValExpr evaluating to boolean	Flag indicating whether this form should prepend its ID to its children's IDs when their client IDs are generated. The default value is true.

h:graphicImage

The h:graphicImage element renders an image.

It generates the following HTML element:

There are no possible subelements.

This element supports the following shared attributes: alt, binding, dir, id, lang, onclick, ondblclick, onkeydown, onkeypress, onkeyup, onmousedown, onmousemove, onmouseout, onmouseover, onmouseup, rendered, style, styleClass, title, and value.

It supports the following specific attributes: height, ismap, longdesc, url, usemap, and width (see Table F-25).

Table F-25. *Specific Attributes of h:graphicImage*

Name	Type	Description
height	ValExpr evaluating to String	Value to override the actual height of this image.
ismap	ValExpr evaluating to boolean	Flag indicating that this image is to be used as a server-side image map. Such an image must be enclosed within a hyperlink (HTML element <a>). A value of false causes no attribute to be rendered, while a value of true causes the attribute to be rendered as ismap="ismap".
longdesc	ValExpr evaluating to String	URI to a long description of the image represented by this element.
url	ValExpr evaluating to String	Context-relative URL to retrieve the resource associated with this component. This is an alias for the attribute value.
usemap	ValExpr evaluating to String	The name of a client-side image map (an HTML <map> element) for which this element provides the image.
width	ValExpr evaluating to String	Value to override the actual width of this image.

h:inputHidden

The h:inputHidden element renders an input HTML element of type hidden.

It generates the following HTML element: <input type="hidden"../>

There are no possible subelements.

It supports the following shared attributes: binding, converter, converterMessage, id, immediate, rendered, required, requiredMessage, validator, validatorMessage, value, and valueChangeListener.

There are no specific attributes.

h:inputSecret

The h:inputSecret element renders an input HTML element of type password.

It generates the following HTML element: <input type="password"../>

There are no possible subelements.

This element supports the following shared attributes: accesskey, alt, autocomplete, binding, converter, converterMessage, dir, disabled, id, immediate, label, lang, maxlength, onblur, onchange, onclick, ondblclick, onfocus, onkeydown, onkeypress, onkeyup, onmousedown, onmousemove, onmouseout, onmouseover, onmouseup, onselect, readonly, rendered, required, requiredMessage, style, styleClass, tabindex, title, validator, validatorMessage, value, and valueChangeListener.

It supports the following specific attributes: redisplay and size (see Table F-26).

Table F-26. *Specific Attributes of h:inputSecret*

Name	Type	Description
redisplay	ValExpr evaluating to boolean	Flag indicating that any existing value in this field should be rendered when the form is created. Because this is a potential security risk, the password values are not displayed by default.
size	ValExpr evaluating to int	The number of characters used to determine the width of this field.

h:inputText

The h:inputText element renders an input HTML element of type text.

It generates the following HTML element: `<input type="text"../>`

There are no possible subelements.

This element supports the following shared attributes: accesskey, alt, autocomplete, binding, converter, converterMessage, dir, disabled, id, immediate, label, lang, maxlength, onblur, onchange, onclick, ondblclick, onfocus, onkeydown, onkeypress, onkeyup, onmousedown, onmousemove, onmouseout, onmouseover, onmouseup, onselect, readonly, rendered, required, requiredMessage, style, styleClass, tabindex, title, validator, validatorMessage, value, and valueChangeListener.

It supports the following specific attribute: size (see Table F-27).

Table F-27. *Specific Attributes of h:inputText*

Name	Type	Description
size	ValExpr evaluating to int	The number of characters used to determine the width of this field.

h:inputTextarea

The h:inputTextarea element renders a textarea HTML element.

It generates the following HTML element: `<textarea../>`

There are no possible subelements.

This element supports the following shared attributes: accesskey, binding, converter, converterMessage, dir, disabled, id, immediate, label, lang, onblur, onchange, onclick, ondblclick, onfocus, onkeydown, onkeypress, onkeyup, onmousedown, onmousemove, onmouseout, onmouseover, onmouseup, onselect, readonly, rendered, required, requiredMessage, style, styleClass, tabindex, title, validator, validatorMessage, value, and valueChangeListener.

It supports the following specific attributes: cols and rows (see Table F-28).

Table F-28. *Specific Attributes of h:inputTextarea*

Name	Type	Description
cols	ValExpr evaluating to int	The number of columns to be displayed
rows	ValExpr evaluating to int	The number of rows to be displayed

h:message

The h:message element renders a single message for a specific component.

It generates the <span..>..</span> HTML element if a style is specified; otherwise, it generates template text.

There are no possible subelements.

This element supports the following shared attributes: binding, dir, errorClass, errorStyle, fatalClass, fatalStyle, for (**required**), id, infoClass, infoStyle, lang, rendered, showDetail, showSummary, style, styleClass, title, tooltip, warnClass, and warnStyle.

There are no specific attributes.

h:messages

The h:messages element renders all pending messages.

It generates the <span..>..</span> HTML element if one or more of the dir, lang, style, and styleClass attributes are specified; otherwise, it generates template text.

There are no possible subelements.

This element supports the following shared attributes: binding, dir, errorClass, errorStyle, fatalClass, fatalStyle, id, infoClass, infoStyle, lang, rendered, showDetail, showSummary, style, styleClass, title, tooltip, warnClass, and warnStyle.

It supports the following specific attributes: globalOnly and layout (see Table F-29).

Table F-29. *Specific Attributes of h:messages*

Name	Type	Description
globalOnly	ValExpr evaluating to boolean	Flag indicating that only global messages (i.e., messages not associated with any specific component) are to be displayed. The default value is false.
layout	ValExpr evaluating to String	The type of HTML layout to use when rendering error messages. The valid values are table and list. The default value is list.

h:outputFormat

The h:outputFormat element renders parameterized text.

It generates the <span..>..</span> HTML element if a style is specified; otherwise, it generates template text.

It can contain the following subelement: <f:param../> (zero or more).

This element supports the following shared attributes: binding, converter, dir, escape, id, lang, rendered, style, styleClass, title, and value.

There are no specific attributes.

h:outputLabel

The h:outputLabel element renders a label HTML element.

It generates the following HTML element: <label..>..</label>.

It can contain the following subelement: <h:outputText../> (one or more).

This element supports the following shared attributes: accesskey, binding, converter, dir, escape, for, id, lang, onblur, onclick, ondblclick, onfocus, onkeydown, onkeypress, onkeyup, onmousedown, onmousemove, onmouseout, onmouseover, onmouseup, rendered, style, styleClass, tabindex, title, and value.

There are no specific attributes.

h:outputLink

The h:outputLink element renders a hyperlink to another page or to another location of the same page. For example, this code:

```
<h:outputLink value="#{evaluate-to-a-url}">
  <f:param name="name1" value="val1"/>
  <f:param name="nam2" value="val2"/>
  <h:outputText value="#{evaluate-to-the-display-text}"/>
</h:outputLink>
```

is rendered in HTML with this code:

```
<a href="a-url?nam1=val1&nam2=val2">display-text</a>
```

It generates the following HTML element: <a..>..</a>
Possible subelements are

- <h:outputText../> (one or more)

- <f:param../> (zero or more)

This element supports the following shared attributes: accesskey, binding, charset, converter, coords, dir, disabled, hreflang, id, lang, onblur, onclick, ondblclick, onfocus, onkeydown, onkeypress, onkeyup, onmousedown, onmousemove, onmouseout, onmouseover, onmouseup, rel, rendered, rev, shape, style, styleClass, tabindex, target, title, and value.

It supports the following specific attribute: type (see Table F-30).

Table F-30. *Specific Attributes of h:outputLink*

Name	Type	Description
type	ValExpr evaluating to String	The content type of the resource designated by this hyperlink

h:outputText

The h:outputText element renders parameterized text.

It generates the <span..>..</span> HTML element if one or more of the dir, lang, style, and styleClass attributes are specified; otherwise, it generates template text.

There are no possible subelements.

This element supports the following shared attributes: binding, converter, dir, escape, id, lang, rendered, style, styleClass, title, and value.

There are no specific attributes.

h:panelGrid

The h:panelGrid element renders an HTML table compliant with the HTML 4.01 specification. This component fills the table from left to right and top to bottom with the JSF components it contains. It uses the columns attribute to determine the length of each row, and it keeps creating rows until all contained components have been rendered.

It generates the following HTML element:

`<table..><thead>..</thead><tbody>..</tbody><tfoot>..</tfoot></table>`

Possible subelements are

- `<f:facet name="header">..</facet>` (zero or one)

- `<f:facet name="footer">..</facet>` (zero or one)

- JSF UI components (one or more)

This element doesn't support any shared attributes.

It supports the following specific attributes: columns and width (see Table F-31).

Table F-31. *Specific Attributes of h:panelGrid*

Name	Type	Description
columns	ValExpr evaluating to int	The number of columns to render before starting a new row
width	ValExpr evaluating to String	Width of the entire table

h:panelGroup

The h:panelGroup element is used to group UI components when only a single component is expected.

It generates the `<div..>..</div>` HTML element if the attribute layout is set to block; otherwise, it generates `<span..>..</span>`.

Possible subelements are the JSF UI components (one or more).

This element supports the following shared attributes: binding, id, layout, rendered, style, and styleClass.

It supports the following specific attribute: layout (see Table F-32).

Table F-32. *Specific Attributes of h:panelGroup*

Name	Type	Description
layout	ValExpr evaluating to String	The type of layout to use when rendering this group. If the value is block, an HTML div element is rendered. Otherwise, with any other value, an HTML span element is rendered.

h:select*

There are seven JSF tags to render selections. They are h:selectBooleanCheckbox, h:selectManyCheckbox, h:selectManyListbox, h:selectManyMenu, h:selectOneListbox, h:selectOneMenu, and h:selectOneRadio. In the next sections, we'll show you examples of all these tags and what HTML code they generate (indented by hand for improved readability). The examples are to be placed inside an h:form element with id="form". The faces-config element inside faces-config.xml only contains the following code:

```
<managed-bean>
  <managed-bean-name>myBean</managed-bean-name>
  <managed-bean-class>myPkg.MyBean</managed-bean-class>
  <managed-bean-scope>session</managed-bean-scope>
</managed-bean>
```

Listing F-1 shows you the backing bean.

Listing F-1. *MyBean.java*

```java
package myPkg;
import java.util.ArrayList;
import javax.faces.model.SelectItem;

public class MyBean {
  private ArrayList choices = new ArrayList();
  private String oneChoice;
  private Object oneValue;
  private SelectItem[] selects;

  public MyBean() {
    selects = new SelectItem[3];
    selects[0] = new SelectItem("1", "one");
    selects[1] = new SelectItem("2", "two");
    selects[2] = new SelectItem("3", "three");
  }

  // ---------- Getters
  public Object[] getChoices() {
    return choices.toArray();
  }
  public String getOneChoice() {
    return oneChoice;
  }
  public Object getOneValue() {
    return oneValue;
  }
  public SelectItem[] getSelects() {
    return selects;
  }
```

```
// ---------- Setters
public void setChoices(Object[] choiceArray) {
  int len=0;
  if (choiceArray != null) len = choiceArray.length;
  if (len != 0) {
    choices.clear();
    choices = new ArrayList(len);
    for (int k = 0; k < len; k++) {
      choices.add(choiceArray[k]);
      }
    }
  }
public void setOneChoice(String oneChoice) {
  this.oneChoice = oneChoice;
  }
public void setOneValue(Object oneValue) {
  this.oneValue = oneValue;
  }
public void setSelects(SelectItem[] selects) {
  this.selects = selects;
  }
}
```

Figure F-1 shows you the rendered output as it appears in a browser.

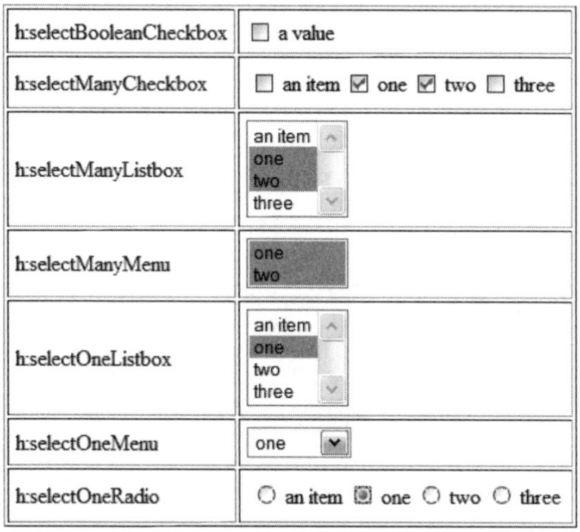

h:selectBooleanCheckbox	☐ a value
h:selectManyCheckbox	☐ an item ☑ one ☑ two ☐ three
h:selectManyListbox	an item ▲ / one / two / three ▼
h:selectManyMenu	one / two
h:selectOneListbox	an item ▲ / one / two / three ▼
h:selectOneMenu	one ▾
h:selectOneRadio	○ an item ◉ one ○ two ○ three

Figure F-1. *Rendering of h:select**

h:selectBooleanCheckbox

The h:selectBooleanCheckbox element renders an input HTML element of type checkbox.
    There are no possible subelements.

This element supports the following shared attributes: accesskey, binding, converter, converterMessage, dir, disabled, id, immediate, label, lang, onblur, onchange, onclick, ondblclick, onfocus, onkeydown, onkeypress, onkeyup, onmousedown, onmousemove, onmouseout, onmouseover, onmouseup, onselect, readonly, rendered, required, requiredMessage, style, styleClass, tabindex, title, validator, validatorMessage, value, and valueChangeListener.

There are no specific attributes.

For example, this code:

```
<h:panelGroup>
  <h:selectBooleanCheckbox id="checkbox" value="#{myBean.oneValue}"/>
  <h:outputText value=" a value"/>
  </h:panelGroup>
```

generates the following HTML code:

```
<input id="form:checkbox" type="checkbox" name="form:checkbox" /> a value
```

h:selectManyCheckbox

The h:selectManyCheckbox element renders an HTML checkbox list.

Possible subelements are

- <f:selectItem../> (zero or more)

- <f:selectItems../> (zero or more)

This element supports the following shared attributes: accesskey, binding, border, converter, converterMessage, dir, disabled, disabledClass, enabledClass, id, immediate, label, lang, onblur, onchange, onclick, ondblclick, onfocus, onkeydown, onkeypress, onkeyup, onmousedown, onmousemove, onmouseout, onmouseover, onmouseup, onselect, readonly, rendered, required, requiredMessage, style, styleClass, tabindex, title, validator, validatorMessage, value, and valueChangeListener.

It supports the following specific attribute: layout (see Table F-33).

Table F-33. *Specific Attributes of h:selectManyCheckbox*

Name	Type	Description
layout	ValExpr evaluating to String	Orientation of the list to be created. Valid values are pageDirection (the list is laid out vertically) and lineDirection (the list is laid out horizontally). The default value is lineDirection.

For example, this code:

```
<h:selectManyCheckbox id="checkboxes" value="#{myBean.choices}">
  <f:selectItem itemLabel="an item" itemValue="999"/>
  <f:selectItems value="#{myBean.selects}"/>
  </h:selectManyCheckbox>
```

generates the following HTML code:

```
<table id="form:checkboxes"><tr>
  <td><input name="form:checkboxes" id="form:checkboxes:0" value="999"
      type="checkbox"/><label for="form:checkboxes:0"> an item</label>
    </td>
  <td><input name="form:checkboxes" id="form:checkboxes:1" value="1"
      type="checkbox" /><label for="form:checkboxes:1"> one</label>
    </td>
  <td><input name="form:checkboxes" id="form:checkboxes:2" value="2"
      type="checkbox" /><label for="form:checkboxes:2"> two</label>
    </td>
  <td><input name="form:checkboxes" id="form:checkboxes:3" value="3"
      type="checkbox" /><label for="form:checkboxes:3"> three</label>
    </td>
  </tr></table>
```

h:selectManyListbox

The h:selectManyListbox element renders a scrollable HTML option list. It shows a scrollbar on the right-hand side, and you can select more than one item as usual by pressing the Shift or Control key while clicking.

Possible subelements are

- <f:selectItem../> (zero or more)

- <f:selectItems../> (zero or more)

This element supports the following shared attributes: accesskey, binding, converter, converterMessage, dir, disabled, disabledClass, enabledClass, id, immediate, label, lang, onblur, onchange, onclick, ondblclick, onfocus, onkeydown, onkeypress, onkeyup, onmousedown, onmousemove, onmouseout, onmouseover, onmouseup, onselect, readonly, rendered, required, requiredMessage, style, styleClass, tabindex, title, validator, validatorMessage, value, and valueChangeListener.

It supports the following specific attribute: size (see Table F-34).

Table F-34. *Specific Attributes of h:selectManyListbox*

Name	Type	Description
size	ValExpr evaluating to int	Number of available options to be shown at all times. If not specified, all available options are shown.

For example, this code:

```
<h:selectManyListbox id="listboxes" value="#{myBean.choices}">
  <f:selectItem itemLabel="an item" itemValue="999"/>
  <f:selectItems value="#{myBean.selects}"/>
  </h:selectManyListbox>
```

generates the following HTML code:

```
<select id="form:listboxes" name="form:listboxes" multiple="multiple" size="4">
  <option value="999">an item</option>
  <option value="1">one</option>
  <option value="2">two</option>
  <option value="3">three</option>
  </select>
```

h:selectManyMenu

The h:selectManyMenu element renders a scrollable HTML option list. The difference from h:selectManyListbox is that it doesn't display a scrollbar, and, by default, it only shows a single item at a time. You can still scroll through the items with the up and down keyboard arrows and with the mouse wheel (if you have one). To display more than one item, you can change the vertical size of the component to the appropriate value, as in style="min-height:30px".

Possible subelements are

- <f:selectItem../> (zero or more)

- <f:selectItems../> (zero or more)

This element supports the following shared attributes: accesskey, binding, converter, converterMessage, dir, disabled, disabledClass, enabledClass, id, immediate, label, lang, onblur, onchange, onclick, ondblclick, onfocus, onkeydown, onkeypress, onkeyup, onmousedown, onmousemove, onmouseout, onmouseover, onmouseup, onselect, readonly, rendered, required, requiredMessage, style, styleClass, tabindex, title, validator, validatorMessage, value, and valueChangeListener.

There are no specific attributes.

For example, this code:

```
<h:selectManyMenu id="menus" value="#{myBean.choices}"
    style="min-height:30px">
  <f:selectItem itemLabel="an item" itemValue="999"/>
  <f:selectItems value="#{myBean.selects}"/>
  </h:selectManyMenu>
```

generates the following HTML code:

```
<select id="form:menus" name="form:menus" multiple="multiple" size="1"
    style="min-height:30px">
  <option value="999">an item</option>
  <option value="1">one</option>
  <option value="2">two</option>
  <option value="3">three</option>
  </select>
```

h:selectOneListbox

The h:selectOneListbox element renders an HTML option list.
Possible subelements are

- <f:selectItem../> (zero or more)

- <f:selectItems../> (zero or more)

This element supports the following shared attributes: accesskey, binding, converter, converterMessage, dir, disabled, disabledClass, enabledClass, id, immediate, label, lang, onblur, onchange, onclick, ondblclick, onfocus, onkeydown, onkeypress, onkeyup, onmousedown, onmousemove, onmouseout, onmouseover, onmouseup, onselect, readonly, rendered, required, requiredMessage, style, styleClass, tabindex, title, validator, validatorMessage, value, and valueChangeListener.

It supports the following specific attribute: size (see Table F-35).

Table F-35. *Specific Attributes of h:selectOneListbox*

Name	Type	Description
size	ValExpr evaluating to int	Number of available options to be shown at all times. If not specified, all available options are shown.

For example, this code:

```
<h:selectOneListbox id="listbox" value="#{myBean.oneChoice}">
  <f:selectItem itemLabel="an item" itemValue="999"/>
  <f:selectItems value="#{myBean.selects}"/>
  </h:selectOneListbox>
```

generates the following HTML code:

```
<select id="form:listbox" name="form:listbox" size="4">
  <option value="999">an item</option>
  <option value="1">one</option>
  <option value="2">two</option>
  <option value="3">three</option>
  </select>
```

h:selectOneMenu

The h:selectOneMenu element renders an HTML option list.
Possible subelements are

- <f:selectItem../> (zero or more)

- <f:selectItems../> (zero or more)

This element supports the following shared attributes: accesskey, binding, converter, converterMessage, dir, disabled, disabledClass, enabledClass, id, immediate, label, lang, onblur, onchange, onclick, ondblclick, onfocus, onkeydown, onkeypress, onkeyup, onmousedown, onmousemove, onmouseout, onmouseover, onmouseup, onselect, readonly, rendered, required, requiredMessage, style, styleClass, tabindex, title, validator, validatorMessage, value, and valueChangeListener.

There are no specific attributes.

For example, this code:

```
<h:selectOneMenu id="menu" value="#{myBean.oneChoice}">
  <f:selectItem itemLabel="an item" itemValue="999"/>
  <f:selectItems value="#{myBean.selects}"/>
  </h:selectOneMenu>
```

generates the following HTML code:

```
<select id="form:menu" name="form:menu" size="1">
  <option value="999">an item</option>
  <option value="1">one</option>
  <option value="2">two</option>
  <option value="3">three</option>
  </select>
```

h:selectOneRadio

The h:selectOneRadio element renders a set of input HTML elements of type radio.

There are no possible subelements.

This element supports the following shared attributes: accesskey, binding, border, converter, converterMessage, dir, disabled, disabledClass, enabledClass, id, immediate, label, lang, onblur, onchange, onclick, ondblclick, onfocus, onkeydown, onkeypress, onkeyup, onmousedown, onmousemove, onmouseout, onmouseover, onmouseup, onselect, readonly, rendered, required, requiredMessage, style, styleClass, tabindex, title, validator, validatorMessage, value, and valueChangeListener.

It supports the following specific attribute: layout (see Table F-36).

Table F-36. *Specific Attributes of h:selectOneRadio*

Name	Type	Description
layout	ValExpr evaluating to String	Orientation of the list to be created. The valid values are pageDirection (the list is laid out vertically) and lineDirection (the list is laid out horizontally). The default value is lineDirection.

For example, this code:

```
<h:selectOneRadio id="radio" value="#{myBean.oneChoice}">
  <f:selectItem itemLabel="an item" itemValue="999"/>
  <f:selectItems value="#{myBean.selects}"/>
  </h:selectOneRadio>
```

generates the following HTML code:

```
<table id="form:radio"><tr>
  <td><input type="radio" name="form:radio" id="form:radio:0" value="999"/>
    <label for="form:radio:0"> an item</label></td>
  <td><input type="radio" name="form:radio" id="form:radio:1" value="1"/>
    <label for="form:radio:1"> one</label></td>
  <td><input type="radio" name="form:radio" id="form:radio:2" value="2"/>
    <label for="form:radio:2"> two</label></td>
  <td><input type="radio" name="form:radio" id="form:radio:3" value="3"/>
    <label for="form:radio:3"> three</label></td>
  </tr></table>
```

Shared Attributes

Table F-37 lists in alphabetical order all the attributes that are available in more than one component.

Table F-37. *Shared Attributes*

Name	Type	Description
accesskey	ValExpr evaluating to String	Access key that, when pressed, transfers focus to this component.
action	javax.el.MethodExpression	The expression must evaluate to a public method (without parameters) that returns an Object. The NavigationHandler uses the result value, converted to a String, as outcome to decide the next page.
actionListener	javax.el.MethodExpression	The expression must evaluate to a public method with the signature matching void actionListener(javax.faces.event. ActionEvent). This method is executed when the user activates this component.
alt	ValExpr evaluating to String	Alternate textual description of the element rendered by this component.
autocomplete	ValExpr evaluating to String	The browser should disable its autocomplete feature for this component when this attribute is set to off. This is useful if your component does autocompletion and you don't want the browser to interfere with it. Default value is on.
bgcolor	ValExpr evaluating to String	Name or code of the background color for this table.
binding	ValExpr evaluating to javax. faces.component.UIComponent	The value binding the expression linking this component to a property in a backing bean.
border	ValExpr evaluating to int	Width (in pixels) of the border to be drawn around the component.

Continued

Table F-37. *Continued*

Name	Type	Description
captionClass	ValExpr evaluating to String	CSS-style class or a space-separated list of CSS-style classes to be applied to any caption generated for this table.
captionStyle	ValExpr evaluating to String	CSS style to be applied when this caption is rendered.
cellpadding	ValExpr evaluating to String	Definition of how much space the user agent should leave between the border of each cell and its contents.
cellspacing	ValExpr evaluating to String	Definition of how much space to leave between cells and between the outer cells and the edges of the table.
charset	ValExpr evaluating to String	The character encoding of the resource designated by this hyperlink.
columnClasses	ValExpr evaluating to String	Comma-delimited list of CSS-style classes to be applied to the columns of this table. Each class refers to a column. If there are more columns than classes, they remain unstyled. For each column, you can write a single style class or a space-separated list of classes.
converter	ValExpr evaluating to javax.faces.convert.Converter	Converter instance registered with this component.
converterMessage	ValExpr evaluating to String	A message to replace the default text of converter messages.
coords	ValExpr evaluating to String	The position and shape of the hot spot on the screen to be used for client-side image maps.
dir	ValExpr evaluating to String	Direction indication for text, to override the default. Valid values are LTR (left-to-right) and RTL (right-to-left).
disabled	ValExpr evaluating to boolean	Flag indicating that this element must never receive focus or be included in a subsequent submit. A value of false causes no attribute to be rendered at all, while a value of true causes the attribute to be rendered with disabled="disabled".
disabledClass	ValExpr evaluating to String	CSS-style class to apply to the rendered label on disabled options.
enabledClass	ValExpr evaluating to String	CSS-style class to apply to the rendered label on enabled options.
errorClass	ValExpr evaluating to String	CSS-style class to apply to any message with a severity class of ERROR.
errorStyle	ValExpr evaluating to String	CSS-style[s] to apply to any message with a severity class of ERROR.
escape	ValExpr evaluating to boolean	Flag indicating that characters that are sensitive in HTML and XML markup must be escaped. The default value is true.
fatalClass	ValExpr evaluating to String	CSS-style class to apply to any message with a severity class of FATAL.

Name	Type	Description
fatalStyle	ValExpr evaluating to String	CSS-style[s] to apply to any message with a severity class of FATAL.
footerClass	ValExpr evaluating to String	CSS-style class or a space-separated list of CSS-style classes that will be applied to any column footer generated for this table.
for	ValExpr evaluating to String	Client identifier of the component this element refers to.
frame	ValExpr evaluating to String	Code specifying which sides of the frame surrounding this table will be visible. Valid values are none (no sides), above (top side only), below (bottom side only), hsides (top and bottom sides only), vsides (right and left sides only), lhs (left-hand side only), rhs (right-hand side only), and box or border (all four sides). The default value is none.
headerClass	ValExpr evaluating to String	CSS-style class or a space-separated list of CSS-style classes that will be applied to any column header generated for this table.
hreflang	ValExpr evaluating to String	The language code of the resource designated by this hyperlink.
id	String	The component identifier for this component. This value must be unique within the closest parent component that is a naming container.
immediate	ValExpr evaluating to boolean	Flag indicating that this component, if activated by the user, is to be processed during the Apply Request Values phase rather than during the Invoke Application phase.
infoClass	ValExpr evaluating to String	CSS-style class to apply to any message with a severity class of INFO.
infoStyle	ValExpr evaluating to String	CSS-style[s] to apply to any message with a severity class of INFO.
label	ValExpr evaluating to String	A localized user-presentable name for this component.
lang	ValExpr evaluating to String	Code describing the language used in the generated HTML for this component.
maxlength	ValExpr evaluating to int	The maximum number of characters that may be entered in this field.
onblur	ValExpr evaluating to String	JavaScript code executed when this element loses focus.
onchange	ValExpr evaluating to String	JavaScript code executed when this element loses focus and its value has been modified since gaining focus.
onclick	ValExpr evaluating to String	JavaScript code executed when the user clicks the mouse button over this element.
ondblclick	ValExpr evaluating to String	JavaScript code executed when the user double-clicks the mouse button over this element.

Continued

Table F-37. *Continued*

Name	Type	Description
onfocus	ValExpr evaluating to String	JavaScript code executed when this element receives focus.
onkeydown	ValExpr evaluating to String	JavaScript code executed when the user presses a key with the cursor positioned over this element.
onkeypress	ValExpr evaluating to String	JavaScript code executed when the user presses and releases a key with the cursor positioned over this element.
onkeyup	ValExpr evaluating to String	JavaScript code executed when the user releases a key with the cursor positioned over this element.
onmousedown	ValExpr evaluating to String	JavaScript code executed when the user presses the mouse button over this element.
onmousemove	ValExpr evaluating to String	JavaScript code executed when the user moves the mouse button within this element.
onmouseout	ValExpr evaluating to String	JavaScript code executed when the user moves the mouse button away from this element.
onmouseover	ValExpr evaluating to String	JavaScript code executed when the user moves the mouse button onto this element.
onmouseup	ValExpr evaluating to String	JavaScript code executed when the user releases the mouse button over this element.
onselect	ValExpr evaluating to String	JavaScript code executed when the user selects text within this element.
readonly	ValExpr evaluating to boolean	Flag indicating that the user is not allowed to change this component. The element may receive focus unless it has also been disabled. A value of false causes no attribute to be rendered at all, while a value of true causes the attribute to be rendered with readonly="readonly".
rel	ValExpr evaluating to String	The relationship from the current document to the anchor specified by this hyperlink. The value of this attribute is a space-separated list of link types.
rendered	ValExpr evaluating to Boolean	Flag indicating whether this component should be rendered (during the Render Response phase). The default value is true.
required	ValExpr evaluating to boolean	Flag indicating that the user is required to provide a value for this input component.
requiredMessage	ValExpr evaluating to String	A message to replace the default text displayed when the user doesn't submit a value for a required input component.
rev	ValExpr evaluating to String	A reverse link from the anchor specified by this hyperlink to the current document. The value of this attribute is a space-separated list of link types.

Name	Type	Description
rowClasses	ValExpr evaluating to String	Comma-delimited list of CSS-style classes to be applied to the rows of this table. Each class refers to a row. If there are more rows than classes, the list restarts from the beginning. For example, with a list of two classes, the first class applies to all odd-numbered rows, while the second class applies to all even-numbered rows. For each row, you can write a single style class or a space-separated list of classes.
rules	ValExpr evaluating to String	Code specifying which rules will appear between cells within this table. Valid values are none (no rules), groups (between row groups), rows (between individual rows), cols (between individual columns), and all (between all rows and all columns). The default value is none.
shape	ValExpr evaluating to String	The shape of the hot spot on the screen to be used for client-side image maps. Valid values are default (entire region), rect (rectangular region), circle (circular region), and poly (polygonal region).
showDetail	ValExpr evaluating to boolean	Flag indicating whether the detail portion of displayed messages should be included. The default value is true for h:message and false for h:messages.
showSummary	ValExpr evaluating to boolean	Flag indicating whether the summary portion of displayed messages should be included. The default value is false for h:message and true for h:messages.
style	ValExpr evaluating to String	CSS-style[s] to be applied when this component is rendered.
styleClass	ValExpr evaluating to String	CSS-style class or a space-separated list of CSS-style classes to be applied when this element is rendered. This value is passed through to the generated HTML as the class attribute.
summary	ValExpr evaluating to String	Summary of this table's purpose and structure, for user agents rendering to nonvisual media such as speech and braille.
tabindex	ValExpr evaluating to String	Position of this element in the tabbing order for the current document. This value must be an integer between 0 and 32767.
target	ValExpr evaluating to String	Name of a frame where the resource retrieved via this hyperlink is to be displayed.
title	ValExpr evaluating to String	Title information about HTML elements generated for this component.
tooltip	ValExpr evaluating to boolean	Flag indicating whether the detail portion of the message should be displayed as a tooltip.

Continued

Table F-37. *Continued*

Name	Type	Description
validator	javax.el.MethodExpression	The expression must evaluate to a public method with the signature matching void validate(javax.faces.context.FacesContext, javax.faces.component.UIComponent, Object). This is a validator method that is executed during the Process Validation phase.
validatorMessage	ValExpr evaluating to String	A message to replace the default text of validator messages.
value	ValExpr evaluating to Object	The current value of this component.
valueChangeListener	javax.el.MethodExpression	The expression must evaluate to a public method with the signature matching void valueChange(javax.faces.event.ValueChangeEvent). This is a value-change listener method that is executed when the user sets a new value for this input component.
warnClass	ValExpr evaluating to String	CSS-style classes to apply to any message with a severity class of WARN.
warnStyle	ValExpr evaluating to String	CSS-style[s] to apply to any message with a severity class of WARN.

APPENDIX G

■ ■ ■

Eclipse

In the preceding chapters, we showed you how you could realize web applications by putting together HTML, Java, JSP, XML, and JSF modules. We intentionally relied on simple development tools because we wanted you to "get close" to the code and see in detail how the various pieces fit together.

Although it's possible to compile a Java module from the command line in order to check its syntax, or to look for inconsistencies between modules by studying their listings, it's more efficient to use an IDE for all such menial tasks. This way, you can concentrate on the more creative part of developing software.

An IDE integrates all the applications that you need to develop software—from a source editor and a compiler, to tools to automate the application building process and a debugger— into a single environment. When developing in Java or in another OO language, an IDE also includes tools to visualize class and object structure as well inheritance and containment. Another advantage of using an IDE is that it propagates changes you make to individual modules. For example, if you rename a class, the IDE will automatically update its occurrences throughout your project files.

IDEs are also increasingly supporting the development of GUIs in graphical mode, allowing you to drag and drop interface components. IDE extensions also support you in the design of OO applications by providing Unified Modeling Language (UML) diagrams.

In this appendix, we'll introduce you to Eclipse, which is an extremely powerful and extensible IDE, well suited for web application development. The Eclipse Foundation makes a new release of the Eclipse IDE once a year. Each yearly release has a different name, and that of June 26, 2007 is called Europa. The fact that Eclipse Europa fully supports JSF is of particular interest.

Once you've installed Eclipse to develop web applications, you can use it for any other software development task, including, for example, developing and debugging applications written in Java or C++.

Furthermore, Eclipse is a development platform that is comparatively easy to extend. Therefore, whatever task related to software development you need to perform, it's likely that somebody has already developed an Eclipse plug-in for it. Eclipse's official plug-in site (http://www.eclipse-plugins.info/eclipse/plugins.jsp) lists more than 1,500 plug-ins organized in 60 categories. In fact, Eclipse itself consists of a core platform that executes plug-ins, plus a series of plug-ins that implement most of its functionality. Therefore, the standard packages available for download from the Eclipse web site already include dozens of plug-ins.

In this appendix, we'll only talk about the standard Eclipse package for Java EE development.

One third-party plug-in that you should be aware of is Exadel Studio (`http://www.eclipse-plugins.info/eclipse/plugin_details.jsp?id=1023`). Exadel released version 4.0 of Exadel Studio in August 2006 to provide an extensive palette of functions, including the handling of JSF, which was not yet available in the standard Eclipse package. It supports drag-and-drop of JSP and JSF components in graphical mode, which significantly speeds up the composition of your pages. Exadel Studio also supports Facelets, which extends the JSP/JSF functionality.

Furthermore, to support database persistence, Exadel Studio includes a Hibernate wizard that extracts the structure of an existing database and generates the corresponding peer classes automatically.

Now that Eclipse supports JSF, it's likely that Exadel will soon release a new version of Exadel Studio with still more powerful functionality. We tested Exadel Studio with the Callisto release of Eclipse, which preceded the current Europa release, and it worked well.

■**Caution** Don't install Eclipse unless you've already installed everything described in Appendix A!

Eclipse is only one of many possible IDEs suitable for developing web applications. Some of them already support JSF, and some others probably soon will. Some, like Eclipse, are free, and some others are not. We chose Eclipse on the basis of our personal preferences, but, without any doubt, other developers will recommend other packages. In any case, Eclipse is probably the most widely used IDE for Java development.

How to Install Eclipse

Execute the following steps to install Eclipse:

1. Go to `http://www.eclipse.org/downloads/` and click on the `Windows` link at the end of the line that starts with `Eclipse IDE for Java EE Developers - Windows (125 MB)`. It will download the file `eclipse-jee-europa-win32.zip`.

2. When you expand the zip file, it creates a folder called `eclipse`. It's not really important where you place it, but the traditional place for it is in the `C:\Program Files\` folder. Eclipse is written entirely in Java. As it doesn't fiddle with your operating system, you can move around its directory as you like.

3. Launch Eclipse by executing `C:\Program Files\eclipse\eclipse.exe`. Eclipse will ask you to select a workspace. The workspace is the folder where Eclipse stores your development projects. Therefore, it makes sense to place it on a drive or in a directory that you back up regularly. Before clicking on the `OK` button, check the box marked `Use this as the default and do not ask again`. It will make your life easier.

When opened for the first time, Eclipse starts with a splash screen. Close that, and you'll see the window shown in Figure G-1.

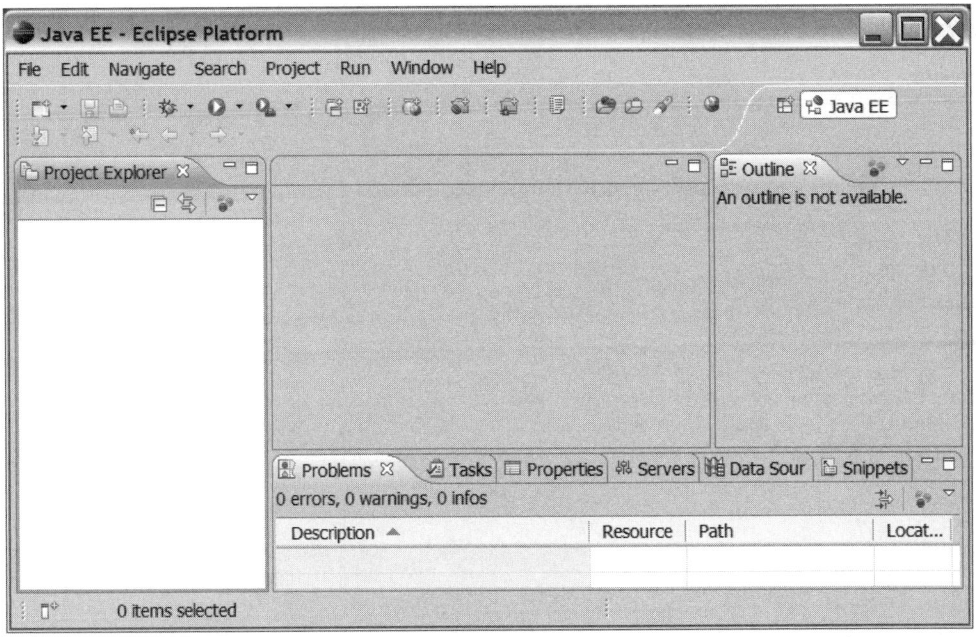

Figure G-1. *Eclipse's default window*

With Eclipse, you create a project for each application you develop. The initial window is obviously empty because, immediately after installation, you haven't yet created any new project. It will become more interesting in a moment. In the rest of this appendix, we'll refer to the unnamed subwindow in the middle as "Eclipse's main window."

Importing the Eshop* Projects into Eclipse

Rather than show you how to create a project from scratch, we'll tell you how to import into Eclipse the example applications we showed you in the previous chapters. We'll start with Eshopf, which includes JSF functionality.

First, download the example code from the Source Code/Download area of the Apress web site (http://www.apress.com). After expanding the zip file, you'll see that we've created a folder for each chapter and appendix containing example code. The file you're interested in now is eshopf.war in the folder for Appendix G. If you place it inside Tomcat's webapps folder, you'll see that Tomcat will expand it to the application folder named eshopf, so that you can execute the application by typing http://localhost:8080/eshopf/ into your web browser. But we digress, because you don't need to place eshopf.war in any particular folder to be able to import it into Eclipse.

In Eclipse, click on the File menu and select Import. You can also access the Import menu item by clicking the right button of your mouse anywhere inside the Project Explorer sidebar. Usually, Eclipse gives you more than one way of performing any operation.

In any case, after selecting Import, you'll see a dialog with a dozen different possibilities. Select the WAR file option inside the Web folder, as shown in Figure G-2, and click on the Next button.

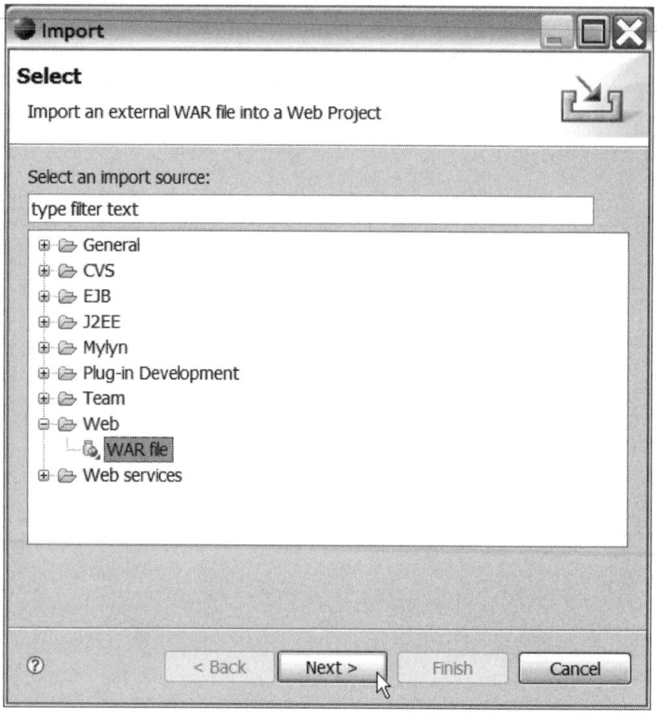

Figure G-2. *The Select dialog*

This takes you to the dialog shown in Figure G-3. We took the screenshot after selecting eshopf.war as the WAR file and typing eshopf as the name of our Web project.

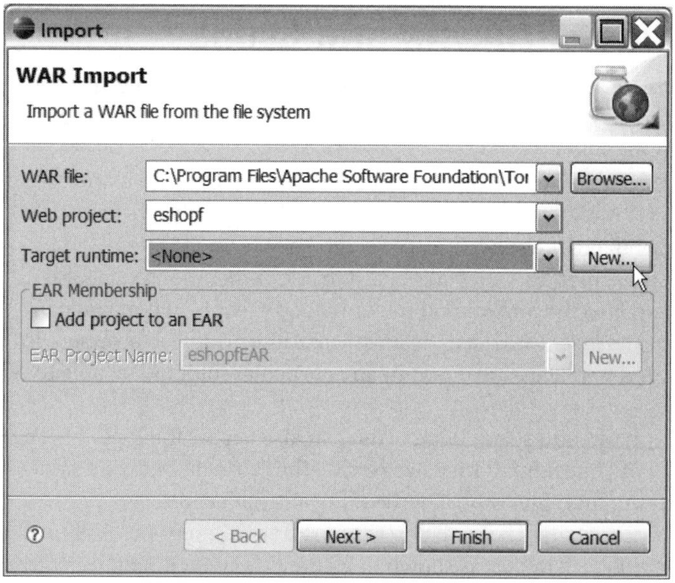

Figure G-3. *The WAR Import dialog*

In addition to filling in the fields WAR file and Web project, you also need to specify in which environment you want your new Eclipse project to run. To do that, click on the New... button to get to the dialog shown in Figure G-4. Note that the title of the dialog is New Server Runtime instead of the expected Target Runtime. Fortunately, this is inconsequential. Select Tomcat 6.0 as shown, and click on the Next button.

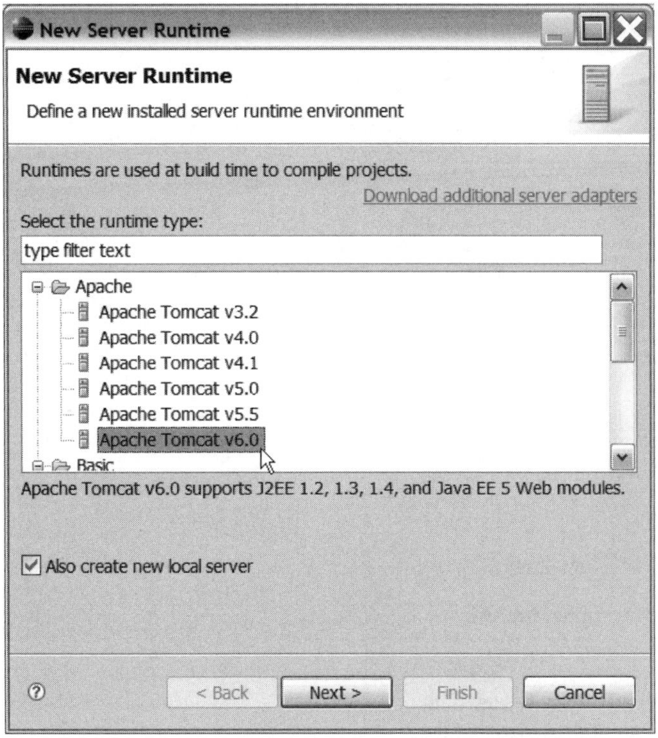

Figure G-4. *The New Server Runtime dialog*

You'll see a second New Server Runtime dialog, as shown in Figure G-5. You must fill in the Tomcat installation directory field and select the JRE as shown.

Click on the Finish button. This takes you back to the WAR Import dialog. Click on Finish again to complete the import.

During this import process, Eclipse opens the dialog shown in Figure G-6. When this happens, you must click on the I Agree button. You'll only see this dialog the first time you import an application that includes JSF.

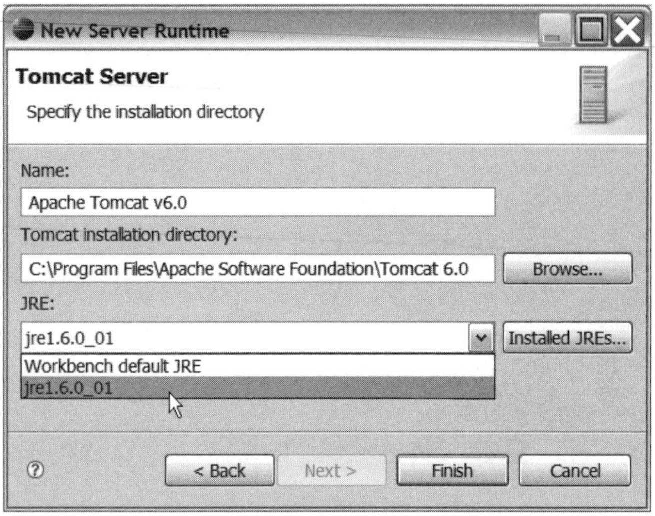

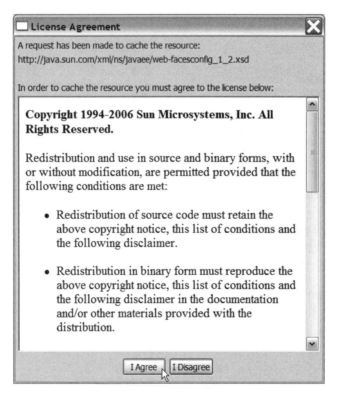

Figure G-5. *The Tomcat Server dialog*

Figure G-6. *Licensing the JSF application configuration file*

You can import the remaining applications (eshop, eshopx, eshopfn, and testf) in the same way. It will actually be simpler, because Eclipse will automatically set the Target runtime field of the WAR Import dialog (see Figure G-3) to Apache Tomcat v6.0.

The Project Explorer Sidebar

Once you've imported the Eshopf application, you'll find that the Project Explorer sidebar is no longer empty, as shown in Figure G-7.

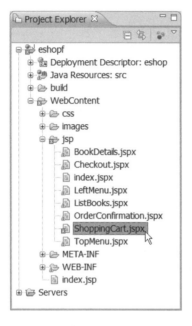

Figure G-7. *The Project Explorer sidebar in JSP*

As you can see, it looks similar to the Folders sidebar of Windows Explorer. Eclipse creates the standard folders Java Resources: src, build, and WebContent for all web applications. The Servers folder only contains the definition of the Tomcat 6 web server that we created while importing Eshopf.

The yellow triangles with an exclamation point inside them that appear on the bottom-left corner of some of the icons indicate that Eclipse has one or more warnings to report on the corresponding item, while the red squares with the Xs indicate errors. Unfortunately, these problems are not always real. In Eshopf, Eclipse reports 1 error and 49 warnings that aren't justified. We'll talk more about this in the next section.

Figure G-8 shows how the Project Explorer sidebar displays Java modules.

Notice that it lists all the attributes and methods of a class. You only need to double-click on one of the listed items to open the file in Eclipse's main window with the cursor positioned on that item.

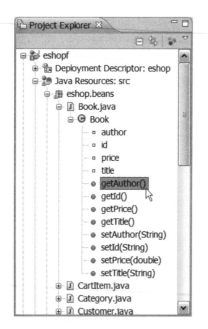

Figure G-8. *The Project Explorer sidebar in Java*

Eclipse Errors in Error Reporting

If you double-click on a module shown in the `Project Explorer` sidebar, Eclipse will open it for editing in Eclipse's main window. Open `ShoppingCart.jspx`, scroll down to display the line with the error, and move the mouse over the part that Eclipse underlines with a jagged line. Figure G-9 shows the result of doing this.

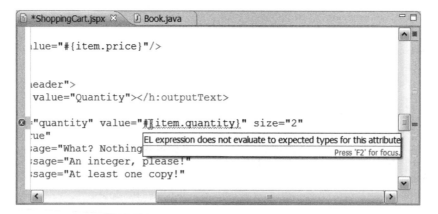

Figure G-9. *Erroneous error in ShoppingCart.jspx*

Eclipse reports this error because the getQuantity method defined in CartItem.java returns a value of type int, while the value attribute of the element h:inputText is defined as being of type String. Eclipse shouldn't report an error, because the results of EL expressions are automatically converted to the expected type, and the conversion to String is always possible. Fortunately, Eclipse reports this error in a JSP document, which it doesn't need to process in any way. If Eclipse had "invented" an error in a Java module, we would have had to implement a workaround to remove it, because Eclipse would have aborted the compilation. Tomcat correctly recognizes that there is no error and processes ShoppingCart.jspx without any complaint.

If we wanted to prevent Eclipse from reporting this error, we could have modified CartItem.getQuantity to return a String value. This would in turn require a couple of other minor modifications (for example, in putQuantity). We decided not to do it, in the hope that the next version of Eclipse (due in 2008) will take care of it.

Figure G-10 shows you an example of an erroneous warning.

Figure G-10. *Erroneous warning in ShoppingCart.jspx*

If shopManager really couldn't be resolved, the Delete button beside each item in the shopping cart wouldn't work. Indeed, this element in WEB-INF\faces-config.xml makes it visible as a session-scoped bean:

```
<managed-bean>
  <managed-bean-name>shopManager</managed-bean-name>
  <managed-bean-class>eshop.beans.ShopManager</managed-bean-class>
  <managed-bean-scope>session</managed-bean-scope>
</managed-bean>
```

You should aim at developing software without errors or warnings. For many programmers, 100% clean compilations are a matter of honor. Nevertheless, it isn't reasonable to complicate the code only to work around unjustified warnings. It could cause confusion later, and you would probably remain stuck with overengineered code long after the fix became unnecessary. Ultimately, it's up to you to decide how far you want to go in order to have a "clean bill" from any tool, including Eclipse.

In any case, these examples show that Eclipse has powerful checking capabilities. If you select the `Preferences...` item of the `Windows` menu and then click on `Validation`, you'll see the list shown in Figure G-11.

Validator	Manual	Build	Settings
Application Client Validator	☑	☑	
Classpath Dependency Validator	☑	☑	
Connector Validator	☑	☑	
DTD Validator	☑	☑	
EAR Validator	☑	☑	
EJB Validator	☑	☑	
HTML Syntax Validator	☑	☑	
JPA Validator	☑	☑	
JSF Application Configuration Validator	☑	☑	
JSP Content Validator	☑	☑	
JSP Semantics Validator (JSF)	☑	☑	
JSP Syntax Validator	☑	☑	
ModuleCore Validator	☑	☑	
War Validator	☑	☑	
WSDL Validator	☑	☑	...
WS-I Message Validator	☑	☑	
XML Schema Validator	☑	☑	...
XML Validator	☑	☑	

Figure G-11. *The validation list*

This gives you a further idea of the amount of checks that Eclipse performs on your code. Don't ignore the problems Eclipse reports, because they're really there in perhaps 99.9% of the cases.

Eclipse's Main Window

You've already seen that Eclipse uses its main window to let you edit source code. It highlights the code with different colors, checks the syntax as you type, suggests element attributes and function parameters, indents automatically, and completes your code.

Figure G-12 shows you an example of the information Eclipse displays when you move the cursor over an element.

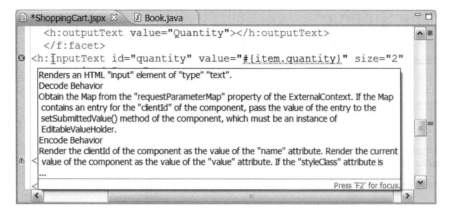

Figure G-12. *Information pop-ups*

You can edit XML files in normal source mode, but also in design mode, as shown in Figure G-13.

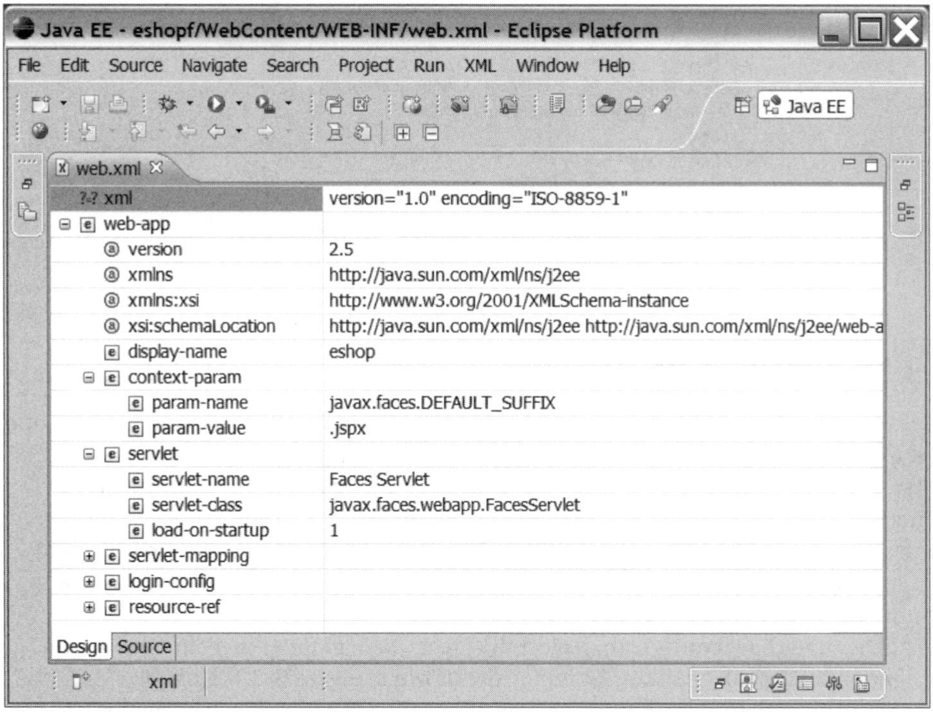

Figure G-13. *Editing XML in design mode*

The Outline Sidebar

The Outline sidebar on the right-hand side of Eclipse's main window shows the structure of the file you're editing. For example, Figure G-14 shows its content when you open ShoppingCart.jspx.

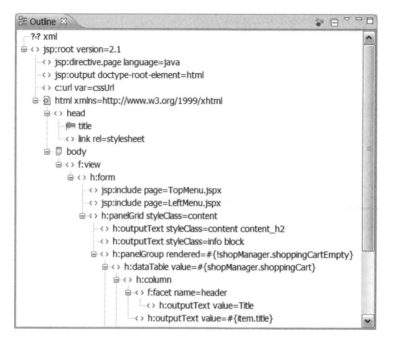

Figure G-14. *The Outline sidebar*

How to Make a WAR File

You've seen how to import a WAR file into Eclipse. In this section, we'll show you how to do the reverse: export a project to a WAR file that executes within Tomcat.

First, you need to ensure that the project is ready to be exported. To do so, select the Clean item in the Project menu. This opens a dialog with a list of all your projects. Select Clean projects selected below, check the box beside the name of the project you want to export, and click on the OK button. Eclipse flashes a series of operations in the status line at the bottom of the window (e.g., JSP Content Validator).

Once the status line returns blank, select the Export item in the File menu. You'll see a dialog almost identical to the dialog for importing shown in Figure G-2. Select WAR file in the Web folder, and click on the Next button. This opens a dialog like that shown in Figure G-15 (after resizing).

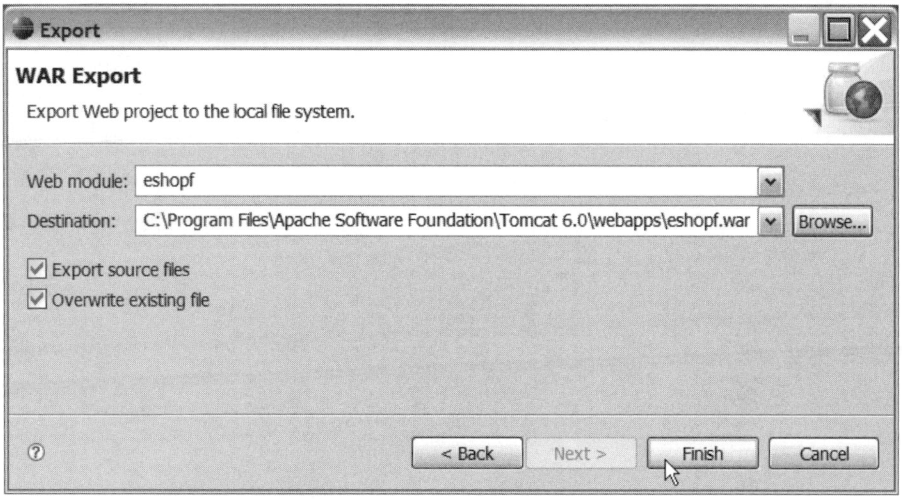

Figure G-15. *The WAR Export dialog*

Fill in the Destination field as shown, check both boxes, and click on the Finish button.

To verify that everything works, wait while Tomcat expands the WAR file into a normal folder, and type http://localhost/eshopf/ into a web browser.

APPENDIX H

■■■

Abbreviations and Acronyms

Here you'll find all the abbreviations and acronyms used in this book, even if some are pretty obvious!

Abbreviation/Acronym	Description
ACID	Atomicity, Consistency, Isolation, and Durability (the DB properties)
Ajax	Asynchronous JavaScript and XML
AJP	Apache JServ Protocol
ANSI	American National Standards Institute
API	application programming interface
APR	Apache Portable Runtime
ASCII	American Standard Code for Information Interchange
ASF	Apache Software Foundation
BLOB	binary large object
CEST	Central European Summer Time
CGI	Common Gateway Interface
CLI	command line interface
CPU	Central Processing Unit
CRUD	create, retrieve, update, and delete
CSS	Cascading Style Sheets
CTI	computer telephony integration
DB	database
DBMS	database management system
DCL	Data Control Language (SQL)
DDL	Data Definition Language (SQL)
DML	Data Manipulation Language (SQL)
DNS	domain name server
DOM	Document Object Model
DOS	Disk Operating System

Continued

Abbreviation/Acronym	Description
DTD	Document Type Definition
ECMA	Originally, European Computer Manufacturers Association; today, Ecma International
EL	Expression Language
EST	Eastern Standard Time
EUC	Extended Unix Code
FTP	File Transfer Protocol
GB	gigabyte (1GB = 2^9 bytes = 1,073,741,824 bytes = 1,048,576KB = 1,024MB)
GIF	Graphics Interchange Format
GMT	Greenwich Mean Time
GUI	graphical user interface
HTML	Hypertext Markup Language
HTTP	Hypertext Transfer Protocol
HTTPS	HTTP Secure
HW	hardware
i18n	internationalization (i + 18 omitted letters + n)
IANA	Internet Assigned Numbers Authority
IDE	integrated development environment
IE	Internet Explorer (Microsoft's web browser)
IEC	International Electrotechnical Commission
IP	Internet Protocol
IPv4	IP version 4, with 32-bit addresses expressed as x.x.x.x, where x = 0…255 decimal.
IPv6	IP version 6, with 128-bit addresses expressed as x:x:x:x:x:x:x:x, where x = 0…FFFF hex.
ISO	International Organization for Standardization
ISOC	Internet Society
ISP	Internet service provider
JAD	Joint Application Development
JAR	Java ARchive
Java EE 5	Java Platform, Enterprise Edition 5
Java SE 5	Java Platform, Standard Edition 5
JAXP	Java API for XML Processing
JCP	Java Community Process
JDBC	Java Database Connectivity
JDK	Java Development Kit
JMX	Java Management Extensions
JNDI	Java Naming and Directory Interface

Abbreviation/Acronym	Description
JPEG	Joint Photographic Experts Group
JRE	Java Runtime Environment
JSF	JavaServer Faces
JSP	JavaServer Pages
jsp	File extension of JSP modules in the traditional scripting format (JSP pages)
jspx	File extension of JSP modules in XML format (JSP documents)
JSR	Java Specification Request
JSTL	JSP Standard Tag Library
JVM	Java Virtual Machine
KB	kilobyte (1kB = 2^3 bytes = 1,024 bytes)
LAN	local area network
LDAP	Lightweight Directory Access Protocol
LOB	large object
LSB	least significant bit
MB	megabyte (1MB = 2^6 bytes = 1,048,576 bytes = 1,024KB)
MD5	Message-Digest algorithm 5
MIME	Multipurpose Internet Mail Extensions
MPEG	Moving Picture Experts Group
MRML	Mind Reading Markup Language
MSB	most significant bit
MSIE	Microsoft Internet Explorer
MVC	model-view-controller design pattern
OASIS	Organization for the Advancement of Structured Information Standards
OCI	Oracle Call Interface
ODBC	Open Database Connectivity
OMG	Object Management Group
OO	object-oriented
OOD	object-oriented design
OOP	object-oriented programming
OS	operating system
PC	personal computer
RAD	rapid application development
RETML	Real Estate Transaction Markup Language
RFC	Request for Comments
RI	reference implementation
RPC	Remote Procedure Call

Continued

Abbreviation/Acronym	Description
RUP	Rational Unified Process
SAX	Simple API for XML
SGML	Standard Generalized Markup Language
SOAP	Simple Object Access Protocol
SQL	Structured Query Language
TB	terabyte (1TB = 2^{12} bytes = 1,099,511,627,776 bytes = 1,048,576MB = 1,024GB)
TCL	Transaction ControL (SQL)
TCP	Transmission Control Protocol
TLD	tag library descriptor
UBL	Universal Business Language
UDP	User Datagram Protocol
UEL	Unified Expression Language
UI	user interface
UID	unique identifier
UML	Unified Modeling Language
URI	Uniform Resource Identifier
URL	Uniform Resource Locator
VB	Visual Basic
W3C	World Wide Web Consortium
WAR	Web ARchive
WTP	Web Tools Platform (an Eclipse project)
XHTML	Extensible HTML
XML	Extensible Markup Language
xmlns	XML namespace
XP	Extreme Programming (see http://extremeprogramming.org); in Windows XP, XP stands for *experience*
XPath	XML Path Language
XSL	Extensible Stylesheet Language
XSL-FO	XSL Formatting Objects
XSLT	Extensible Stylesheet Language Transformations

Index

You Need the Companion eBook

Your purchase of this book entitles you to buy the companion PDF-version eBook for only $10. Take the weightless companion with you anywhere.

We believe this Apress title will prove so indispensable that you'll want to carry it with you everywhere, which is why we are offering the companion eBook (in PDF format) for $10 to customers who purchase this book now. Convenient and fully searchable, the PDF version of any content-rich, page-heavy Apress book makes a valuable addition to your programming library. You can easily find and copy code—or perform examples by quickly toggling between instructions and the application. Even simultaneously tackling a donut, diet soda, and complex code becomes simplified with hands-free eBooks!

Once you purchase your book, getting the $10 companion eBook is simple:

1. Visit **www.apress.com/promo/tendollars/**.

2. Complete a basic registration form to receive a randomly generated question about this title.

3. Answer the question correctly in 60 seconds, and you will receive a promotional code to redeem for the $10.00 eBook.